WALKING BACK

JEAN MOSS

WALKING BACK

Matador
9 De Montfort Mews
Leicester LE1 7FW, UK
Tel: (+44) 116 255 9311 / 9312
Email: books@troubador.co.uk
Web: www.troubador.co.uk/matador

ISBN 978-1905886-920

Typeset in 11.5pt Bembo by Troubador Publishing Ltd, Leicester, UK

Matador is an imprint of Troubador Publishing Ltd

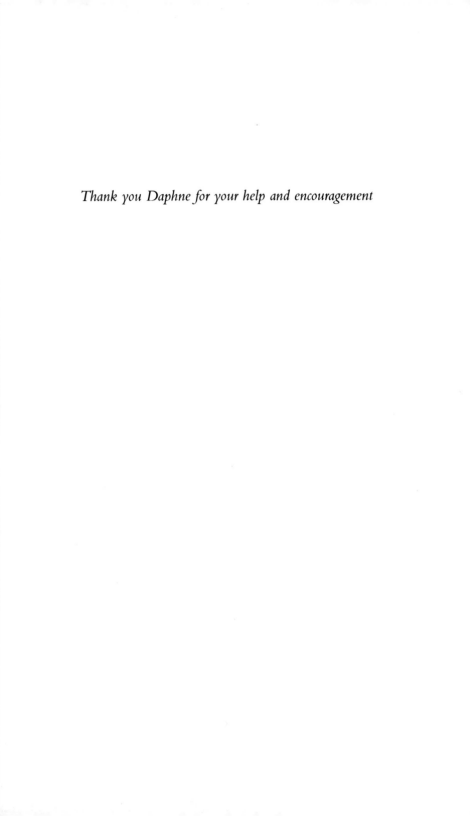

Thank you Daphne for your help and encouragement

MY LOVE

A crunch on the murram her heart starts to pound,
hearing his feet as they tread dry red ground.
Across the veranda he strides through the door
then opens his arms, to the girl whom he saw,
sitting legs crossed on a mat, on the floor.

Having loved one another for most of their life,
he knew he would one day make her his wife.
At the start of each day came a soft gentle kiss,
for years they had dreamed of this wondrous bliss.

So contented they are eating breakfast alone,
crisp bacon and eggs in the old estate home.
Crusty baked bread made into toast,
sweet mellow coffee. Medium roast.

'How much do you love me?' she asks, one more time.
They sit at the table, their eyes glow and shine.
With a smile and a wink came the loving reply.
'How deep is the ocean, How high is the sky.'

A whistle they hear then a bicycle bell,
the rustle of basket, crunched paper as well.
Back from the lake at incredible speed,
it'is Chisolo with fish, on his trusty old steed.

By lamplight they sit at the end of each day,
it persistently hisses refusing to stay
bright, 'til the pump pushed at great speed,
In and out, in and out, gives the light of their need.

In the old days of Africa now known by so few,
their old love developed, nurtured and grew.
Lying quiet spinning dreams at the end of each day,
two heads on one pillow, holding hands as they lay
watching the moon hanging over the hill,
lighting up thunderheads ready to spill,
Distant rains, from the deep velvet indigo night,
overcome by the moment their senses took flight.
Not the noise of the crickets or bats in their flight
can leach out the still of an African night.
The cough of a leopard in the outcrop nearby,
simply adds to the peace as they listen and lie.

What more can be given by God in your life,
in a world overwrought by such anger and strife.
These lives were embroidered and sent down from Heaven,
they were touched by His hand at the age of eleven.

Sleep well my love, now it shall be told,
how life from our teens began to unfold.
All the wonder we've known through all of our years,
so much laughter we had, we knew little of tears.

All the love in my life will always be yours, we
have known we have grown, we have come to this source.
When two lives intertwine as ours have done,
light turns to dark for the one left alone.

And now as I travel through life on my own,
I think of our past, cherish dreams we have known.
With paper and pen from my heart I shall write,
of the millions of stars in our African night.

THE MAN WITH THE GREY GREEN EYES

Where the sun lies behind dark clouds lined with white,
It paints the edges in bright golden light.
This halo of love transferred to the mind
In a passionate whirl makes the eyes become blind.
Tears roll blood pounds with a desire to fulfil
 Deep rainbow dreams their colours to spill
Over naked desires engulfing the heart
Make it scream, make it cry as it sees in the skies
A vision of longing in sad grey green eyes

Forever you'll be for the rest of my life
In the golden white clouds at the front of which lie
Grey vaporous masses over which I must fly
All the sadness I'll shed, as I empty my tears.
Kiss the lips I have known for so many years.
Your arms will enfold me again I shall feel,
The love and the comfort as gently I heal.
With love always present my gaze will arise to the man up above
With the kind, grey green eyes.

Our lives are like pebbles washed up on the shore
A change of the tide we're together no more
I now have to lie in the sand all alone
There are no arms to hold me
My heart is like stone
For a time I shall walk in voluminous shroud
Torn from the grey, of underneath cloud
Ere yon golden edges draw me to the skies to the man
With the smiling grey green eyes.

For Jim

CHAPTER 1

It was 6.30 a.m. on a dark, bitterly cold morning quieted by a blanket of white hoar frost. I opened heavy eyelids. 'Margie, time to get up,' my father called from the bottom of the stairs. Minutes later he tapped on the door 'Come on, time to get up', he insisted. I answered with an almost inaudible grunt. I stretched my legs drawing them back quickly as they crept towards a chilly untouched area of white sheet at the end of the bed. Looking over the bed covers I turned half closed eyes towards the window, and involuntary shivers swept through me. From the pavements outside, street gas lamps were shooting weak streaks of light across the glass, creating delicate frost-lace patterns as fingers of ice stretched across cold window panes.

The day had begun. Getting out of a warm, cosy bed was a great effort. It took every bit of courage I had to lift the feather eiderdown and to wrap it round my body and heave it up to my ears in an attempt to ward off the icy air. Once beneath the eiderdown I used my well rehearsed skills to find and put on my warm slippers. On the way to the bathroom I scratched the frozen window with the tip of my finger nail, breathing hard onto the scratched surface. As I peered warily through the melting ice my body became racked by goose pimples, my eyes took in the cold scene of glistening frost encrusted pavements. I closed the bathroom door firmly; the air from the paraffin stove was warm and vents in the top cover reflected fern-like patterns of light and shade onto the ceiling.

Slipping from under the eiderdown I washed quickly, wiped the steam from the mirror with a towel. A dressed reflection looked back at me. 'Not bad' I said to myself with a wry smile. A final pat to my wavy black hair, a tug of my gymslip and I was ready to start the day. I felt comfortable in the black and gold school uniform; our blazers, hats and the boys caps had a band of blue, purple, red or green, depending on which school house we were in. I was in Delves, my house colour was purple.

My father was the only person who called me Margie, to my school friends and a few select others I was simply 'Cog', a nickname derived from my failure to define this particular object, when it was drawn on the blackboard of the science laboratory. It never died, other people called me Jean. A coal fire in the kitchen range burned brightly, warm air rose to greet me as I walked down the stairs.

Ladling steaming hot porridge into a dish I covered it with brown sugar, a little milk and a lot of cream. I ate my breakfast quickly in order to catch a green Well's bus from outside the house to Harecastle station. The train left at 8.00am. Its destination was Crewe, and school. My long-suffering mother stood patiently waiting in the hall holding my satchel, gas mask, and hockey stick. She was tall, straight and elegant. 'Do hurry Jean' she said anxiously as she pressed money into my hand for school lunch and 10.00am tuck. With a kiss and a 'Goodbye mum,' I scurried out into the frosty air.
Well's bus was on time and the train was too. As I ran from the bus stop to the station, I almost lost my hat in sudden gust of wind 'Oh Heck 'it was a hard and fast rule that hats must always be worn to and from school.

The train drew slowly into Harecastle station, stopping with a screech of metal wheel on metal rail. Leaping into the carriage I was greeted by warm damp air jetting from beneath the seats as it steamed up windows and spectacles. Passengers hurried past to other carriages, opening doors then hastily closing them, in an effort to keep out the icy blast. Everyone huddled, shivered, and

2

wiped dripping red noses, as they pulled up their collars and blew warm breath into their woolly gloves before settling down.

I tucked myself into a corner and noticed the cold, red chapped faces of fellow passengers and I wondered what the day had in store for some of them. Workers wearing heavy boots, stretched blew their noses on red spotted handkerchiefs and yawned noisily as they swayed in rhythm to each movement of the train. Alongside them office workers clutched well worn brief cases. 'The-knees-together-brigade' were stifling yawns with frustrated sighs, tapping their lips rapidly with gloved fingers as they looked out of the window into the misty haze which hung over damp fields, before drifting through the hedges as it crept into every distant corner, painting an indistinct, chill landscape.

At two minor stations on our way to Crewe, the train picked up a daily contingent of commuters who mostly looked sleepy and grumpy. I wondered if it had something to do with the noise of the chattering students whose breathy words hung shrill in the chill morning air. The older travellers stepped sedately and with care into carriages; the younger contingent struggled with their bags calling loudly from one to the other, commenting on a recent date, or giving a shove in order to hurry the others along. Flopping into their seats, they greeted me rowdily, 'Hello Cog' they chorused. The conversation touched on the difficulties of last night's homework, as backwards and forwards we discussed what we felt was right and what was probably wrong. Everyone seemed to have found it difficult. Oh dear, maths!

We drew into Crewe station which was alive with people. There were parcels of every shape and size all of which were in the process of being heaved from guards' vans and piled high onto station platforms. Leaving the warm carriage was a cold skin-chilling experience. We made our way quickly through chattering hard-nosed porters who were intent on pulling flat-topped, open wooden trucks by their long metal handles, to the mountains of goods which were standing on each platform. Their job was to transfer every item, including milk churns, to the part of the platform which was marked out for its on-going destination.

It was a 15 minute to walk to school, so there was no time to waste. Out of the corner of my eye I noticed the wave of a green flag and heard a shrill whistle -blow. The guard leaped back into his van, closed the door and stuck his head out of the window as the train chugged out of platform two.

His face would soon be enveloped by a cloud of steam as the engine pulled slowly and noisily away. Skipping up the steps from the platform to the forecourt, we hurried along broken uneven pavements leading to school. We deposited ourselves in the warmth of the assembly hall with some relief and time to spare, becoming lost amid the sea of boys and girls who diverted the attention of a sharp-eyed headmaster from the figure he eagerly sought to ridicule. My mother had chosen this school for me. I felt it was a drain on her finances, fees, reading books, text and note books, and of course uniform all had to be paid for.

This was in late autumn, October 1940, during the second world war which raged despite Chamberlain having given many promises to the Germans in exchange for, 'Peace in our time'. Most pavements in the streets were decorated with smoke screens. Huge barrage balloons hung high in the sky. Sirens screamed to warn of air-raids, when people would disappear into Anderson shelters, holes in the ground, and pub cellars. Others braved it out. There were slogans of every description 'Dig for victory' was one; 'Is your journey really necessary?' was another. Chamberlain had collapsed. Churchill's speeches and rhetoric kept everyone 'fired up', getting us through what appeared to be an impossible situation.

There were ration books which covered everything from food to clothing. Imaginations were stretched as people wondered what to bake, what to sew and what to make out of the little they had. In the North West people dreaded the Germans aiming a direct high explosive hit on the station of Crewe, because its huge network of lines was a vital link with the rest of Great Britain. Crewe Works and the Rolls Royce factory were both prime targets; so many of our cities had almost been reduced to rubble.

My father became a member of the Home Guard, he took his duties very seriously and he bored my mother to tears with 'do's' and 'don'ts'; my brother cried a lot. I went to climb trees and play cricket with the local lads in nearby woods to get out of the way. Dan Bolton knocked on the door 'Coming to play cricket Jean?' he called. Nodding, 'Yes, I'm coming' I replied, whilst hurriedly lacing my shoes. There was no holding me back. 'Don't be late Jean' mother would call, with meaning. 'Okay' was my usual reply as I grabbed my cricket bat.

Most people dreaded Crewe station but I liked its distinct smell of oil, smoke, engine grease and something else which I could never quite put a finger on. I liked the jostle of the crowds, the hustle, bustle and noise which seemed to give it an air of mystery, and seductive romance. The lights of the station were dim, to some a little daunting. Trains drew into their scheduled platforms, guards gave an ear-splitting cry, 'Crewe, all change at Crewe'. Sleeping passengers shot back to life, tumbling out still drowsy onto greasy platforms. They squinted through the dim lights in an effort to spot a porter. Some sought the exit, others platform numbers for a connection to on-going destinations. Each platform had tiny shaded light bulbs squinting onto signs revealing doors to the toilets and the way to newspaper kiosks. 'Careless talk costs lives', said posters on the wall. People cupped their hands around warm mugs of steaming drinks bought from the small waiting-room cafés on every platform. As trains pulled out slowly they were chased by late passengers running with coats flying, towards the nearest door of the train. Puffing and blowing they pulled down the door handles, leaped in and slammed the door behind them, just in time.

Massive engines coupled to passenger trains, goods carriages and rolling stock moved endlessly along the network of lines which made up Crewe junction. Smoke and jets of hot steam belched from below the engines. Passengers and troops jumped from trains at the end of their journey, leaving others to wait wearily for a little longer. Some perhaps to wait for connections which may not arrive at all. It was the norm in this frenetic hub of railway travel in the North West during the war years. The platforms were usually a heaving, moving mass of humanity. Blobs of civilian colour were interspersed with khaki, RAF blue and navy. There were posters, porters and billboards advertising everything from cocoa to sausages displayed on walls alongside platform numbers. Tension merged with staccato cries of wild excitement, some faces wore broad smiles in their expectancy, others with heads hung low said farewell to their loved ones.

In Crewe town most streets were blacked out, windows were draped with dark heavy-duty curtains to prevent chinks of light from spilling out into the night. Some cars ventured out, drivers nose to glass peered warily out of steamy windscreens into almost empty streets. Hooded headlamps were of little help. The one exception to this darkness was at the time of an air raid when brilliant fingers of light stretched from strategically placed search lights on the ground, reaching up, spreading out and penetrating the inky black sky in search of enemy aircraft. Positive sightings would result in a whip lash crack of anti-aircraft fire. Long metal barrels pointing up to heaven fired shells which split the night skies, to finally explode like giant fire crackers.

One autumn night, sirens wailed their all-clear, high explosives and incendiary bombs had fortunately failed to hit their intended targets. A small explosion quite near to Crewe Grammar School created a flurry of activity, creating considerable chaos. Lessons were disrupted, staff were in confusion, pupils were excited and in high glee. Teachers instructed pupils, and the pupils reluctant though they might have been, followed the instructions without hesitation.

It was during this time that one day, during a period of private study, I sat on the shaded side of the assembly hall with my legs curled beneath the desk, reading, when suddenly I noticed the handsome boy a little older than myself who was sitting opposite. The sun was directing a shaft of light onto his fair wavy hair, giving emphasis to his broad shoulders and the stocky frame beneath. I gave a little shiver, it was my first inkling of how suddenly 'lightning can strike'. We lifted our heads at the same time, our eyes met and a future was born. Little did I think that this small seemingly unimportant incident would have such an impact on my future. Our eye contact was followed by the quick flick of a note from the end of a ruler, the paper was folded into a tight pellet which landed alongside my foot. With pounding heart I bent to pick it up. I unfolded my treasure carefully stroking it out over the desk top. The message in small neat handwriting said, 'Can I walk you to the station?' I looked up and he gave me a tiny smile. I was flushed, overwhelmed and in a dreadful flap. I replied without hesitation 'Yes'.

Each day after this, Jim Moss collected his green bicycle from the boys' cycle rack and walked to the top of the drive which led from the gate of the girls entrance, to wait for me. He leaned relaxed and patient by the wall, his head slightly to one side, a fair uncontrolled curl lying softly over his forehead. He never seemed to mind waiting, he said 'If I want something badly enough I shall wait, forever if that is what it takes'. Catching sight of me he winked, and his face broke into a shy smile. He lifted his bike and walked towards me; taking my hockey stick, gas mask and satchel he tied them to his cross bar. We sauntered along in a dream walking over broken misshapen footpaths which led to Crewe station, down the luggage ramp to platform No 2. It was here that we made plans for future dates. Each day became magic.

The next day, as on all other days we walked to the station together, it was raining but we barely noticed. The headmaster had decided the whole school was to go to the cinema to see the film 'Stanley and Livingston' which he felt would be a good geographical learning curve, a diversion during the bomb disruption. Each group upper, middle and lower school walked in crocodile to the Plaza cinema. The line buzzed with excitement. Wangling seats side by side had not been difficult. Dreams began to unfold before our eyes. The big cinema screen led us into Africa, in our imagination we were exploring Africa together. The continent seemed to hold everything we loved and had so often talked about. We could visualise animals wandering in herds through wide tracts of bush country hung over by vast moody skies. There were risks to be taken, isolation and unforgiving heat, the people, their way of life and all the mysteries of their folklore. The film gave substance to our dreams and the belief that one day destiny would lead us there. 'I love you Jean Brindley' and 'I love you Jim Moss'. We were fifteen years old!

During the war our cities were devastated, Crewe on a smaller scale was part of this national picture. Sirens wailed, shrapnel fell, the streets were turned into rivers of bricks and rubble. There were smouldering 'skeletons' which had once been lines of street houses, shops and factories were standing like jagged teeth against the skyline, their very fabric lying amongst the watery debris littering the streets below. Fire engines and firemen fled in all directions in their efforts to douse flames which threatened to take hold and devour everything in their path. Winston Churchill offered us, 'blood, toil, tears and sweat' for however long it took to win the war.

Jim, along with other boys from school was recruited into the Crewe sea cadets. I stood amongst my friends and others who went to watch them on parade, I made a point of jostling to the front. It was a jaunty, jolly affair, at times they were a little out of step as they marched down the main street of the town but Oh! we were so proud of them. They looked very smart in their naval uniforms. The sight 'fairly made yer toes curl!' In their enthusiasm they looked as though they could change the whole course of events and we went along with this image.

We walked over the fields of Cheshire gun in hand, accompanied by Rover the dog. Rabbit pie was a good source of protein and meat was rationed. We had every excuse to catch rabbits. On warm sunny days we were tempted to sit in the long cool grass as we talked and we dreamed. Sometimes Jim made me long daisy chains, putting them over my head. 'Suits you' he would say wistfully'. We sat talking of Africa, of our hopes for the future and, more relevant to the moment, of our next date. Later with fingers entwined we ambled our way home, bending to pick wild mushrooms on the way.

I loved going to the pictures even though it usually meant me waiting, with racing heart and baited breath beneath the clock at Smith's bookshop come rain or shine. The bus always seemed to be late, which threw me into a complete panic. In time the red double decker bus would appear round the corner from Victoria street and there he was, swinging on the bus rail, with not a care in the world. A smile on his face, a wink in his eye, and his curls blowing in the wind. Seeing him was the cue for me to dash to the bus stop excitedly.

Queuing at the Odeon cinema meant standing beside many other folk in the alley which ran alongside the wall from the back of the cinema to the foyer. The wind howled relentlessly down this narrow opening. Regardless of the season, the cold air sent people jostling in the gusts of wind. I put my back to Jim and he slid his arm around my waist to protect me against the onslaught of the draught! Our chances of getting the seat we preferred were better when we were at the front of the queue. In the entrance to the foyer an attendant stood waiting to welcome the patrons; he was always resplendent in a green suit with ornate gold epaulets and trimmings of gold braid. His shoes were black and shiny. His face shone, his fair wavy hair was Brylcreemed and neatly combed back. He allowed two, four, sometimes six people at a time to approach the cash desk to buy tickets. Green clad usherettes standing at different points in the cinema switched on torches, checked the tickets and then tore them in half. They led people through the haze of blue tobacco smoke to their seats. We always chose to sit beneath the finger of light stretching from the projection room at the back of the cinema to the screen beyond. Beneath this light an intimate darkness beckoned all young lovers. We settled down in a rosy glow of contentment. I felt an arm reach over my shoulders. Here and there, girls dressed in the same shade of green carried trays secured around their neck by a canvas cord. The trays displayed drinks and goodies for sale. As more people arrived the place buzzed with excitement and chatter, which competed with shrill whistles from boys when their eye caught sight of an attractive girl. There was the noisy sound of people sucking at straws from empty bottles. Added to all this matches and lighters flared and cigarette ends glowed in the dim light.

When the show began an organ rose slowly from the dark crevice beneath the cinema screen, both player and organ picked out by a spotlight. The organist who was always immaculately dressed, played 'God save the king' with great aplomb. This was followed by assorted music for some minutes, then a burst of introductory music heralded the film. As the curtain was slowly drawn back, the organ began to retreat into the inky blackness from which it had previously ascended.

No one ever seemed to see that special someone secreted in the projection room; the man who set the spools rolling and the screen blazing to show the latest news of the war by Pathe Gazette, together with the assorted advertisements and excerpts from films soon to be shown. There were previews of westerns, thrillers, love stories and musicals of the time. It was the age of the big band sound. We had seen Glenn Miller in 'Orchestra Wives' . At that time, there were so many soft and sweet songs. 'Serenade in Blue' became a tune with very special meaning. It evoked heart-wrenching memories of each phase in our lives, the gentleness, passion and love which always burned so brightly in our hearts.

The light thrown from the screen and projection room pierced the haze, picking out patterns of uneven lines, hazy featureless heads some upright, some side by side, others stealing a kiss. At the introduction of next week's film there was a momentary silence in the cinema, on this occasion it was to be 'Now Voyager' the theme tune was 'Wrong'. We decided there and then, that we would see it. Also coming soon was 'Casablanca' starring Humphrey Bogart and Ingrid Bergman; it made such an impression on us that we walked out of the cinema in a dream, especially me! In the future at some of the most poignant times in our lives, Jim, would look into my eyes and say quietly, 'Here's looking at you kid.' His delivery of this short line was so full of meaning that I almost turned to jelly.

Some Saturdays we went to the Astoria ballroom in Crewe, and sometimes to the town hall. My mother never seemed to mind or worry if I was with Jim. This was very odd, she was usually so particular as to where I was going and with whom. In those young halcyon days, we danced misty eyed to some of the tunes of the day, our looks spoke volumes. Other faces we knew from school stood around, some alone, some with girls, a few having visited the pub were a little bleary eyed and slightly worse for wear.

The war continued to rage, changing the course of events. Churchill encouraged us to go forward, towns were still suffering, ravages of the blitz. Our risks were pretty remote compared with city folk. Danger was always around the corner, it could strike anywhere, with no warning. As summer came we took to the hills, we rode on our bicycles to Beeston and Bickerton hills. Sitting amongst the heather we picnicked on sandwiches and boiled eggs all washed down with tizer. It was a good and simple life. Caught in a summer storm, we sought shelter beneath big oak trees, or in a hole in the hedge. Always we emerged sodden, but happy.

Slowly our lives moved on to another phase. Jim's finals were fast approaching, he had chosen after completing them to go to agricultural college. Tropical agriculture would be included in his studies. We still met as often as possible, though we did not have the close proximity of the past. There were times of quiet desolation as I tried to get to grips with the changes. The green bicycle was replaced by a B.S.A. 650 motorcycle for greater ease of travel between college and home.

 Due to an eighteen month age difference my exams were a year after Jim's. We became a little gloomy over events Jim asked me what I had in mind for the future. Nursing I told him. We had discussed this many times in the past, now the crunch had come. Nothing was the same, the bubble had burst, no hand turned inwards to give me chocolate when girls passed boys on the school gallery. Our 10a.m. break was no longer something to die for.

Each day I walked to the station following the same worn pathways. Now, unaccustomed to struggling with luggage, I hauled it over my shoulder only to find it would persist in slipping down, almost driving me frantic. My friends made 'sad' comments 'What a state you are in,' 'Come back Jim all is forgiven' they muttered, helping me to heave the bag straps back into position. In the train I put my baggage onto the rack, Jim had always done this for me, 'For goodness sake buck up' Brian called from the corner opposite, 'Just hush' I replied. His brother Tony picked up my hockey stick which had fallen from the rack. 'Thanks Tony.' I smiled at him, Brian said 'Not again', he had often noticed how his brother came to my aid. I sat and stared vacantly out of the window, miles away.

Suddenly we were in Alsager. 'Cheerio Cog' they all chorused. 'See you in the morning'. 'Bye I'll look out for you'. Looking out meant pulling on the door strap which let down the window and sticking my head out. Running towards the carriage. 'Hello Cog,' they would yell, piling in and flopping down. It would be the start to another day. I was brought out of my reverie by the porter yelling Harecastle station. Grabbing my luggage, I stepped from the train and set off to walk the odd mile along the canal side, to the village of Hall Green.

A small Cheshire village, Hall Green had, at this time, a chapel, a pub and a village store which sold literally everything. It belonged to my friend Alby Pierpoint. There was a tennis court and a club house which was approached by a particularly narrow path over bad tempered Mr Maddocks' fields. A little further down the road in Scholar Green, a small village hall was a meeting place for locals. It was here that residents rehearsed and performed in light opera. Everyone gave of their best. The village audience, seated on wooden chairs, cheered and clapped with infectious enthusiasm as each participant appeared on stage to do their 'bit.'

Silence fell as the production began, broken by fervent chattering during the ten-minute interval, before the second half. At the finale the audience clapped again whilst a local dignitary handed flowers to the principal players.

Everyone enjoyed these 'get together' times, the wail of sirens doing little to quench their enthusiasm. The village hall was also used as a meeting place by the local village band. Each week they practised for the annual garden party held at Rode Hall. Music from 'The Gondoliers', 'The Merry Widow' and other such 'gems' rung out over the grounds, guests dressed for the occasion sat at small tables, ate scones and drank tea from china cups. The garden party was fun. There were coconut shies to tempt accuracy and pride, trinket stalls, lucky dips, ice cream, pop corn and cream teas. Boat trips were taken on the lake, teenage boys and girls paid their money and a boat was chosen. The boys, in a show of fierce masculine energy, rowed away from the tiny jetty, flirting madly with the girl sitting at the opposite end.

Always, as I left the house to go to this event, mother called, 'Keep out of trouble Jean.' I was never quite sure what she meant, but felt that had Jim had been with me the comment would not have been made. Those were the days! The days when in nearby Moreton Hall, a beautiful Elizabethan house, surrounded by a moat, pageants were staged. The days when the cubs and scouts, brownies and guides, paraded with the brass band, marching their way to church for the Armistice service.

Mother had given a temporary home to an evacuee, Sam. He was enjoying a different way of life and had become much more relaxed since living with us in the village. There was no blitz to fear, no blood, no sweat, no tears. He took well to the country and country ways and was sad to leave his new family when the time came. A desperate wish to see his parents helped the sadness.

With Jim at college I found other ways of whiling away my time. I visited my aunt at the Moors farm. Here, on the kitchen beams hams hung to cure; eggs, milk thick with cream and other perishables stood on a marble slab in the huge walk-in larder. One of my chores was to carry out 'baggin' consisting of tea and a basket of sandwiches, to the men working in the fields.

At this time in my life my most relaxing hours were deliberately spent in a green and verdant valley not far from my home. It was called 'Sandy Desert' and this was my bolt hole from prying eyes; the noise of people, the place I went to when I wanted to be alone and in peace. I could search my thoughts without interruption, I could daydream, sing, read, draw, paint and weave dreams in this magical place. Undisturbed on the grassy slopes I could think of the past and make plans for the future. My faithful, battered old school bag carried sandwiches and a bottle of water, or lemonade if I had pocket money to spare. Despite the heat of summer, the stream rippling through the trees at the bottom of the green slopes could be soporific and relaxing as it danced its way over stones and pebbles, swirling its way round marsh marigolds and cuckoo pints which had strayed from the banks to the water's edge and beyond. Usually I placed a piece of grass between my teeth, lying down in an effort to juggle with my uppermost thoughts. Up popped a face, it was Jim. Gazing up at white vaporous clouds scudding over a blue sky, I wondered if he too was looking up at these same clouds. We often watched and commented on the sky together. So many emotions raced through my awakening body on these occasions.

One day whilst lying there, memories came flooding back to the time of my fifteenth birthday party; mother had decided to take a group of my friends for afternoon tea to Moreton Hall. Jim was late and I had refused to move until he arrived. I could visualise it so clearly. Suddenly there he was, arriving just moments before the bus. Blonde curl bobbing he sped round the corner, deposited his bike and ran, running, puffing and blowing, full of apologies, towards us.

Still lying idly on the grass, watching the clouds, my imagination flew to the evenings when he had ridden over to the market town of Sandbach to see me, having first helped his father to wash and put away the glasses after the bar had closed. He had thought little of jumping onto his bike, peddling like hell as he sped over the five miles of country lanes, in order to arrange a future date and give me a much awaited hug and kiss 'Goodnight.' Only to be off again, back into the darkness on his return journey, a street lamp revealing his quick wave as he disappeared round the far corner. Wistfully I gazed after him humming, 'Serenade in Blue.' On the above occasion I had been staying overnight with my cousin, her husband had an ironmongers-cum-fix-it shop in the high street. There was a narrow entry running up the side to the back entrance, in which we could hide!

I snapped out of my dreams, time to sit up, come back to reality and concentrate on my drawing. I paused from time to time to make sure the shading was in the right place, giving the effect I wanted. A bee buzzed by flicking my cheek as it passed, back again, around my head it went. I swung out my hand. It disappeared. I could not have been happier, alone with my thoughts, dreams, sketch book, pencils and a picnic. In the gentle breeze my imagination drifted to the soft touch of a hand reaching out to give me a bar of chocolate. Suddenly there was a nip in the air. I gave an involuntary shiver. 'Time to move,' I said to myself. It occurred to me to visit my artist friend she could comment on my sketching. Snapping out of my reverie I picked up sandwich paper and rubbish and stuffed it into the bag. It was now late afternoon, time to make my way home.

As I climbed over the stile I shivered again, it was becoming even cooler. I felt I needed a little constructive criticism of my drawing, work must be finished and presented to the art master within the next few days. Ambling absent mindedly along the sandy lane towards the main road and my home, I was suddenly drawn to a halt. 'Mm coffee,' I murmured to myself, as the smell of delicious percolating coffee drifted over the air. I was approaching Maria's house, she had seen me coming along the lane and was leaning against the gate. Huge tortoiseshell glasses and long brown hair framed her dark handsome face and her slim fingers were adorned with enormous silver rings and tipped with blood red nails. In her mouth she held a delicately balanced cigarette holder; protruding from the holder was an aromatic Passing Cloud cigarette, its tip gently glowing like a fluorescent bead. Her dress as always consisted of slacks and a shirt covered by a paint slashed linen smock. 'Calling in for coffee?' she asked. 'Lovely thanks, could you give me an opinion on my drawing?' 'Sure, come on in.' We went into her tiny room in which there were seats topped with chintz covers; a small table covered with a lace cloth and set with china teacups patterned with small pink roses. Beyond this room, her cluttered studio held everything from brushes to paints, huge easels and canvases, she was a very successful artist.

We sat down and over coffee discussed my drawing. She felt it was well drawn, of good content and pleasing, there was little she could find fault with. We sat chatting in this cosy atmosphere until the bewitching crepuscular light appeared, as darkness began to fall. 'Time to say goodnight,' I feel I should make the short walk home. 'Thanks for coffee and for your comments'.

'Goodnight, sweet dreams, may see you tomorrow,' Maria chucked me under the chin, a habit of hers. I went out into the now dusky moonlight, closed the little wooden gate and continued on up the lane. Maria was a divorcee, I felt a little apprehensive as to mother's reaction on hearing of my visit to her home. My fears were unnecessary, she was dancing attention on my younger brother. I crept in unnoticed. The following day I followed my usual routine and caught the train to Crewe.

Jim, by this time, was having new experiences, meeting new people, making new friends, he was learning from a different and unfamiliar curriculum, his horizons were widening. He was enjoying college and making the most of his time there. Many opportunities opened up and were directed at him, his finals had been a great success. He weighed up the pros and cons of what he wanted from life. His choice was to go overseas. Lurching from day to day I travelled backwards and forwards on the train to school. Life did not hold the exciting events of the past. One day merged into another, all seemingly alike with no light and shade, no quick heartbeats. Come the end of the school day, how I missed the lonely figure standing on the platform waving until the train was out of sight. I had put my head out of the window, frantically waving back, until I could no longer see him through the billowing smoke belching from the engine's chimney. Then sitting down I had read the little note scribbled for me on the back of my mirror, just before the train was due to leave, 'I love you Cog.' Those were happy days.

These days I settled into a corner of the carriage, and gazed through a haze of smoke thrown back by the old steam train. My thoughts persistently dissolved into a dreamlike quality, imagining a life with Jim. Meanwhile I had exams to pass, and my future to attend to. I had chosen nursing as a career I had better get on with 'things'. Oh how we rejoiced when the war was over. How we danced on V.E. night. The streets were full of revellers, everyone had a party and most streets had a communal party. In every conceivable hall in the country people danced, their faces wreathed in smiles, to a weary standstill.

CHAPTER 2

The time had come to re-weave our lives. One day, having decided to do a little shopping I caught a train into Chester. Looking longingly into a shop window, deep in thought, I suddenly heard, 'Hello Jean, fancy seeing you.' Turning round quickly I found myself looking into the face of Jim's mother. 'Good gracious, Hello,' I managed to stammer. When I asked how Jim was she pointed to a timbered restaurant nearby, 'Shall we sit and talk over a cup of tea.' Taken aback, all I could say was 'Yes please'. And so over tea and scones I learned of his future intentions. He had made up his mind and was applying for positions in Africa, now with great anticipation, he awaited replies. I knew this was going to happen eventually, what I had not realized was that it would be so soon.

The following weekend I decided to stay with with my cousin, so when the time came off I went in high glee. 'Bye mum.' 'Bye love, enjoy yourself' smiling she watched me leave. Jim would ring me, perhaps we could meet; from Sandbach it was so easy to hop onto a bus into Crewe. I gazed through the bus windows in joyful anticipation of the next 48 hours. I felt a telephone call in the air. Bright and breezy I arrived at the shop. Mary was married to an ironmonger, his shop was used by all the local farmers, there was everything to root for and anything to buy, a veritable Aladdins cave, lots of nooks crannies with walls made up of tiny drawers each having a little worn brass ring to pull on.

My bedroom at the back was over the kitchen, cosy and warm,; old fashioned striped paper decorated the walls, a smell of cooking pervaded the house and shop. I plonked my case down in the bedroom and was immediately called down to supper, we were on the verge of sitting down when the phone went, a tall, black old fashioned phone, it had an upright stand with a swollen latticed piece on the top for speaking into, the cradle attached to the side of the stand held another smaller black rounded oblong with a convolution at one end used to hold by the ear to receive conversation.

I rushed to pick up the phone immediately recognising the voice, 'Hello what a lovely surprise' I heard my voice say, it belied my inside pounding. 'Hello love when did you arrive?' 'Quarter of an hour ago, how are you what are you doing?' I said. Something told me things were not quite as they should be. 'Mum told me you met in Chester, she enjoyed the chat over tea and I think she said scones.' I heard myself say 'Jim why did you not tell me you were thinking of going overseas in the immediate future and had already started to put out feelers in Africa' The next sentence I could not believe, I was simply flabbergasted. 'I saw you having an animated conversation with a Yank when so I was passing through Sandbach, I hardly knew if you would be interested in what I was doing,' he said. Jumping to my own defence immediately, I told him 'Jimmy', another Jim! was a friend of the family who visited the house when he was sad and homesick; mother used to talk to him about his family. This was our first disagreement over anything and proved to be a turning point affecting many years of our lives. I also saw he could be was jealous, which amazed me.

Strolling to the post box deep in thought, just a few days after this telephone conversation, I looked up at the approach of a motorbike, instantly recognising the familiar figure coming towards me. What I did not expect was the girl sitting behind in the pillion seat, flaming red hair streaming out in the wind. I was racked with jealousy, it felt like the end of the world, how could he do this? The only thing I could take heart from was the special little wink always kept souly for me. I felt this act was his way of saying 'See how it feels?' Watching him disapear into the distance was a nightmare. I put the letter into the post box, had the most dreadful night invaded by dreams and fantasies. I was grateful when the dawn came through. Within a short time he had left for Africa. My life continued on in a melee of confusion.

My exams completed and successful, I decided to spend some time in the Land Army as I had a year to spare before I could commence my nursing career. I enjoyed working the land, muck spreading, harvesting, milking, dairy work, calling in the cattle, washing down the shippons and generally slopping about in 'wellies'. Coming from a farming family I found no difficulties in this way of life. In fact I enjoyed it immensely. Too soon I felt, the time came for me to pack my bags, leave home and start nursing. It was a far cry from any discipline attempted in the past, there were so many rules which had to be obeyed and so many restrictions, the list of 'Can't do's' was endless and very daunting.

Hospital uniform consisted of thick black stockings with black laced shoes below a long heavy gingham dress, over this a snow white apron. We had cloaks to throw over our uniform when we walked along open windy corridors from ward to ward, to the dining room or to our 'rooms'. Never were we allowed to step outside the hospital in uniform. Attempting to stuff my wiry black hair into a well-starched nursing cap proved an almost impossible task. 'Are you ready?' this was Daphne my friend, 'Yes I am' I lied nodding to myself 'Yes I'm coming'. 'Well hurry, we are late for the lecture.' 'Okay,' I replied, lacing up my shoes hopping about on one foot. I was still doing battle with the hair, not one hair must show. I literally fell out of my bedroom door, Daphne was now very impatient with me as we walked briskly down the corridor, never running. 'Nurse, you only run in fire and haemorrhage.'

My nails had always been my pride and joy, now they had to be filed short, there must be nothing for germs to hide behind. Periodically they were inspected just to make sure. The first year was hard, made worse by inadequate food. Things did not bode well, ward work, lessons, studies and vitually no free time were not the things life was made for. I felt life should not be such a drudge. There were of course those who were dedicated to this spartan existence, my friend was one of them.

On the wards I looked after my patients with all the skill and care I could muster. There was much jealousy, bitterness and frustration among the senior staff with the resulting unfairness which angered me deeply. Many had trained and remained, hence their word was always above reproach, no other claim would ever be considered, what they said was carved in stone. At the end of my first training period I took the preliminary exams and passed them. I now knew that this was not really what I wanted out of life. When the time came I sat in edgy silence for some minutes before telling my long-suffering mother of my decision. She was not at all pleased, it was, it must be said the career she had always wanted for me. I have to admit Jim's absence seemed to make it difficult for me to form positive decisions; for most of our formative years we had made so many future plans together. When I mentioned this to mother, her retort was 'Piffle'.

Suddenly my parents decided to leave our 'roots', our village home. Home now, was to be near to the cousin with whom I had spent so much time in the past. The more I thought of this, the more I became obsessed with disbelief at how the misinterpretation of a simple situation could turn two lives around. Once settled in our new home I felt the time had come for action. I rang Jim's mother periodically to catch up on his news. He always seemed to be in good spirits, she said, enjoying his new life and experiences. He had written to me, he told his mother. Where was the letter, I wondered.

Having put the nursing career behind me I decided to explore new territory. After a night out with a friend currently training as a metallurgist in a local factory a course of action was taken. Shortly afterwards I heard there was a vacancy in the laboratory, and tentatively I approached the senior metallurgist as to the possibility of my becoming a trainee, I underwent one or two formalities and to my astonishment after this brief interview found myself accepted. I enjoyed the work as it was challenging, and demanded considerable concentration and application, exactly what was needed at this time. When not bent in concentration over an experiment or a long line of analysis, we all shared a great deal of laughter. Don proved himself to be an understanding fellow, he painstakingly explained each delicate procedure until it became second nature. This appointment, at this time, was a finger pointing, it had a dramatic influence over my future life.

The early morning brought rain, but now it had increased to a heavy downpour not at all conducive to leaping from a warm bed into a cold bathroom. I washed and dressed quickly, then mended the ravages of the night with a spot of makeup. Whistling a little tune I hurried downstairs, and a glance at the grandfather clock told me the truth, 'Heck, only fifteen minutes to catch the bus' I said out loud, often I cycled to work, impossible in this deluge. Hastily I boiled the kettle, made tea and put a slice of bread under the grill. Tea made, I took a cup upstairs to mother and bade her, 'Bye, see you later.' In a race to eat the toast, 'If only I had hauled myself out of bed a few minutes earlier,' I muttered. I spread on vast quantities of salty farm butter, topping it with a spoonful of honey. It was scrumptious, I would have liked more. Grabbing my mackintosh and umbrella from the hall stand, and sandwiches from the larder, I called 'Goodbye mum,' and fled through the door into the rain and a nearby bus stop.

Rain pounded the umbrella, within a few minutes the bus had arrived. Damp bodies of passengers steamed up the windows, sleepy distorted faces peered through hand-rubbed-off moisture to see where they were. The bus came to a halt in the midst of a large muddy puddle; in order to get in or out of the bus the puddle had to be manoeuvred; inside there was much chattering with the odd peel of raucous laughter thrown in. In the corner, on the back seat, sat an extremely large lady she wearing a canary yellow hat and bright red lipstick, sitting next to her some young blade gave a snigger, she gave a huge guffaw. I felt she had passed on a shady joke, after which she closed her eyes and promptly fell asleep, mouth open, yellow hat wiping the steamy window. People around smiled, obviously amused by the partly-heard incident. A man arrived at his destination and as stood up his glasses tumbled to the floor his sole comment, as fumbling he stooped to pick them up, was 'Bugger it'.

Inside the bus it smelt alarmingly of damp clothes and stale tobacco, people appeared to be enveloped in a blue haze. The next stop was mine and it would be a relief to get off the bus despite the heavy rain outside. Umbrella up, head down and jumping puddles I raced through the rain towards the laboratory. I heard and saw nothing. I did, however, run headlong into an individual on a bike peddling towards the factory repair shop. There were cars, bicycles and people all over the place, all streaming into the works at the buzzer's last wail. Peering from beneath a now misplaced umbrella, 'I am so sorry' my face was red, 'No harm done. Who are you, what is your name, are you okay?' I hardly knew which question to answer first. 'Jean, yes I'm fine thanks, just wringing wet.' I felt covered with embarrassment as I thought 'what an odd-looking chap', his hair was greased down in dark wavy squiggles. 'My name is Tom, can I take you for a drink tonight at the Old Hall, 7.30p.m., just to show there are no hard feelings?' For some reason, I shall never know why, I said 'Yes, thanks' then sped off in the rain. 'Yes' delivered so swiftly and without thought, consumed me for the rest of the day, it was so out of character.

A little research told me Tom's father was in charge of the repair department, he was held in some regard by management, and eventually he was elevated to Overseas sales, which was to take him to all parts of the world. I did not realise the impact this short encounter would have on my future. Out of curiosity I kept the date at the Old Hall, noticing as the evening wore on that Tom was rather more than a two-pint-a-night man! Over the next months we met often, attending grass track meetings in which Tom always took part, this with his insatiable desire to quaff beer seemed to be the sum total of his interests. At times my mind spun, wondering what on earth I was doing in this situation. Often my thoughts went out to Jim. One evening when in a particularly vocal mood he told me something of his past, of his time spent in France during the war and of a French girl with whom he had fallen in love. I told him my story of Jim, explaining my feelings and how I knew they would never change. My inference was that if Jim and I did meet again, there would be no alternative but to be together as we had in our school days.

Within ten months Tom asked my parents for permission to marry. Mother's reply had been a resounding 'No'. Father gave in, 'Yes'. I was accepted by his family, he was never a part of mine. I felt in no-mans land, perhaps I could re-direct his interests? Quite the reverse happened. Hence this story can be told.

CHAPTER THREE

Setting out a life remembered is no simple task, the memory plays tricks with light and shade. The one positive thing I understood at this point, was that the answer to my unhappiness lay many thousands of miles away. I made a secret resolve. With this at the back of my mind, questions were asked of myself, answers were sought.

Presently life was destined to be difficult, at times downright impossible. Despite this I decided giving up hope was not an option. Destiny was to play a big part in my future. At this point painting, drawing, dancing and reading became an integral part of my life; being a member of the local amateur dramatic society provided an outlet for my inner turmoil and confusion. The stage was an ideal place on which to release the frustration of mistakes, and give vent to my boiling wrath.

On a hot summers day in 1948 I married Tom. It was a small, simple no frills wedding, in tune with the dreary pattern of our courtship. The only exciting bit of the whole episode had been my knocking him off his bike in the rain! My mother, who was not, in any sense happy with the event, sang sotto voce 'You little fool' with every hymn. I seemed to be unaware of what was happening to me, nor had I the remotest idea of its significance. My wedding to Tom was an informal, quiet affair with just family and friends at the church.

'Oh! look at Jean,' I heard people say as I walked past. I had on a long 'New Look' skirt, the top was jacket type, there were buttons down the front; it had a nipped in waist and long sleeves. The collar had a trim of white appliqué, the material was heavy navy-blue silk. Navy kid court shoes completed the outfit. The hat I borrowed, but now. I cannot remember it at all. My hair at the time was longish and wavy. All the usual compliments were offered. Guests and people round about were in a happy and buoyant mood, whereas I began to have some inexplicable misgivings and so had my mother by the look on her face. I felt like running away but I calmed down and the wedding went without a hitch. Suddenly for a reason I could not explain, I had an urge to run away somewhere, anywhere would do. My mother looked irate, she was opposed to the whole event and made it very obvious. The reception was held in a small hotel nearby. People were seated, wine poured, toasts drunk, food enjoyed. There were the usual speeches with endless innuendos, more glasses were raised. Reminiscent of rehearsals from a recent play the whole scenario was dream-like.

After the reception people stood around, wished us good luck and waited for us to leave for the honeymoon in a car which Tom's father had kindly lent us for a few days. Our journey to Morecambe was one of almost complete silence despite my attempts to make a little conversation. 'Do you like my outfit?' I asked. I had topped my navy-blue suit with a smart coat. The reply was a grunted 'Yes its okay'. 'Is that all you have to say?' No reply. What an uneventful journey. Before we had travelled very far my new husband complained of a headache. This made me smile, the thought crossing my mind that only women were supposed to suffer headaches on such occasions.

We drove around for sometime and eventually found the hotel. The porter took our luggage to the bedroom which turned out to be a smart suite which took me completely by surprise. We talked a little and read for a short time. Tom decided that perhaps a rest would ease his aching head so he lay down and went to sleep almost immediately. He snored, grunted, twitched, and looked, well, pathetic really.

Feeling somewhat at a loss, I suddenly felt an overwhelming urge to fill my lungs with cold, fresh stinging sea air, something to clear the collected fuzz in my brain. Putting on warmer clothes I departed hastily, hands in pockets and head down, into a salty wind which stung my face and blew away the cobwebs. I walked along the promenade and made my way down to the beach. I was one of the few hardy souls facing the bracing sea air; gingerly I picked my way between salt water pools lying fresh and clear, as the tide went out it left ripples of sand and stones in its wake. I bent down and carefully chose a number of fine smooth flat stones, polished them with my hands then put them into my coat pocket. I rolled them around slowly, feeling their velvet softness. I heard each dull bump as my fingers jostled one stone against the other. I took the stones out of my pocket one by one, placed them with precision between my thumb and index finger, took a deep penetrating breath of salt air, then with some force deftly skimmed them across the sea, counting the number of times I could make them jump as they sped over the water. Strolling back along the sand, I splashed in tiny pools and kicked at pebbles, reeling in the knowledge of the ghastly mistake I had made, glaringly aware of my inability to turn back the clock. My walk back to the hotel was accompanied by deep thought and absolute confusion.

Pushing open the swing doors I came into full view of the bar where Tom was sitting squarely on a stool with a pint pot in front of him. 'Oh heck, not a good start to the evening' I thought to myself as I made my way to the bed room to change and generally titivate. Afterwards, I took a leisurely stroll towards the lift stepped in and pressed the button. Its descent to the sitting room was rather bumpy and when it reached the ground below the door slid open to reveal Tom, he was still sitting in the bar. It was almost time to eat.

We ate as I remember, a reasonably tasty meal. It was well cooked and well presented, accompanied by a bottle of wine. My now father-in-law had been the instigator of this extravagance, it had been arranged in advance of our arrival. I thought it was a wonderful gesture. Dinner was eaten almost in silence and there had been a great deal of head holding. By this time I was fast becoming frustrated by the lack of conversation. 'Thank goodness I don't bite my nails, they would be down to the wick' I heard myself say. 'What do you mean?' asked Tom, 'Just forget it' was the only reply that I felt capable of.

Our meal over, Tom went back to the bar and I decided to go up to our room. I read for a short time and drifted off to sleep quite quickly. This was to be the pattern of our four day 'Honeymoon.' What a catastrophe. We had both made a monumental mistake.

Our families (not my mother), awaited our arrival home and they were bursting with curiosity about what we would have to say, they wondered about our enjoyable (or so they thought) last few days. Gradually their features became more and more crestfallen, news-starved faces surrounded me, and I resorted to light-hearted small talk. I was so very unhappy. Later in the day we moved into a small house which had in the past been a privately owned school. Tom's father had arranged for the rental of the property, which belonged to a friend. He also bought most of the furniture from yet another friend who happened to be in the business of furniture making. The family had worked hard to make it comfortable during the four days we had been away.

It made a comfortable little home. The various gifts received were put to good use, bits and pieces given to us by relatives helped to give it a cosy finished look. A Rayburn cooker had been installed in the kitchen. We were lucky, so many people had so much less in 1948. The larger part of the school house was occupied by the Britains, whose friendship became invaluable to me. With them I could laugh and be my normal self. I enjoyed animated conversations with their many friends. Peg was a confident and superb cook; she cooked succulent roasts with vegetables from the garden, grown by her own fair hands. We ate game, which was, at her at husband Martin's insistence, left hanging in the cellar to become high. Martin was a Civil Engineer and a great raconteur. We had good times together. Sometimes during the summer we went for picnics in Martin's huge, open Alvis car. We put a packet of shortbread and bananas on the seat to eat later in the field.

In 1949 I began to put on weight, and each morning I was very sick, I told Peg who laughed and said 'You my girl, are pregnant'. It was the last thing I wanted at this time. I moaned and groaned 'I am not', I said with conviction, 'You are my dear' she replied with equal conviction. My mother was a little non- plussed, so was everyone else who knew me. All were convinced I would never cope but I was determined that I would. Each day I became bigger; each month I felt I was going to pop, but I was assured popping was out of the question. I became huge in every sense of the word, my walking became a waddle. I longed to be 'normal' again. Throughout the whole nine months mother and Peg supported me in every way possible.

When in February 1950 I went into labour, Peg took me into the nursing home. I gave birth to Elizabeth on February 20th and it was a long and arduous birth. When the time came for us to leave the nursing home it was Peg who drove us home. If I had a problem with the new baby it was my mother and Peg who came to my aid. My mother was an enormous help; each day she cycled or walked from her house to mine. I had help from so many people, I don't know how I would have managed without them. I certainly could not rely on Tom. Never generous with money, he spent most of it in the bar of the local pub, his home and family taking second place. Time went on.

Tom's father had become quite fond of me. Every Saturday morning he came in his car to see me and we chatted and drank coffee. He knew of my frustrations and was aware of Tom's drinking problem. He enjoyed a drink of course but was in a very different league from his son. There were occasions when Tom arrived home late at night in such a state of inebriation that I felt my only solution was to take Liz out of her cot, wrap her up well, put her into the push-chair and walk one and a half miles to my mother's home.

By this time, Tom's father was actually in Overseas sales. One Saturday morning during his usual visit to see me, he mentioned that a vacancy had arisen for a teaching mechanic in Africa. 'Which country?' I asked, as I held my breath. 'Nyasaland, The Nyasaland Transport Company,' he replied. I was stunned. It must be a dream. I swallowed hard in an effort to contain my excitement. Here was a door through which I could perhaps leap. A rush of adrenalin created a kaleidoscope of vision; this job opportunity for Tom could steer me to my goal. More importantly, he felt it would be a good opportunity. I agreed wholeheartedly. 'Yes, a wonderful opening to a new future,' I replied, trying to hide my dizzy excitement. Waves of joyous anticipation took hold; this could well be my passport to something very special, something wonderful. It was an opportunity I must nurture. I had been given the mould, what I did with it was up to me.

After some persuasion from his father, Tom accepted the position overseas and flew off to Nyasaland. In a state of frenzied excitement and expectation, I spent the next weeks packing and arranging for the shipment of all our essential needs. Furniture was provided by the company. We were to stay in a private hotel until our bungalow in Limbe had been vacated and our sea luggage had arrived. When the time came for us to leave for Africa our tears were tinged with happiness as we anticipated our new life. My mother, who was very close to Elizabeth, felt the parting deeply, but I knew that she understood why I had to take this step as she smiled gave us a hug and waved us off. Liz was a little bewildered as she left Nan, but after a minute or two and a few comforting words she calmed down.

Our journey was interesting and mind boggling. We travelled on a small Airwork aircraft, which had to stop frequently to refuel. We visited France, Corsica, Malta, Wadi Halfa and Johannesburg. They were fascinating overnight stops, where the people and their cultures were all so diverse. In a high state of nervous tension we landed at the small airport of Chileka. Tom met us in the Citroen light fifteen which he had bought soon his arrival in Nyasaland. Airport formalities were quickly over, in that era they were virtually non-existent. We collected our luggage, greeted Tom, clambered into the car and set off for the hotel. On our arrival we were allocated a small suite in the private hotel, which was to be our home until our new home was ready for us to move into. The hotel was comfortable. It was a long low building with a veranda running along the back, which looked out onto a garden and lawns. At the front there was a small garden surrounded by paw paw, mango and avocado trees. Beyond the garden and out towards the nearby Blantyre-Limbe road there were many eucalyptus and flamboyant trees. It was a mass of colour. Isabel and her husband, whose name escapes me, were relaxed and friendly, thoughtful and very kind. They had lived in Nyasaland for many years and had seen changes which they had great difficulty in accepting and getting used to. Many of the 'Old Timers' found that the changing times created a great deal of anxiety and frustration. The new ways had intruded on their well ordered and peaceful lives, to the extent that they were finding the situation unbearable at times.

It very quickly became obvious to me that I was quite unprepared for the culture shocks I was to experience. My first introduction to this was when I saw a cow which had recently been slaughtered, lying on the back of an open box body; the throat had been cut, its eyes were wide open, its head lay limp and lifeless, bouncing about over the back end of the battered truck. Passers by were unimpressed and continued on their daily round. Men never carried loads, they walked ahead, hands free and without any burdens. Following behind, straight upright, women chattered incessantly. They were all draped in colourful kitenge cloth, and all carried heavy loads. To enable them to carry their loads they had 'doughnuts' of tightly rolled grass which they put on their heads, placing whatever they had to carry on top of the 'doughnut'. Some of the women exposed large bulbous breasts, suckling babies as they walked. The babies were securely tied by a piece of kitenge cloth placed beneath their behinds, brought forward and firmly tied in front rather like a hammock, so making it easy for the woman to haul the baby over onto a hip across to a waiting nipple. It seemed simple, easy, uncluttered and natural.

There were many different ethnic groups living in Nyasaland, coming from every corner of the globe. Many of the shops (doukas) were owned by Asians. Almost all the shops were dark, dingy and fly be-specked. Despite this they had a wide range of goods essential to the indigenous people and the expatriate community. They could produce the most obscure items, from shadowy alcoves and previously unnoticed shelves, all small, all vital and found only in these tiny little doukas. From their stocks they could produce lamp wicks, candles, prickers for primus stoves, coca cola bottles with a rubber teat on the end, which were bought by the local people to feed their babies, and by the farmers to feed young stock. The list was endless. Each shop had its own spicy smell; every ingredient for mixing curry hit the nostrils and titillated the palate, which when added to the smell of burning joss sticks was pungent and exotic. Almost always the approach to these shops was hair-raising. Battered uneven, crumbling red brick steps led up from the road to the shop, around which were festooned hundreds of various cooking pots and pans in all shapes and sizes. They were mainly used for Dover stoves, and the wood burning stove found in the outdoor kitchens of the European homesteads. The Africans used the pots on their wood fires in the villages; they were a useful commodity and extraordinarily efficient.

There were Asian shops, which specialized only in kitenge cloth in brilliant shades of every colour. Some were printed with bright African slogans, some had flowers, others trees, some were in patterned swirls, most were made in India. The cloth hung from the high roof inside, along the lower shelves and onto the counters. It spilled out onto stands in the street. Bright, colourful and busy, these shops were always surrounded by 'lookers,' 'feelers,' and 'buyers,' I had entered yet another very extraordinary world.

In the African markets, sellers stood before every vegetable which could be conjured up by the imagination. On tiny peanut stalls surrounded by litter and rubbish, a few enterprising locals shelled, salted and roasted peanuts over a wood burning brazier, afterwards dividing them into small heaps. Every heap was placed onto its own square of old newspaper, deftly rolled into a cone and sold for one penny. The markets were hot, often there was the smell of rotting vegetables and rancid cooking oil; it was essential to keep 'eyes down' to avoid stepping into stagnant puddles and their often unsavoury contents.

Our hotel was on the main road between Blantyre and Limbe. I quickly taught myself to drive the Citroen and passed a full test. I could now come and go as I wished. Driving gave me free access to the market. It gave me free access to life! Intrigued, I would visit the market on most days. I found the seemingly aimless trailing around the different stalls, despite the cacophony of sound, in some way relaxing and fascinating. Vegetables on the stalls were replenished on most days, they were usually fresh and crisp. The bits of decayed greenery, from previous days, hung about the floor and were to be avoided. All the vegetables we bought from the market were well washed in permanganate of potash when we got home.

Africans from the villages took eggs to the market, usually wrapped up in an old piece of cloth. Alongside the eggs a bucket of water was placed. An easy way to test for freshness; float, they were not good, tilt, they were suspect, sink and stay, they were fresh. All around there was the din of individual stall holders urging people to buy their wares. Most of the market stall 'table tops' were built from slats of uneven, sagging branches stripped of shoots and cut from nearby trees; these were nailed to an equally bent uneven leg at each corner. The tops were generally covered with banana leaves or old pages of the *Nyasaland Times*. Some of the stalls displayed freshly killed meat, it was open to the air and all that the air contained. Every purchase was wrapped in banana leaves. Enquiring about the quality and possible contamination, I was told that animals killed for consumption always bore a vetinerary department stamp.

Lining each side of the market, tiny Indian shops sold paper coils of spices, popadums, chapattis and home made samosas which were usually delicious. They sold everything for every type of curry and would willingly cook a curry to take away. Also for sale they had powder, seeds, leaves, pestles and mortars, made from brass, stone, or wood; pots, pans and coconut grinders. The list was endless. In the main streets there were more sophisticated shops selling mainly imported goods in big well laid out stores. Usually these shops were a European domain. Chemists, bookshops and shops selling groceries catered especially for the farming community. Hardware stores sold everything from big farm machinery to the spares needed to keep it in order. All the hospitals and schools were excellent, each ethnic community was catered for.

A Greek, Yiannakis, sold wine by the bottle or by the jug, they also sold fish freshly caught and brought from Lake Nyasa. They made the most delicious bread. The shop rarely closed its doors.

The whole scene was a kaleidoscope of colour which I found enchanting. The clatter, the chatter and the laughter, all the people vying for attention as they endeavoured to catch the eye. It was amazing to walk through these sights and situations. It was enthralling and not at all life threatening in those days, in fact there seemed to be a sense of overall happiness and well-being.

Hating to spend the days in idleness, I managed to find work in the pay section of the Nyasaland Railways office in Limbe. At first I walked to the office from the hotel. In the cool season I wore a loose cream coat. The dark hair and this particular coat caught the fleeting glance and attention of an admirer. Feeling this was a momentary flight of the imagination, and impossible, I realized the admirer had driven on. It was Jim!

Moving into the bungalow and passing my driving test made life more flexible, moving about became much easier. I was able to drive to work, dropping Elizabeth into school on my way. Life was becoming more organized and I found I was enjoying it. Liz had met new friends and had settled into school. 'Having a lovely time,' she said. Work deprived me of a lot of my previously 'spare' days, but I still found time to go to the markets.

I noticed the local people could and did fend for themselves. Each family had its own garden, with chickens, goats and sheep for meat; some had cattle. All had an *nkokwe,* a round hut built on stilts in which maize was kept to dry. It was pounded by the women who made it into flour, boiling it to a thick stodgy gruel, 'nsima', which was the main carbohydrate in their diet and which they ate with everything. The maize was kept to dry in this way and was used should the rains fail. Famine was not common and the European farmers were always on hand to help. Indians kept small shops in the bush, usually near to the villages for convenience. The Africans could buy any commodity they needed, and these nearby stores were their life-line.

Outside, on the verandas of these far-flung shops, there were

Africans alongside Indians, sometimes two, four or even six sitting at old treadle 'Singer' sewing machines. They made clothes, they patched and mended, laughed and talked and called to passers by. They were almost always very efficient and were used to everyone, whether rich or poor.

N.T.C. buses travelled the countryside. They were always bursting at the seams. The rack on the top of each bus carried bicycles, chickens, goats. pigs, fruit and vegetables. Inside the bus passengers were jammed into seats – some held chickens or a piece of luggage for which there was no room on the top. There were women, babies and children in all different stages of dress or undress, the noise was awesome and the smell at times nauseating! In all seasons these buses travelled the roads, through the mud of the rains and the dust of the dry season, at any time of year the roads were different. A few roads had strip tarmac, one strip for each wheel, always a difficulty if something approached from the opposite direction!

From the first day I arrived in Nyasaland I started to ask questions and put out feelers. I made many enquiries, asking people during conversations if they knew, or had heard of an estate manager by the name of Jim Moss. I always awaited the answer with both baited breath and hot sticky palms. I eventually had a positive reply. I often wondered what Jim's reaction would be if at some point I could go up to him, touch his shoulder and say, 'Hello Jim, it's me'. He had after all said, in his last letter, which I had received many years ago, how he looked forward to seeing my dark head walk past his window! It happened that events moved in an unexpected direction.

At a party given by a friend, I met Bill who was in the Public Works Department, employed by the Crown Agents. Suspecting he may know a lot of people in the area, I asked my usual question, and he gave me a somewhat quizzical look replying, 'Yes the name is familiar'. He was not at all sure of the name of the estate, but was convinced that it was in the Lunzu valley.

One evening there was a temporary fault with the generator in the compound. Leaning back into my chair, under a meagre wedge of light thrown out by the moody pressure lamp, reading had been impossible. One word tended to merge into another. The spasmodic power from the generator had spluttered and ground to a halt, ceasing to penetrate the undiluted peace of the African night. How quiet it had suddenly become. Watching the flickering shadows I found myself transported back to our arrival some months ago. I had come here full of hope, anticipating events which I was 'willing' to happen in this small, fertile, landlocked jewel called Nyasaland.

The journey with Elizabeth – Liz aged five – to this country had been a great adventure revealing many culture shocks. Not surprising, when one considered the swift and somewhat disorganized migration from Cheshire to Africa. Flying in a twin engine aircraft in 1955 had meant that the flight was, by necessity, staggered and constant refueling was necessary. Each landing in different countries had been fascinating and eye opening. A short stay in Paris, a night in Corsica and Malta, the next landing had been in Wadi Halfa in the Sudan.

On arrival in this dry arid country, a badly bent, seemingly unroadworthy bus, had been driven wildly to the only hotel used by airways in Wadi Halfa.

Here I was told by a long-faced lugubrious receptionist that a cabin had been reserved for us on a river boat on the Nile. I remembered saying to myself 'This is not for the faint hearted'. Two local youths with overpowering body odour had carried the luggage over a sandy path which was littered with stones. It ran between shining sun-baked boulders and led to the deep murky waters of the Nile. On the shore, a river boat bobbed with a compelling swoosh. We had been allocated a small cabin which was badly in need of decorating. Liz had to be consoled; she did not like the boat at all. There had been little time to relax, shower and change. Space was at a premium. As dusk was falling we had cautiously negotiated the rough track back to the hotel. Stone steps led up to a heavily carved wooden door with highly polished brass handles. A fine looking Sudanese waiter had swept us into the hall, which was covered with brightly coloured carpets, giving warmth to the uneven stone floor. Feeling very hungry, we had walked straight into the dining room where we were immediately escorted to a table. We chose soup followed by chicken. It was served quickly and efficiently, by waiters who wore a long white kanzu and a red fez. They each had a folded white napkin over one arm; their faces shone like polished ebony.

As we were enjoying the meal we had suddenly become overwhelmed with swarms of tiny flies which had descended on the dining room, silently and in clouds. Floating and gyrating, their wings shone like a myriad gossamer cobwebs as they caught the light of the chandeliers. They had sunk into the soup, rested on the food and found their way into our eyes. It had been extremely irritating and uncomfortable. Leaving the table we helped ourselves to fruit and a bottle of water from the trolley before making our way back to the boat.

Not a lot of sleep had been possible despite our weariness. Any peace had been offset by an antiquated fan, which determinedly screeched its way through the night. A little lavender oil applied to the cog wheel had not had the desired effect. Liz occasionally gave the odd whimper of discomfort, but had been calmed by me using a fanning movement with some old magazines. With the morning light, the flies and mosquitoes seemed to have disappeared, thankfully. We eventually made our way up to the hotel where we had a leisurely, enjoyable breakfast, with no flies!

When the time came we were taken from the hotel to the airport on the same old dilapidated bus. After a short wait we boarded the tiny plane to Johannesburg and touched down in Khartoum. Elizabeth's chatter during the flight had been incessant with endless questions. The ride in a taxi from Johannesburg airport to the hotel was a hair-raising experience. Lights were ignored, corners hurtled round and pedestrians were scattered in all directions. Was the driver a mad fellow? We almost fell out of the taxi with relief when we arrived at the first class hotel, The Johannesburg Hotel. The food was excellent and the beds were large and soft. Morning tea had arrived complete with a small plate of biscuits. The breakfast table had groaned with food of every description. It had been overwhelming, after the austerity which to some degree still existed in post war Britain.

After breakfast was over coffee was served on the veranda. Liz made a little friend. His family had come from Scotland to the Transvaal. It was very relaxing looking out into the sunlit garden and watching the children play. In no time at all, it seemed we had to return to Johannesburg airport. Was it Jan Smuts airport? The name slips my mind. This time a calm and very pleasant driver had taken us on a less nail-biting journey.

The small aircraft in which we had arrived, had to back track to Nyasaland. The short walk over the tarmac had been a heart-lurching affair. I had wondered with each step I had taken, what the future held for us. After take-off, I gave Liz some books and pencils to play with. Then it had been time for me to sit back and think. There had been so many thoughts, so many questions! Gazing out of the window the landscape had seemed to rise to greet each gaze. We saw undulating hills, and hundreds of miles of seemingly empty bush. Colours of the recently burnt-off grass lept up to the eye, black and umber, raw and burnt sienna, the cadmiums of dried and parched bush grasses broken by the green of miombo bush and dense, flat topped acacias used by game for shelter in the heat of the day, rising up striking and delicate. Then there had been the dark green mopani forests. Rivers had writhed along like silver snakes undulating in the mosaic of colours below. Scattered lakes shone like bevelled mirrors glinting in the sunlight. Excitement and anticipation had grown with every mile. Thoughts of this past journey ended abruptly.

A glance through the window revealed the compound now lightened by a brilliant moon. Cast shadows moved eerily, playing and flitting like ghosts over the ground as a slight breeze stroked the leaves of nearby trees. The bungalow in which we now lived was near the small town of Limbe. It was one of five or six situated near the main bus depot and repair shop. Bougainvillea grew alongside other local shrubs, giving a colourful air to an otherwise dreary setting. Daily there was the noise of perpetual transport. Oil constantly spilt and trodden into the ground caused the red murram earth to compact to a hard almost granite-like surface, giving it the appearance of glass, perfectly reflecting the surrounding flora.

Because of the temporary fault with the generator, Tom had asked me if I would like to join him in a 'Sundowner', he was going to The Shire Highlands Hotel in Limbe. Liz was spending the night with her little friend Cherry. Reading was an impossibility. Why not go out? It was a lovely starry evening I noticed, as we slid into the Citroen light fifteen. It was with dogged determination that I had learned to drive this car. There was very little traffic on the roads at this time, and in a less than ten minutes we were driving into the hotel car park. The Shire Highlands was a long low building, on a slight rise up from the road. The main approach was a narrow pathway leading from the road to the front doors. It was covered by an archway of riotous orange and deep fuchsia bougainvillea flowers which shone like the glow of a million sequins in the silver moonlight. In the lobby of the hotel there was a paper shop; amongst the many papers and magazines they sold, presented in a yellow dust cover, a months edition of the ever popular *Daily Mirror* which was read avidly by all the expatriates.

There was also an exclusive boutique belonging to a lady of French origin. She had excellent taste, which was evident in the exquisite and expensive lingerie that she sold. Opposite these two shops a highly polished corridor led down to the swing doors of the hotel bar. Pictures on the walls were of local scenes and dignitaries. The air was filled with a smell of polish, cigar and cigarette smoke, cooking and ale. It was warm, welcoming and friendly. The bar was a meeting place for the farmers, particularly on Friday evenings.

We walked down the corridor leading to the bar and I wondered what the outcome of the evening would be. Usually it was disastrous, no doubt I would have to drive home. A buzz of voices and rising laughter drifted on the air, a sign of farmers enjoying their Friday night out. After taking a step through the swing doors, I immediately noticed three figures standing opposite in the subdued lights of the bar. One of these figures stood a little to one side of the strategically placed lamp above, throwing out an instantly recognisable silhouette. Gazing intently at the tall erect body, noticing the enigmatic smile, the slight incline of the head as he concentrated on the conversation of his two friends, I came to an abrupt halt, the world stood still and I was rooted to the spot.

Instinctively, he gave a half turn of his head, looked towards the doors, paused for a second, looked away, then quickly back again 'Cog' he said in total disbelief, 'Is it really you?' a look of total bewilderment, surprise and joyous recognition crossed his face. He put down his glass, walked towards me, took me in his arms and planted a kiss on my lips. I went into shock at that moment, I was unable to move or to speak.

For a second or two we stood, each assessing the other, then his lips parted, revealing the same even white teeth which had always emphasised his disturbingly good looks. I could only utter 'Jim', I trusted neither my voice to speak, nor my legs to move. Again taking me in his arms he swung me around dizzily. I looked into his eyes as he winked that slow knowing wink which 'spoke volumes.' Looking up at his fair wavy curls, I noticed a grey streak had claimed the curl which persistently fell over his forehead; his steady grey eyes gazed from a bronzed handsome face, his mouth was still gentle and beautifully shaped, something I had always been very aware of. He had grown a moustache which suited him admirably.

A startling white shirt covered his broad shoulders and wide chest. It emphasised the colour of his skin, darkened by the African sun into a healthy glowing tan. Beneath khaki shorts, strong muscular legs were lightly covered by blond silken hair. His feet were pushed into brown leather boots.

That old and familiar little wink had completely disarmed me, the years rolled away. Meanwhile, the overwhelming tenderness of this encounter had spread to the hard, tough sightseers. The atmosphere in the bar was charged with so many different emotions; all around there was silence, all the chattering and laughter had stopped as they waited and watched. Hands moving down had paused, interrupting the movement of glasses to lips. In what seemed to be slow motion we lifted our arms and embraced. I rested my head in the crook of his shoulder, drinking in the warmth and the old familiar 'Jim' smell which I remembered so well. He held me to his chest pressing his face against the top of my head. Eventually he released me. He put his arm through mine as he steered me to the bar.

Following these explosive moments, people in the bar once more resumed their tireless chatter and accompanying peals of laughter. Glasses were lifted, knowing glances were passed our way. For us a new life had begun, the meeting was painted in our memory forever. We were both completely bowled over by events. Tom, in this commotion was leaning on the bar, pint in hand, talking to one of his colleagues. Our lives were transformed forever.

From the time I joined Jim at the bar, the rum and coca cola he introduced me to had the taste of nectar. I wanted those exquisite moments never to end. We had both been quite oblivious to our surroundings and everyone in them. After our drinks Jim suggested that we go to 'The Flamingo', a tiny bar–cum–restaurant situated on the road between Blantyre and Chileka airport. 'The Flamingo' belonged to a Greek by the unlikely mane of Tony Pope, I was told that he served an extremely good, succulent piri piri chicken with a cabbage salad. There was a tiny floor for dancing, whilst listening to the sweet music of those days, which was loved by everyone.

Everything was so inclined towards 'the romantic', in some strange way it cast a spell onto a situation already charged with every known emotion. This battered little place was up an incline from the road. As we got nearer the smell of roast chicken hung in the air, greeting us from the open windows and doors. We could hear the sound of soft mellow music playing on an old gramophone in a corner. Jim parked the car that he had brought by boat from England, and driven up from Capetown. It was a Vauxhall Wyvern, this had replaced his B.S.A. Bataam. He could travel into Blantyre in covered comfort now, leaving the bike for estate work he told me. He held the door open for me and I slid out of my seat, as I stood up his arms came round me, and looking into each others eyes we kissed and were transported into further emotional turmoil.

From the balmy night air we walked into the restaurant. The floor for dancing had been made from polished concrete and was surrounded by small wooden tables, which were covered with red check table clothes and matching napkins. On each table was a wine bottle festooned with wax 'droppings'; over time they had become so dense and uneven they appeared to have been sculpted. We chose to sit at a table by the window, scent from a nearby frangipani drifting over, the moon was brilliant. Tony came over to the table, Jim introduced us. Tony was short, he bore little resemblance to the Greek Cypriot of my imagination. He was gracious, helpful and accommodating.

Holding hands we ordered our meal and sat glancing round the room. I was surprised to see how many people there were. The 'Flamingo' was obviously very popular with many of the farmers known by Jim. Softly the music played, and suddenly I heard the strains of 'Serenade in Blue', the Glenn Miller sound. I looked at Jim, he was standing at my side his hand stretched out to take mine and together we moved as if in a dream to the dance floor. In each other's arms we danced, as we had before, so many years ago. Wandering in a dream back to the table we sat down and the euphoria continued. We ate the delicious chicken, 'hot and spicy' which went so well with the cabbage salad, thinly sliced onions, feta cheese and olives, dressed with thick green olive oil and a little vinegar. An ice-cold bottle of wine completed our meal. I have never, either before or since that time, experienced such a pleasurable meal.

Looking over to the bar, Tom was with, of all people, the Viviers brothers, the two men who had been standing with Jim at the bar in the 'Shire Highlands'. He was well into his beer. It was with some relief I noticed he had no interest in what I was doing as I did not want any intrusion. Life was now wonderful, nothing must spoil it.

It was late when Jim took me home. Tom followed much later. Tommy Viviers drove him home in the Citroen, his brother Jan following in their Chevrolet box body. I heard nothing, I had drifted off into a sleep induced by perfect peace. This was something that had not happened to me for a very long time; indeed, this was a new beginning, my life was starting again. I have always maintained that fate had a hand in everything. Our life is charted out for us from the day of our birth.

After this encounter we met in secret, or whenever I felt Liz could be left safely with Tom, or she was able to stay with her school friend Cherry, whose mother, Gypsy, was a South African of my age. She worked alongside me in the offices, she was without bias and would always help when she was able. I never felt remotely guilty, everything seemed so right. We both had confessions to make, it would be madness to think otherwise. Jim had always been the love of my life, I had always been his. Together. This is how we had always intended our life should be, though never in our wildest dreams had we imagined it would happen in this way. We travelled over the roads of Nyasaland, hoping the Public Works Department had taken the tops off the corrugations of compounded earth. They removed them by using a tractor behind which branches and twigs were tied, forming a huge brush which they dragged along to smooth off the bumps and corrugations. It worked well, making travel easier, but if we came across a tractor on a murram road, which we were unable to pass, the vehicle and those inside would be swathed in red dust. This brushing was a simple, cheap and reasonably efficient way of solving the road problem. What is a little dust?

At a later date I was introduced to a right turn along this airport road which led us to a long murram road going some way into the bush, and gradually as the road forked and petered out, it became part of the driveway to Namisu estate. Jim's home. Presented with these situations and others we had to overcome, when I look back I smile whilst revelling in the thoughts of all the challenging experiences. It was a simple life, there were no complications made by idealists or radically motivated individuals to suffocate the soul. Whenever we met, Jim always told me how pleased he was to have me with him. There were times when I thought my heart would explode, it raced through such torrents of love and excitement. Being together again was something so very special. During the following two weeks Jim 'phoned me at the office as often as he could and it was then that we arranged our meetings.

Hearing his voice was a huge shock; he sounded exactly as he had in the past. We were excited by thoughts of the future but we were also aware of the problems we were to face.

We often met at the Limbe Cemetery. I parked my car alongside the cemetery walls, beneath the eucalyptus trees. I was always wildly excited at these times as I crept into Jim's 'Wyvern' and sat beside him before we sped off to the 'Ntondwe Bar', a small, intimate bar/restaurant. It was a quiet, remote little place, between the towns of Limbe and Zomba. In this secluded hide-away we ate fish, chambo from Lake Nyasa and salad, accompanied by a glass of chilled Chardonnay from South Africa. Here we were far away from the eyes of the world; here, as we sat holding hands and gazing into each others eyes, we made plans for our future. It would have been nice to sit there forever we thought, as we lingered and burned the midnight oil until every drop was drained. We wanted the clock to stop. When the time did come for us to leave, we left arm in arm, hugged tightly together. We drove back slowly to the Limbe Cemetery and then Jim walked me over to my car, the Citroen, and followed me back home in his car. As I pulled over he came up to my car and said with great tenderness 'I cannot believe this has really happened, here we are together again, this time for always.' I went into the house and crept into the spare room, which had become my haven of peace.

It was a hot starry night, so by invitation from the moon, I made the decision to take a stroll to give myself some uninterrupted time for thinking. I was happy, excited and a little confused as I ambled along in deep thought. Suddenly I became aware of a car travelling slowly alongside me. Through the open window a familiar voice called my name and the door opened. In disbelief I slid in beside Jim.

This was how I met Geoffrey again. 'Hello Geoffrey' I said. He was standing alongside the bar, tall wide-eyed and handsome. 'You managed to find him at last' he said taking two strides towards me, then he gave me a big hug. 'Yes, I found him' I answered quietly, my arm linked into Jim's. I had last seen him as a rather serious young boy. He kissed my cheek and gave me a big smile, one I shall never forget. I was amazed at how he had changed; he was tall now and had dark floppy hair. His concerned dark eyes looked first at me and then back to Jim. This look became so frequent, and so familiar. The look, I gradually came to understand, was standard either when he was overwhelmed, or when things had really gone beyond his belief or comprehension. It became known as 'Geoffrey's look.' He became a tremendous support to us, a wonderful friend who was always totally loyal. We loved him very much and he loved us in return, never wavering in his efforts to help. Much of what was asked and needed of him sometimes, caused his eyes to become very large indeed! He had known and heard of me for many years. He also knew of my sudden appearance in Nyasaland, and of our meeting some days ago. Secretly he was delighted, it seemed to give him great joy to see us together. There was little he did not know of our past. He also knew of our liaisons during the years of separation. I of course (by getting married) had made rather more of a mess of things than Jim. He had been a whole lot wiser than I had, as was always the case. Nor did he jump into things unthinkingly. This was his way.

Saturday morning, on the 3rd of August 1956, became a special day. It happened on the day after I had met Geoffrey in Ryall's hotel. Elizabeth and I were walking down the hill, past a cluster of shops on the right hand side, in the main shopping area of Blantyre. We had been to the bank. A voice from a shop entrance called, 'Jean.' It was Geoffrey, he had called in to see Michael the local hairdresser who was a friend of Jim's. Michael was a Greek who oozed charm. He was considerate, discreet and understanding; his replies to inquisitive clients were always in the negative. In a small community of Europeans, news travels quickly and curiosity is easily aroused. As the years passed our friendship grew and they came to regard him with great affection.

Geoffrey's next words were unbelievable. Walking across the road he asked, 'Would you like to come to Namisu with me, I am going to deliver a bag of red beans and some groceries to Jim'. Unsure of my actions, my knees considerably weakened, I got into the car and sat in the front with Geoffrey. Liz hopped in the back. Surrounded by shopping, we made our way over the dusty roads to Namisu, talking incessantly throughout the whole journey. From Blantyre we took the main Chileka airport road, which was in reasonably good condition. Some way past the 'Flamingo' we suddenly took a sharp right turn onto a very bad road. We bounced and bumped our way along the corrugated surface and we were surrounded by dust thrown up from the wheels which found its way into every conceivable crevice. A cloud of red dust filtered into the car, penetrating our eyes, ears and noses', the shopping in the back was also covered by a film of fine red powder.

After some miles the road became less pot-holed and less dusty though it was still stony. We were approaching Namisu. This was obviously the domain of the estate, as it had been well tended and the storm drains had been cleared in preparation for the next rains.

The road led to the estate drive. To the left of the drive we passed a bwalo, or compound, in which there were a number of buildings for housing tractors, together with field equipment, bulk sheds, tobacco barns and an office; there was also a clinic for the workers. At the far end of the bwalo, a reasonably large hut, made from mud and wattle, belonged to the Headman of the estate.

The whole area was surrounded by tall, sweetly pungent, and well-kept eucalyptus trees. It was welcoming and had an air of colonialism. From the compound the long drive was lined on either side by tall jacaranda trees, covered in clusters of blue bell shaped flowers which eventually fell to the ground creating a beautiful, brilliant blue carpet. The drive rose gradually to the

Namisu homestead. Its approach was in grassed tiers and on each tier grew bushes of frangipani, plunbago and poinsettia.

On the left of the driveway stood the homestead. It was long and low and was approached by three steps leading to the veranda which ran along the length of the bungalow. On either side of the main front steps a low wall had been built. The walls ran along the front and round to the side of the house. Flower beds lay below the walls, each bed planted with tall brightly coloured, dark red and deep orange canna lilies, their heads peering over the veranda in a splash of brilliant colour, breaking up the green of the creepers and potted ferns.

On the veranda were cushioned wooden chairs, each with its own small table. The windows were open, a gentle breeze danced on the lightly woven curtains, making them flutter. In front of the house the views were spectacular, a huge seemingly endless lawn leading down to rocky outcrops which stood like sentries to the dark green mopani forest beyond. The distant hills were indigo and blue, hazy in the heat of day, far away land seemed to merge into the sky. Immediately opposite the house, beneath the shade of a group of bluegum trees, there were chairs and a small wooden table. Flower beds here and there gave the appearance of scattered rugs. Nearby was a paddock for the horses. To the left there was a garage, nearby were the sheep and cattle bomas. Other outbuildings situated near a rocky outcrop were used mainly for rearing chickens and ducks. Trees were everywhere.

I was convinced that this was Heaven. Now, in the shimmering heat of day the slight breeze had become warm and the spasmodic rasp of the cicadas in some way emphasized the silence of the surrounding bush as it embraced the scene in a blanket of peace and tranquillity. Sheep grazed on nearby sparse grass. A herd boy with a stick in his hand and an infectious grin on his face was in charge: he wore old leather sandals, his spectacles had only one lens. He called the sheep by name. He hummed or he sang, depending upon his mood at the time. He called to passers by, perhaps the boy tending the garden, or the one carrying wood to the water drum. Each conversation ended with a long high pitched, 'Ehh, ehh, ehh, ehh.'

'Jim may be in the garden,' Geoffrey said as he disappeared through the house to call him. After a few moments we heard their voices, and there he was, tall, handsome, tanned and smiling. He walked over to us and gave us both a hug. 'Welcome to Namisu' he said. We remembered this embrace for the rest of our lives. This was a new life, a new, wonderful and peaceful life. One which we have loved and cherished for every precious moment. Gradually amongst all the excitement, disbelief and exhilaration, it dawned on me that we had absolutely nothing with us; no toiletries, no personal belongings of any description! 'Can we manage?' I queried, 'Of course,' came the reply. We could cope for a short while I supposed.

Wondering 'out loud' what our next move should be, Geoffrey asked me to write a list of what was needed, and where they could be found in the bungalow at the compound. He said he would give the list to Tom. I saw no problems arising from this and felt pretty sure that there would be no opposition to my request – I was right! Essentials would be collected first, the rest could come later. On the following morning Geoffrey and my friend Gypsy went to the house in Limbe to tell Tom where I was and what was happening. When they went to the house there was no resistance from Tom, in fact he helped with the task in hand. I realised that the only thing he might lose was a little 'face'! This negativity came as no surprise. I did feel great relief however, particularly when I learned that a date had been arranged for them to collect further items.

I never went back to the office. Gypsy gave a partial explanation, covered by a few excuses. I gathered that the head of department was a little put out at my sudden disappearance. Who could blame him? I seem to remember I sent a written apology some time later.

After a busy weekend Geoffrey drove back to Ndata estate, some way on the other side of Limbe. He was a temporary manager. The Boddy family, who were normally managers of the estate, were in England. Their return journey was by sea. They were bringing Geoffrey's fiancee back and were due to arrive shortly. Their marriage as to take place in Nyasaland, after which they would manage and live at Mudi estate, which was approximately one and a half miles from Namisu. Jim had initially overseen this estate. He was presently in charge of both until Geoffrey and Shirley were settled into life there.

Standing on the writing desk in the sitting room of Namisu house, was a large black and white photograph of me, taken as I was about to start my first year's nursing. It was in a wooden frame and he had taken it with him wherever he went. This affected me deeply; putting my hands on his cheeks I gave him a warm kiss. In return he gave me his wondrous smile. Then, with his arm round my waist and taking Liz's hand, we explored the house and garden together.

The house was mellow with an aroma of polish and gun oil. It was clean and well looked after. In this masculine home it was possible to detect a whiff of what I now know to be 'Old Spice.' From that moment on, all I needed to be transported back to that wondrous time is one small whiff of that very personal aroma. It always evokes pure nostalgia and overwhelming love. The floor of the large entrance hall shone. It was covered by a leopard skin rug. In the corner an umbrella-stand held walking sticks and a shot gun, in its case.

From the hall a door to the right led to the sitting room, which was simple, comfortable and adequate. There was a large round maize mat on the floor, with chairs and a green-cushioned sofa beneath the window. The curtains were light beige, toning in with the maize mat. By the wall, as we went in through the door, Jim had his desk with the photograph of me on it. Alongside this was a large bookcase with a varied selection of books. Many were first editions. There were stories of past African hunters and I noticed a 'Breath of the Veldt' and endless books on the life of Winston Churchill.

An avid reader many of Jim's books were ordered from Heffer's in London, and transported by sea. In the corner on a coffee table there was a small vase of frangipani flowers from the garden, which looked and smelt exotic. Many personal bits and pieces were scattered about the house. It was evident from the 'feel' of each room that this man was a homemaker who enjoyed the comfort of his home.

Sitting on the sofa under the window I noticed that there was a view of the distant hills, and three other chairs were strategically placed. Beneath the side window there was the old battery radio from which we could listen to romantic, nostalgic music sent over the air from Rhodesia. We danced as we had danced so many years ago.

The 'World News' came from London and every European listened to it. We always felt that it was honest and reliable, and based on fact. Often then, while sitting on the veranda enjoying our 'Sundowner' in the balmy twilight of evening, we would be moved to dance to the music as it filtered through the open windows. It was all too wonderful for words.

A door in the far corner of the sitting room opened out into the dining room which also had a door leading into it from the hall. There was a large dining table, with a bowl of fruit in the centre, dining chairs and an enormous sideboard on which there were condiments, small silver-framed photographs, decanters and a soda syphon (the old wire covered type). Again, on a small table in the corner there was a small vase holding flowers.

Jim introduced us to Harrison, his cook-cum-house servant – a Nyasa – he was setting the table for our evening meal. Hunger making smells drifted from the kitchen.

At the far end of the hall, a door led to the back veranda and the kitchen. Each door on the left-hand side of the hall led to the bedrooms. The first led to the master bedroom and the second to the guest room which had been turned into two rooms, one large, one small for convenience. Doors from each of these bedrooms led to a very large bathroom. All the rooms were high and airy. The ambience of the house was warm and welcoming, quiet and relaxing. Instinctively I knew that Namisu was going to be a haven of peace.

We strolled from the house to the kitchen garden, which was obviously tended with care. The soil was rich black dambo soil which was well fed with manure from the estate cattle. A stream ran through the garden which provided Lemon, the Nyasa who attended the garden, with water for the growing vegetables. Alongside the garden there was a field of sweet maize. A nearby borehole pumped water to the house.

Any water to be heated went through pipes into a drum which stood on a three-sided wall made from bricks and approximately four feet high. A fire beneath the drum was fuelled with logs. It fed hot water into the bathroom taps. The borehole also provided cold water to the taps and the lavatory. A septic waste tank was highly efficient and virtually trouble-free. Any problem with the pump could be repaired quickly, as spares were always to hand.

We ambled around the homestead and its surround in total bewilderment. A destiny had been fulfilled from our past youth. We had predicted it could and would happen, and it had! Here we were together, all our hopes had come to fruition. Jim had waited in hope, I had found him. As for Elizabeth, though she did not realise it at the time, she was to be given an unselfish love for the rest of her life, with opportunities she would otherwise never have known.

When we arrived back at the homestead from our tour, darkness had begun to fall and a delicious smell of chicken roasting drifted through the air. It was almost time to eat. We bathed and smartened ourselves up a little. Jim appeared, just as I remembered him, rubbed, scrubbed and smelling gorgeous; he was casually dressed and looked very handsome. I felt I wanted to rush over and give him a hug. Liz and I, whilst clean and smelling of soap, our hair combed and tidy, were still in the clothes we had worn all day. We would have to wait until the next day when Geoffrey and Gypsy would arrive with other things to wear.

We sat on the veranda, listening to the crickets and watching stars in the southern sky. In the still warmth of the African night the sweet smell of frangipani drifted over on the evening breeze. Jim was preparing two brandy sours and lime and soda for Liz. We sat totally relaxed and contented, the joy of being together was greater than even we had anticipated. Strange how love lets you see things that you have not already seen, in such a small space of time. 'I am pleased you are with me now' he said. So many times in our life he has used these words. From now it would always be not 'my life' but 'our life'.

Harrison stood to attention, 'Dinner leady bwana'; many Africans have difficulty in pronouncing 'r'. He had made chicken soup. We then had roast chicken, baked potatoes, spinach and sweet potato mashed with butter. All the vegetables were from the garden. It was delicious. He then served, of all things, steamed pudding with egg custard. An old favourite. We left the table to have coffee on the veranda. In the lamplight we listened to the wild beat of the drums floating in on the soft night air and watched the tiny lights of fire-flies, as they appeared to mingle with all the stars in the Heavens.

Pressure lamps burning brightly in the house gave a soporific hiss. We could hear the voices of the cook and his helper as they cleared the dining room. The chink of china and clatter of cutlery ebbed and flowed. Liz looked tired and was yawning, it was obviously time for bed. She had no complaints when I suggested that perhaps it was time for sleep. After saying goodnight to Jim I took her into the guest room and put one of his pyjama tops over her. We rolled up the sleeves, then as she cuddled down into bed I gave her a goodnight kiss and tucked her up; she looked comfortable in the glow of lamp light. Jim came in, and he put a torch under her pillow, gave her a kiss and made sure the mosquito net was tucked in. She went straight to sleep and it was quite late when she awoke the next day.

We ambled back to the veranda arm in arm, then we sat down, and slowly we drank another cup of coffee. Our feelings were a mixture of elation, comfort and disbelief. We were more than a little overwhelmed by events as they moved so swiftly from wishing and hoping to sudden reality. By seizing heaven-sent opportunities we had reached our ultimate joy.

Time does not stand still. The staff had left and gone to their huts, the pressure lamps had become dim. Jim pumped up the sitting room and bathroom lamps; one was used for carrying, the other stood in the bathroom. Torches and candles were very much in evidence, though never matches. In their place was a cigarette lighter, candles were only used when all else failed. What a calamity, I had no nightwear! I used a pair of Jim's pyjamas and noticed they had a large split in one of the seams. I made a mental note to repair them the next day. Looking like Wee Willie Winkie I made my way to the bathroom, where my teeth were cleaned by courtesy of Jim's brush. Later walking to the bed I crawled quaking beneath the mosquito net. By this time, for obvious reasons my mind was in a state of turmoil.

In what seemed like an eternity, though in fact it was only a few minutes, Jim joined me under the mosquito net. For a while we just lay and looked at each other. It was wondrous and seemingly impossible that we, two people who were not at all innocent to the facts of life, should suddenly become so overwhelmingly nervous and shy. After all, it had plagued our imagination and been in our thoughts for so long. This was how our new life together had started.

Little did we know at the time, but we were to have a lifetime of total and enduring passion, which was to include every colour in the spectrum of a rainbow. We had a gourmet recipe for our future and our fidelity never wavered or waned. Despite the stumbling blocks we were to encounter, from that moment, on, our future was assured. A spark had burst into flames when we, two teenagers looked across a school hall, one sitting in the light of the sun, the other in the shade. Chemistry took over and reshaped our lives. 'My love,' became my name for Jim.

CHAPTER FOUR

Namisu 1956

From the 3rd of August, 1956. Namisu became our home. Namisu was a tobacco estate of some 12,000 acres, lying 1,200 feet above sea level, in the Lunzu valley of Nyasaland. It was a restful valley surrounded by the distant hills. The cool of evening gradually gave way to the shimmering heat of midday and beyond. As the heat became more intense everything shone and became distorted, with one object merging into another, and in this mirage the whole of the valley seemed to wilt. The cicadas in the trees were noisy and agitated, humans and animals became lethargic, their energy depleted in the heat of the day.

Gradually as the cool of evening approached and with its profound peace and accompanying tranquility everything revived. Then the whine of mosquitoes and the distant cackle of scavenging hyenas would come, offset by a high moon and myriads of constellations. The surrounding hills added great beauty to the valley. Trees and local flora grew in uneven steps on their slopes like giant stairways leading the way to Heaven.

In between the vegetation huge grey boulders lay. Hill streams glittered like shards of mirror in the bright sunlight as they wound their way down to the river below. Above the hills, a blue sky embraced white puffs of cloud. The sun caught their vaporous edges and created a halo of light as they floated majestically above, to be carried on by the wind as though they had never existed.

With the coming of the rains, the scene took on a dramatic change as black and thunderous clouds advanced towards us like a mighty army, unfolding the drama of an impending storm. Bolts of lightning lit up the sky, thunder bellowed, retching out a black swirling mass of water which soaked everything in its path. Sitting rapt in wonder on the veranda of the homestead, it was bewitching to see seasonal changes unfold. Spreading out in front of the hills the lawn led to a rocky outcrop and wooded area. The woodland continued on to the foot of the hills. It was home to a large variety of game, both large and small

To the right of the lawn, two geldings fed and frolicked in the paddock, alongside this there was more woodland which continued on for five miles or so to Larangwe, the home of our hunter friend and fellow tobacco grower, Jock. From there it continued on to the river and beyond, narrow game tracks led down to the water where the trees were full of chattering monkeys. The rocks were a sunning place for lizards and iguanas and a haven for leopards. Kudu in this area were always on the alert. There was an abundance of guinea fowl and qwali on the estate whose cackling calls could be heard through most of the day Added to this, in the early morning, were the deep guttural calls of the ground hornbill.

The heat of day was always accompanied by the staccato noises of cicada beetles on nearby trees. At the close of evening, the sounds change, crickets chirrup, hungry mosquitos buzz and whine. Penetrating the still night air, barking dogs from a nearby village make themselves heard.

Each day we walked amongst the tobacco fields where plants grew higher than our heads. Like sergeant majors inspecting a parade we took out suckers, topped the delicate white and pink flowers and picked off insects which would damage the plant. One of the tobacco fields lay alongside the drive which led from the house to the bwalo; the tobacco barns, grading shed, office and stores. When darkness falls, as it does so quickly in Africa, the moon rises over the distant hills coating the earth with a luminous silver light, bringing with it the mysterious silence of the African night. A silence intensified by expectancy and intrigue, as the strange haunting noises of the wild are heard from the surrounding bush.

Harrison tapped on the bedroom door, it was 6 am. Jim's daily reply was a sleepy, 'Come in. ' The door opened and a tray was placed on the small table immediately to the left by the wall. Sometimes I would pour the tea, but usually it was Jim, as he had to go to the compound in order to give the estate staff their tasks for the day. It was necessary to talk to his headman about any foreseeable problems. Machinery had to be checked every day to make sure that it was in good working order. Any spare parts had to be written down, to enable us to buy them on our next visit to Blantyre. Wood piles must be checked regularly throughout the season, wood had to be brought in, cut to a certain size and measured by the mendel, then it was stacked by each tobacco barn, ready for the tobacco curing process when the time came. There was also re-forestation to be considered and attended to. Each day people were crowded around the dispensary door, tablets were handed out for malaria, headaches, limb pains, sprains, cuts and bruises. Medicines were given for constipation, diahorrea, stomach ache and sickness.

Harrison knew what we would like to eat for breakfast, the bread had already been put to rise in a large tin. Each day a few warm fresh buns were put out into a basket on the table, to one side of the buns a small bowl held curly butter pats. The glorious smell of baking pervaded the house. Every morning I waited for Jim to walk up from the bwalo and the moment he came into sight, I set off to meet him smiling and waving with joy. We put our arms around each other, kissed and then chatting, we walked to the house. At this time we usually made our way to the sitting room where we listened to the news from the BBC. Afterwards came breakfast. Our breakfasts were tasty and sustaining, a choice of cereal, porridge or fruit salad. Homemade bread or toast, or both! Bacon, eggs, liver and tomatoes, followed by Rose's clear marmalade, Jim's favourite, I preferred the coarse marmalade. Tea or coffee was served either in the sitting room or on the veranda.

Side by side, we held hands, linked arms or, at times, Jim put his arm around my shoulder, or my arm would be around his. We loved to hug. We did almost everything together. I went into the fields with him and into the barns when they were curing. The smell of tobacco curing is wonderful, though difficult to describe, in someway it has the sweet mellow aroma of malt and honey.

There was great excitement at the time of the tobacco auctions. They were a joy to visit, the speed with which the auctioneers sold the tobacco defied belief. Each bale was open, the contents were smelt, felt and fingered. The colour and texture were noted. Jim's tobacco usually sold well. We had great fun with the farmers and the auctioneers. Mostly we had a 'get together' at the end of the day after the rooms had closed. It was usually in The Shire Highlands Hotel, we laughed, talked and, needless to say, the odd risqué joke would be told. We were often teased, which was inevitable under the circumstances. They were hard cases but a good bunch. On auction days we called in at the 'Flamingo' on our way home and tucked into piri piri chicken. Then replete, we would make our way back to Namisu, blissfully content.

Later we bathed, went to bed, cuddled, and went to sleep in each others arms to be awakened at 6 am by Harrison, tea and the joy of another day.

Often I wondered, could life always be this way! Elizabeth, now at school, had to be taken the 20 miles from the estate to Blantyre everyday and collected in the afternoon. She was not in her original school. After much thought, we felt this particular school would better for her, it was fee paying, and Jim knew the matron well. If Gypsy was visiting us at the estate she would pick her up and bring her home, sometimes Liz stayed with Gypsy and her daughter Cherry, Liz's friend, in her small house in Blantyre.

Eventually, for the sake of continuity and for the sheer convenience of all concerned, when there was a vacancy for a weekly boarder at the school, we took the opportunity of placing our name at the top of the vacancy list. We went to see the matron and the headmistress and it was arranged that at the beginning of the next term, we would take advantage of the place. Liz was excited, she knew a number of children there. Many people living estate lives had their children at the school as weekly boarders, so she was not alone in these circumstances and she adapted to the routine and school life without any problems.

Once a week on our visits to Blantyre for work or shopping, we made a point of visiting her, usually taking a 'treat' of some kind and making sure she was her happy and her usual chirpy self. Liz was taken great care of as the matron, like everyone else who knew him, had been bewitched by Jim's magnetic charm. It has to be said, he was special and quite unique.

Friday was marked in most peoples' diaries, if they lived up country, as it was the day we called at the library to return books and collect others for reading during the following week. It was a ritual. It was on Friday that we all 'met up'. We called into the 'Times Book Shop' in Blantyre for magazines, which were mainly from Rhodesia or South Africa (though there were also British monthly magazines, which were much more expensive and not so in touch with Africa as some others). Sometimes we bought small trinkets from the bookshop, usually it was for the house. From the jewellery section Jim bought me a very pretty dress ring. It was silver with a circular top encrusted in marquisate – I still have it to this day. We also bought ornaments and pretty little lamps. They were no use at all for reading, but very attractive, giving a soft glow in some dark corner, throwing out gentle patterns onto the walls.

Usually there was a visit to the Limbe Trading Company for Rose's lime cordial, Rose's Lime marmalade, wine and other basics of life; flour, sugar, fat, Koo melon and lemon jam which we ate by the spoonful! Then of course we visited our post box to pick up the mail. We collected and delivered mail for Old Jock, our neighbour. Jock was a great friend, he had taught Jim all he knew about the bush and bush lore. They had tracked and hunted many times, often in wild and dangerous territory and there was great rapport between them. Our 'sundowners' were often taken with him on his veranda at Larangwe estate, when we would listen to hair raising tales of the past; he was a master raconteur.

On our way home we collected Liz from school, then we headed back to the peace and quiet of Namisu. She often brought her school friends home to stay for the weekend. They found lots to do; they tended the animals, had picnics, cooked their own food outside under the eagle eye of Ferrison the herd boy and sometimes they ate with him (much preferring to eat the grey mess he cooked in his old tin pot than the food prepared for them in the house), they thought it was wonderful to sit, as the Africans do, on some old flat stone round the fire, stirring the contents, usually thrown out by Harrison, consisting of tomatoes, onions and beans cooked to almost a puree. Most children were skilled at rolling posho (a thick stodgy porridge made from maize flour), with one hand. A hole was made by the thumb which formed a receptacle for the bean mixture as it was dipped in and out of the pot. They preferred this to what they called 'ordinary food'!

There were times when Tom collected Liz from school and took her out for the day. We picked her up in the evening sometimes calling at the 'Flamingo' on the way home. If it had been a long, hot exhausting day we went back to the estate to eat omelette with fine chips, vegetables from the garden and crispy fried onions. It was always delicious, even more so with a glass of cold wine from the charcoal fridge which stood on the veranda at the back of the house. Harrison's omelettes were like ambrosia, by comparison my efforts failed miserably. Afterwards, as always, we sat on the veranda with our tray of coffee, talked of the day's events, discussed the crops and laughed together.

We talked of ourselves and of all the things we hoped to do and the places we would like to visit. We talked of our hopes and dreams and of the family we might have. I had been told, after the birth of Elizabeth, that my chances of having more children were slim, whilst I found this difficult to accept, Jim refused to believe it at all. We discussed all these things while the stars shone in the heavens and the moon shed its light over our paradise. It cast moving shadows all around, making it even more eerily beautiful than it already was. A little later we would move into the house and lie side by side on the sofa beneath the window reading our books, we moved only to pump up the dimming pressure lamp. Suddenly I would feel his gaze upon me, these times I shall never forget. These were the moments when the tenderness of love wrenched at my heart. So often this was how things were, words would have been an intrusion.

At home in England there was some worry and confusion, despite the fact that both our families knew of, and accepted, our situation. We told them of our intention to marry as soon as possible. In less than a year we had found, and made a friend of, a solicitor who we asked to represent us. After some unpleasantness, I was divorced and given custody of Elizabeth. Financially we found it rather draining! Tom was very 'sloppy' about it all, the magistrate at one point suggested that he stand up straight and take his hands out of his pockets! When the divorce was over, he stayed for a short time in Nyasaland, then flew home to England. His family were not surprised by the outcome. Some time later he met and lived with a Welsh divorcee, they remained together until she died.

One year exactly from the date I went to Namisu we were to be married. The date was the 3rd August, 1957. The day we would reach up to the sky and catch pennies from heaven. My name would become Jean Moss.

Back at Namisu, we put up a swing for Liz beneath the blue gum trees opposite the house. I loved to take a swing in the heat of the day, the gentle flow of cool air was light and refreshing. It was a great success. Alongside the swing, the chairs, the long wooden seat and a small table were used continually at all times of the day and for all sorts of reasons. In particular we liked to sit there for morning coffee when Jim arrived home from the fields.

One very hot morning, as the sun shone from a crystal clear sky, my heart skipped a beat and my head reeled. I felt nauseous and lethargic and I wondered what the problem was. The next day Jim took me into Blantyre to see the doctor. I was told I had low fever and must rest and to see him again if there was no improvement. I did not improve. On my next visit he told me I was pregnant. We were full of joy and very excited. Despite the prognosis given by the doctor in England, I could conceive, we could have babies! We felt our life was complete, I just had to take a little care and make sure I went full term.

To celebrate we bought a bottle of champagne and went to a small chalet on the shores of Lake Nyasa. It was a long weekend of undiluted bliss, the thoughts of our future and our lives together filled us with joy. Sunsets and sunrise from the lakeshore were spectacular, its glistening water rippled with the golden orange glow of early morning sunrise, later becoming a mirror of brilliant blue as it caught the sky's reflection. At evening time, a blood red sky glowed from the polished darkness as the sun sank below the edge. Now the lake became a moving glowing mystery of brilliance, gradually dissolving into deep indigo, overshot with crimson.

Each morning, a chorus of birdsong heralded the day. Monkeys chattered, as they dashed madly from tree to tree, as usual they made a general nuisance of themselves. The rustle of palm trees, swaying in the lake breeze, was soporific and beguiling. Their huge leaves, as they became dry and of no further use, fell onto the sandy beach or floated down onto the chalet roofs, where they rested with a dry crackle. During our time at the lake we lay under the palms and read, we swam and we paddled in and out of the water, sometimes we decided to fish. In the heat of day the answer was to siesta. Our chalet was on the beach, where gleaming waters shone through the open door, trees sighed and cicadas screamed. Gradually our eyes closed and we slept.

In the evenings we might share 'sundowners' with friends, we might eat in the beach restaurant, where the menus were mainly 'fishy' though chicken dishes were usually available. The ferry back and forth was an accepted part of this trip! After a few days of high emotion, which would always remain with us, the time came for us to make our way back to Namisu.

The sun glistened on the lake and palm trees rustled on the lake shore. With sand in our toes, we moved between cottage and car sadly. A little wistfully we put on our sandals then popped back into the cottage to make sure nothing had been left behind. The car slid along the sand road from the lake. Lining the road were huts and villages, all of which were surrounded by palm trees. Many of the local men were making boats, rasping and cutting out the centre of a whole tree, using only an axe and a worn rasp as tools to complete the task, and cutting them in such a way as to enable a man to sit on the back whilst paddling. Fish was their staple diet, voices were carried in a haunting echo over the water. Cries of encouragement, excitement and laughter exploded from the shores as they hauled in their catch – food for the hopeful waiting families was assured for some days to come.

Women tended the gardens within the vicinity of each hut; hoeing, weeding and building up ridges. There were children of all ages, usually assisting with various village chores, they chewed on sugar cane, spitting out fibrous residue after extracting all the sweetness. Some gnawed on maize cobs, milk from the juicy niblets covering their dark faces. They ran after the car as we carefully dodged pot holes in the sandy road. Clouds of dust, thrown up by the wheels, stuck to their milky mouths and cheeks. They called after us as they ran, rubbing in the accumulated milky mess, attracting hundreds of flies, which they happily ignored.

Babies tied to the backs of women appeared to defy gravity, as mothers bent forward to weed and hoe. They were happy living their communal life. They sang and called to each other whilst tending to their daily chores (some of them were pounding maize to make posho, which they ate with fresh fish caught by the men). Usually it was baked over the village fire for their evening meal. Men drank large quantities of beer which was made by the womenfolk; they played drums, danced, whirled and writhed around the red glow of the village fires - ululating, singing and chanting, the mysterious sounds rang out over the lake. Their celebrations lasted well into the night.

The road was sandy and uneven, Jim eased the car over the ruts. Eventually after much manoeuvring, we arrived at Liwonde to cross the river by ferry. One look at this manually manipulated, broken down piece of equipment which was responsible for transporting the car and ourselves over this enormous flow, did not inspire blind faith. However everyone appeared to be relaxed, so I adopted the same attitude. Everything seemed to be taken for granted – after all, we had used the ferry on our journey to the lake. Jim drove the car onto the ferry and we were heaved laboriously over this vast expanse of water by a group of Nyasas, pulling ropes over squealing dry pulleys. Holding onto the side of the ferry, cool air blowing over the river raised goose bumps, on what had previously been hot wet skin. It took some time to reach the other side; it was a lengthy, painstaking part of the journey. Despite the ferry journey we loved our visits to the lake.

After our arrival back home from the lake, plans for our big day began to get underway. Many nights found us snuggled on the khonde until the early hours of the morning, spinning stories and watching mysterious shadows move around us as the silver moon made its way over the African sky. One evening Jim gave me a sketch of his first voyage to Nyasaland in 1947. It had taken a month to sail from England. After arriving in Cape Town he had travelled overland by train through South Africa and Rhodesia, to Nyasaland, eventually reaching Limbe, his final destination. Presenting himself at the company offices and exchanging formalities, he was given a briefing about his work and the company's expectations. This included guidelines on the management and direction of the African work force as well as information with regard to the house and estate. He was given the names of neighbours on nearby estates who were also employed by them. Nothing else was forthcoming. It was essential that Jim learned the local language as soon as possible, in order to make himself understood by the Nyasa work force. After the briefing, transport and a driver were made available to enable him to collect his luggage, buy essential groceries and basic commodities and to drive him to the estate house, which was already furnished.

He decided to spend his first night relaxing in a hotel in Blantyre, they set off early the next day and, with a loaded truck, made their way to the estate. Fortunately the driver spoke a little

English. They stopped to buy bananas and tomatoes from a roadside stall. Arriving at the estate Jim was greeted by a watchman who handed him a large bunch of keys, clapped his hands and, looking at the truck, offered his services which were gratefully accepted. Jim was now on his own, it was up to him to point himself in the right direction. That was how it was in those days of sink or swim situations. He quickly got to know the managers and owners of nearby estates and discovered they were always ready to help. His first task was to find a house boy, preferably one who could cook.

The first evening was spent at Namisu, he had been invited to supper with the then manager of the estate. (I think his name was Ron.) Jock, the old hunter from a nearby estate, was instrumental in helping Jim with the many difficulties and hiccups that he would encounter over the next few weeks. He was particularly helpful in teaching him to speak the language, he was also a master in the art of tobacco growing.

Order in the house and on the estate came quickly and a routine was soon established. An area manager from Limbe made regular visits. Mudi estate had a house which was thatched and really appealing. It was surrounded by huge lawns and indigenous bushes, but there was one big problem – snakes! There were many of them and many different species in the area. My dear Jim seemed to have the ability to go along with these setbacks in such an unhurried laid back way and with meticulous efficiency. His positive outlook and grim determination to get things right, paid off.

Apparently one evening he had been sitting back comfortably reading when a sixth sense told him to glance up, there slithering towards him was a huge cobra. With what I considered to be great presence of mind, he had picked up his gun quickly from the floor and killed the snake instantly with robust enthusiasm! In those days everyone carried a gun for just such an event.

With the help of Jock, his advice, the books he lent, coupled with his knowledge in the field of agriculture, Jim produced splendid crops of tobacco. The workers liked him and he picked up the language very quickly. In the four years he was there, his main diversion had been discussions with Jock whilst sitting on the khonde of the Larangwe house, enjoying a 'sundowner' of whiskey and soda. They talked of their hunting safaris, ad infinitum. At home on the estate he read for relaxation most evenings.

During the dry season he and Jock went off into the bush, usually to the lower river country, to shoot the meat needed for the estate, themselves and the Africans. Dogs also benefited from their hunting. All his hunting techniques he learnt from Jock who was originally a professional hunter (he had gone out to Portuguese East Africa in 1918). Jock was a hardened, wily old timer, able to judge the moods and movements of every species of game encountered in the bush. With Jocks's wealth of knowledge behind him, and his meticulous attention to detail, Jim could not have had a more able teacher.

I loved listening to these stories and adventures, in some respects it was reminiscent of our exchanges and conversations held in the past. In conversations touching my past, I attempted reluctantly to unraval the tangle I had made for myself, without attaching any undue blame on anyone in particular. My aim was to re-weave my life, to bring back and nurture the young joy we had shared in the daisy fields of Cheshire during the wartime years.

At the time Jim had been taking the boat to Nyasaland, I was seeing, courting and had married Tom. It made no sense. Alternatively, had I not taken this course our life would perhaps not have turned out as it did. I remained convinced that it was all pre-ordained. What I struggled to grasp was that all this had happened because of a platonic friendship involving an American soldier. Now, Jim admitted he had been a little hasty in his judgement. I explained all the ins and outs of my marriage; the meanness, the drinking and the general unhappiness. I had no idea why it happened. It was a lesson held in reserve for me I supposed, just another lesson which I had to learn. I did however, when the time came, turn it to my advantage with dogged determination.

The fact that we were together was all that really mattered, though Jim was repenting the lost years. After all these years in Nyasaland, Jim told me of his sudden urge to go to Nigeria. One evening whilst reading an agricultural magazine he had noticed a cotton cultivation officer was needed in Nigeria with the Crown Agents. After seeing this he thought hard and long, and discussed it with the company in Nyasaland, they were prepared to re-employ him after his tour in Nigeria. He then put in an application for the position and was successful. When the time came for him to leave Nyasaland, Jock took his dogs and pet baboon. It was tame and quite friendly, as a youngster it often sat on the back of his dogs as they walked in a crocodile line to the vegetable garden. There was Tiny, Jim's favourite dog who had the heart of a lion and loyalty to match and Sheila, his other dog, was like her name, defensive but flighty. As the baboon grew into full adulthood it became dangerous and very aggressive and difficult decisions had to be made!

I listened intently to all these stories and I was always hungry for more. I had a great weakness for wanting to know everything about him, to the very last detail. It was necessary for me to know, he had spent so much time in my imagination. I felt that every unanswered question must be called upon and tied in. And now, it was midnight and we decided to call it a day. I had learned quite a lot this night about the man I was to marry. We each wandered off to the bedroom clutching a glass of Roses's Lime Cordial, always our bedtime drink. We crawled under the mosquito net, feeling deeply warm inside and very conscious of our close proximity, to fall into joyous sleep. We were in eager anticipation of the huge happiness we knew the next day would bring.

CHAPTER FIVE

That morning we awoke full of excitement and overwhelming enthusiasm for our coming event. In four hours time we would be married! We fussed and we fumbled, making ourselves look splendid for what was, to us, an earth moving occasion.

Geoffrey and a heavily pregnant Shirley, who by this time were married, arrived in a flurry of dust. We had to dash to meet the 2 pm deadline in Blantyre. Within a few hours all our dreams would come true. This thread, held onto for so long, had not broken, we could float through life on a bright cloud of happiness and contentment., We would go over, under or through any dark clouds we might encounter, basking in the warmth of the love we had, in such abundance.

We had originally hoped to marry in the church of St. Michael's. We approached the rector who refused to marry us, the church would not marry a divorcee. So, we had a civil wedding performed by a registrar. We emerged happy and completely content, on this previously mentioned date of August 3rd, 1957, and this is how we remained.

As we walked from the registry office, Geoffrey gave us his lovely wrinkly smile, he gave me a kiss and shook Jim's hand fervently in genuine joy, his eyes were as big as I had ever seen them. He really did love us both, the relief of us getting married seemed almost more than he could bear.

Also at the ceremony was one of our neighbours, Jack O'Hea, a good friend from a nearby estate, afterwards he walked over to his car and on his return we noticed he was carrying a package under his arm which he handed over to us with his love and best wishes. The box held a Royal Doulton coffee service which I have to this day. He was delighted that at last we had become an 'item.'

Jim and I revelled in these dizzy moments, albeit we were a little shaken with incredulity at the fruition of all our hitherto made plans. Holding hands, hot and sticky, we walked happily towards the car. After a big kiss, the car door was opened for me and I sat down, completely content.

We laughed, reminisced and made our way noisily to 'The Flamingo', no other venue could possibly have been considered. It had been our first 'experience' together in Nyasaland. We were greeted by Tony who made an immense fuss with much kissing and shaking of hands, his attention was second to none.

Champagne was 'on the house'. We made our way to a table tucked away in an open alcove, it was closed in by walls of bourgainvillea, nearby doves cooed softly as cicadas played their castanets. It was a perfect setting for a perfect day. Our piri piri chicken seemed like food from the Gods on this day. The accompaniments and lots of crusty bread were washed down with crisp white wine. We felt closeted in a dream world. Geoffrey and Shirley who ate with us had sandwiches, chilli gave Shirley indigestion and Geoffrey did not like 'bones,' he would never 'pick' a bone. He used to think that we were quite out of line, 'cannibalistic' I think was the word he used. In our book, it was sheer bliss.

I remember it was with some relief that I removed the 'cowpat' from my head. It was a hat borrowed from Shirley for the occasion. A light loose coat covered my dusky pink dress, the outfit was finished off by a pair of black court shoes. Jim looked incredibly smart in his grey suit. I wanted to put my arms around him and stay there forever. It had been a magical day, a day of floating unreality. We were day dreaming and we found ourselves talking, laughing and drinking Greek coffee with Tony until late afternoon, when at last the time came for us to make our way home to Namisu.

Jack O'Hea, Geoffrey and Shirley had left, leaving us to further our romantic interlude in the alcove. Elizabeth was with Gypsy and Cherry who had taken her to visit friends in Mulanje and were staying the night. Jim and I had told her of our of our plans. We explained our hopes and dreams for our life in the future. It would be a happy life full of love and excitement. She may have been small, but she trusted me; we had always done everything together, been everywhere together. Jim was sweet and kind to her and she loved him as though she had known him forever. She never stopped loving him.

On our way home from 'The Flamingo' to Namisu we saw bush buck nibbling at crops in a nearby field. Meat at that moment was in great demand on the estate so Jim took his gun from the car, we thought it was a good idea to take a shot. Buck was on his license. In those days rules were made and must be followed, it was not wise to bend them, there could (and would) be problems ahead. The game department were very keen, the European game rangers were attentive to the job in hand, and their responsibilities.

Bushbuck could be a nuisance, they consumed vast quantities of young shoots as they pushed their way through the ground, decimating the crop if they were not controlled. So, on our wedding night, I clambered over furrowed fields in my wedding gear and high heeled shoes, with Jim regaled in his one good suit we carried the bush buck to the car and heaved it into the boot. This exertion really made us puff and blow. Afterwards we dropped it at the house of the headman, Makolo, who dressed it and delivered it to the house the next morning. He had his share, some we gave to Geoffrey and Jock, some to the house servant, the rest we put into our charcoal fridge. The meat was very good.

Rarely a week went by without our visiting Jock, usually we went on Sunday. At times other old friends also appeared, families whom Jim and Jock had known for years. Sometimes Geoffrey and Shirley came along too. These were great times, they were always such fun, with much tale telling, banter and laughter. Sometimes the tales were mild but at others they were appallingly raucous. The latter occurred mostly when Jock decided to reminisce, which was often. He was an accomplished raconteur and had an enormous belly laugh. He had defied death many times and in many ways. He was a wiry, muscular and shrewd man who did not give a damn for anyone unless he deemed them a proven and genuine friend. He was very particular in his choice.

Jock always bought his milk from an Italian who had a large herd of cattle and lived on an estate nearby. Much of this milk was taken to Blantyre, however, he did provide a few locals with a daily quota. Bison, Jock's cook, collected two bottles of milk each day. The lady of the estate, who was always waiting at the point of distribution, kept a 'beady eye' on the receptacles into which her milk was being poured. She looked down into the bottles which Bison had handed to her and made a comment as to their lack of cleanliness. 'Bwana Simpson's bottles are not clean.' Poor Bison, on his arrival back to Larangwe he handed the bottles back to Jock not forgetting to reiterate the comments as to the doubt of their cleanliness! With a loud bellow, accompanied by considerable blasphemy which was all delivered in a strong Scots accent, Jock roared with a stutter of sheer indignation, 'The bottles are clean enough to put her bloody dirty milk in.' Come the next day, on his visit to the estate, Bison took great pleasure in repeating, with exaggerated emphasis, Jock's reaction to her comment on the state of the bottles. The lady was incensed. For some time Jock's occasional evening visits to the farm ground to a halt. Dried milk had to be bought from a Blantyre store and Bison was almost 'Out on his ear.' This story was told to us on one of our Sunday 'drop ins'. Life was never dull.

As I write this story it occurs to me that the date is February 4th 2003. I am gripped with an all consuming melancholy when I realise that Jim and I gave each other our last kiss two years ago today. The thought wrenches at my heart and I am weighed down with a blanket of disbelief, and an almost unbearable grief. What must I do? I must live on, write some more, and I must relive our life as I remember it.

There were times when visiting Jock for a quick coffee could become a marathon event. Listening to his tales, of which he had a never ending store, the time flew by. He would get up from his chair quite suddenly and disappear into the kitchen without a word being spoken. When he returned a short time later he sat down with a smile, Bison following on his heels carrying a huge tray covered with fingers of warm sardines on toast and welsh rarebit. We all drank Castle beer as an accompaniment to these tasty morsels. We had more anecdotes, exchanged with tips of the art of tobacco growing, tobacco seed beds, fertilizers, insecticides, pesticides, planting, ridge building, the breakdown was endless. In the midst of all these mental meanderings, he again called Bison. Jock had decided we must stay to supper. It was difficult to refuse, particularly as he was never in the mood for refusals! The more people there were around the more he revelled in it. Bison was told to catch either a chicken or a turkey depending upon how many people had arrived. He had to catch, pluck clean and cook the bird, and then go to the vegetable garden, collect vegetables and prepare them. There was always a huge variety of everything in the estate gardens. With the meal, potatoes were inevitably mashed, unless there was a special request for roast, in which case we had both. It was always delicious. To follow there were usually pancakes, stewed fruit (everyone had stewed fruit of some kind to hand), steamed pudding as light as a feather, and served with custard was a favourite.

Jock had hugely varied tastes, His table was always immaculate. There were always damask napkins and beautiful shining glassware. Everything was served to perfection. A far cry from what one would immediately expect. The room adjacent to the dining room had become Jock's library, it was full of eclectic and interesting books, ranging from big game hunters to cookery, medicine and poetry. There were others with somewhat risqué titles! Jock's books were his pride and joy. For years he had sent to Heffer's of London for books and he had many first editions. His serious reading was always done sitting bolt upright at the table, with the book on a clean cloth and his hands freshly washed. Each book had a dust cover and all were on the shelves in alphabetical order.

This extraordinary man was a strange mixture, a brave wild Scot and a hunter who could live under almost impossible conditions. He was a relentless womanizer and a great lover of beauty, his heart, though tough and strong, could also be soft and caring. His lurid stories of hunting and sex whilst in Portuguese East Africa took one's breath away – as did his carnal desires. Jock's wife Mia was an African princess of the Yau tribe, they had one daughter Annie. It was a happy marriage, generally accepted, and it lasted until the day he died of black water fever. It was his third and last attack. Mia had nursed him through the other two from which he fully recovered, the final bout was fatal, there was nothing she could do to save him. His two previous attacks were cured by native medicine, constant attention to his fever, and the unswerving attention Mai gave to his water intake. I gather he was not an easy patient!

Fortunately Jock had taken a liking to me which was a huge bonus. I was given to understand that often in the past he had asked Jim 'When are you going to marry laddie?' Pointing to my photograph on his desk his reply was always, 'Not until this girl comes along, I can wait until then.' It was almost as though he knew. He waited for me, I obliged and came along. Geoffrey always made the comment that our feelings poured out all over the place.

Once, it happened that I was driving Geoffrey's car and I broke my collar bone. I knew that I was approaching a bridge, which lay astride a deep gorge, and that the bridge had no sides. The roads at this time were dry and dusty and visibility was very bad. I was almost at the bridge when a car coming from the other direction, exploded from a cloud of dust ripping by at an alarming speed, reducing visibility to nil. Dust flew like a sandstorm. I had to make a quick decision, was it the bank or the gorge? I chose the bank, hitting my collar bone on the steering wheel. Jim, who was following behind was beside himself. The break was a perfect nuisance. No one was at the hospital to attend to it at the time, so we tied back my arms to straighten the bone. My poor love had to do so much for me. I felt sure he was sorely tried, though with a smile, he denied it. I still have a blimp on my collar bone as a reminder of those days.

One evening following this, whiskey in hand, I said to Jim 'Tell me more about Nigeria' I requested, I loved listening to his stories, getting to know more of the man for whom I had always had such a fascination.

So, his story began. In 1951 he set sail for Nigeria, arriving in Lagos he was sent to Kano in Northern Nigeria, this was essentially his base. However his travelling was far flung, it was mainly in the northern interior, Agedez, Zaria, Kaduna and Kontagura were the main places he had contact with but for almost three years he was almost entirely alone in the bush, only moving into civilization to make reports and to collect mail. His only mode of transport was a horse, no house had been provided, it was not in the contract.

Accommodation and porters were provided by village headman of whichever district he was in at the time. He slept mainly in mud and wattle huts and his comforts consisted of whatever his porters were able to carry. There were no amenities in the huts. A cook was part of his entourage and essential. Sanitation left a lot to be desired, some villages had water, in others it had to be carried. Fortunately, Jim was a loner, he did not really feel the need for people. He loved his horse, he bought an African Grey parrot from one of the district officers who was to leave for the UK. The bird became his pal; it entertained him and made him laugh as it talked frantically whilst sitting on his shoulder during his treks. He travelled through the bush for many, many miles singing 'Slow Coach' to his horse, often the parrot would join in an a 'sing-along'. At other times it chatted loudly, always vying for attention.

The only Europeans he came across were on the mission stations where he always received a warm welcome. They like everyone else who met him, fell under the spell of his charm and his stoic determination, with that certain indefinable quality and inner glow that he seemed to radiate. He was comfortable to be with. He was also very kind. Add this to his good looks and the results are pretty amazing, he was quite irresistible. These are my sentiments. The nuns took him to their hearts knowing how he dealt with some of the hardships he had to cope with as he toured the cotton growing areas. Rivers had to be manoeuvred by holding onto the horse's mane as it swam across. The parrot sitting on his head making the most frantic of noises. Crocodiles lay in and alongside the river, imitating giant floating logs! On reaching the opposite bank they would shake themselves off and head for the nearest village, where the headman arranged for a hut for him to sleep in, water, a fire to cook on and help from the odd villager wanting to earn a shilling or two. In the villages he bought chicken and yams to make palm chop stew. Spinach, tomatoes and sweet potatoes were for sale. Some of the women made and sold bread, it was light and fluffy and raised with fermented beer.

He told me of sitting around the fire in the evenings alongside the headman. Villagers passed by and handed him mugs of village beer, his conversation was made possible only by words he had picked up, and the odd bit of English known to the headman. With supper over, it was time for bed. The horse was tethered, his parrot was on it's perch. Now it was time to nestle into the sleeping bag placed over a thick pallet of dried grass. With the door closed he drifted off to sleep. There were times during the hot season when Jim slept in a hammock, at these times he had to be alert to any strange or unrecognised sounds penetrating his shallow sleep. At cock crow, the village started to move. Bed, luggage, horse and parrot were rounded up ready for the road, a cup of goats milk, a mealie cob, beer bread and honey made up his breakfast. With an all round 'Thank you' he rode off to make as many calls as were possible on that side of the river before dusk. With the day over he went back to an organized camp on the other side, his carriers were attentive to his basic needs.

As his tale unfolded, I thought 'What a hard life.' Only someone of his patience and strength of will would carry it through for any length of time. Fortunately his physique matched his courage. There were also times when he had to face the Hamatan in the Niger Province. They were violent windstorms, dust enveloped everything, leading to great discomfort. It occurred to me that 'Old Jock' would have made it his business to cope with those hardships too.

★ ★ ★

Again, as my mind wanders, and I reflect on the suffering Jim had latterly. These same characteristics were always displayed as he carried on, stoically doing whatever he had to do, never complaining and never giving in to his illness which we all knew must have been devastating for him. His love, his giving, his discomfort, his pain, his grief, we all shared but, and I have to say this, we all thought that this illness was a temporary hiccup, to us he was indestructible. Jim still is, and always will be, guiding us, taking care of us; the family he loved so very much. In return he was loved in equal measure and he always will be.

★ ★ ★

One morning Jim was awakened by considerable discomfort. He had a sore throat and his neck was very stiff, he also had a throbbing headache, nausea, dizziness and a feeling of disorientation. Headquarters had apparently warned him of an outbreak of meningitis in the area and had suggested that should any of these symptoms manifest themselves he must head for the nearest mission hospital. With great difficulty and considerable discomfort, he assembled his carriers. They rolled up his bed, collected the parrot and with help he mounted his horse, whose name I cannot recall. From the village he rode for almost the whole day until he reached the mission. Immediately they took one look at him as they took his temperature and made necessary tests. He was gently washed, put into clean pyjamas and into a soft bed with lovely clean white sheets. This Jim said with such depth of feeling! My goodness – I could sense the bliss he must have felt at the sheer comfort and the relief of cleanliness. He had needed and received at this time much attention and nursing; he was sufering from tick typhus, not meningitis. The American nursing nuns had taken great care of him. He was allowed to do very little and made to stay and recuperate for two or three weeks. The sickness had taken its toll, he was weak and had lost two stone in weight before being discharged in reasonably good health. He carried on with his duties at first, but it was recommended that he leave for England before the end of his contract, as he needed recuperation in Europe.

On arrival home he recovered quite quickly. He bought a new Vauxhall and spread his wings a little. He met a girl who was completely besotted with him. This girl has been mentioned in a previous chapter. She knew nothing of me at the time, but he said I was still tucked away in the recesses of his mind and that my photograph was always within grasping distance. He never gave up, he was sure that one day I would appear from somewhere, somehow.

During one of our reminisces he told me of the time he went to the Emirs durbar, where the horses charge towards the visitors stands. They are then suddenly brought to a halt by the spiked bits that were used in those days. He told me of camels he used to ride at times, and of the Fulani tribe. All this he told me as we sat holding hands in the moonlight. The skies were brilliant, the bright evening stars; the Southern Cross, Orion's Belt, The Milky Way, Big Bear, Little Bear, were pointed out to me almost every night. How I loved this life. Every blissful day held a wealth of love and happiness, every night was untold magic. I just revelled in the deep warmth, comfort, safety and absolute contentment. No one could want more or could have more love, adventure and kind consideration than my love had given to me in our years together. We shared everything.

It transpired that after spending a few months in England, once again 'Africa called', it is always said that once you have tasted the waters of Africa, you will always return. How true this is. Jim wrote to his old employers asking them to consider his re-employment, asking if they had a vacancy in Nyasaland in tobacco production. He explained his position with them in the past and their insistence that should he write to them if he ever wished to return. The reply was favourable and everything was set for him to once again leave England. So, in 1954, my love once more set sail for Africa and Capetown. This time he knew and understood what lay ahead of him, he was becoming an old hand in the vagaries and upheavals created by a love of Africa. The Vauxhall, bought whilst in England, was in the hold and he was looking forward to driving from Capetown to Nyasaland. Well rested from the voyage and the time spent at home, he was fit but had not made up his weight. After embarcation he booked into an hotel within walking distance of the docks, preferring to be near when the car was unloaded. On the release of his car he inspected the parts which he felt might be in need of attention, checked the oil, filled up with petrol and was raring to go. Shopping was packed alongside luggage, and the spare parts which were shipped out with the car were packed. A box of tools was always kept in the same place for easy access, a wise practice when covering the roads of this vast continent of Africa. Water was a must, so were basic foods, just in case! Fruit, maize and nuts were for sale in the villages, people displayed their wares alongside the road.

Here and there, usually just in from the road, small well-built wooden stores owned by Afrikaners, and mainly used by Afrikaner farmers in the area, sold all the bare essentials. Each store had its own tiny bar, around which stood a few battered, well-worn stools, strategically placed to accommodate the large backsides of nearby farmers, most of whom used any farm vehicle at hand to nip to the nearest local bar where they could enjoy a tot, a pipe of tobacco and exchange news. They were huge, hard, bearded men who roared out their grievances and lewd conversations in a guttural Flemish dialogue. There were always a few spotlessly clean tables and the home cooked food was exceptionally good. They served tasty soups, pickled fish, bobotie, salads and excellent fresh bread and butter.

It had taken two days of re-organization, planning the route and making enquiries as to any pitfalls he may be up against. He told me of his overwhelming enthusiasm to set off on this long, dusty journey through the Cape Province, Orange Free State, Transvaal, Southern Rhodesia, Mozambique and on to Nyasaland.

Sometimes he slept in the car, at other times in some small hotel. The roads were dusty and potholed, at times they ran through tunnels hewn out from under mountains at others through scrubland.

Along the roads he encountered scattered groups of women, their bodies swaying rhythmically as they walked. They carried pots of water on their heads and babies on their backs and they were usually pregnant at the same time. In addition they also had other children walking at their heel. Most were heading for the nearest stream to start the daily ritual of washing. They spent most of the day here, calling out news of nearby villages, and talking of any scandal heard from the local white people. Their clothes were washed by beating them on smooth worn rocks, rubbing vigorously on each item with a piece of hard soap usually bought from an Indian douka (shop) nearby, later swishing them through the stream water many times to remove any surplus soap. They rang them out and hung them to dry on nearby branches until the time came for them to leave for the village. People arriving late carried their wet washing in large enamel bowls, it was the task of the elder children to carry it back to the village. Each woman carried back a full pot of water which was mainly used for cooking. Washing sessions and collecting water was at times perilous. Many natives had been taken by hippo, crocodiles and, at times, by a hungry old lion.

The journey was interesting and without hiccups or problems. Travelling through the bush, he told me, he had seen a lot of plain game, Thompson's gazelle, wildebeest, sable and, at times, eland. Warthogs ran with their tails erect, babies followed along behind their mother, tails up. If the mother stopped to stamp her feet in agitation, so did they, all their actions mirrored those of their mother. Elephant fed in the bush alongside the road, pulling and pushing at trees and ripping off bark with their trunks. Herds of buffalo, heads raised, stood staring, their fierce penetrating eyes shone black from beneath the thick boss of the enormous horn span. With their head up and thrust forward they seemed to say, 'Is anyone looking for trouble?' Jim told of snakes slithering over the road as the car approached. Nearby hyenas tugged and tore at the flesh from a recent kill, screaming in their greed at any others in the pack who attempted to steal from them.

During the journey he stopped to give a lift to a white farmer living in the Transvaal, this proved to be useful as he pointed him in the right direction and gave him a considerable number of tips; where to head for and what to avoid. The farmer was visiting a relative near the Rhodesian border, hitching a lift in order to drive a vehicle back to his farm near Johannesburg.

CHAPTER SIX

Jim told me how he looked forward to arriving in Nyasaland, greeting 'Old Jock' and his dogs, and to the hunting which he knew would have been planned for him. It was wonderful to be returning to the Lunzu valley and Namisu, Geoffrey was recently arrived on the next door estate, Mudi.

It was not difficult to settle into the relaxed atmosphere of Namisu and his surrounds. The dogs had not forgotten, they followed him wherever he went, it was almost as though he had never been away. He bought sheep, goats, chickens and ducks and erected appropriate sheds for each. The vegetable garden was established quickly, the estate and house workers were quickly and quietly organized. Life fell into place, Jim's needs were met and gradually everything moulded into a pattern. He and Geoffrey were neighbours, Jim taught him the way of life in Africa, he became acclimatized and eventually loved it. He was at first a little taken aback by 'Old Jock', although later became one of his greatest fans. He learned the art of tobacco growing and of living in Africa. Dear Geoffrey, he attempted to learn to hunt with Jock and Jim, walking for many miles and never giving in, but it was soon established that he was not really hunting material, although if Jim went he was always willing to follow.

Things changed for a while, some way out of Limbe was the Ndata estate the domain of the Boddy family, Geoffrey had been asked to manage the estate whilst they were on leave in the UK. The Boddys were to escort his fiancee, Shirley, on the boat journey from England to Nyasaland. Shortly after her arrival they were to marry. It was during this time that Jim and I met again in our unbelievable chance meeting in The Shire Highlands Hotel. Just a short time afterwards, I met his brother, it was a momentous time for all of us.

Hastily sent letters and telegrams sped backwards and forwards from Nyasaland to Cheshire for weeks, neither of our families were at all surprised at the outcome after hearing the news of our meeting. It was not quite the thing to do in 1956, but all who knew us would expect nothing less.

From the 3rd August 1956, our lives were inextricably bound, we were blissfully content.

CHAPTER SEVEN

Quite suddenly the company announced their intention of re-roofing Namisu house, it was to be carried out more or less immediately and completed well before the rains in early November. For this reason it was necessary for us to erect a large grass hut to use as a temporary home. It was built on the lawn in front of the house and was quite adequate for a short time, it had three and a half grass walls and was interwoven with bamboo. The roof was made from palm fronds. We made a good sized dining room which had two windows, the spare grass framing each window was pulled back and rolled to form a rounded window frame. Each window was covered with mosquito netting. Next door was the bedroom which had a grass dividing wall with a small space midway for access from room to room. In the bedroom we did not have a full outside wall, one quarter of the wall was used as a door and was our only source of light. During the night this space was covered with framed mosquito netting . Tiny, the dog basket, was in the corner. From the dining area a small mosquito door led to a path which wound its way to the kitchen. It was slightly away from the house for safety reasons. Taking everything into consideration, we were adequately equipped. Our furniture which we had brought over from the house, together with any equipment we felt we might need, was constantly covered with dust from the dry grass floor. The rest we tucked away where it was easily retrievable.

Our battery radio was essential and one of the first things to be moved over, we placed it on the sideboard, high and handy, alongside the pressure lamp. We must have our news, stories and radio shows from the BBC not forgetting the sweet nostalgic music from Rhodesia. Whilst living in our temporary home I made lots of feta cheese from a recipe given to me by Poppy, the hairdresser's wife. Cheese lying in brine was in every conceivable corner.

Jack'O Shea, our neighbour, often came to visit us, Geoffrey came whenever he could. We picked at cheese, drank coffee or wine, depending on the time of day. We held lengthy discussions and covered many diverse subjects, topical and otherwise. Our views and thinking differed widely at times, the more agitated we became the more cheese we ate and the more wine we drank! It was great fun, even though it sometimes became a little raucous!

At this time of the year workers were busy stumping the land and hoeing ready for the coming tobacco crop. Each field was rotated. All this activity disturbed a large number of snakes. The air as ever, became filled with the noise of cicadas in the still heat of afternoon, forms in the distance shimmered and became distorted. I made Rosella jelly, which we ate with homemade scones and cream. Our life was one of bliss! I put great effort into making Jim's favourite meals, and revelled in the joy of success as he savoured each mouthful.

Now was the time for preparation of the nurseries and for making tobacco seed beds. Each bed was approximately 30 yards long by four feet wide. Generally one bed produced sufficient seedlings for one acre. The seeds were tiny, the size of a pin head. There were petrie dishes everywhere. They were divided up into sections with each section holding a seed of a different variety of tobacco in order that the rate of determination could be noted. The seedbed soil had to be fine and worked, then it was injected with fumigants before sowing. Once the seedlings had appeared, they were covered with a grass mulch and watered regularly. The mulch protected them from the sun and from any direct force of the sprayed water. Geoffrey's eyes at times were orbs of consternation at the delicate and complicated process of it all. What of tobacco now, I wonder, as I write? Jim never did smoke, but he loved the challenge of producing a good crop. Each time he went into the fields or to the nurseries, I went with him, holding hands as we walked along, always very aware of each other – electricity had a habit of passing between us on most occasions. Outside each nursery a small wooden stand was erected and on the stand an enamel bowl holding water and disinfectant. Hands had to be washed before entering.

Each evening before the short twilight Jim came over to me, hand out, and off we would go to inspect the tobacco nurseries before 'Sundowner' time. We were still able to use the bathroom in the homestead, it had been a later addition and was still in a good state of repair. We were fast asleep one night when we were suddenly awakened by the most blood-curdling sounds. Outside, quite near to our grass home, a leopard had attacked the dogs, killing one and badly wounding the other. Tiny, who was getting old, was in his basket in the bedroom. Jim grabbed his gun, I held the torch, but it was too late, the leopard had sloped off into the night. The dog who had been attacked had the most awful wounds which Jim treated each day with permanganate of potash mixed in water. After much care and attention, the dog did survive but it was a struggle. The attack left him cowed and timid, poor 'Wolf'. The leopard was very much in evidence for some time. It came into the kraal stealthily during the night and killed four sheep. We sat up one night watching and waiting with baited breath and gun in hand. We glimpsed him once by the light of the moon, flitting in swift retreat behind the rocks. It was necessary to be absolutely still and deadly quiet. I merely rustled the paper in which I carried a sandwich (in case the wait was long and we became hungry), it was the end of our vigil for that night, leopards have good hearing. Yet again the kraal had to be reinforced, each night the sheep were driven in before darkness had fallen and the gates were firmly closed. During the night the watchman made regular visits to make sure everything was intact.

Jim's beloved Tiny became very sick, a deep sadness enveloped us all. We knew he was old and we knew he was fading fast, but this only served to cement the gloom we felt, he had been so loyal and gutsy. He had hunted with Jock and Jim, flushing out game which would have had the other dogs fleeing in the opposite direction. He attacked a civet cat which had been taking chickens, a ball of spots and brown fur rolled out thrashing in every direction, squealing and growling, barking and hissing, stopping at Jim's feet the civet cat was dead. Tiny was spattered with blood from claw gashes on his face. He was triumphant in his success. Looking at Jim he shook his massive scarred mastiff head, and limped off back to the house. He was quite a dog. He followed his master everywhere. Tiny was not a handsome dog just beautifully ugly. Still in our temporary grass home, Tiny lay in his basket in the corner. One night he came over to Jim's side of the bed. There was a slight mewling noise followed by a scratching on the side of the bed, we were not fully asleep, but dozing fitfully because we both felt the dog had a problem. The scratching stopped, and then started again, it was louder this time. Jim patted Tiny's head, 'Lie down, old friend, lie down and rest' I heard him say quietly. Tiny was saying 'Goodbye,' in the morning he lay dead. Jim was devastated, his old friend had died. It took some time to get over this, not seeing him around and having to come to terms with the fact that we would never see his ugly old face again which it had been so full of character, with his ragged ears and his battered scarred old face. He was buried in style. Walking from the little grave Jim looked at me sadly, I took his hand detecting the odd tear as we slowly walked back to the house. His sadness affected me, I hurt for him, there were somersaults in my stomach and an ache in my heart which I had almost forgotten could exist.

Life went on. Sometimes we went into Blantyre, just for books and magazines and to see Liz. If Jim needed to have his hair cut we would call in to see Michael. We drank Greek coffee and ate biscuits with him, his mother and his wonderful wife Poppy always greeted us eagerly. Michael's mother was a handsome old Greek lady who dressed in black 'widow's weeds'. She had been over to Greece and had chosen Poppy as a wife for Michael, she then took her back to Nyasaland. Fortunately he had fallen in love with Poppy, they had a hard but happy life together. As time went on they had two sons and were devoted to them. My wedding ring was purchased from a little Goan jeweller next door to Michael's shop. It was made up of tiny white gold hearts between two bands of yellow gold. I have never moved it from the day Jim put it onto my finger!

At the moment changes were being made for the following year; the company approached both Geoffrey and Jim, they were given the choice of remaining on tobacco production or moving onto a tea estate. Jim chose to remain where we were, he loved the challenge of the tobacco crop. Geoffrey opted for tea. He and Shirley were to move to Mpeni, through Limbe, on the Mulanje road, towards the Mozambique border. The move was not immediate. These changes were a sign of things to come, it was difficult if not almost impossible to comprehend. At this time almost everyone smoked. the company knew a whole lot more than they told us of the anti-smoking campaign now being waged world wide. We did not query it, we were happy and could not, at that time, ever imagine that it would all come to an end. We dreamed on.

On the estate there were a great many flocks of guinea fowl and qwali (partridge). Often we walked into the bush, past the stream and way up into the hills. Jim took his shot gun and I took the 2.2, we usually went in the afternoon, though not until the great heat of day had passed. We walked along the estate roads, checked the tobacco barns, chatted with the alonda (watchman), making sure everything he had been set to do for that day had been completed, then on through the trees. In the dip before the rise I saw a flock of guinea fowl, 'Look Jim, shall I take a shot', 'Yes, keep it low', came the reply. I kept it low, took a shot and the bird fell to the ground. I took aim again, I shot and another one fell. 'Good girl, that was clean shooting,' I felt pleased as we walked over to pick up the guinea fowl, which would be our dinner for the next day. Jim shot pigeons for Liz when she was home, she loved them roasted. She used to sit on the veranda steps and pick away at them until the bones shone. The walk into the bush on the estate was very beautiful, we went through glade after glade, sometimes in the distance, looking directly at us there were two kudu, I had seen them near the house. The handsome male with his huge curved horns could often be seen peering over the rocks which lay at the back of the cattle boma. Sometimes the female was with him. She was beauty incarnate with her big sad eyes and huge rounded ears. Of all the antelope I love the kudu. Usually we arrived back from these walks in the evocative crepuscular light of evening.

I took the birds into the kitchen and handed them to Harrison,
'For supper tomorrow please Harrison,'
'Yes, madam, I hang them up,'

The next day they would be brought to table, beautifully roasted, served with game chips which we had taught him to prepare. He was in fact an extremely good cook, he did not drink beer which was an added bonus as so many of the African staff drank pombe in the villages to the point of stupidity. Pombe or beer is always made by the women who also make a potent spirit called cachasu, which is quite lethal. It was in fact illegal to produce this in the villages, however it still went on. It was always very obvious when they had been drinking this spirit, they were quite out of their minds, and made the most awful noise walking back from an evening's session to their huts, loud wails, shouting, singing and cries carried over on the night air. Work the next day was impossible. It was a tribal custom they followed, or so it seemed, and if they fell foul of the behaviour befitting the tribe, then the headman of the village or the village chief would deal with them accordingly.

Jim prepared our drinks, I placed nuts in a small dish, some shelled, some unshelled as Jim liked the shell them himself.

'Your drink is ready love.'

'Okay, just running the bath water.'

It was not long before he walked onto the veranda bathed, clean shirt and shorts, a pair of moccasins on his feet. He looked so fresh and good and smelt of soap and aftershave. It was a special smell he carried throughout his life. There was something evocative about it, something masculine and something everyone noticed, certainly the family did, even his grandchildren.

I gave him a kiss as I passed on my way to the bathroom and noticed that Harrison had turned back the bed and put down the mosquito net. A slight breeze was blowing the curtains, and the crickets were chirruping. The moon was half full. I took off my clothes quickly and lay for a while soaking in the bath, the water was slightly brown, this was always the case as a residue built up in the water drum, despite this the water was soft and relaxing. Afterwards I put on a kaftan which I had made from some colourful cloth which I bought from one of the Indian shops in Blantyre. Feeling clean and relaxed I sat down on the khonde to enjoy another unforgettable and tranquil evening.

We talked for some time of the annual safari planned by Jock, we hoped to accompany him. He would leave a little earlier than Jim and I. It would be necessary for us to find a bush guide. We both hoped we would never have to leave Africa, it was certainly never our intention. In our retirement we had thought it might be a splendid idea to farm on the slopes of Kilimanjaro, where the cattle and game virtually lived as one. Our temporary grass home had now been taken down and we had moved back into the house, the only signs of our having been there was the scuffed grass which would recover in no time at all.

After moving back we decided the bathroom needed decorating, there was not a great deal of choice. One of the estate carpenters painted the walls with white wash, mixed with cochineal. I was in charge of the mixing. As I stirred frantically Jim came along, commenting that my pink was just a little too pink! It was a much lighter shade when it was dry, the end result was quite attractive. We painted the outside of the bath black, together with the legs and a small stool. It all sounds quite dreadful and yet it looked very nice! We went into one of the Indian doukas in Blantyre and bought a few yards of light cotton, which was dotted with tiny sprigs of roses. I made curtains and a cloth for the small table near the hand basin. Originally the house was without a bathroom however Jim, who liked his home comforts, decided that he must have one, and it was to be ensuite. I loved gazing through the bathroom window onto the drive and the coloured bushes and trees lining either side. I often sat on the stool at breakfast time and watched Jim walk up from the bwalo.

We decided to have an early night. Harrison had cooked a splendid meal. Deciding against coffee. 'Bed love?' asked Jim. What a good idea I thought. I had visions of being curled up beside him. Thinking these lovely thoughts I decided an early night, listening to the sounds of Africa, would be just wonderful. Hand in hand we walked to the bedroom.

Suddenly it was morning, Harrison knocked on the door, 'Come in,' I called. He opened the door quietly and put the tray on the table. I opened one eye and saw him creep out taking great care not to make a noise. It was Saturday, not a great deal was happening, Jim turned over peered through one eye, propped himself up on his elbow, crooking his finger, beckoning. Leaning over I kissed him, 'Good morning'.

'Stay where you are for a while, you don't have to get up early this morning.

'Let's lie in and chat and listen to the doves,' I suggested.

'Can you smell the bread baking Cog? What could be better than this, you and me, tea in bed and all to the aroma of hot bread?

Happiness welled up inside us. Reluctantly we eventually rolled out of bed and decided we would go over the Larangwe to see Jock.

As ever we took coffee on Jock's veranda and the conversation turned to books, references to past hunters, 'The shooting man's bedside book,' and so on. I found everything they had to say interesting and listened intently. The conversation changed to poetry, Burns, Kipling 'The Complete Verse,' the latter always lay alongside Jim's bed, its advice and quotes made a great impact on his life. In particular Kipling's 'If' seemed to hold great meaning for him. Almost as though he felt, somehow, the world had lost its way. Then conversation turned to the bush as it so often did. Jock reminded Jim of the time we took the short road back to Namisu after drinks and supper. It had been quite late and we left around midnight. As we walked along in the moonlight we could hear the sound of small animals and birds, owls and nightjars which were accompanied by the sound of distant village drums, broken at times by the unearthly bloodcurdling laugh of a hyena, which had been attracted by the smell of meat cooking on the village fires. From the side of the path we were taking there was an ominous grunt; our hearts skipped a beat, looking round we saw the shadowy outline of what was obviously a fully grown male lion walking alongside us. It was a mere three to four yards away in the bush. It padded along for half a mile, grunting with each step. The gun that Jim always carried gave me some modicum of comfort on these occasions. Eventually, walking directly in front of us, the lion crossed over to the other side, disappearing into the undergrowth. We did not dare to sigh with relief. We just continued apace until we reached Namisu, where we sat down with a large whisky and soda. Of course the account was embellished considerably by Jock.

It was decided that Jock was to leave for safari to Chikwawa on the 10th of August for three weeks, we were to follow on the 17th August with a guide and carriers. Liz was to stay with Geoffrey and Shirley, Jack O'Hea would tend Namisu. We left Larangwe quite early having decided, as it was so very hot, to return to Namisu. The afternoon was spent on a reading siesta. The cicadas made the most dreadful noise. In the evening we were to have super with Geoffrey and Shirley.

Outside we could hear the chatter of Harrison and the herd boy, the thump of the charcoal iron pressed onto clothes, when the iron cooled, the sound changed to shaking and blowing which was necessary to awake its dying embers. This primitive piece of equipment was used by everyone in those days, it was really quite an efficient, but a time consuming chore.

As the afternoon wore on the herd boy Ferison wandered past to gather and count the cattle and sheep before putting them in the kraals, simple rudimentary enclosures, which often had to reinforced to keep out the leopard and hyena. There were times during the dry season that the leopard made frequent visits. At such times a bait was set and a hide built in the tree above. Jim often took Makolo, the headman, and sometimes he went alone to wait, hoping it would come and take the bait. There was very little the villagers could do if their sheep or goats were taken, other than bang drums, scream and make noises in an effort to deter and perhaps drive it away.

Often, it occurred to me how well Jim had trained the Africans on the estate, they were willing, loyal and always polite. I also realised how this life appealed to me, it gave me the inner sense of peace for which I longed. My life had been miraculously re-directed, we were sharing our love of Africa. It was a love which was never to leave us. As the afternoon drew on we knew that Harrison would soon knock on the door asking where he must put the tea tray. We raised ourselves slowly, dressed and went onto the veranda, our tea was waiting, there were ginger biscuits – our favourites. The recipe was taken from the 'Nyasaland Cookery Book and Household Guide.' It was a splendid book which even has instructions on how to frost windows (brush with a hot solution of Epsom salts and water!).

After tea we took a sharp walk down to the bwalo (compound). Everything was in order. It was still hot and the cicadas were no less noisy, the grass was dry and frizzled. The huts were alive with naked and raggedly dressed children, all rushing hither and thither, some helping their mothers to grind maize, some playing, and some helping to prepare the evening meal. Duties were allocated in order of age.

Makolo appeared from the door of the biggest hut in the compound, he and Jim discussed the tasks to be completed on the estate and prepared the duties to be carried out whilst we were on safari. We walked back to the house, bathed, changed and with a bottle of wine under one arm, we got into the car and went over to have supper at Mudi with Geoffrey and Shirley. When we arrived, we saw Old Jock had also been invited. This would make an interesting night, and a late one!

CHAPTER EIGHT

Old Jock was really on form that night, it was a riotous evening with peels of laughter ringing out through the night. We talked lightly, touching on a number of subjects, mainly Jock's life before we knew him. He had his usual whisky and Jim joined him with a whisky and soda. The rest of us had our brandy sours adding lots of fresh lemon to them.

After a delicious meal, we wandered through to the veranda, it was a balmy night, the hot air was tinged with a slight breeze, which carried on it the incomparable fragrance of Africa. Handing Jim my empty port glass I placed a cushion at his feet and sat cross legged with my head resting on his leg, in my favourite position, it made me feel safe and loved. The two places in which I could take advantage of this familiar comfort was in our own home and in Geoffrey's. Added to this there was a wonderful soporific sensation as my hair was gently twirled from above.

We were entertained by stories of the early days of Jock's career, he seemed to have spent so much time battling between bouts of malaria and near starvation. His sole means of survival had been from the meat and ivory he had shot and sold in nearby small towns and villages. There appeared to have been many days at one point in his life when he was unable to rise from his bed, at these times he would write up his diaries as the rain pounded on the roof of his hut. It had been necessary for him to move from camp to camp in whichever area he chose to hunt, this was usually dictated by the knowledge of the local people who knew the number and the variety of game in the vicinity. Carriers were employed to distribute whatever he managed to bag, they were based in the camp and delivered from wherever they were to the nearest townships. In some of the more permanent camps he had goats and poultry to be used for his own consumption. His carriers brought him mail when they went to Fort Jamieson and his sisters in Scotland wrote to him regularly. They always asked when he was going home. He never did. Africa was his home, he loved, lived and breathed it. Even at this time, he ordered books from Heffer's. The service was reliable despite the time it took for them to arrive. All this direct mail went to his post box in Fort Jamieson. His stories were fascinating. There was his marriage to Mai who had nursed him through so many attacks of fever of differing kinds, the birth of their daughter Annie, his buffalo hunts and near encounters with death. He deprived himself of all the comforts and trappings of outside life, he was adamant in the defence of his choice, he in no way regretted his chosen path. I have his diaries and , knowing him as I did, they move me greatly whenever I re-read them.

After all the tales were told for that night, we had to discuss going to Chikwawa. The final date was settled, Jim and I would leave on the date we had originally planned, the 17th August. At midnight we said 'Thanks' and 'Farewell' before leaving for home. We took Jock home on our way. Mai met him at the door as she heard the car arrive. We greeted her and apologized for our late 'delivery.' She smiled, clapped her hands and kissed us both on each cheek, then, waving goodnight, she stood alongside Jock as we drove away.

CHAPTER NINE

The following week I visited the doctor, plans were being made for the hunting safari into the bush, in the valley beyond the Chikwawa escarpment. The doctor seemed to think I would be fine, there was no reason at all why I should not go. I was getting very excited at the prospect of going out into the blue. Whilst we were in Blantyre we bought supplies, ammunition, spares for pressure lamps, batteries and other essentials. Soon we would be out in the Chikwawa bush, it would be dry hot and dusty.

The library was also essential to us, I felt that books must be available whilst Jock and Jim were out hunting. I intended to write my diary each day. There would be so much spare time in camp - little did I know! On the way back home to Namisu, as we approached the tiny dirt road on the right leading to the 'Flamingo,' we gave each other a knowing look, we turned right up the incline and with a smile drove up to our favourite haunt and ate our favourite meal together.

As we drove home from the 'Flamingo,' we both remarked at the number of fire flies that danced alongside. Bush babies eyes shone from nearby trees as the car lights reflected in them. Night jars swooped in front of us, a jackal ran out of the bush and dashed over the road, disappearing into the night on the opposite side. We stopped the car and held hands, whilst we listened to the sounds of the bush, both drinking in the beauty of the African night. It was warm and exotic, with a waxing moon shining down from a deep indigo sky which was alight with shimmering twinkling stars.

These moments were so full of meaning, I would have liked them to last forever. Slowly we approached home, still in our dreamy state and we parked beneath the two eucalyptus trees which cast long ghostly shadows across the drive. We walked up the steps leading to the veranda of the Namisu house. The sensible thing would be to go to bed early. Tomorrow would be a busy day. Harrison was to bring tea at 6 AM. Though it was still quite early, we drank our tea in haste as Jim had to organize the estate workers. He and Makolo had many things to discuss and much had to be attended to whilst we were away. We had to leave in two days time.

The prospect of our first foot safari together filled us with excitement. I was determined not to disappoint Jim despite my ignorance of bush lore and all that it entailed. I was a willing learner and I knew that my duties lay in organizing the camp whilst he and Jock were hunting. Had I not been pregnant I would have gone with them. At the moment it was impossible, their intention was to walk many miles if necessary in search of buffalo.

Jim left for the bwalo and I went into the kitchen to ask Harrison to prepare breakfast. I wandered to the bathroom in a daze, looked at myself in the mirror and saw a message written in lipstick reflected over my face. 'Cog, I love you, your Jim. X'. Our little messages to each other were frequent and could be found anywhere.

I went into the cupboard and took out a packet of green jelly cubes which he loved. The whole procedure of pulling them apart, rolling them around his mouth, eventually getting them to the stage where they could be chewed, gave him such pleasure. I remember as a boy he often had a packet in his pocket.

When Jim came home to breakfast I was sitting crossed-legged on a large, round, maize mat which covered the sitting room floor. I was taking the sleeves out of one of his old shirts, having decided it would be ideal for safari, cool and loose. I had gone through his shorts and taken out two pairs which were now too small for him. Two small tucks in the back were all that was needed. I had a pair of rope soled boots which were easy and comfortable to wear. I would be wearing a topi, Jim his soft bush hat.

After breakfast large quantities of water must be boiled, put through the candle filter and then into water bottles. We had to carry drinking water, the filter went with us as part of the luggage. Taking out a mosquito net that was to be used in the bush, it was obvious by the number of small holes that it also needed attention. On hearing the familiar crunch of Jim's footsteps, my heart gave a jerk. As he came through the door his arms opened. I leapt up from the floor and fell into them. Such peace, such comfort, they fitted me so well. We ate breakfast, then sat on the veranda drinking coffee. We had a full schedule for the next two days and much to organize. Our household and garden workers were to organize the paraffin, lamps, petrol, cooking utensils etc., Everything was to be put into the garage ready to be piled onto the truck when we were ready to leave. Meanwhile I mended the mosquito nets and organized the clothes I thought we might need. I also packed two woollies, having heard that the nights can be quite cool in the bush, particularly if a slight wind gets up. That day everyone appeared to have worked hard, even through the heat of day we had persisted with our tasks. I even made a sticky ginger cake, cooked in the Dover stove. It was good.

It was with splendid contentment we bathed, dressed and relaxed with our sundowners on the veranda. Hand in hand, as ever, we listened to the night sounds of Africa. So, with our safari plans in our head, and with hearts flowing over, we poured out two lime juice drinks, turned off the pressure lamp, then followed the shaft of light that led to our bedroom. Jim gave the bedroom lamp a vigorous pump or two which enabled us to read before drifting off to sleep.

CHAPTER TEN

It was a glorious morning, the rising sun was gradually penetrating through the smoke haze of recent bush fires, painting an ethereal, golden glow over the distant hills. Two monkeys chattered in a nearby tree. The chill night air had not yet lifted, the atmosphere of peace with which night turned into day was both bewitching and romantic. Jim walked out of the bathroom dressed in his old bush clothes, he looked tanned and handsome and had a merry twinkle in his eye. He stooped to kiss my cheek, 'You are going to love this Cog. Remember as we walked over the fields in Cheshire how we made our plans for Africa, and imagined how it would be?' He asked.

'Will it be very exciting?' I queried.

'It will be wonderful, we are doing what we always wanted to do, we are doing it together and you will love it,' he said. He smiled and his grey eyes gazed at me and my knees turned to jelly! As he moved past, the air carried the old familiar trace of leather, gun oil and a touch of Old Spice. It lingers with me always.

I felt comfortable in the bush gear I had organized, 'You look gorgeous in that outfit,' Jim told me. I found that difficult to believe, but welcomed the comment with a smug smile. We each had our own tasks to perform. I was in charge of the food, cooking utensils and any other incidentals which might be needed. Jim organized the main bulk of the luggage, ground sheets, hunting gear, guns and enamel wash bowls. These were needed to carry portions of salted meat back to the estate. All the other necessities, including beer, which he automatically collected from experience, he now put together with the rest of the luggage. I despaired of my memory and my ineptitude, but Jim reassured me!

The two Africans we were taking along were Maspiah, Jim's gun carrier, and Harrison the cook, both were wildly excited at having been chosen to accompany us. To them it meant much food, not only eaten whilst in the bush but meat from the trip would be dried, enabling them to carry it home to their families. They felt privileged at having been given this opportunity, and were the envy of most of the Africans working on the estate, although they too would get their share of the spoil on our return. They both busied themselves manipulating a lot of the equipment into a little space. The truck was beginning to creak under the strain. Thus, laden to the hilt, with the odd things to still pick up in Blantyre and Maspiah and Harrison sitting on boxes with their legs straddled over the luggage in the back, we moved off slowly.

As we left we saw small groups of women and children on either side of the drive, they were standing staring and giggling with hands over mouths. The women were draped in coloured kitenge, they obviously had not been up long. Some wore bent old shoes, some had rubber shoes, others were barefoot. Children smiled and waved and ran alongside as we moved slowly forward. Everyone was calling 'Nyama' (meat). They knew we were joining Jock in the hunting area. It was their way of asking us not to forget them.

It was a glorious morning, the air was filled with the sweet smell of frangipani, still coated in the cool wet dew of night. Its scent hung in a cloud of red dust thrown up by the wheels as they rolled over the dry ground, throwing fine powder into motionless air. It covered everything in its slow gradual fall back to earth, shining and glinting in a red gossamer cloud, the rising sun penetrated each colour in the kaleidoscope.

Our screaming monkeys scuttled backwards and forwards in front of the truck. In agitation they jumped up and down scratching and chattering, eventually tiring of their pursuit they ran back to the house. On our journey to Blantyre we travelled carefully to avoid bumps and potholes. Corrugations in the road had to be covered at some speed, in order to avoid the tooth rattling judder experienced when travelling at a slower pace. Jim parked in Blantyre and dashed over to the chemist's shop to buy insect repellent and tablets of carbolic soap. He threw the parcel into a basket in the back of the truck, smiled, patted my hand and we were on our way again. Conversation was limited due to vehicle rumble and clatter. It opened up our thoughts to the intricate and coloured pattern of how the rest of our life would be, and to the immediate experience ahead of us, which to me was absolutely new. I was filled with intrigue as my imagination ran riot. Here and there we passed local people walking from village to village. Some with loads on their heads, though mostly at this time of day they appeared to be carrying water from the streams to their village.

The riotous whirring of my brain was suddenly brought to an abrupt halt as we approached the Chikwawa escarpment and then started our descent. We wound our way down and around this prescipitous and virtually unmade road cautiously. The panoramic vistas unfolding before our eyes to the side and in front were bewildering, the sheer beauty and the breathtaking magnificence unfolded for as far as the eye could see. A vast wilderness spread out like an endless carpet. It was an enormous patchwork of glorious sunlit colour. There were shining yellows in every hue; light and dark browns of the burnt off bush, all the greens, dark, light, bright and the lime green of new growth. Here and there some of the greens were tinged with red. Blobs of colour seeming as though thrown from a painter's palette were immediately below and around us, clear and bright before they gradually faded into the recession of the land, to a faintly cloured haze in the far distance. This was the lower river country leading to Chikwawa, Jock's camp, our hunt and the Mozambique border. Alongside wispy spirals of smoke gave way to small brown dots, these were huts belonging to distant villages. Each hut was surrounded by tiny green squares of maize.

Down the escarpment we went. The great Shire river snaking into the distance. Where bright glints of sun skimmed the river they appeared like shards of broken mirror flashing their morse code to the sky. Were we really heading to invade this vast, breathtaking wilderness, with only the sharp eye of a native guide to lead us to Jock's camp, somewhere in the bush? Jim assured me that all would be well. He knew I relied on him entirely, as I did for the rest of my life. I could feel him analyzing my thoughts as we edged our way down the escarpment. My hand wandered to, and rested on, his tanned knee. I laughed out loud with happiness as we bumped over the winding, stony, boulder ridden road. Lower and lower we travelled towards our destination. In the heat of the day the journey took on a dream-like quality, Jim eased his way over dips and boulders, I gathered the journey to our overnight stay took longer than usual. To me this was a huge adventure; time stood still. I was enthralled by the surrounding vista.

The two Africans in the back seemed oblivious to the dust which had enveloped them from head to foot. We could hear their chatter and laughter. They were spattered from nose to chin with milk from the sweet maize cobs they were eating. We had bought some from a village alongside the road on the way. By now we were almost at the bottom of the escarpment on the approach to our first night's stop. 'What are you thinking of Cog?' Jim asked, my reply was simply, 'Buffalo.' I rubbed his knee.

We arrived at our first stopping point mid afternoon. It was very hot by this time, particularly at this low altitude. We parked beneath a wild fig tree in a Mesamali village at the edge of the bush. Here we were to stay overnight. Despite the water we had drunk from our canvas water bottles on the way, we were very thirsty, 'Tea please Harrison,' I heard Jim say. Water was poured into our small safari kettle, it was put onto the embers of one of the smouldering village fires. We had parked under a tree and there was a large tent behind it. This was where Jock kept all his vital stores, together with all the things he thought he might need. We were to put anything that we felt we would not need alongside his stores. There were always trackers to fetch and carry should anything be needed in camp.

We wanted to stretch our legs so we strolled off arm in arm to the stream near the village. We took our boots and socks off and cooled our hot feet in the water, this was a simple way to cool off. Energized after our brief foot bath, we walked back to the village to find Harrison and Maspiah had almost unloaded the katundu (luggage). Harrison had unpacked the two canvas chairs for us to sit on, he had also utilized two smaller boxes by putting the enamel tray on the box. The tray was covered with a small napkin, one of six which I had recently sewn. It had on it two enamel mugs, the teapot and a jar of powdered milk. To the side was the biscuit tin! I could not believe how organized we had become in such a short time. Of course Harrison had accompanied Jim on many occasions in the past. He obviously knew the ropes! This was perfect, again it all seemed like a dream. We were here in the midst of the bush, in an African village. We sat under a huge fig tree and were oggled by villagers as we sat drinking tea and eating biscuits casually, our feet were wet and so were our boots.

Later we had to sleep in the store tent on a straw mattress. It was covered by a large mosquito net, and to finish the furnishings we used a box as a side table. Maspiah had arranged all the loads for the carriers as we were leaving at cock crow. Jim knew exactly what was needed. After eating with the people of the village, Harrison took our camp mattress and mosquito net and I helped him to arrange them. We were all quite busy, Jim was hungry so I made him a cheese sandwich. We had brought two homemade loaves with us and flour to make bread whilst we were in camp. Afterwards we ate bananas.

Before supper, we wandered down to the river again with soap and towel in an attempt to wash off some of the dust from the journey. All in all, we felt good, we were content with the world.

We had taken a bottle of whisky, a bottle of brandy and some beers with us, not just for ourselves but with Jock in mind, we also put in a soda syphon and gas cartridges. All the villagers sat around a large fire in the centre of the compound, inscrutable dark faces picked out by the flickering flames. Standing to the side over red glowing embers, a cooking pot of mshima (maize porridge) was constantly being stirred by one of the older girls until it became malleable and ready to be hollowed out with the thumb in preparation for the relish into which the bread would be dipped. The relish was usually made with onion, garlic and tomato and was eaten with either fish or meat. As they ate and drank their voices were raised, seemingly in anticipation of their next bite! Their laughter was loud and, to my untrained ear, raucous, although I quickly learned that this was their way, rather like children they became excited by events. There were white people sleeping in the village. Plenty of food was at hand and their men could earn money as carriers. This was life as they knew it and they were quite happy. Whilst we were there the villagers spent much time standing around us, they stared and giggled, their hands covering their mouths in a shy, coy gesture.

Mesamali consisted of some fifteen or more mud and wattle huts. They all had an uneven grass roof, some had tiny windows, others were without windows. They all had bamboo doors, most of which hung crazily askew. The headman had a larger hut, set slightly away from the rest. Everywhere there were goats and chickens, with the result that all the small bushes on the outskirts of the village were decimated. Goats stripped leaves from any tree or bush they could reach, completely destroying it. It was the responsibility of the herd boys to drive all the goats into the bush away from the village to prevent so much damage to vegetation. Goats are restless, they continually bleat and rush about. Add to this the noise of the women, their shrill calls echoing through the village as they called to each other whilst they swept outside their huts with a twig broom, pounded maize or brewed beer from maize, banana or guinea corn. The beer is a thick glutinous broth and very potent. Signs on the roadside indicate the whereabouts of kachasu, an illegal, highly dangerous spirit. Despite this, it was made in some of the villages. A woman's work is primarily to hoe the small maize or vegetable garden alongside the hut, it is usually surrounded by an uneven broken fence, made from branches in a bid to keep out the goats. The village chickens scratch around frantically pecking at each tiny morsel in their path. They in turn are followed by noisy, crowing, highly oversexed cockerels chasing and fighting in an effort to quell their never-ending desire. The noise continued until night took over, when villages and animals slept.

Some of the huts had a small kraal into which the animals were driven each night. Families without merely shared their hut with whatever animals they possessed. Each family had many children and each hut appeared to house an extended family, all of whom gave the appearance of being busy but in reality, doing very little, other than to call the latest news. Everyone tried to outdo the other in conversation and advice.

Everywhere there were small children who were coated in dust and grime, playing happily in the dirt. African children are usually very contented, they amuse themselves. Hours are spent pushing and playing with round stones in the sandy soil. A favourite past time is one in which bits of wire are bent deftly, tied, stretched and joined until they become bicycles, carts or barrows, these they attach to a stick, pushing or pulling them along. Any string they use is made from the softened bark of a tree. It is mainly the male children who play in this way with their worn shorts exposing a dusty backside and often much more! Women and girls if not hoeing in the fields are at the stream washing clothes, carrying water or making beer. Men of the village are mostly absent, they work outside the villages. They are the carriers of news from one village to another. Whilst on these missions they are quite capable of drinking copious quantities of beer before they return to the village with much shouting and singing.

As evening approaches they sit around the communal fire, their faces dark in the flickering flames. A great deal of time was spent nose picking! This was the time to pass on the news of the day, whilst eating food prepared by the women. More beer was consumed. Women walking along the road almost always had a baby on their back and another in her belly. At the least sign of hunger, the infant on her back was hauled to under one arm and suckled as she walks along. Often in the heat of day she sits under the shade of a nearby tree. African women walk with great ease and dignity. To us looking out into the village as we sat on our camp chairs drinking tea, their life appeared uncluttered and simple. This is how they were, these were their customs. They were happy and their needs were small. This was in the month of August, in the year 1957.

Harrison was busy preparing supper. Contented, we sat and watched the intrigues of African life. Some of the villagers had lit fires alongside their huts temporarily deserting the communal gathering in the middle of the compound. The chatter was incessant. There was every indication that complete darkness would soon be upon us, twilight hardly exists in Africa. We lit the pressure lamp and placed it on the upturned box. I was warned to be careful as I tried to haul our safari mattress onto the heaps of straw that Harrison had laid over the hard earth floor of the tent.

There was very little room amid all the stores. We made up the bed, plumped up and placed the pillows, attached the mosquito net to the roof of the tent and then tucked it well under the mattress. We sprayed for insects, shut down the flap and went to our camp chairs. It was sundowner time!

'How's that for organization love, what would you like to drink?' Jim said.

'Brandy and soda, small brandy lots of soda please,' I replied. I was really going to enjoy this. Jim had whisky and soda. We felt we had earned our sundowner! Once more, sitting outside the tent on camp chairs we continued to watch the end of day activities in an African village. The sun went down and the moon rose to join the stars in a deep indigo sky. The world was wonderful, we were happy, we held hands in a romantic mood as day turned into night.

Meanwhile Harrison was cooking supper, he had made a hole in the ground into which he put hot embers from the village fire, feeding it with wood from a nearby pile previously collected from the bush. Over this he placed a sheet of tin, forged from a hammered out paraffin drum. It was used as a hot plate, on which he cooked our evening meal. The sun, sinking in the west, shed a golden red glow over the scene. The carriers were silhouetted, shuffling about arranging their beds under the trees. In front of us the fire crackled, sparks flying, as Harrison fed it with more wood. On the other side of the village, women made posho in preparation for their evening meal. Their fires threw up spirals of smoke, their dark faces watched us and we watched them. The fire in the centre of the compound sent up brilliant cascades of sparks which seemed to rise high in the sky on their way to mingle with the Southern Cross, Orion's belt, the Milky Way and all the other stars which danced in the sky of the southern hemisphere. The whole atmosphere was romantic, bewitching and ethereal. As we sat side by side our heads gradually became closer, the grasp of our hands tighter, this was a magical moment, one we would never forget, words were not needed.

The smell of cooking filled the night air, we realized suddenly how hungry we were. Harrison had roasted maize cobs, which we coated in butter and seasoned well. They were delicious! To follow there was bacon, eggs and tomato, delicately flavoured with wood smoke. It was a simple meal eaten in primitive surroundings. A meal which always springs to mind with great clarity. I was destined not to forget this night, it brought home to me the meaning of true happiness and the joy of a simple life. The glorified trappings of the West were not necessary in this stress free way of life, it was a basic primitive 'back to nature' way of living of which we now, sadly, know nothing. It was the end of another day in an African village where life drew to its slow, easy and unhurried conclusion. With the night came a bright moon, it spun shadows of the surrounding trees onto the village compound. Dark ghost-like people followed their nightly rituals without hurry. Chickens went to roost, some dogs lay sleeping, others sloped towards the fire in search of discarded bones. Men, women and children gradually disappeared into their huts. Frustrated goats bleated as they were driven into the kraal, the persistent noise of crickets penetrated the now cool night air. Jock's carriers lay wrapped in their blankets on bamboo mats by the embers of the fire. Their loads were arranged in neat piles in preparation for an early departure.

We wandered into the tent longing to lie down, hoping to sink into a peaceful sleep. Again I was enveloped in a dream-like aura as I walked alongside this beloved man to our bed on the floor of a tent in an African village, surrounded by snoring natives. Chattering monkeys leapt into the wild fig tree above the tent. Jim was worried in case I became tired whilst walking as the sun rose and the heat of day built up. We had a considerable distance to cover the following day, the estimate was approximately 15 miles. He wanted to walk as far as possible before sun up. Everything was enveloped in the ethereal beauty of bright silver moonlight and millions of twinkling stars. Here we were, loving every minute of this adventure. Lying relaxed and dozing, we became aware that the village had fallen into silence, the chatter had stopped the fire had ceased to crackle. The carriers rolled up in their blankets snored fitfully. In the distance we could hear the call of the hyena, nearby a dog barked, the crickets continued to chirrup and night apes pelted the roof of the tent with wild figs from the tree above. We fell into a deep sleep.

Suddenly as I write I find I am jerked into the present and reality. My senses reel, as broken-hearted I attempt to complete my daily chores, suspended between past and future, pulled backwards and forwards by remembered joy and fulfilment, inching forwards with temerity and apathy to an unknown and unimaginable future without Jim. There are times when I feel it is too difficult to endure. I weep, paint, write and try to forget. But do I want to forget? I am unable to comprehend that he is no longer with me. The ever empty driving seat which I have to fill. The quiet of the door lock in our home, as no key releases it other than my own. No familiar manly frame and lovely smiling face to greet me. I am alone.

CHAPTER ELEVEN

'Morning bwana, morning memsahib, breakfast ready', Harrison called us at 3 am. He put the tea and ginger biscuits onto the small rickety table by the door of the tent. Water had been carried from the river and poured into half of an old, open 5 gallon drum. Lying alongside was a towel, a tablet of carbolic soap, a bottle of fresh water and our tooth mugs. We stretched, yawned and shivered. I poured the tea sleepily and handed a mug to Jim. Running my fingers through his tousled hair, I gave him a kiss, then shivering, jumped back into the warmth of the bed. When tea was finished we gradually came to life, leapt up from the mattress and were ready to face the day.

The river water was cold, making our faces tingle, a fresh early morning nip in the air greeted us. Outside, the hurricane lamps hung low on the branches of the fig tree, surplus fruits thrown at the tent by night apes, lay in the sand.

Freshly kindled fires blazed, throwing flames and sparks up into the dark morning air, casting moving shadows onto black eager faces poking up from lean bodies, knees huddled to chin, all swathed in thin grey blankets. From time to time, hands with long tapered fingers stretched out towards the heat of the fire.

Cocks crowed, dogs barked, goats bleated. The village stirred to a cacophony of sound. People yawning rubbed eyes and noses stumbling out of the dark doorways at the centre of each hut. A smell of bacon and percolating coffee drifted into the tent. I had to shake myself. I supposed this was real and not a dream. Africa plants its rare seed into the psyche with a lightness of heart, it survives, thrives, becomes evergreen and lives forever. The free, slow and irresistible rhythm of this simple life takes hold, burning interminably into the memory.

In the tent, shivering, we washed and dressed. Jim looked very comfortable in khaki shorts and shirt. Cotton socks covered his feet which were pushed into soft veldskoen boots. On his head he wore a floppy leather bush hat. I was dressed in shorts, altered to accommodate my figure, a sleeveless shirt, socks and rope soled boots. Breakfast was a bacon sandwich, made even more tasty and tempting by a slight hint of wood smoke and crispy burnt edges curled by leaping flames which had licked the sizzling fat. By the light of the hurricane lamp we rinsed our plates and mugs, assembled luggage, and rolled the bed. Jim drove the Land Rover through open tent flaps into what had been the bedroom space. The time had now come to find Jock and his camp. Carriers who were still huddled around the fire were patiently awaiting our departure. One man stood barefoot under the tree, apart from the rest. He was a slender 6ft tall African. His features lacked the blunt profile of the local people, his were more inclined towards the finer features of the tribes living in the north. A brightly coloured cloth, anchored with a shoulder knot covered his lithe body. He was the headman from the Chikwawa village, Harrison told us whilst showing his respect for the man whose name was Fabrica, a tracker of great skill, who was known and trusted by Jock.

We left the camp at 4 am. it was a little later than we had originally intended. Maspiah called over the twelve carriers. Each one had an orderly load, each knew his position in the safari line. Fabrica, as tracker, was at the head. I set the pace, with Jim alongside carrying his rifle. Maspiah walked behind us with the other guns. Harrison followed the carriers, who were now chanting as they walked, until a rhythm was set. Fabrica's mesmeric, rhythmic sway and effortless gait gave the impression of his being able to continue on to the end of the world, he never wavered.

Leaving the village behind, we were led down to the river, passing through native sambas (gardens). Huge maize tassles rustled in the breeze of dawn. We followed small hard trodden native paths which gradually petered out, leading into 8ft high dambo grass which descended almost to the rivers edge.

It was here that Jim became concerned. Taking my arm he led me to a smooth washing stone which was used by the women of the village as a surface on which to pound clothes. Sitting me down gently on the stone, he removed our socks and boots and handed them to Harrison. We crossed the river hand in hand, put on our boots again and set off with determination, into the distant bush on the other side.

Away from the villages we moved deeper into bush and game country. It was here that the line began to move in silence and ceased to chant. It was fast becoming daylight, the sun's rays became blood red from the eastern sky, picking out the fusion of fine branches like intricate black cut outs on a backcloth of red, turning gold as it rose further into the sky, shedding silver rays onto cool dew-soaked grass. Each drop shimmered like a precious jewel, laying a carpet of transparent watery beauty. Cobwebs hung delicate as lace in nearby bushes and birdsong broke the silence. Ground hornbills gave their deep guttural call, echoing eerily over the land. Timid gazelle stood graceful and doe eyed beneath the flat topped acacias as they emerged from the morning mist. Monkeys chattered, covered in confusion at the sight of our group. Slowly the bush began to come to life.

The climb was gradual as we left the river, leaving behind the easy walk on the green vegetation bordering its banks. Now we came onto stony ground littered with thorn thickets and flies were becoming a nuisance. We walked along game paths, human and animal tracks mingling in the sand. All around us, as far as the eye could see, there was bush, although we had passed one or two huts as we moved up from the river. In their gardens were huge green and yellow pumpkins waiting to be cut, sweet potatoes spread their leaves green and dense over the ground. Beans had ripened and were ready for picking. All around pigeons softly cooed. Peace enveloped the surrounding bush.

We moved on to stony ground, climbing over rocky crags, side-stepping small springs of water seeping from the ground. We came across old and fresh spoor of game. Jim took my arm to give me support if he felt I might stumble. The cool of early morning was stealthily substituted by mind numbing, 'slow down a bit' hot air, the soft hum of insects would soon be replaced by cicadas in the heat of the day. As we trekked again, I felt transported back to the old black and white movie in which we were the players. Our tracker had been told by a man passing by that Jock had a kill, this meant lion would never be far away from his camp and its surrounds.

Fabrica saw things that were 'invisible' to us; newly broken grass, faeces – hot, cold, damp or dry. Old and new spoor, broken branches on nearby bushes – he knew when they were broken and by what animal, he was always on high alert; to me everything was new and bewildering. I sensed the carriers were edgy. All around us there were bushbuck, klipspringer and impala, easy prey for a lion. The odd comment from Jim indicated that for the past hour he had noticed I was becoming tired. I was actually very tired and wet with sweat, the moisture invading my underwear was making my skin smart. I was sticky and extremely uncomfortable. On the flat it had not been a problem, the long rocky incline was difficult to negotiate. A short rest was indicated so we sat on top of a large flat-topped boulder. Harrison who had the primus to hand, boiled water quickly in our small tin kettle, he dropped in the tea leaves. Patting his knee Jim suggested I put my feet up, removing my shoes and socks he massaged my feet with methylated spirits and talc from the medical box, they tingled but felt good and refreshed. Jim explained that when we resumed our trek my muscles may be a little sore, they would have to tone up after the stop. Actually they felt good, brand new and ready for anything.

We drank tea from a tin mug and ate a few more ginger biscuits. Jim slipped his arm around my shoulders, I looked into his grey eyes which were flecked with tiny specks of green. Tenderly he pulled me to my feet. It was time to trek. The carriers picked up their loads, heaved them onto their heads and fell in line. We moved on. We continued our trek into the bush our pace was intentionally slow at first, it was easier on the muscles I was told. The toning up experience after our short stop was really quite painful.

Gradually the pace quickened. Fabrica silently pointed to lion spore, huge cat like prints in the soft sand, some were quite visible others could only be seen by a sharp, trained eye. A pride had recently passed by. Looking down I noticed Fabrica's bare foot tracks showing cracked heels which had left rugged indentations in the sand.

I was still doubtful of ever finding Jock in this huge wilderness. Fabrica paced on, sometimes giving a low whistle to alert us to nearby game. The sun was relentless in its climb. My back had begun to ache. To the right of us a jackal slunk along, occasionally jerking its head to the side, diamond bright eyes in a sharp pointed face took sly stock of any intruders in his territory. At times, he sniffed the air, we wondered what he had scent of, there were no vultures in the sky. I came to the silent conclusion that perhaps it was the smell of humans, our smell. Swishing his tail he headed off in another direction going further into cover. He would still be watching us craftily from a distance.

Fabrica pointed out a family of hyena beneath a nearby tree. Jim had noticed them and was telling me quietly to look to the right under the acacia tree. It was a large pack and they made no attempt to move. One or two raised their heads lazily for an instance, then shuffling into position gave a loud grunt and settled down to sleep whilst digesting the food in their distended bellies. They were fat and well fed and, to my mind, disgustingly ugly.

By now the sun was almost at its zenith, it was very hot, the tetse flies were a menace. They landed unobserved, inflicting unpleasant bites, gorging themselves with blood until they were hugely fat. When they were caught and squashed, their gory feast splattered in every direction. The tetse is responsible for transmitting sleeping sickness, caused by parasites taken from the blood of big game to man. They carry a disease called 'nagana' to horses and cattle. For this reason there are few domestic cattle in the 'fly belts'.

The shrill monotonous noise of the cicadas in the heat was almost deafening. I understand this noise is made only by the males, and by two tiny muscles clicking on either side of the abdomen. Crickets have the same action, but on their front legs. At one point we side-stepped to avoid a puff adder, they are thick short and deadly. It was reassuring to know we always carried a Fitzsimmon's snake bite outfit. Serum was regularly updated, it was bought from South Africa.

Just past midday we arrived at Jock's camp, we were welcomed by a blue towel hanging in a tree at the camp entrance. This was to let us know we had arrived at the right place! The camp was a settlement in the bush. A circular clearing amongst the trees with a river nearby. We took a look around. A few yards from the camp, secreted behind the rocks, a long drop approximately 4ft deep had been skilfully put together. Over piled earth recovered from the digging a large wooden box had been placed and a round hole cut from the centre. Jock had overseen and fussed over the task. It was kept from view of the camp by a grass screen. Nearby a branch held a blue/grey toilet roll, this refinement was to please me. My one fear was snakes, and they like dark, moist holes!

A huge fig tree grew in the middle of the camp clearing and beneath the tree was where the 'boys' sat, talked and slept. At night they unrolled their grass and cane mats under this tree and slept like the dead, well fed and tired. A mattress was almost unheard of by the local native, it was not part of their way of life, they were able to roll up a mat, put it over their shoulder and move on.

Alongside the tree a campfire burned. There was a pile of kindling nearby. The camp fire was a meeting place, sitting in its rosy glow there was much talk by Jock and Jim of their years together. Jock had transferred much of his knowledge to Jim, during the long arduous hunting safaris they had shared together. On many occasions each one of them had been at the others mercy, luckily both could hear the least movement in the bush. The glow one felt when listening to these bush sensitive and fearless souls was inwardly invigorating and yet in a strange way relaxing. Their conversation was interesting and packed with knowledge. It was thrilling to sit around the camp fire in the evening with a gin and tonic, listening in wonder to some of the stories they had to tell, all sprinkled with experiences they described so well. Enthralled, I sat and listened to them discuss the strategies of past hunts and of how they would utilise them in future hunts should the same situations arise.

A few feet away from Jock's bed, half a dozen boxes contained various foods; tinned beans, beers, toilet rolls etc., they were used as makeshift tables on which to put books, candles, torches and note books. At Jock's fanatical insistence, there was always a pencil Beyond the boxes, a grass hut had been built, this was the bathroom, in it there was a tin bath and two small tables, made from branches of different thickness tied together with bark strips.

On one side of the entrance a table held an enamel bowl and a hand towel, together with a piece of carbolic soap (which was a 'must' on safari). Towels and clothes hung on twigs sticking out from main structural branches. The floor was covered with a split cane mat. Our shower was a watering can with a fine tobacco sprinkler rose, it was filled with warm water and the neck was ledged between a forked branch. The handle tilted by man power outside, showered the bather beneath. Harrison attended to this primitive procedure with professional efficiency. It was necessary to stand on a cane mat in the shower, otherwise sand spattered up onto damp washed feet and legs. It was crude but worked very well.

The next hut was our private domain, our bedroom. We were surrounded by thick grass walls and a grass pallet had been laid on the floor ready for our mattress. In the corner opposite the bed, a hen had chosen to nest, each day she laid an egg. Jock had bought her from a villager in Mesamali, for some reason he had decided he must eat an egg each day. Despite our concerted efforts to rout the chicken, she refused to move. Her rustling and clucking were very disconcerting at times. I threatened her with the pot. Eventually we became quite fond of her. Jock took her back to Larangwe. At the back of our hut and for as far as the eye could see, there were rocks, bush and an omnipotent silence.

Opposite, and some way past the central tree, there were racks for drying game meat brought in from the hunt. Branches tied at equidistant intervals formed racks on which to place the meat. It was then hoisted up onto six forked branches which were knocked firmly into the ground. Beneath the racks a smouldering fire dried the strips of meat and gut slowly, rendering them virtually imperishable. The meat process was repeated many times, most of it we carried back to the estate for use in the villages. We used a little ourselves. Any surplus was fed to the dogs. With some of the better cuts we made biltong, seasoned dried strips of meat, considered by some to be a delicacy. Geoffrey used to shave off wafer thin slivers with his pocket knife, 'Very tasty' he would comment after almost every morsel. We were not great eaters of biltong. Jim munched on the odd stick. I decided to leave it for them to enjoy!

In all there were five racks for meat, all of differing sizes, they produced much smoke and many overwhelming smells. The 'boys' in camp were responsible for turning the meat, keeping the fires low, and at the right temperature. Beyond the racks there was the cooks' domain, here were the fires on which either Harrison or Jock's cook (Bison) prepared our meals.

Again there was an improvised table for pots and pans, a water filter and a lantern. From this area a small well trodden path led to the river. This completes the circle of the camp. There was, of course, the odd camp bed here and there, they were essential for rest in the heat of the day. Jock was out hunting when we arrived. He had left at dawn and had not yet returned.

CHAPTER TWELVE

With seemingly little effort the carriers removed the loads from their heads and put each one into its appropriate place. This was carried out under the supervision of Bison, Jock's cook, who had previously been issued with instructions by Jock before he left. Jim and Maspiah put up two camp chairs and another small bed alongside the hut. Our mattress was put onto the grass pallet. We quickly made up the bed. For me this had always been, and for some reason always would be, a priority. Harrison put the kettle on to boil, he organized and put away all the foodstuffs we had brought along. The Africans accompanying us on the trek placed their sleeping rolls beneath the central tree. Soon, they sat down and ate fresh milky maize cobs bought from a villager before leaving Mesamali. Harrison gave them something to drink. We fell into our camp chairs and drank large mugs of tea.

The two cooks worked together very well, dividing chores and helping each other when it was needed. Water brought up from the river each day, was put onto fires in readiness for our evening bath. Cold water was always kept in containers nearby.

It was almost 2.30 p.m when Jock returned to camp, he appeared not to have a trace of exhaustion. At 65 years of age he was fit and hard muscled. He was however extremely frustrated, telling us in his inimitable way and at great length, how he had lost the spoor of a big buffalo bull he had been following. He felt it had deliberately led him off trail by disappearing into thick ingalanga bush, which to all intents and purposes is a no go area for the hunter with any sense. Here it waits motionless, and having waited, it will charge on sight of its aggressor. There would be little chance of escape in this thick dense thorn bush. The almost inevitable fate, was to be tossed into the air and trampled into the ground. Despite these dangers both Jock and Jim revelled in the thrill of a buffalo hunt. They were always careful and cautious, never underestimating the devious, wily ways of this huge and dangerous animal. He told us of coming across a herd of zebra, and of the anxious old mare who, on sensing danger, had thrown back her head, nostrils flaring, eyes round and black as she leaned back on her hind legs, ready for flight as she gave her warning bark. The heard now alerted scattered in all directions in a cloud of dust and disappeared into the bush with an echo of drumming hooves.

Sitting on a camp chair, a very thirsty Jock drank three beers with relish and at great speed. He ate two fried eggs, bacon, tomatoes and a tin of baked beans, he talked almost continuously. In fact, we all three talked, we discussed everything that that had in any way remotely touched or influenced our lives. Our discussions were mainly topical and interesting. Our conversations were influenced a great deal by the books and the papers we read, whether we were in agreement or otherwise. Deciding it was time to read and take a little siesta, the heat by this time was tiring and debilitating. We had earned a rest, it seemed an eternity since leaving Mesamali. The camp became still and quiet, everyone dozed in wilting inertia, it was sensible to give movement a miss until the sun had taken its full toll on the day.

In our grass hut the air was motionless, we were wet with perspiration, however we snatched a little sleep, only awakening as the sun began to sink into the west. I was content and comfortable and did not want to move. There was movement in the camp, Harrison had water ready for the showers, I was intrigued as to how effective our contraption would be. It was good and very efficient. Harrison's timing with the watering can was perfect, our ration was three cans per person. With a great effort I made my way to the shower, sandy soil stuck to the soles of my feet. Inside I took off my wrap, hung it onto a protruding snip of branch, then a little bewildered by the sudden impact of the whole situation, I stepped onto the rough uneven surface of the bamboo mat. This was my introduction to a makeshift shower in the wide open spaces of the African bush. I loved it, carbolic soap and all.

An early evening breeze wafted through the doorway in which Jim stood guard. It brought a shiver of goosebumps to my wet body, laughing as I steeped from the mat, he opened a towel and wrapped it around me. I melted as he rubbed me dry, after using a dusting of talcum powder I slipped on a loose cotton robe.

Jim prepared to shower, taking his clothes as he stepped into the shower, I buried my face in them, there was no escaping the evocative scent which had brought me such comfort and delight in past years. It haunted and 'cosied' me for all of our future years together. I washed his back and gently massaged the broad shoulders, then handing him a towel I went back into our bedroom, laying out clothes for the evening across the bed.

Jock sat on his camp bed in shorts and white vest waiting for his turn. With a towel over his shoulder, he eventually made his way to the shower, talking all the time, he had so many questions to which we must always have answers. Bison took his clean clothes and hung them over the wall of the hut. Amazingly refreshed and dressed appropriately we sat with a sundowner in our hands, overwhelmed by a sense of wonder and sweet contentment. Lamps had been lit and were hanging from the trees, we watched the comings and goings of the camp. Our two cooks had re-organized the shower hut and were now preparing the evening meal.

The Africans cooked their maize meal beans and meat as they sat beneath the central tree. Their meat hung over the fires, the venison juices falling onto red embers, sizzled, smoked and smelt ambrosial. Before our arrival Jock had shot a small antelope for use in the camp.

Our supper was ready, we were looking forward to the meal. Harison put it into metal dishes and placed them onto the table made from spare boxes. We helped ourselves. It seemed extraordinary that 'out in the blue' we were served onion soup, sausage, chips and spinach, followed by tinned peaches with evaporated milk. The spinach together with a few lettuces, we had picked from the garden just as we were about to leave. We had put them all into a greaseproof bag, where they remained fresh and crisp.

It was a hot balmy night and the lamps were throwing shadows over the camp. A light rustle of leaves and crackling of small twigs and shoots alerted us to the possibility of the 'old man' being uncomfortably near, our nerves tingled at the thought. There was a little fear and a deal of doubt as we sat around the camp fire enjoying our evening meal. Each tree, each bush was silhouetted against a backdrop of stars. Our talk was of impending independence in this British Protectorate of Nyasaland, it was too difficult to comprehend as we sat here under the stars taking in the experience of the African bush.

Our hearts were pounding with the thrill of our close proximity to game wandering in the surrounding bush, their pungent smell drifted towards us on the night air, penetrating our over sensitive nostrils. Hyena whooping in the distance, accompanied the sounds of nearby snuffling and crunching made by the animals around us treading dry brittle grass and twigs, straining eardrums, and breaking up the silence. Smoke spiralling from the camp fires, at times overcame the scent of game, crowding our nostrils with the sweet, tangy fragrance of burning wood and roots. Sparks flew up into the night, fires crackled and flames danced as Harrison fed the red embers. We wondered what changes the sabre rattlers for independence might bring. We hoped very few!

The Africans under the tree had finished their meal, they were jabbering loudly, some picking their teeth, others their noses. Litter was everywhere. Some of the carriers started to sing, soon the others joined in. They had been drinking chibuku and they danced and stamped their feet well into the night, singing of the buffalo, of its crafty ways, of its history and of their wish for the bwana to shoot a big bull.

We decided to tuck away thoughts and political upheaval for another day, perhaps another year! Very relaxed, tired and yawning, we decided the time had come for bed. After a prolonged 'Goodnight' to Jock, we made our way to the mattress. Lying down caused the grass pallet beneath us to rustle and murmur. Bed felt very welcome. We lay beneath a panoply of stars, a hand of love touched my shoulder. Spreading our arms we embraced in the African night, our love was a many splendoured thing. We snuggled down to the sound of Harrison and Bison clearing up the camp, humming softly as they worked. In time the camp became silent, we drifted off into a dreamless sleep.

'5.45' Jock boomed, 'Time to get up laddie' (Jim was often his laddie). Harrison arrived with a tray of tea, he put it down quickly and dashed off to prepare breakfast. Today it was a hurried affair. At 6.15 a.m. the two men set out to hunt, taking with them four carriers. My lot was to lie and worry, wondering if they would have any success and feeling that had I not been with them, they would have been up and away much earlier. Before they left I had been told to take care and not to worry, they would be back in no time at all. My instructions were not to stray too far out of camp and to look out for buffalo bean. I put my arms around Jim's neck and begged him to take no chances. Buffalo bean is a creeper which after flowering, is covered by a mass of beans covered in tiny hairs. If lodged in the skin they can cause a severe reaction, it is said to drive a person mad. Only applied mud will remove the hairs. My brain had been washed with warnings of this plant.

I crawled out of bed, popped into a shift and stood outside waving. The men disappeared into the bush. They were well shod and well armed, with an obvious purpose in mind, each stride was long and confident. Seeing no reason to go back to bed, I took my time washing, dressing and generally fiddling about. Breakfast was relaxed and slow, I ate two rounds of toast with honey and drank two mugs of coffee whilst reading my book 'Where men still dream', by Lawrence G. Green. Soon, flies were becoming tiresome. 'Time to stretch your legs Jean', I said to myself. I decided to wander off to the river with my .22 rifle. I had a fancy for roast pigeon. Harrison had been told by Jim not to let me wander off alone, in view of this he tagged along behind me chewing on a piece of sugar cane and noisily spitting out the sucked dry fibre.

As I approached the river it became obvious that hippo were nearby. Sounds of blowing, grunting and snorting echoed over the water. Harrison voiced his concern and felt we should return to camp but I refused. Poor fellow, he was convinced the bwana, if he knew, would be very angry. There were many hippo and a number of crocodiles lying in the river, all looking relaxed and harmless, eyes blinking in soporific slow motion it seemed. I had no desire to tempt fate despite my burgeoning curiosity. Lion had been to the river to drink, either during the night or in the early morning. Spoor along the river bank was everywhere. A herd of buffalo, impala and what appeared to be eland had also walked down to the river quite recently. The whites of Harrison's eyes were round with fear and dread 'Fools rush in where angels fear to tread' he was no doubt thinking. Perhaps I was a fool I thought as I kicked a piece of dry buffalo dung through the air. The elephant grass lining the path to the river was at least eight feet high, it rattled and chattered as we made our way through. Tinder dry grass and sand under foot pushed my thoughts over to our families in England who were always aching for the sunlight we enjoyed so much in this verdant little country of Nyasaland. Where were Jock and Jim I wondered, no doubt following spoor somewhere towards the Mozambique border. I felt anxious about them, hoping upon hope that their trek would have positive results. They were good intrepid hunters, very sure of their weapons and hunting techniques. Once, having found spoor, they inevitably followed it to its ultimate end, even so it could be a chancy sport, one never really knew what the outcome would be - they could even be attacked by buffalo bean!

My luck was out with pigeons. I did however, manage to shoot two guinea fowl as they walked by. Flocks abound in Africa, even so it was quite a good shot! I had two very good tutors in Jock and Jim. Target practice was a way of life, it made them more comfortable knowing my aim was straight, particularly as I made a point of going into the bush whenever possible, usually if Jim went, so did I. Supper tonight would be guinea fowl, either roasted or stewed, hopefully they would not be tough and sinuous, although one did appear to be old and suspect, it was short of an eye.

We made our way back to the camp walking through the bango reed. Harrison was somewhat relieved, he took his responsibilities very seriously, in this instance I was one of them, despite my steaming disapproval and vociferous rantings as to why I was not in need of a chaperone, he followed. I liked him – he was a rogue, he stole food, I often found him with cheeks stuffed like a hamster. Had he not heard my approach chewing would have given the game away. Soon after arriving back in camp, we were set upon by two Americans who looked rather like Laurel and Hardy. They were escorted by four guides, I could scarcely believe my eyes. They needed water they said, so we handed them each a glass of water followed by coffee. Arriving unannounced 'out of the blue', I don't know who was more surprised, them or me. They said their camp was on the Mozambique border and that so far they had been unsuccessful in their hunting. I noticed that they were flabby and obviously out of condition. They were also alarmingly over armed, and completely overdone with the trappings of hunting. Their shirts were wet and salt stained with red dust clinging from ankle to knees. It was getting very warm, now the air was barely stirring. They felt they should travel on, I said 'Goodbye', and wished them luck, they disappeared into the bush amid the shimmer of dead heat.

I could not wait for the men to return to tell them of this bizarre camp incident. The watu (Africans) who were left in camp tended to Jock's previously shot antelope. They were taking it from the drying racks and packing it for their return journey to Larangwe. Firstly it would be taken to Mesamali and packed into the store tent until the end of the hunt. I guessed they were in high glee at the amount of meat they would be able to safely pilfer or perhaps sell. It would be wise of them to remain undetected, Jock's wrath could be awesome.

It was midday, the heat was intense. I wandered to the edge of the camp and peered out into the bush. In the distance two figures, sliced by a mirage, walked towards the camp. As they drew near I could sense their disappointment, obviously the hunt had not been successful. They came back with an impala and nothing more. Both decided that they had been far too late leaving camp, next time it must be before 'cock crow'. The carriers quickly seized and cut up the meat, laying out the liver and guts over one of the racks. The smell of this African delicacy as it dried and cooked over the fire was appalling. It permeated the whole camp penetrating my nostrils and making me gag, it was everywhere with no breeze to direct it. Later, watching them make their ensima, roll it, and eat it with the half cooked gut almost turned me green! At this time my senses were delicate, I did eventually become acclimatised to each situation as it arose.

Reaction to my camp callers was not quite what I had expected. Apparently my two men had been aware of, 'wandering hunter' signs whilst out in the bush, these signs had indicated that whoever they were, they were not even remotely professional hunters. They did however raise their eyebrows at their venturing into the camp. It occurred to me that Africa was a complete revelation, a world that in the past I could only have guessed at. Each day brought something new, something which became etched deeply into the mind, never to be forgotten. Sometimes, it might just be the sound of silence!

The rest of the day was to be taken easy, tomorrow would be a very early start. We all flopped into our camp chairs with a can of beer. There was a small charcoal fridge tucked away in the shade of the bush, it kept drinks and perishables quite cool. A little later, on our meal consisted of beans on toast with grated cheese on top. River water was boiled in order to conserve the clean water we had brought with us, sometimes after drinking river water, we were sent helter skelter clutching our gut to the 'loo amongst the rocks', blue toilet paper flying in all directions. This slight emergency was a nuisance in that it tended to interfere with our relaxation, usually reading!

I watched Matilda the hen scratch up bits around camp, she had a wonderful time scratching in the dust, pecking at insects and scraps lying under the tree. Each day she laid a large brown egg. Seeing her reminded me to ask the carriers to bring back eggs from the village on their return. Eggs were always for sale in the villages, they could also bring manioc and water melon. On our immediate arrival in camp there had been times during the night when I sat bolt upright in bed, startled by the rustle of crisp dry leaves nearby. Flashing on the torch I had expected to at least see a snake but it was only Matilda blinking her red eyes in the light, shuffling to ready herself for the rest of the night. Making sure the mosquito net was well tucked in, I once again descended in to oblivion. I slept until a voice, strident in its delivery again carried the message, 'Tea is up laddie'. Wobbly and disorientated, we would awake from a deep sleep.

Dawn was not far away, the game would be moving. The carriers began to stir and chatter. Fire embers, still red from the last 'feeding', were given more dry wood and flames leaped Heaven ward. Jock's bi-Aladin lamp swinging from a rope beside his bed, was still alight. It had been for most of the night. A number of lion had been padding on the outskirts of the camp, emitting spine chilling grunts! We had guns at the ready in case of emergency. I felt quite safe with the two men about. 'The old man', Jock's name for an old male lion in the area, had been lurking around, for this reason we had quite a large fire near to the huts, fed by wood, by two of the Africans during the night. Whenever it was necessary for me to get up in the night, Jim followed me with a torch. My real fear is of snakes.

After a disappointing trek yesterday the men had cleaned and polished their guns. Each day they rod the barrels with gun oil, wiping the surplus over the stock and outer barrel. I loved the smell of gun oil, I still do. Their guns were always in tip top condition, the inside of the barrels shone. I can see the two men now, holding up guns to their eye, to inspect for pits.

The lamp hung from the branch of a short sapling, the rest had been utilized in the making of the hut, Jock's voice boomed as he tried to make a conversation with us. I often paused to wonder how many men of his age possessed the cranky humour, stamina and ability to walk for so many miles into the bush in pursuit of game. In the past he had been pushed to the limit. He had lived this life since 1918, initially under severe deprivation, over the years his life had slowly improved. I have Jock's diaries secreted away, in which he reveals some of the trials and tribulations encountered in his early life. Many are quite awesome. Not at all for the faint hearted.

With bath time over, now dressed and relaxed, we called to say we were going for a short walk, 'Take the gun laddie' so, we took the gun. We came across a bridge of natural rock stretching over a dry stream bed. If you listened hard it was possible to hear water running deep beneath the stream bed, somewhere further on it would resurface. We would come across this same phenomenon in later years in another country in the continent of Africa.

Time for a 'sundowner'. Conversation over this pleasantry held me spellbound, hunting stories were varied and endless. We decided on a second drink. We again had three courses for our evening meal, eaten with hot flat bread baked in an underground oven by Harrison. The food was simple and tasty, the surroundings and atmosphere were added seasonings. We noticed ants were invading our food supply each foot of the charcoal fridge was placed into a can of water.

Now it was time to pump up the lamp, to go to bed and to read for a short time before we slept.

CHAPTER THIRTEEN

Time to get up, the bush was alive and vibrating with the early morning song of birds, frogs and crickets, from the distance came the deep guttural call of a ground hornbill which echoed eerily round the camp. The boys were still asleep under the tree, and the fires were in need of kindling. I ventured to the door of the hut, Jock was sitting on the edge of his bed, mug of tea in hand. He was talking to the Africans in Nyanga rousing them from their deep sleep. It never ceased to amaze me how they did sleep, their sleeping positions looked anything but conducive to sleep. I am assured that their sleep is both much deeper and much more relaxed than mine will ever be. This had been proved to be correct on many occasions!

I poured a mug of tea and took it to Jim, assuring Jock I would be responsible for waking him. He looked so comfy I felt guilty at having to disturb him. I organized his clothes and his water for washing, whilst he wandered off to the loo in the rocks. Jock strolled off in the same direction muttering loudly. By this time everyone in camp was dressed and ready to head off into the bush for the hunt. Maspiah joined the hunting party as Jim's gun bearer. With determined strides they all marched away from the camp towards the distant Mozambique border.

I waved them off wondering what success they would have today Feeling the pull of my bed I decided to lie down and doze for a little while longer. At last with great effort I struggled up, washed my face and combed my hair, which made me feel a little more lively. Harrison prepared breakfast. I ate chips and egg with great relish. Bison and Harrison went off to the river to wash the clothes, they are the only two left in camp, the other remaining two had gone to Mesamali village, carrying salted and dried meat to the store, and to bring back eggs, green maize, bananas and manioc. The rest of the men are with Jock and Jim.

Having decided that to do nothing would be self defeating I took some of the load from Harrison's shoulders by making the bread. This was put into a biscuit tin, then placed on the wire mesh rack over the fire to bake. I decided Bison could be responsible for making the manioc patties. Writing up my diary, tidying our bedroom and the camp was quite a feat as the heat built up. The bits of meat drying on the rack stank. The camp was very quiet apart from the din of the cicadas, it was now hot, hardly a leaf stirred. The men would not leave my thoughts I awaited their return in anticipation.

Eventually after what seemed an eternity, the quiet became punctuated by distant voices. I clambered up to the rocks and stood looking out into the bush. In the distance I saw the men approaching, they were split into jagged pieces by a heat mirage. Soon they would arrive in camp, I squinted as they drew nearer, I thought I could see the tracker carrying what appeared to be an animal's tail. Now, they became whole and were well within vision, it was clear to see their trip had been successful. Jim was in the middle, he looked quietly satisfied despite his bedraggled appearance. He had bagged an eland bull. It had been a hard chase they said. Everyone looked hot and sticky. The elation of success had taken over from the earlier exhaustion they had apparently experienced. Each and everyone was wet through with sweat, they were covered from head to foot in dust, thorn prickles, blood and dried grass. Thank goodness I had thought of putting a debbie of water onto the fire. The carriers rushed down to the river to wash and refresh themselves.

It was well after midday and the men were thirsty. Time for drinks and relaxation, they spruced themselves up a little then tucked into bread and bananas, they had not eaten whilst away from camp. The bull had been shot some distance away and had been cut up and hauled into a nearby tree with the aid of ropes. Some manageable pieces had been brought back to camp. To bring the rest of the animal in meant a five mile back track. I was looking forward to seeing the head – a trophy would always remind us of this hunt in Chikwawa, and my first safari with Jim.

The Africans were jabbering incessantly about the hunt and all that it had entailed. How it had been shot, the initial approach and how long it would take to carry it back into camp. Maspiah had remained behind as a guard but it still meant an immediate trek back to the shoot. They took their knives and disappeared once again into the emptiness of the scrub. Bison and Harrison went with them. Three hours later they returned arriving in pairs, each pair carrying different portions. I was amazed at the size and weight. Harrison and Bison came back with a hind leg laced to a pole. They both looked very tired, they were not used to this type of work and it showed. The pole had rubbed Harrison's shoulder skin and it looked red and sore.

Nevertheless, regardless of the weight they had to carry, each man had woven a small bag of reeds, the bags contained stomach, gut, lungs and all things 'smelly', as part of their prize for carrying. All the meat must be laid onto the prepared bed of twigs we had prepared during their absence. The African carriers once again headed towards the river and again, they came back looking surprisingly refreshed. Bewilderingly, they made another journey to collect more meat and the eland head, to return just as the sun was going down. I was never able to understand how so much was done in such a short time.

Now, there was still a great deal to do, so much meat to attend to in order that it be kept fresh. Jim had to concentrate and work on the head immediately, to preserve it. It was very impressive, a splendid trophy. More racks had to be made, to take the volume of meat which must be dried before we left. Jock had a little more time, he intended to stay for another week. There was excited chatter and everyone had a job to do. In fact, many jobs to do.

We decided to 'pick' at the guinea fowl with our drinks. One was very scant fare, so the men suggested that I put a piece of eland undercut in a tin to roast, they also asked me to throw in some potatoes. Their idea was a roaring success. It was a delicious meal, eland meat is manna from the wilderness, it melts in the mouth. Venison at its best.

Jim decided that some of the meat should be salted and put to dry, this way it was easier and more convenient to transport. The rest was covered with salt and again hung by ropes into a nearby tree out of the reach of hyena until we could attend to it the next day. Jock was to remain in camp for another week which gave him more time to cure his meat. There was plenty for everyone, it would last for a long time. We rendered the fat down and put it into tins.

The boys cut wood and made fires. It was indeed a busy camp. A lot of water was needed for baths that night. We were all so tired and there was still a lot to do before we could go to our beds. Jock decided to bathe there and then. He bellowed with anger at his estimated one and a half inches of bath water, complaining bitterly of sand in the bottom of the bath, which he insisted was going up his backside. He rubbed, scrubbed, muttered and moaned, then rounded the whole lot off with a whistle, 'Loch Lomond'. When the time came for our bath we had lots of warm water. We made audible comments as to how much we needed this good soak and how much better we felt for it. These comments were made for Jock's benefit. 'Aye, its okay for you two buggers' he roared. We laughed.

A little later it was nice just to sit with our 'sundowner'. We all enjoyed our supper immensely. Jock was persistent in his complaint at the scarcity of bath water, he told Bison in Nyanga that he could, 'Roll up his mat and bugger off' before lapsing into an unusual state – for Jock – of silence. I can repeat his threat in Nyanga but I cannot spell it! Bison turned away with a smile, he had been on the receiving end of this sentence for years. Tonight not a lot of talking went on, we fell into our bed in utter weariness. In the near distance, no doubt with the smell of blood in their nostrils, the hyena cackled hideously, their cries punctuated by the distinctive yelp of a jackal. The moon was riding high and the 'Old man' padded around nearby. Matilda was nesting in a corner, the crickets were doing their bit. With the smell of meat in the air, animals lurked around for most of the night. The fires burned, guns were to hand, I had heartburn! Sleep came slowly, we were very aware of the mosquitoes. They sounded like castanets in their frustration at being unable to land on juicy nearby flesh which was safely guarded by a well tucked in mosquito net. After a kiss 'Goodnight' we faded into oblivion. Our sleep was deep and undisturbed.

Now, dawn was breaking. It was time to get up. Stumbling from our mattress in a state of exquisite semi-consciousness and what appeared to be a ton of sand in each eye, we struggled into our clothes. Face rinsing was a great reviver. We walked over to Jock, who by this time, was fully organized, having given each of the boys specific jobs for the day. Our day was also scheduled. No hunting for Jim as he was to organize the final cutting and drying of the eland meat. Having digested what was expected of us that day, we said farewell to Jock who had decided to walk some distance into the bush, just in case!

He was fit, absolutely awake and walked with the gait of a man who knew exactly what he was about. He was hard, lean and dark eyed, A whisky drinker with many varied experiences under his belt. We ate eland liver, kidneys, tomatoes and eggs for breakfast. It was food for the Gods. Afterwards, feeling a little more human, we set upon tackling our chores before the heat built up. We investigated a loud grunting and scratching nearby and discovered a bush pig with a family of piglets, rooting near the rocks.

I pottered around, generally tidied up the camp and then salted enough meat to pack into two large enamel basins for use on the estate. Afterwards, under Jim's beady eye, I helped to salt and hang more meat to dry for Jock. I then prepared some meat for a stew and decided to add dumplings for extra umph! Afterwards I boiled the remains of the liver, and made scones.

When Jock returned he looked tired and frustrated. He wondered if the big bull had left the district, gone into dense forest or thick bush with his scent. Poor 'Old Jock' I thought giving him a beer. We still had quite a lot to do; the workers were a great help, they took down the huge limbs from the trees and cut them up under supervision. I noticed that Fabrica was very efficient in the salting. Bison prepared food for Jock, still angry at his lack of success. It was a great relief to sit and chat for a while, with a mug of coffee.

More surprises. Into our midst, seemingly from nowhere, strode a white man accompanied by two natives. In a controlled voice he introduced himself and then in a very authoritative manner, he asked to see our game licences. He had heard we were in the area and had come to check our shooting. We were quite in order, neither of the men had overshot, there was only one of each of some animals on their yearly licence. We offered him a beer and something to eat which was followed by coffee. He was with us until 3.30 p.m. when he left us to walk to a native village near the Mozambique border. He left us a friend for life, our visitor explained how the government were clamping down as too many animals were being shot by over zealous people, some without a licence. We wondered about the two Americans! After the game ranger had gone, we rested for a while, it had been a hectic twenty four hours. Meat was drying under the supervision of the boys. There still seemed a lot to do and we were leaving the next day. The journey from camp to Namisu had to be made in one day, with no overnight stop at Mesamali. Meat had to be transported as soon as possible, I supposed, we could do it. I felt I had well and truly gone through my initiation.

We managed a refreshing little doze on the camp beds. The day was hot, the camp was at peace and the meat was organized. The boys were all around to keep the fires burning. Why not lie down, relax, read and doze? 'Panga tea Bison,' came the cry. When it came it was a very good cup of tea, we drank it thirstily. The usual banter ensued and the nattering went on for some time. Before the fall of darkness which is so sudden and dramatic in the tropics, we took our usual bath. For supper we ate the stew I had made earlier, with dumplings. We decided to go to bed early, we had a long walk and a long journey ahead of us the next day.

My feet had started to swell and Jim was concerned. I told him 'Please do not worry,' I felt quite well. It would be necessary to leave camp at about 5.30 a.m. We could cover most of our walk to Mesamali in the cooler air of morning. We said 'Goodnight' to Jock and went to the little grass bedroom that we were destined never to forget. Everything had been prepared and packed for our trek, Jock would attend to anything left behind as his larger vehicle could carry any surplus. Two of his carriers were to take our salted meat to Mesamali. For a while we lay talking, mulling things over, at the same time feeling sad that our hunting safari was almost at an end. It was a relief to know that everything had been packed into boxes and bags. Harrison had worked splendidly. The fire crackled, the boys coughed, the lion grunted and the night jars cried but we were oblivious to it all, we heard nothing until 4 a.m. then ,'Come on time to get up,' it was the usual call from Jock.

Thinking dreamily of the slumbering world outside, we fell from our mattress, fumbled for our clothes, dressed, then staggered to the rocks, still under the cloak of sleep. For the last time we washed, drank tea and ate a little breakfast.

★★★

Once again I am taken over by the reality of the moment. It is Sunday, I prepare a little lunch and decide to have a gin and tonic. It occurs to me, that for all our life, Jim had always made me a perfect gin and tonic. At this thought, I become enveloped with despair. At times like these I become bereft and desolate, and wonder just how I can go on without my love. Life appears empty and meaningless without his being here. Having carried my tray into the conservatory, I open the door and windows, I need air. Gazing out of the glass, I become over emotional, plunging into a state of total disbelief at all that has happened to separate us. Looking out into the empty shed opposite, I see tools that are no longer in use, the beloved head no longer bending, eyes cast down over the work bench. Gone is the warm sunny smile shining through the window, glancing up to make sure I am there standing painting alongside my easel, we were comfortable and content in our love. My heart sinks at thoughts of the future, at the loneliness and grief which I know I must face. How I miss the whimsical remarks and the kiss as he passes by, the wit and the leg pulling. I miss his charm, his good looks, his guidance and his intrepid approach to life. I marvel at the love given to me over the years. There is no solution, I know that, but I cannot accept the knowledge. I go back to my writing, back to living in the past, knowing it will take me forward. I must live with my beautiful and evocative memories, they will comfort me.

★★★

Our loads are now placed ready for the carriers, everyone in the camp is awake. We are quieter than usual, feeling sad at leaving our

142

'bush life'. Despite the frantic meat preparation the bush had been peaceful, tranquil and very different. However we had to return home. And so, in the cool of approaching daybreak, with Fabrica leading the way, and the boys ready to follow, we said a fond farewell to Jock. I felt that he was sorry to see us go. Taking up our positions behind Fabrica we left camp at a steady three miles an hour. Cutting off in another direction, Jock disappeared into the bush with his three carriers in search of game. He shot a sable. We saw only small game on our trek back, the bigger game had made their way to the river to drink, we came across all kinds of spoor.

Walking at a steady pace, I felt fine. I found myself turning round frequently, sometimes walking backwards in an effort to talk to Jim. He suggested with a smile that I walk forwards in a straight line in order to conserve my energy. The trouble was, I had so many questions to ask. I forgot his words and almost tripped over a stump. After this I decided to keep quiet and walk in a straight line which was almost impossible with my enquiring nature. I knew I must heed his words.

Fabrica decided to take us to Mesamali via a 'short cut'. It was an infinitely more interesting path. We slowly descended into a dambo with a tiny running stream, it was quite breathtaking. For some distance we walked along the bed of the stream. All types of tropical creepers and ferns formed an overhead archway. The ferns formed 'walls' on either side, helped by green lacy bushes. The creepers climbed over the bushes, joining and intertwining. It was deliciously cool. The water in the stream glistened, its bed was sandy and pebbled. The pebbles gleamed like marbles when the rising sun's rays caught the ripples. I felt I would like to sit and watch the water wend its way into the distance forever, with a total disregard for time as I wondered how much of it's course ran through such beauty. I was very quickly brought out of my reverie. A voice called 'Nyoka,' silently and stealthily a mamba slithered from the bushes, crossed the stream and disappeared into the undergrowth on the other side.

Continuing along the streambed, Fabrica took a sharp turn right. Suddenly in front of us there was a very steep incline, luckily, there were numerous bushes on either side, I managed to haul myself up by them, with the help of Jim giving me a push from behind. As we reached what I felt must be the end of our climb, we were confronted by an enormous rock which had to be negotiated. Again Jim helped me, aided by a bush growing alongside. I made it though I felt a little jaded by that time. Even the boys were flagging, they sat on the boulders to take a breather before we resumed our journey. The only person showing little sign of fatigue was Jim. I was determined not to rest after the experience of our outward journey. I just leaned heavily against him, whilst the boys took a few moments rest.

Time beckoned; we carried on into the bush for probably two miles on a gentle incline. Just as I was thinking, 'How much farther?' to my great joy we started to descend. The crisp dry grass was becoming malleable. Beneath the grass previously loose dry sand was pliable and spoor more obvious. Quite soon we came upon the first shoots of green. We were approaching the river. Now, the air was filled with bird song. Damp air rising from the river was laden with perfume from a beautiful bush, rather like the English lilac, and smelling just as sweet. I cannot remember its name. The change of atmosphere and scenery after the long walk, brought a lighter, quicker step, we were quite near the village. We passed through tall elephant grass, bango reed and more sand. At last we reached the river, it looked cool and refreshing as it lay gleaming in the sunlight. We removed our shoes and socks and waded across knee high water which gave us a new lease of life. The only ache was in my back! The journey had seemed much more tiring than our outward trek.

On reaching Mesamali, we all flopped. The primus stove refused to light so it had to be 'pricked'. The boys ate their food with the villagers. We had our tea and ate liver sandwiches, which had been made earlier in camp, there was a dry scone to follow. Afterwards, with great effort, we loaded the truck. I quickly wrote a note to Jock, to be delivered by the carriers on their return to camp. All was ready, Harrison and Maspiah climbed into the back sitting amongst the boxes, bags and the meat. The vehicle creaked alarmingly, on our return there was the added weight of the meat, the head alone weighed 50 lbs. I wondered how on earth we were going to motor up the escarpment.

With a last farewell to the villagers, we drove away.

CHAPTER FOURTEEN

On our way home it was necessary to cross the Shire river at Liwonde, this from the south, a different approach to the Shire than the one from Lake Nyasa. A bund had been built recently to give traffic easy access to the other side, the engineer however, decided this may cause flooding because the river was too big to interfere with permanently in this way. So, it was decided that the bund had to be breached, which resulted in a massive flow of water. On our approach to Liwonde we were greeted with much commotion. We had commented on two loud bangs heard a few moments ago, not really giving it much thought, until a number of locals waved us down, frantically shouting and gesticulating. The bund they told us was in the process of being blown up. We must wait until after the third and last explosion. We all groaned, Harrison's tongue was wagging incessantly. It could be a long wait.

Strange how once on the way home, the aim is to get there as soon as possible. I seem to remember we were held up for a little over an hour. Then it was the antiquated hand-winch and rope ferry again, to take us over to the other side. Leaning on the rail, Jim put an arm around my shoulders, at the same moment we both considered the possibility of the rope slipping. 'It would be the beginning of a long journey by Shire to the Zambezi, non-stop, if the rope slipped', he commented. He was smiling which gave me confidence! It took some time to get to the other side, 'Ee's' and 'Eh's' echoed over the water as the boys voiced their dislike of the ferry.

Once over, we soon reached the foot of the thirteen mile long

Chikwawa escarpment. I had originally been worried about finding Jock in the bush, now I was very concerned as to how on earth we were going to get up this escarpment with our heavy loads. Jim seemed quite confident. We looked at each other and laughed at the sight we were confronted with, two figures shrouded from head to toe in dust and grime. Starting our ascent, Jim was full of glowing confidence. Now, we badly wanted to get back home to the estate. I still had a feeling of foreboding. Slowly, we manoeuvred the slopes, at times the offside was sheer. We rattled along beautifully, the boys in the back had, amazingly dropped off to sleep. As usual we were admiring the stunning scenery around us, this particular view we felt must be one of the most spectacular in Nyasaland. All of a sudden we came to an abrupt halt, the engine gave a few chugs, moved forward a little, gave a few more chugs, a few splutters and then ground to a juddering halt. We were one quarter way of the way up the escarpment, I had visions of total disaster!

My dear Jim. He and the boys secured the vehicle at the back. Needless to say, I was on my feet and out of the truck in no time at all, I had an enormous fear of it rolling back over the edge. He lifted the bonnet, investigated the innards, then raising his head and with a pained look on his face said, 'Oh no, it's the plugs'. Apparently we were running on three plugs, strange because we had replaced old plugs for new before we left Namisu. After some fiddling around, the engine started and with a heave from Maspiah and Harrison and much gear changing, we moved, travelling slowly, ever so slowly, with everyone waiting with baited breath for the engine to cut out again. I looked at Jim for reassurance, he gave me his confident smile and squeezed my hand, repeating the sentence I was to hear so many thousands of times throughout our life together, 'Don't worry love, Jim will look after you', and he always did.

We edged into Blantyre in a three plugged struggle calling in at the nearest garage, fortunately they happened to have what was needed. Soon, with the engine running smoothly, we drove away with a huge sigh of relief. Later we discovered there had been dud plugs amongst our last buy. These things often happened. By now we had the most abominable smell hanging around us, perhaps because we had been so engrossed in trying to get our transport up the escarpment, it had not been noticed before. The eland head had really begun to smell despite all the salt. We hurriedly bundled it into a sack, tied it securely and were delighted that momentarily, at least, we had cut out the stink. Perhaps the fact that the air was now much cooler would help. In the valley it had been so hot.

We now had to collect Liz from Geoffrey and Shirley, they were now living in Cholo, at least 25 miles from Blantyre. We gave Harrison and Maspiah money to buy food in Blantyre, with instructions to wait for us at a given point. As soon as we arrived at the house, Liz ran out, she was wildly excited to see us, we gave lots of hugs and kisses, Jim swung her round and she laughed happily. As I stepped out of the car, I was greeted by hoots of mirth, 'Only you could get away with looking like that, our Jean,' Geoffrey commented, he always called me 'Our Jean'. No doubt I did look a bit odd, my dress was unconventional to say the least. I was pregnant, dirty, bedraggled and very hungry, not a pretty sight. Feigning a 'hurt' expression I looked at Jim, he told me I was beautiful. Always the vain one, it was all I needed to hear.

Luckily tea was ready. Amid much laughter, talk and leg pulling we devoured round after round of cheese sandwiches, followed by scones and gooseberry jelly. We had three pots of tea and decided that this was by far the best afternoon tea we had eaten for a long time. It was quite dark then, thank goodness we were off the escarpment. We talked of our stay in the bush, the eland bull, of Jock, of the camp and of all our comings and goings, also of our struggle to get home. We had so much to say and so little time to tell it all. Much would have to wait for another day. Talking so intently, we missed the time. Now we must leave, pick up the boys and wend our way home. We arranged our next 'get together', then piled into the car, Liz was sitting on my knee. She talked incessantly all the way from Cholo to Namisu. I was exhausted. Half an hour later than we intended, the boys were waiting. All we wanted at this time was to get back and to become organized. There are times for everything. Unmolested from Blantyre to Namisu, we arrived home at approximately 9 pm.

We washed, had a cup of tea, then we all literally fell into our comfortable beds, sinking into a dreamless sleep.

Harrison awakened us the next morning at 6.30a.m. It was so quiet without Jock. As we drank our tea we thought of the past happy days spent in the bush. My first hunting expedition. I hoped not the last. With a big hug and a kiss, we braced ourselves for the workload of the coming day. The stinking head was worrying me a little, Jim had asked Makolo to scrape it off. He had always helped with these tasks, he was very keen and took a great deal of care and trouble to attain perfection in what he was doing.

The 25th August 1957 was a very busy day indeed. With a vehicle laden with ulendo trappings, where on earth did we start? Obviously the meat must be our first priority. We ate a little breakfast and then quickly set about our various chores, roping in a number of the estate staff. Jim walked off down the drive to the bwalo (compound) to organize the work force, to find someone to oversee them, and to talk to Francis Makolo.

Lemon, Harrison and myself set about the task of emptying the truck, we set out related items in some semblance of order. Harrison took out a roast from the packed basin for our evening meal. The rest we divided up. Jack O'Hea arrived to collect his meat, a local Italian family benefitted from out hunt, together with Makolo and other estate workers. By this time the main bulk of the meat had been divided up. The rest was well salted, spiced and dried at the back of the house with Harrison and Lemon keeping vigil.

Washing had been kept to the minimum, the old tin trunk had kept the dust out. In camp clothes had been taken down to the river each day, washed quickly dried and ironed with the old charcoal iron. All the cooking utensils had to be washed and put away. The mosquito nets and safari bedding needed attention, the nets had acquired many more holes, they must be sewn, then washed and put into store. Boots and shoes were, needless to say, in a dreadful state. Many things which were of no further use, were thrown away. Everything else went into the store room. The truck was almost empty, only the eland head remained. I drove to the bwalo and Makolo removed it, he appeared to be delighted at the thought of sitting scraping all the rubbish from it! The vehicle I left to be washed down, we would collect it later on.

Jim and I walked back to the house arm in arm, we had a lovely 'cosy' feeling, everything had been organized and cleared up. Time for coffee we decided. Jack O'Hea from the tobacco estate next door, arrived on his B.S.A. Bantam, he had decided to call in to drink coffee with us and to catch up on our hunting news, also to pick up his roast. Jack wanted to talk, our conversation turned to changes being made by the company, a lot was happening. We had known this before we left for the valley. Jim and Geoffrey had been confronted with a choice, would they like to move from tobacco to tea? Geoffrey had chosen the latter and went to live in Cholo. Jim was not at all interested in tea, he loved the challenge of a tobacco crop. 'And if we decide not to grow tobacco, and to dispose of the estate?' They queried.

Jim's reply was, 'Then I suggest you lease it to me'.
'Oh dear.' I thought.

We, of course, had to prove our worth and our capital assets, which were sadly depleted after the divorce and its consequences. A great deal depended on whether or not we could procure a loan from the Land Bank. Jack O'Hea when presented with this, decided to depart the services of the company and moved to Tanganyika.

We approached the Land Bank, attended various meetings, filled in numerous forms and eventually the loan was approved, stipulating that it must be repaid from our first sales of tobacco. With this security the lease was agreed for the following years crop. We must settle down, finish the present crop and make plans for the next. It was all rather daunting. We knew it could either make or break us, so much depended on the right weather and the stretching of our finances. We felt we were able to achieve this, after all the last crop had been a bumper and had fetched huge prices. I had learnt as much as possible about the crop in the short time I had been at Namisu. During the night when it had been necessary for Jim to check and regulate the barn temperatures, I had always gone with him. Day after day he had answered all the pertinent questions I put to him, he had also explained refinements at each different stage in the crop. Poor old thing he seemed inundated with chores at times, there was so much work involved in growing and producing a crop of good grade tobacco.

There was the important selection of a site for seed beds. The rotation of these sights, the size, preparation and soil treatment. The fertilizer requirements. The fencing and the windbreaks had to be organized. Then of course there was seed bed hygiene, sowing, shading, watering, clipping and weeding. No sooner was all this organized and carried out than the thinning and pricking out had to be done. Each process required meticulous handling.

Everything had to be geared towards the transplanting of the pricked out seedlings, they must be planted into previously prepared fields two weeks before the rains. Each planting station, depending upon the type of soil, needed from 1.5 to 4 litres of water to enable the seedlings to grow with as little 'shock' as possible. Much of this water had to be carried over a period of time, and poured into big drums, placed at strategic points in the field. Afterwards there was the infilling, replacing weak or dead plants with new seedlings, this had to be carried out within a week of the original transplanting to ensure an even crop. The list was endless. We had the short rains and everything went as planned.

Shirley had given birth to Sarah in September. It seemed the Moss brothers were high in the fertility stakes. My baby was due in mid December. At the end of most days, after darkness had fallen, we sat on the khonde and remarked on the contrasts in the sky. The storm clouds had gathered, stars peeped from the clear sky between. I could 'feel' Jim looking at me, we sat side by side, quite oblivious to the world outside. Bats had started to fly, crickets chirruped, night jars called, mosquito's whined with aggressive persistence. Waves of perfume from the bush flowers floated over on the night air. This was our world, we were quite content in it. We hoped it would last forever. When supper was over Harrison went to his hut. In the silence, the hiss of the pressure lamp which fed us with reading light, seemed momentarily intrusive. My mind began to wander to the crops, the weather and the tobacco auctions.

Then on a simpler note, to our shopping list. In the morning we had to visit Blantyre and Limbe. I had to remember to buy samosas. We were going to meet Geoffrey and Shirley, perhaps we would have lunch together. Liz was going to stay with her school friend and I hoped we could call in at the 'Flamingo', on the way home, and so, my mind ran on. Drying alongside us on the veranda was the eland skin. Jim had cleaned and salted it, it was now on a frame, where it went through a stretching and drying process. When it was completely dry it would be softened, this was achieved, by a long and drawn out method of even rubbing. A stone was kept especially for this process.

We wondered if we should go to bed, but neither of us wanted to move. We were comfortable, reading, talking, making plans and putting the world to rights, or so we thought! Jim felt the crop should be a success, the seed beds were looking splendid, bursting with strong, upright, healthy looking seedlings. The rains gave every indication of arriving when they should. We hoped this would be the case, so much depended on 'good' rains. I badly needed to ease my position, the baby was moving energetically. He gave my tummy a little pat. His eyes were full of meaning.

There was a call from a nearby leopard, we collected the dogs and fastened them up, took the gun from the hall and headed towards the sheep kraal. The leopard had approached in complete silence and had skilfully taken a lamb. Whilst sitting on the veranda we had heard nothing. In the past few months it had taken a number of sheep, the herd boy had done none of the repairs he had been asked to do, everyone else had been busy preparing the fields, seed beds, barns, stumping and cutting grass, whilst also attending to a hundred and one other jobs. Jim was not at all pleased. He had asked Ferison if these jobs had been done his reply had been 'Yes'. Tomorrow it would have to be done, the fences must be strengthened and reinforced. I heard mention of the carpenter and gathered he would be asked to make the repairs. My thoughts turned to the female kudu I had seen walking quietly through the rocks near the house. It had raised its head over the top and we had come face to face. I remembered the huge limpid eyes gazing down at me, bright and alert. I hoped it would not fall pray to the leopard. There was nothing more we could do that night after being disturbed. We went off to the bedroom, pumped up the pressure lamp, attended to last minute calls, then slept.

After breakfast the next day, we picked up our books which must be returned to the library, our shopping lists, and whatever else we thought we might need. Excited and full of enthusiasm, we set off for our Friday shop to Limbe and Blantyre. Everything was in order, jobs allocated, and the kraall fence under repair. As we moved to the car we sensed a change in the weather. The heat seemed to be building up as if for the short October rains but it was much too early for this, even so, clouds hung heavily over the hills. It had been in our minds to spend a weekend in the 'Kuchawe Inn,' on the Zomba plateau before the real onset of the rains and before the pressure of the crop got under way. This was food for thought. Our last visit to the inn had been one of relaxed bliss, spent glancing up from the dappled shade of the hotel veranda, with a glass of wine to the side and a book to hand, we had looked out at the panoramic views which were so breathtakingly lovely. It was equally so at night when the landscape was aglow from the moon. The crickets strangely added to the ethereal magic of this wonderland, which was approached by a steep tree lined escarpment from the town of Zomba below.

Zomba at this time was H.Q. of the government. Consequently there were quite a number of well-equipped stores and a Greek shop of some note which sold delicious bread and cakes.

Back to our shopping trip. We had taken great care and some time in choosing our books at the library. We went to the Limbe Trading Company for various 'goodies' and to the market. Mandala provided any spares we needed for the machinery on the estate. As always, we visited the bookshop in Blantyre. I was browsing around, picking up and putting down and being generally curious about everything, when Jim told me he had to nip to the office, 'See you in Yiannakis in fifteen minutes,' he said. This was fine, we had decided to meet Geoffrey and Shirley in this café cum bakery, it was very good and not expensive, so ideal for cheese, a Greek salad, fresh bread and a glass of wine. I walked down to the bakery with Geoffrey, he had just walked over from the library opposite. Shirley had remained at home with their daughter Sarah who was a little 'off colour'. We sat at a table near to the window and ordered a jug of wine, this was how the Yiannakis served their wine, it was very popular. We passed the time of day and in a few minutes Jim arrived.

We told Geoffrey of our plans for the estate and the crop we hoped to grow. His eyes grew ever larger at the mention of every difficulty we had to overcome. There was the renting of the estate, land bank loans, the challenge of the crop, the make or break situation and many other things which we must overcome to make it a success. Spelling it out in this way, the whole venture did sound a little daunting. He suggested we move on to tea! Our big worry was the weather, always a problem to tobacco farmers. We all had to keep our fingers crossed. Our lunch was simple and delicious, the wine perfect. Geoffrey suggested they come over to Namisu for the weekend.

In the meantime we had decided not to go to the 'Flamingo,' we would pick Liz up from school and wend our way home to check that all the tasks allocated for that day had been completed, the kraal being uppermost in our minds. Liz would no doubt spend her time playing on the swing and talking to Ferison, who at the moment was tending the sheep quite near to the house.

Harrison would cook our usual Friday night omelette, some vegetable or other from the garden, served with tiny chips. With all the chores completed, we bathed, settled down to read, had a tasty supper, then moved on to the veranda with coffee, spending some time watching the stars and fireflies. Liz dashed around trying to catch them in a jar, she wanted to make a 'fire fly lamp! In a short time we went to bed. Jim and I of course had to discuss the coming year and its prospects, yet again!

After all was said, the quiet gradually took over and we dozed off. The next day Chisolo brought us fish from Lake Nyasa, gleaming chambo, so delicious, fresh and good. We ate it for supper, it had been cooked well and tasted good. Each week Chisolo cycled backwards and forwards to the lake, his basket overflowing with fish on his return. He sold it on the estate and in the villages, he was very popular and everyone looked forward to his visits.

Geoffrey and Shirley did not visit us during the weekend, Sarah was still a little under the weather, however the Boddy's arrived with their three children who, to put it mildly, were a complete nightmare! Ken and Bev were splendid people, I am not quite sure what happened to the children at this stage. We had been walking around the tobacco nurseries explaining our plans and intentions to Ken, suddenly we sensed all was not well. We went heading back towards the house and were greeted by the most horrendous uproar. We dashed through the door and found all of Jim's priceless books on the floor and the children lying in the bookcase, our jaws dropped, whatever would their next move be?

Jock paled at the very thought of a visit from them. We were all very fond of the Boddy family, they were such kind, helpful people, but the kids took not a scrap of notice of anyone seemingly to go all out to disobey and be disruptive. One visit had been catastrophic, the whole family had been jammed into the car, Ken had enjoyed the odd whisky with Jock and was a trifle 'worse for wear'. When the time came for them to leave and return to Ndata, the family scrambled into the car, waving frantically and calling a hundred 'goodbyes'. Ken drove slowly down the drive and into the rocky ford nearby. 'My God,' said Jock, 'They were crossing the ford when we heard a gunshot, Ken the silly bugger had not unloaded his rifle', Jock was in total disbelief at this breach of the rules. He went on to say 'The rocks in the ford, must have set the trigger off, he had shot poor bloody Bev through the Achilles tendon.' There was a complete and utter uproar, Jock sent Bison running over to us, with literally a note in a cleft stick, it was a hurried note asking us to 'Please help.' He gave a brief explanation and asked us to hurry.

We arrived in a flurry of dust and debris. Ken was full of remorse, a potent mixture of love and alcohol. We took Bev to the hospital in Blantyre, they found that the tendon was badly shot but not severed. It took years to repair, leaving a hideous scar. Despite all,

Bev always forgave Ken, they were as mixed as liquorice allsorts and yet so compatible and loving towards each other. When things did go wrong, which was rare, it was better to flee in the opposite direction until feathers had stopped flying.

From that day on Jock always referred to Ken as 'That silly bugger Boddy.' Ken was in fact of enormous help to us during the growing of our next crop, he had a very inventive mind. He built a frame onto an old 'Chevvy,' which he had found lying around Ndata. It carried much of our tobacco from fields to barns during the season. The big trailer had not been included in our lease, so we must make do! The early rains came and with them came the work. There were workers everywhere, scuttling around like ants, as plants from the seedbeds were carefully pulled, carried to the fields and planted. Capitoa's called their orders and the workers jumped to attention. We worked like hell and prayed. Every procedure was carried out with meticulous care, nothing was left to chance, every skill in the book was put into the crop. We had to rely on the weather to do the rest! All the tobacco in the fields looked green and good, a few wilted plants had to be re-planted with new seedlings, this was always the case. Rain clouds collected over the hills and drifted over the farm dutifully shedding their moisture. Everything looked in tip top condition, our sometimes faint hearts were becoming not so faint. Even so our eyes were glued to the weather and the crops. Our efforts were spent in keeping everything up to date and workable, they appeared to be paying off.

Each evening we relaxed with our sundowners and kept an eye on the clouds over the distant hills. By this time I was enormous. I was convinced that I could not carry this baby for much longer, it bobbed about inside causing a great deal of discomfort at times. I commented to Jim that perhaps if we patted it less it might fall asleep and rest for a while!

These days our morning tea was arriving much earlier than it had in the past, there was so much more to attend to before breakfast.

Harrison was roped into doing all sorts of things. I helped with the cooking. Jack O'Hea called to see if he could be of any help, he was to leave for Tanganyika soon. I think he felt he would like to give us what assistance he could, knowing we had literally put our all into the project. We asked him to oversee the workers who were busy taking off grasshoppers and other insects from the tobacco, it also had to be suckered and the delicate pink flowers had to be removed, weeding was necessary and the ridges had to be built up, the list was endless. Tobacco does not like too much rain. With flagging spirits we watched the clouds build up over the hills. They marched on towards us, despite all the mental effort we put into pushing them back they persisted, bringing with them the inevitable insect infestation. Our crop went from an exciting stand of tall green upstanding tobacco soldiers, to bent, yellow diseased plants. We bowed our heads and rung our hands in disbelief. The tobacco harvested before the downpour was good and fetched high prices, however daily deterioration, due to the rain, meant there was much which could not be rescued.

We paid the rent and our debt to the land bank. Sadly we were not in a position to fully finance a crop for the following year. The cards were on the table, we had to move on. We made enquiries, viewed other tobacco estates for rent and did our sums over and over again. We were clutching at straws. But, 'Never say never' it was one of those mountains which we had to climb in order to reach the other side. The time would soon come when we would have to leave Namisu. I would go ahead we decided, whilst Jim organized the closure of the estate and sold the remaining crop. Everyone pulled together and Geoffrey was a 'gem'.

Amidst all these comings and goings, I was taken to hospital, where I was delivered of a baby girl on the 27th December, 1957. We called her Sally. There was great excitement, Jim and Liz grinned from ear to ear when they saw her. Their smiles were huge. It was a wonderful time for us despite all of our crop worries. I was in hospital for a week, I returned home hoping I had not forgotten how to deal with a new baby. In particular a new baby in the tropics. Despite all the precautions and fuss I made, or perhaps, because of them, who knows? We had to rush her off to see the doctor, as we thought she had dysentery. It cleared up quickly and I realised that life could be made too 'sterile', even for a new baby! Liz fussed with Sally all the time, I must say she was a wonderful Christmas present to us all. This year we had celebrated Christmas with Geoffrey and Shirley before I went into hospital. I thought of the past year Christmas 1956, when we had all celebrated at Mudi, Jim in black tie and me in my off the shoulder black velvet dress. How we move on!

Jim was still selling some reasonable tobacco, we struggled on with the estate and estate work. For the coming months life went on as normal, we carried on doing the things we had always done, but now we had a basket in the back of the car when we went shopping, cuddled up in this tobacco basket was baby Sally. The weeks flew by and as the time gradually grew closer to my leaving Namisu, there were many 'Get togethers' and many 'Goodbyes'. At times I had great difficulty keeping my self control. I was deeply saddened, so much had ridden on this venture and when I looked at Jim I felt my heart was being torn out, he was such a good efficient and enthusiastic grower of the crop, but when he had needed the weather most, it had failed. My eyes welled up with tears of disappointment for him, and for our having to uproot from this heaven that we had found together and for all the other emotions burning up inside. Eventually we accepted the situation and then became resolute. We would start again, in some way we felt we would surmount the problem facing us.

Telegrams flew backwards and forwards, we flew back to England in July leaving Jim behind. It was quite dreadful. Jim's mother and father met us at Heathrow, they took complete charge of Liz and Sally, who was their first grandchild, and were kindness itself to me. They could sense I was completely drained by emotion and extremely tired from the weariness of traveling with the children. On the train Sally cried and cried and grandad, not to be outdone, took her bottle along to the dining car and asked them please to rinse it well and fill it with boiling water, 'The baby is thirsty,' he explained. They even gave him a jug of cold water, in which to stand the bottle to cool it.

Gently they took over, and we travelled by train to Crewe station with its many memories of the past. My goodness all this seemed impossible. Our bedrooms had been prepared, there was lots of room in their home. The Horseshoe hotel. I had been welcomed with open arms and so had Liz. My mother arrived later to welcome us and to take stock of her new granddaughter, needless to say she was delighted to see Liz and made a great fuss. There was so much to say but it would have to wait. Gradually the whole story would be told.

CHAPTER FIFTEEN

In October Jim flew into Heathrow, I met him in a lather of joy, excitement and anticipation. It was an unforgettable reunion. Getting into Heathrow, had been difficult in the early hours of the morning, the underground train had only gone so far. I managed to secure a lift to the airport on a staff bus, with the help of a very amiable air hostess to whom I had been chatting whilst on the underground train. The plane landed after a delay of an hour and a half, when I caught sight of him on the tarmac my heart raced and my knees wobbled. Amazingly, as we looked at each other, we both realised at the same time that we were back where we had started. In every sense of the word we were going back to where we had last been teenagers. So much had happened and now we had a baby daughter. Again we had to plan and map out our future. So, what was different? Just age, experience and a more mature understanding of our inner emotions.

When we arrived at Crewe station, all our memories flooded back with a vengence. We became quite overwhelmed, the boy and girl who had traversed these platforms carrying teenage dreams in their head, were now man and woman walking along them into a new future. Jim's parents were overjoyed to see him. As the taxi arrived they rushed from the house seizing him in an enormous embrace. He kissed his mother lovingly, he had missed her so much. At times I wondered why he had ever gone overseas.

That evening we opened a bottle of champagne and talked well into the night as our story unfolded it jerked many a tear. It was made quite clear that we could stay with them for as long as it took, I felt in their eyes forever would have been ideal. Sally was taken over and loved greatly by one and all. It had taken us less than a week, to realise that our dwindling finances, must in some way be made to earn. We racked our brains and with a little help from Grandy Moss purchased a cream Bedford van, wondering how we could put this to good use. We talked around it and found an answer, albeit a far cry from what we had ever envisaged our future might hold

Nan needed cheese, so we decided to go to Crewe market. We would buy cheese from 'Cheesey Edwards,' he had been at school with us, I had been a good friend of his sister and he had once had a 'crush' on me! His parents had retired and now he had the business. It would be nice to catch up on all the gossip. We were given to understand his reputation for cheese ranked high. As we headed towards the stall, Jim met a greengrocer whom he had known as a boy, I was introduced to Jack Harrison. We stopped to talk, exchange news and tentatively, through instinct, put out a few feelers. The greengrocery business he said was booming, stressing that of course quality was the key. We pricked up our ears, absorbed a little more of what he had to say, then with a 'Farewell, see you again soon,' we went off to buy cheese from a very unhappy, overburdened 'Cheesey Edwards.' His lot was not at all what he wanted from life. The conversation we had painted a picture he could not comprehend. It made us quite sad.

That evening, sitting cosily around the fire listening to the chink of glasses, the chatter, laughter and boisterous guffaws coming from the bar, we hit upon an idea! The idea, was to dedicate ourselves to providing a reliable service and a promise of immediate delivery of high quality produce, fresh greengrocery, fruit and poultry, to any interested person in the surrounding district. Our intention was to introduce ourselves by handing out personal cards, giving our address and our intended attention to detail, of each order received. The white van was outside and waiting! The family thought we had taken leave of our senses.

Not to be deterred we went to see Jack the next day. Sitting in his office we told him of our need to work, of our plans and of our intentions to make them succeed. We asked for his opinion on our idea. Could he give us names and introductions to local suppliers, farmers and nurserymen? He said it was a good way to go forward, wished us luck and promised to would help in any way he could. We took heed and approached all the contacts he had suggested, each one greeted us with overwhelming enthusiasm and support. It was explained that this may only be a short term project but presently it was vital to our existence; they fully understood.

Our white Bedford van was fitted with shelves. My cousin, a member of the farming fraternity, also happened to be a carpenter, he made all the movable shelves we needed. We were ready to go! It was not easy, particularly after the life we had led in Africa! We cut savoy cabbages from farm fields in the frost and snow, which made our fingers blue with cold. We picked tomatoes and cut lettuce at various nurseries, bought and picked dirty carrots, beetroot and celery, Bramley apples, beautiful cauliflowers, broccoli and sprouts to name but a few. I made, packed and sold stuffing. Turkeys, geese and chickens were available from local farmers, either with or without feathers. They were bought and delivered to customers on the day of their request. Our reputation became second to none, we made a good living from our convenient and reliable service. Winter came and we worked to full capacity from early morning until late at night, Christmas was mind boggling!

One day as I cycled through the back lanes I noticed a 'For sale' sign on a smallholding. I had noticed this little place in the past before the sign had been put up, it had always fired my imagination. I made some enquiries and we learned that the land had been passed for building, making it even more desirable! We paid a deposit and went ahead with the purchase. We loved it and were very happy there. We furnished and carpeted the house from local house sales and auctions. Jim and my mother, armed with a hip flask, had a wonderful time together at the auction sales. A friend gave me lots of curtains, all of which happened to fit almost as though they had been made to measure.

We went off to the cattle auction in Crewe and bought two Hereford bull calves, I fell in love with them! Two pigs, chickens, ducks and geese. We had a patch of rhubarb, apple, pear and damson trees, laden with fruit which we picked during a romantic, bewitching Indian summer. I made gallons of ginger beer for home consumption. Our larder was a 'walk in' with marble slabs on bench tops, which enabled us to keep everything cool. We loved 'Rose Farm,' and had such happy times there, but Africa still 'tugged' and tugged hard.

At breakfast one day, I discovered I could not cope with the smell or the taste of tea, this meant only one thing – I was pregnant – no one seemed at all surprised at my announcement. At Rose Farm, we worked hard, we loved, we reminisced and took the *Daily Telegraph*. Our love was transferred to our children who loved us and each other as we had brought them up to do. Sally by this time was toddling, spending a lot of time in nearby fields with the calves, her red ribbon gave her whereabouts away amongst the grass and buttercups. The geese chased her and hung on to her little green duffle coat, they pecked on the door demanding attention. It was an idyllic life. During my pregnancy, our business had to be manned more or less by Jim alone although I helped when I was able. Elizabeth cycled to school each day, she was a great help with Sally. Each Saturday we walked to Nan's house where we met Jim and all ate lunch together, this was the time when we aired our views and exchanged news, it was always a great family get together. On Sundays my mother and father often came to the farm. Mother caught the bus and came to see us during the week, especially if she thought I needed help. Everyone seemed to want to help, my poor solicitor was roped in at one point to change a wheel!

We had an English Chisolo – not on a bicycle as in the past but in a small blue van – he delivered fish each Friday, my goodness how Jim loved his Friday fish and chips, with lemon meringue pie to follow. There was a huge sink in the kitchen by the window, during the cold months I bathed Sally in it. When she saw Jim coming down the lane she became so excited she splashed water in every direction, usually wetting me through, then she demanded to be put down rushing to him as he came through the door, wrapping little wet arms around his neck and rubbing her wet nose against his in adoration.

It was a cool summer evening, we decided to go to see 'The Black Orchid,' at the Odeon cinema in Crewe. Grandad kindly looked after Liz and Sally. Half way through the film I became decidedly uncomfortable, I whispered in Jim's ear feebly and with some trepidation, 'I have a feeling my labour pains have started.' We decided it was probably better to stay and watch the film, It would take my mind off 'things,' meaning the pain! In any case the nursing home was nearby. We stayed until the end and from there I went straight into the Linden Grange nursing home.

Jane was born not long after midnight, a lovely little girl 7lbs 7ozs, she looked just like Jim, another Moss. It was the easiest my three births. Sometime later as I sat up in bed feeling relieved, clean and very 'chipper,' I was handed a cup of tea and a piece of hot buttered toast like ambrosia. Now I was longing for morning I just wanted Jim to come and see us. The next morning the sun shone through the window lighting up my bed as I sat and ate my breakfast. I found myself looking out into the distance, I would perhaps be able to see the van moving along the main road towards Crewe station and on towards Linden Grange. Yes, there it was, I could see it moving along the main road. My excitement grew to extraordinary proportions, so much that my temperature shot up. When he walked through the door our arms just opened and we hugged and hugged. We name our baby Jane Isobel Moss – J.I.M!

Reluctantly I stayed in the nursing home for the next ten days. Jim, Nan and Grandy came to collect us on the tenth day. I was taken back to the Horse Shoe hotel for a few days, where my every need was tended to. Then back to 'Rose Farm,' to take up my daily chores, mother came to help me. I was unable to breastfeed so we took it in turn to bottle feed through the night. I really don't know why as we were both wide awake. We just simply used to do everything together, it was our way.

Every day the *Telegraph* was delivered, quite often by the postman. Each Thursday I scanned through the Overseas Appointments section. Strolling around the farm one evening we had heard something which had sounded like a cricket, it created a great yearning in our souls. 'The waters of Africa were calling.' The following Thursday I picked through the Appointments section with a fine tooth comb. Suddenly, I saw a word which stopped my heart, 'tobacco.' Casting my eyes to the beginning I read and absorbed just what it was they were asking for, without any doubt I knew no one could be better qualified for this position than Jim. Crown Agents wanted a tobacco extension officer for the Western Province in Tanganyika. Now I had the impossible task of waiting for him to come home before I could give him the newspaper which carried the very significant vacancy. It had been underlined with some force by yours truly. Jim arrived home calling 'Cog,' as he always did immediately he put his nose through the door. I put my arm through his and reached up with a kiss. 'This may be of interest to you love,' I said handing him the paper, indicating at the same time that he sit down. It took him some time to read and fully absorb the contents, when he looked up his eyes held tears. I knew then what had to be done.

We talked it over, mulled over the pros and cons of the situation and I encouraged him to apply for the position. This he did almost immediately. There was an interview in London and a medical on the same day. He was accepted without question and scheduled to sail on, I think it was the Union Castle, in six weeks time to Dar-es-Salaam. From Dar he went to Tabora in the Western Province to meet the Agricultural officer and to pick up a Land Rover. From Tabora he must drive 300 miles or so to Kibondo, an outpost, which was to be his station, near the Ruanda Urundi border. I could not accompany him as he was to share a house with an officer who was due for home leave. When he had left, the house would be allocated to Jim. Initially, this was a shock however I must cope and get on with what had to be done, it would have been impossible for me to leave at the same time, there was far too much to attend to. Grandparents looked after the children whilst we organized the closing of the business. We visited each customer explaining the situation with apologies. They were sorry to lose the service we had given, but to every single man they wished us well. It took no time at all to sell the building land, for what at that time seemed to be a lot of money, though now it would be a mere pittance.

We browsed through hundreds of magazines, we must buy and ship a car to Tanganyika for our personal use. The government provided a Land Rover for use in the field. A Citroen 'Safari,' was decided upon, with great excitement we ordered it from the Citroen factory in France. It was built, shipped to Dar-es-Salaam and eventually sent by rail to Tabora in the Western Province, from here it had to be driven to Kibondo, this took a long time. Whilst all this preparation was going on, we gradually ran down our business. From Black's of Manchester we bought equipment and tropical gear, all this must be packed alongside linen and personal things which I felt Jim would need before I arrived. In the meantime we advertised the house and the livestock.

In what seemed no time at all the postman arrived with a huge envelope, the contents were all Jim's tickets, sailing instructions and appointment times etc., Inwardly I wobbled a great deal but pressed on. There were days when, as I watched him walk down the lane towards the farm, I became overwhelmed with an intense desire to protect him. I have no idea why, he was big, capable and incredibly independent. He knew his way around and was in no way reliant on anyone. I thought at times, that our claim of being able to overcome anything together was somehow under threat because the parting was not under our control, it was being dictated from an outside source. It was a strange feeling – but at the time it was very real.

To try to describe our feelings is not possible as (once again), we said our 'Goodbye for now' on Crewe station. The world folded in. I waved until the train had disappeared, a speck in the distance. Even now I was longing for our next meeting. This was a nostalgic role reversal of past years. Turning I walked towards the exit, a last glimpse over my shoulder revealed a platform as cold and empty as my soul. Two weeks after Jim had left, Janey's glands became huge, she had mumps, Elizabeth's glands became huge the following week, she had mumps encephalitis which left her deaf in one ear. On calling the doctor, a family friend, she took one look at me, raised her brows and decided mother also needed help. She took us under her wing visiting the farm on most days, until she felt we were stable and able to cope.

The house was sold, the animals had been taken to market and sold. On the day I had chosen to visit my solicitor, I was late and had much to attend to, getting into the van I found I could only get into reverse gear. Feeling a complete idiot I reversed up the lane and along the road to a nearby garage and collected it in the late afternoon – a wasted day – and I had no time to waste. Thank

God the children were with their grandparents! How on earth was I going to pack what was needed for overseas? My decision was to buy a huge crate which I had put into the back of the van. Carpets, mats, bed linen, kitchenware, china, pots and pans along with a hundred other things. I packed into the crate as I bought them. It was sealed and taken to the freight and goods dept., at Crewe. Here it was weighed, wrapped with metal strapping and then sent on its way, by rail and boat to Dar-es-Salaam. What a great relief, I really felt things were moving.

The family were becoming a little fidgety as our time to leave drew ever nearer, I think they had felt we were back home forever, though they did realise that given the opportunity we would again 'Flee the nest'. I was beginning to dread saying 'Goodbye,' it was heart wrenching for everyone and there were to be so many future years of it!

My tickets arrived, they were to Kuala Lumpur. I was not going to Kuala Lumpur. What was the matter with these people? In frustration I rang London and asked them what on earth was going on. I asked them to please book me on a flight to Tabora via Entebbe. They were full of apologies and re-booked my flight immediately. Sally developed mumps, 'On no,' I decided that willy nilly, we were definitely going to be on that aircraft, mumps or no mumps, in actual fact she was not so poorly as the other two had been, much to my great relief. Mail arrived from Jim, he posted letters at every port. It spurred me on to greater effort, there were times when I needed it. All the furniture from our home was spread amongst family homes, some went to auction. I took the children to stay with Jim's mum and dad before we left. Liz went to stay with my mum. Rose Farm was now empty of Moss's. Sally's face by this time was almost normal, not too swollen. Janey was fast growing out of her carry cot, but it was not yet too small for her, so in all, we just made it in time. The family farewells were quite dreadful. Looking back we had packed a lot into the past eighteen months. We had also achieved a lot!

CHAPTER SIXTEEN

Another time, another place

We travelled by train from Crewe station (yet again), to London Heathrow, eventually boarding a B.O.A.C. aircraft, I seem to remember it was a Boeing. The journey by train from Crewe had been a little mawkish, we all felt sentimental and sad at leaving everyone behind, the children were particularly fidgety, but settled down eventually. Certainly they were delighted at the prospect of flying to see daddy. It was a comfortable flight, the cabin crew were helpful and charming and the children were well looked after and well catered for. The ear pressure bothered them a little, I taught them how to clear the build up by holding the end on their nose tight, then to gently blow down their nostrils, the ears clear with a little pop. This may be one of today's 'Nos,' I only know we did it then, and it worked!

There was plenty of room on the aircraft, the children ate well, slept well and were very comfortable. I closed my eyes and attempted to doze, my mind was in a whirl wondering where Jim would be. I knew he would be on his journey to meet us. I was certain he would be in Tabora for hours before we landed. Just to make sure!

We had an overnight stay at Entebbe before we took off for Tanganyika. I was looking forward to staying in the Lake Victoria Hotel, I understood hippos grazed on the huge lawns which extended to the lake. My attempt to read Neville Shute's *Round the Bend* did not meet with a great deal of success as my thoughts were doing far too much wandering to concentrate on anything for any length of time. Catching the eye of the airhostess I asked for a glass of wine. Having noticed that I had not eaten earlier, I was organizing the children, she suggested a tray of food with the wine. I thanked her and accepted it was very good and I ate it in peace. As a family we have always enjoyed food; good, tasty and wholesome food and a bottle of wine with a good 'nose.'

We were seated in the bulkhead. I looked down at Janey who lay at my feet, fast asleep in her cot. I wondered how she would be in the heat of Kibondo, certainly she would not be tucked up in her pram with snowflakes lying on her lashes as she had been in the past! During the night flight one of the air hostess's kindly made up three bottles of Lactogen milk for Janey, 'Better to be sure than sorry,' I thought to myself before making the request. I felt it would help smooth over our arrival and the settling in at the hotel, particularly as I could speak no Swahili, though Jim had told me in his letters that most of the locals could speak a little English. The air hostess was very obliging, handing the bottles over to me a short time before we were due to land.

By this time I was becoming very excited, ripples of joy were alternating with fathoms of deep love which threatened to overwhelm any sensible judgement lurking within my psyche. The children had slept well through the night, I had spruced them up and we were now prepared for our landing at Entebbe. The aircraft circled and prepared to land, Lake Victoria glistened like gold in the sunlight. I put the three banana shaped glass bottles containing the milk, into a bag. I handed it to Liz emphasizing that she must be very careful not to break them!

The three months on my own had seemed like three years, I knew we were both missing each other very much, the jigsaw did not fit.

Our landing at Entebbe had been very smooth. We waited for the other passengers to disembark, gradually falling in behind to make our way to the steps of the aircraft. Sally clutched at my skirt telling me 'Mummy I am very hungry.' She would not eat her breakfast on the plane, which was probably the reason. One of the cabin staff had relieved me of Janey and the carry cot, and was waiting on the tarmac. Liz followed behind; suddenly there was a loud crash and the sound of shattering glass, down went the bottles from the top steps to the ground, now we had no milk, 'Oh dear,' a little voice said. 'My God we've lost the milk,' I wailed, 'how did you do that?'

'It slipped out of my hand accidentally mummy,' she replied her eyes wide and round. The air hostess who had made the milk up for me, seemed most concerned, I decided that only I could put the situation to rights. I told the hostess not to worry, and thanked her for having made up the milk for me, 'Accidents do happen'. I gave Liz, who was by this time crying, a hug and a peck on the cheek, 'These things happen sometimes darling,' and all was well for a while.

We trailed in 'crocodile' down the steps and over the tarmac to the customs shed. For some reason, I shall never know why, the Ugandan customs officer decided my case was suspect and proceeded to open it. If he had stirred the contents round with a big stick he could not have created more havoc. He picked up a box of tampons, scattered them about and asked me what they were, I had no answer. I heard a whispered 'aside,' he dropped hem like hot cakes, scratched his crotch, picked his nose and pushed the suitcase on. Meanwhile he had broken the lock, everything was totally disorganized and in a mess. I noticed two napkins, twirled them into a kind of rope, then closing the case with as much force as I could muster. Anger had made me very strong indeed. I tied up the open end of the suitcase with the napkin rope, leaving in my haste, a bra partially hanging out. I wondered what on earth Jim would have said? By this time I really did not give a damn if it snowed.

Sally was still hungry, still hanging on to my skirt, Liz was dragging her feet along feeling bad at having dropped the milk. I was feeling pretty agitated, only Janey seemed happy as she beamed up at us from her carry cot. The bus arrived to take us to the hotel, there was standing room only. By this time the air hostess, I think her name was Barbara, realised that I was quite near to bursting a blood vessel in frustration, and sent for another bus. Hence we travelled alone and arrived a little more composed than had previously been the case. The Lake Victoria Hotel, was imposing, breath-taking and very colonial, it lay amongst impressive, lush and beautiful surroundings, the view over to the lake inspired an aura of peace and tranquillity.

We had tea and cakes on the veranda, whilst listening fascinated to the grunts of hippo echoing eerily across the water. Amongst all this splendour I made Jane's milk from the hot water jug, standing by the tea pot on the tray. This time I used a 'new,' shaped upright bottle. I had brought three spares with me. Our luggage had been taken to the room. It was a huge ensuite room, with two double beds and one single bed and it overlooked the lake. If I needed water for milk I merely sent for a tray of tea. To make life easier we had supper in the room, the waiter prepared the table and brought up our food. We tucked into chicken Maryland, and I seem to remember it was followed by apple pie. I enjoyed half a bottle of wine. We all slept like logs.

My eyes opened with Jim's face firmly in focus, I badly needed both him and his support. As this was the last leg of the journey, it would not be long now before we were together again and I would hear the old familiar, 'Come on love, come with your Jim,' as he held his hand out to guide me. The very thought of this brushed away much of the tension which had built inside me since I had said 'Goodbye,' to him on Crewe station, as he left for the boat to sail to Africa.

Everyone seemed to be feeling much better this morning, our tea arrived I made up a bottle of milk, and we sat looking out towards the lake. The hippos wallowed in shallow water near the shore, snorts and grunts carried over on the morning air, they filtered eerily through the windows and into our bedroom. I felt a sense of overwhelming freedom spreading through my body as it succumbed to a massage given by the invisible fingers of Africa. We were all very relaxed this morning as we went into breakfast, we ate lots of fruit, followed by a good simple boiled egg, toast and marmalade and fragrant local coffee. I made up another bottle of milk.

At mid-morning a bus arrived to take us to the airport. We gathered our luggage, piled onto the bus then, with 'fully charged' emotions, headed towards the Cessna, which was waiting on the tarmac for its passengers to board. We were to become very familiar with these reliable little airplanes. Flying over shimmering Lake Victoria we saw it was dotted with hippos. We were becoming wildly excited as we drew ever nearer to Tabora. I knew Jim would have been waiting for hours. As we came in to land I saw him immediately. There he was waiting to walk out to meet the aircraft. After landing we scrambled down the steps hanging on tightly to the carry cot, and with Liz clutching Sally's hand, we rushed with beaming faces towards the man in our life. He walked towards us arms open, so much love emanated from his smile of relief at seeing us, and our safe arrival. He gave me a long loving kiss. Then he kissed the girls looking at each one with untold joy. He turned towards me again and held me for a long, long time, so long in fact that it was not until Elizabeth said, 'Can we go now,' that we began to realise the length of embrace. We had been quite oblivious to time, we simply knew we were together, which was all that really mattered. A little voice had brought us back to reality. Here we all were all together in Tanganyika, a country on the continent of Africa. We were back to the magic of hot sweet nights lit by millions of stars. We had wanted this so badly, for me it was knee weakening, all my frustrations and fatigue had left me, like a coating of thick chocolate melting in the sun, they had dissolved and disappeared.

Our cases, complete with the napkin rope, went through customs unmolested and I did not have to lift a finger. 'Oh the bliss,' the fact that I no longer had to worry about the cases was as soothing as being handed a blank cheque! Jim laughed at my attempt to secure the case. The fact that my other half was with me, meant that all further problems were halved, it was an enormous relief. This tall, handsome and sensual man with whom I had always been so besotted reciprocated in full, we loved each other very much. Life could not be better than this.

Laughing and full of beans we piled he luggage and ourselves into the Land Rover and headed for the Tabora Hotel. It was an East African Railways hotel. All these hotels were excellent and of a high standard and all were very typically colonial. There were always damask clothes with matching napkins and all that went with them. Food and service were good, all the rooms were cosy and comfortable. It was easy to forget the outside world.

After we had settled in our room we decided to go out. Jim put Janey on his shoulders and we all went for a walk. He was amazed at how she had grown and advanced in the past three and a half months. Tabora was a nice little town, we decided a little more shopping would be in order in the morning. Jim had bought one or two vital commodities to take back to Kibondo, before meeting us. Almost as though suffering from withdrawl symptoms, I looked forward to a short browse through the Indian doukas, before we left for up country. Back at the hotel we bathed and fed the girls and we talked to them of our journey the next day, they asked a million questions, some we could answer, for others we had no answer
I would have little time to 'root' around the shops, though they were open very early. We were leaving early the next day to travel the 300 miles or so to Kibondo, over sandy roads peppered with

boulders large and small. Kibondo was a small town/settlement, surrounded by bush, game, swamps, tetse fly and mosquitoes. There were very few Europeans living on this small agricultural station. It was in the land of the Buhar, collectively the tribes were known as the Wahar. One man belonging to this tribe was a Muhar. There was a tiny club which some wit had named 'The Laughing Cow,' it had a bar, and a tennis court. Members of the club were given a blue tie which sported the emblem of a cow's face, in gleaming yellow, wearing a huge grin. Forty years on, the tie still hangs in the wardrobe!

With the children tucked up in bed we were relaxed and euphoric, our delicious meal was taken with a bottle of chilled South African white wine. Our conversation ranged over the past, and through what we hoped for, from our years in the future. A little later Jim took my hand and we danced a slow foxtrot to the strains of Ella singing 'Every time we say goodbye'. At our first opportunity we had decided to buy a battery operated gramophone and the Ella Fitzgerald record. We looked forward to that. That night Jim vowed to never leave me again, I believed it and so did he, but, we are not masters of our own fate are we?

CHAPTER SEVENTEEN

We start again

The next morning we were up bright and early, our loads were packed into the Land Rover before breakfast. Willing hotel workers helped, hoping for the odd 'shllingi'. They carried the luggage, Jim placed it in position in the back, leaving room for Liz and Sally and the rest of our yet unfinished shopping. Janey was to travel in the cab, in her carry cot on my knee. Everything settled, a few bits and pieces bought from the doukas and we were ready to go.

It was an awesome journey, full of bumps, bounces and surprises. Every moment I was aware of Jim easing over each and every boulder as he gently turned the wheels into the drop which followed. We travelled through the sand with some speed, avoiding as many of the sometimes huge boulders as often as possible. The foot and handwork involved as each moved from brake to accelerator, to gear lever, to four wheel drive, filled me with admiration for both our driver and our bush workhorse. We travelled along this rutted bumpy road, surrounded by thick bush on either side, for mile after dusty red mile.

'My God what's that,' I screeched, hoping I had not frightened the children out of their wits. I had not been prepared for a snake of such enormous proportions, there it lay across the road with either end still in the bush. As the Land Rover arrived, the thing reared up smacking against the windscreen, I ducked automatically! 'A black mamba,' Jim replied. 'A snake,' called the children helpfully from the back. Janey cried, in fact she cried off and on for most of the 300 mile journey. She objected to every bump we encountered, despite the fact that I tried to ease the carry cot up whenever I felt that a bone shattering jolt might occur.

I knew Jim always carried spares so I was confident that he could go anywhere without us having too many problems. From dust to slithering mud to breakdowns and through flash floods. My greatest fear was game on the road, particularly elephant, but with room to manoeuvre, it was not a problem. Dense bush on either side gave food for thought. Mothers with calves did not like to be intimidated. Suddenly Jim stopped the Land Rover, just to check that the snake had not coiled itself around the prop shaft, this was usual practise as people had been attacked when stepping from the cab, sometimes fatally.

The children were complaining, they were hungry. We stopped to picnic on boiled eggs, cheese biscuits and a Tusker beer. Janey had a bite or two of a sandwich and a bottle I had prepared earlier. By this time we were all pretty well covered on red dust. Jim 'Just hoped Abdallah the cook had remembered to heat the water'. So did I! The house had an old Tanganyika boiler, which was a large drum of water heated by wood from below, exactly like the one we had at Namisu. I was looking forward to arriving at the house. The basic furnishings were courtesy of the British Government. Our shipment, when it arrived, would add the finishing touches. Apparently it had arrived in Dar-es-Salaa and now had to be sent by rail up country to Tabora, and by road to Kibondo.

It was dark when we arrived at the house, Abdallah had the pressure lamps pumped up and bright, the water was hot, and a meal had been prepared. Mahingamo the house servant unloaded the Land Rover and under my supervision put most things in their place. Our suitcases were in a mess, they would have to wait until morning. We bathed both the children and ourselves in record time, put on our pyjamas and a robe, then we ate a good supper. I do remember the soup, it was splendid, I think we had roast to follow. Then, exhausted we all fell into bed and slept like the dead.

We were happy in Kibondo, its isolation was absolute. We were surrounded by tetse fly and game. Should anyone ask, 'Where are you stationed,' the person on the receiving end of our reply ('In the Western Province, Kibondo') usually shook their head in pity, 'What have you done to be sent there'? We loved it, no one could understand why, of course they had no notion as to how it could be. Everyone in the station enjoyed relative peace, the 'home made' fun and the excitement of game being in such close proximity. Almost every day was an adventure.

After some palaver Elizabeth was enrolled into Mbeya school, in the Southern Highlands Province, this meant taking her to Kigoma, on Lake Tanganyika, where she boarded an East African railways train, there was always an official escort and other girls joined the train at stations along the line to Mbeya. It was a two day journey which could be pleasant in the 'dry' and awful during the wet season. The road to Kigoma consisted of mud, elephant, elephant dung, buffalo and buffalo dung. There were also sitatunga, eland and topi. They were all heading for the Moyawosi river and the swamps.

It was sensible to stay in Kigoma overnight, we always stayed with a Polish lady who was a splendid cook, larger than life and flamboyant to an extraordinary degree. Her home was made up of a medley of exotic lace, velvet and damask drapes, an organized pandemonium of brilliant colour lying beside more subdued and subtle colours, each playing its part in bringing seductive comfort and serenity to her guests. Each small table was shrouded with a long delicate cloth. Flowers, ferns and potted plants grew in profusion. The garden was lush, watered and green. Orange, lemon and grapefruit trees gave shade to chickens as they frantically pecked at morsels thrown amongst them. For breakfast we ate lovely brown eggs with coarse brown bread and salty butter. Coffee beans were picked from bushes in the garden, roasted and ground by Olga for our breakfast coffee. We all loved this house. Delicious lake fish was the norm at suppertime.

Janey was now into all sorts of mischief so it was necessary for us to employ an ayah to keep an eye on her persistent wanderings. Everything she picked up went into her mouth. She had Jim's colouring and curly hair. She was a happy, chatty little girl but a handful. She and Sally played happily together, they had missed Liz when she left for school and always looked forward to holidays and Ziza, their name for her, coming home. If there happened to be a rest house within the vicinity, we always accompanied Jim on his working safaris. We remained in camp making it into a comfortable little bush home with our heavy canvas camp equipment. In Nyamirembe, alongside the Tobacco Board, there was a rest house. Just beyond it grew all types of fruit trees which were part of the citrus trial in the area. We picked the fruit and made lots of fresh fruit salad. There were pigeons to shoot, which we sometimes spatchcocked and roasted. Pigeon stew, was also often on the menu. If we had time we went to Biharamulo market, coming home with fish from nearby Lake Victoria, meat and almost always vegetables. No matter where we were we ate well and enjoyed what we ate.

During the day we sometimes went for walks, at other times the children read and played games. In the heat of the afternoon we all had a siesta, then prepared for daddy to come home to a little comfort after a long hot day. We had a bath (our canvas camp bath) ready, hot water to hand and clothes for him to change into. He would relax in his chair then Abdallah, the cook, whom we always took along with us, handed him a Tusker beer and a dish of salted peanuts. When Liz was with us she organized the little ones and herself, my work was to help cook the supper. When we sat down we bombarded each other with questions and indulged in idle chatter, until lights out and bedtime.

One hot afternoon I decided to take a siesta. I picked up my book and wandered off into the rest house. I shuffled up my pillow and as I lay down thought that given the heat of the day, the only answer was to be horizontal, vertical was a 'No, No,'. Feeling comfortable I opened my book glancing upwards before my eyes hit the page. To say I was startled is to underestimate my sheer terror as peering down at me, wrapped around one of the beams in the roof of the rest house, was a very large snake. Its beady eye weighing me up, one quarter of its length was gyrating overhead, mouth (or are they jaws?) wide open, forked tongue flickering. I was terrified, I knew Jim was outside beneath a tree writing his notes. I called, or perhaps squeaked, 'Jim, bring your gun, snake in roof'. In what seemed like an eternity, in fact it was in no time at all, he had appeared in the doorway, raised his gun and fired, as he did so I leapt from the bed, 'Hell that was close,' the snake uncoiled and dropped onto the bed. I was so relieved he had been within calling distance, I dreaded to think what would have happened had he not been around! The bed was well invested with snake blood. To this day the stain is still there. The bed is still in use by our grandsons when they are out camping with friends, they could spin a fine and truthful yarn, fired by the imagination the story could know no bounds!

Our community in Kibondo was small and intimate, we visited each other, exchanged recipes and met in the tiny club but rarely stayed late. Quite near to the house, down a narrow sandy road, there was a small extremely efficient hospital, where a friendly Irish doctor was in charge. He and his South African wife had quite a number of good looking children. The hospital had a European matron, her husband taught everyone on the station to speak Swahili. Their son was never allowed to drink Coca Cola, I remember their son (Charles) telling us vociferously, 'Coca Cola makes your teeth drop out,' he delivered this in utter sincerity, in a high pitched voice with a slight lisp. This snippet was never forgotten by our girls, even now if their own children ask for Coca Cola, Charles is remembered and quoted.

The bush fires in Kibondo were absolutely spectacular, some I felt were too near the house for comfort! It was enthralling to sit on the veranda in the evening light, looking over to the leaping flames as they created a brilliant blood red glow, throwing millions of golden sparks heavenwards to float down on the tinder dry earth below, setting light to trees and bushes which glowed orange in the darkness. The smoke billowing upwards temporarily blotted out the stars. Our children sat watching from the veranda steps, in wide eyed wonder. Arms around each other, Jim and I looked out into the distance, watching and listening to the roar of the fire as it made its way greedily towards the fire break. Each year before the rains, the Africans set fire to the bush, almost overnight green shoots appeared in preparation for the onset of the wet season. As we sat there I turned to look at Jim's face and for some reason my thoughts went back to the gorgeous black French silk nightdress and negilgee that he had bought me from the boutique in the Shire Highlands hotel in Nyasaland. I had found it lying on my bed alongside a record of Glen Millers 'Orchestra Wives,' as a surprise. There was also a little note which told me all I ever wanted to know. I hugged him very tightly and he gave me one of his wondrous enigmatic smiles. The bush fire was now becoming less intense so we 'scooped' the children up in our arms and put them into bed. In a whirlwind of deep content we found our way to the huge bed which awaited us.

★ ★ ★

Now, as I write these words, my mind wanders back to those days. Snake were such small fry compared with the danger and violence which surrounds us at this time. Old age is not sad for me, my sadness is being alone in my old age. It is a relief not to be involved in the torment and dissatisfaction of life as it now presents itself. I have learnt much in my three score years and ten. I have been far away and done many things, and all these things I have experienced and lived through were played out with a perfect and loving partner.

★ ★ ★

Our safari now over, we returned to Kibondo to find a message from the District officer, problems had arisen in Iringa, a huge tobacco area, and the officer in charge had a heart condition, he was in hospital and must return to the U.K. We were to be transferred from Kibondo to Iringa in the Southern Highlands. Iringa we had heard, is a post to be envied. It is the next township to Mbeya, so not so far for Liz to go to school. On the day following our return, we were told of the delivery of the Citroen 'Safari,' it was waiting for us in the sidings at Tabora. Jim's assistant took him in the Land Rover to Tabora. The paperwork presented no problems and the car was in perfect condition, I must say we had wondered many times about this! It took them three days in all to collect the car and complete the journey there and back. We were very proud of our car, each night we sat on the veranda with a 'sundowner,' looking at our sleek motor car, the colour was, I think, 'Mediterranean blue.' We could not believe after the failure of the tobacco crop in Nyasaland, that this gleaming beauty belonged to us. With initiative, hard work and a guardian angel at our side, we had made it. Never had a car been tended with such loving care, it was polished until it glistened.

The Director of agriculture may have had his doubts about its use in the bush but we never had any problems. The suspension was a huge bonus and added great comfort, for our private use it was ideal. The Land Rover was the government workhorse. Before leaving for Iringa we made a point of going to Mabamba, a tobacco area near the Ruanda border, it was wild, very wild. We slept in a tiny mud and wattle hut near to the market place. I remember we bought hand made copper bag needles, which we later used to sew up baskets of fruit with string, to be taken home by the children to their grandparents, on their way back to boarding school in England, at the end of their school holidays.

Fortunately we had taken Abdallah the cook along with us and he went to the market to buy whatever we needed, tomatoes (binongwe), spinach, sweet potatoes etc., We had taken beans, rice, a loaf of bread and lots to drink with us. Abdallah had baked the bread in the wood stove of our outside kitchen at home in Kibondo. He was a splendid cook; always making something out of nothing The little girls gave him no peace, the Africans are good and very patient with children, he gave them little jobs to do. Our outside kitchen was smoky and black, I was mortified when I first set eyes on it. I gave Mahingamo a bucket of whitewash and a brush, he painted it twice and within a month it was back to its original dark grey, enhanced with patches of midnight black within the immediate vicinity of the stove. From then on I kept away deciding the kitchen was not my territory.

Before leaving the Western Province we also went to Bukoba on Lake Victoria, it was delightful and very picturesque. We visited many beautiful areas and felt rather sad at having to move on. On the other hand, with problems fast arising in the Congo and armed troops passing through Kibondo on their way to Kinshasa, perhaps we were destined to leave after all.

We would miss Mr Patel and his dirty little douka, we had to buy everything from him, he had the only shop for miles and everything he sold had to be brought by bus or truck the 300 miles from Tabora. There were times when the bacon and sausage were in dire straits, particularly if they had been carried in the hot season and the journey had taken many more hours than was actually necessary through breakdowns, or the driver may have had a beer drink along the way. Everyone still bought the stuff, it was well wiped with a vinegar cloth and put into the paraffin fridge to cool off and that was the end of the story, we never queried it and we never became sick.

Anno Heckker, a man of many children and his long suffering wife, provided much of the game meat in Kibondo, a good thing. The market meat left a lot to be desired at times. Anno was in game and tetse control, which meant that he was away for weeks at a time. I have his game liver pate recipe which is superb, and a great favourite of all who have tasted it.

We spent a night in the Moyowosi swamp area, on a hill surrounded by buffalo, we had no gun so we all slept in the Land Rover. Jim and I were up and down the whole night, listening to the buffalo graze, bellow and snuffle. In the early morning after the 'buff,' had left to drink, we had a breakfast of sardine sandwiches with the children. Below us at the bottom of the hill, a huge herd of eland now wandered along. Some way in the distance a big herd of elephant moved towards the river. They were shrouded in the swirling mist of the swamp, they appeared to be sliced in two, their huge head and bodies carried along on a grey cloud. It was an eerie and ethereal scene, one that we would never forget. The girls do not really remember it, which is a great pity. Again it was something we felt we had to do before leaving the area. It had been recommended by Anno Heckker!

On one of our safaris to the tobacco area, we had to stay overnight at Kakonko, here there was a government rest house which had a 'long drop,' lavatory some yards away from the accommodation which was not at all conducive to getting up in the night if nature called, which it inevitably did on such occasions. The bed was sprung and the springs had collapsed which gave it a well in the middle. What a bed – Jim thought it was great! Janey at ten months old had her first Coca Cola sucked through a straw here, it was bought from a tiny Indian douka in the midst of the bush, her little face peered out from beneath lovely springy curls which were blotted out by the red powder from the murram roads. Sometimes I opened a tin of beans which she tucked into with a little blue plastic spoon. Sally sitting alongside her looked almost as bad, although she did wear a hat! A bath, and a cuddle, with supper to follow always put things right. Life was never boring!

Gradually we prepared to leave Kibondo, (this name means, 'Infant child'). Eventually everything had been crated and had gone by road and rail to Iringa. Anything we needed before our departure would be provided by the government emergency box which was used for just such occasions. Any further shortage would be covered by friends. We had enjoyed this remote little station which was situated amongst the hills. It was one of the smallest in the territory, there was no air route, no railway and only handful of Europeans who were all friendly and helpful. Before leaving we all enjoyed a party in the 'Laughing Cow.' The following day, we said 'Goodbye,' to our friends with a great deal of sadness. It would take almost a week to get to Iringa. The Citroen was blissfully comfortable. The seats were down in the back for the children where they could either play or sleep. We could travel in peace with my hand on Jim's knee in comfortable silence. In the Land Rover it was almost impossible to hold a conversation. The Department of Agriculture had a workhorse waiting for us on our arrival in Iringa. We had dressed in 'comfort,' clothes for this long journey and with Liz at school we just had the two little ones to attend to. We had roughly planned our route and where to stay when accommodation was available. Our aim now was to head for the Southern Highlands.

I loved Jim's beard, he had had one on and off since Nyasaland. I had always liked beards, so wanting to please me there it was, and there it remained. He always made me feel needed and very proud. Delving into my mental larder I thought of the years which had inadvertently slipped us by. There must have been a reason for this, a need to learn the lessons of life, to grow up and mature and yet even then, young though we might have been, we had known that if we were to be content, we had to be together. There were times when listening to comments and conversations of others, we felt in some way different. The determination and passion we both had for an unusual, exciting and varied way of life, had been mapped out while walking over the fields shooting rabbits for pies and wandering amongst the daisies. What wild and extravagant plans we had made and they had come to fruition. We had fallen in love in our early years and so it had remained. Words were not needed between us, we both knew the thoughts of the other; eye contact was enough in any situation. And so, as we left Kibondo behind, we set our sights to the journey ahead, new vistas, new experiences and new people.

Our first stop was Kisulu to fill up with petrol. Small garages were dotted all over the countryside, some had hand cranked pumps, others were a little more sophisticated, they were all kept by Indians who had an extremely efficient network. Delivery tankers were mainly under the management of Indians. The main Citroen agency in Dar-es-Salaam, belonged to Mithani, his enthusiasm and directions when we made enquiries about anything at all in connection with our 'Safari,' were clear and concise. The vehicle was the only one of its type in Tanganyika at the time. The regular service needed to keep the car ship shape was exceptional. When in Iringa it was a good excuse to visit the coast for a long weekend!

On a whim, 'Shall we vere off to Kigoma and Ujiji,' I asked as we drew away from Kibondo, it meant adding many miles to our journey. It was in Ujiji that Stanley met Livingston. Lake Tanganyika is very restful the scenery around it magnificent. We were sorely tempted but we decided to make Mpanda, our first stop. 'Not a great deal here,' we both decided. There was very little of interest in the town, its surrounds were mainly miombo woodland. There was a small airfield serviced twice weekly by East African Airways. It also had a silver/lead mine on the outskirts, which in itself speaks volumes, there is nothing to appeal to the eye in a mining area. Our overnight stop was at the Mpanda Hotel, it was basic but adequate and homely, and ideal for the children who were fussed over a great deal by the Polish couple who kept it. Each day after the car journey we took the girls for a little walk to stretch their legs. Janey always needed a beady eye kept on her, I think her main aim in life was to disappear in order to scare us out of our wits. 'Where are you,' we would yell. 'Janey we can see you,' Jim called, ever hopeful, and it usually worked. She would trot back arms open towards him, waiting to be twirled around. Sally hearing her chuckle with delight would demand the same treatment.

The next day, early in the morning as I slept, my unconscious mind absorbed the voices of the children. Jim's voice stirred me into wakefulness. I was aware of turning over to hear a voice say, 'Jane will you please come her at once,' the 'Jane,' brought me to my senses because it had a 'y' attached usually and the lack of it was not a good sign. She came over to me pulling my hair, 'Mummy wake up,' she lisped. Sally not to be outdone chirped 'We are hungry mummy.' 'Alright, just do as daddy says, both of you,' I said firmly. Half asleep I staggered out of bed, which was unusual for me, and gave kisses all round. I lingered a little longer as I melted momentarily into the open arms awaiting me, he looked at me and ruffled my hair. Wobbling into the bathroom I took a shower and rinsed my face with cold water. I was suddenly wide awake!

We all trooped into the austere little dining room, with its green walls and bolt upright chairs, including a high chair for Janey. We ate cornflakes followed by boiled eggs and crispy toast. They were home reared eggs, the best ever. The packed lunch requested by us the night before was put onto the table. The old man carried our case to the car, we paid the bill which was a pittance, thanked them very much, then waving goodbye, we went on our way.

'Where are we heading for today love?' I asked.

'If you promise to leave your hand there you can go anywhere you like,' I had my hand where it always lay, on his knee.

'Daddy, Janey wants to do a wee,' the eternal cry as we started our journey, we drove on. 'Daddy, I want to wee,' we went a little further.

'Daddy we both want to wee, badly,'

'For God's sake,'I said, turning round to look at them, they looked like two little dolls! 'Round the next corner and then we'll stop,' ruled Jim.

The next corner was upon us in no time at all. For speed and convenience Jim took Janey and held her out, I kept my eye on Sally.

'Look mummy,' she said 'Ants.' Sure enough, there was a line of soldier ants heading towards us. Jim moved quickly, resulting in Janey wetting his shoe, 'Mummy, mummy she's weed on daddy's shoe, look,'

'You dirty little toad' murmured Jim with a smile, before giving her a big hug.

Finally we put them back into the car with, Sally was still pointing to Jim's shoe and still making comments. She gave her sister a poke, 'Naughty girl,'

Janey started to cry. 'Be quiet both of you,' we called back in unison.

Moving off Jim took my hand putting it on his knee, 'We'll head for Abercorn on the Northern Rhodesian border,' he said looking at me closely, he knew I was keen to visit Abercorn. I squeezed his knee in approval.

'There is something in my shorts.'

'Really?' I quipped.

'I am being bitten he replied giving me cheeky, quizzical look.

Feeling it could perhaps be a red ant we sprayed the car and shot a little up the leg of his shorts, they can be quite vicious, a bite was the last thing we wanted! Sally was as vocal as ever, 'Let mummy kill it daddy.' Daddy raised his eyebrows!

Mid-morning we stopped beneath a huge shady tree alongside the road for a drink and the girls had a short doze. In all, they were very good and had travelled well. On our way again. We passed through Sumbawanga, a remote station and somewhat inaccessible. There were superb views of the forest clad hills, above the Rukwa trough to the east, and the grassy uplands to the west, the climate was delightful. We called at a small Indian douka to buy cold bottled drinks for ourselves and the children, we all had Coca Cola, despite Charles' highly vocal predictions of the dire consequences of such lax behaviour.

The Citroen was indeed very comfortable, living up to all the advertising 'blurb' which had sold it to us in the first place. Its suspension carried us with a balloon effect, over corrugations, bumps and rocks with an elegant ease. I remember what had really appealed to us in the Citroen advertisement were the four red balloons at each corner of the car. It made you 'feel' the comfort experience, particularly after being on the receiving end of the battering delivered by a Land Rover travelling over African roads! One of course was a work horse and would tackle any terrain, the other a luxury car which still held its own in the bush and on the many rough roads over which we had to travel. We had nothing but praise for our 'Safari.'

It was hot as we drove into Abercorn in the early afternoon, the children had been good, Sally taught Janey one or two new words, we stopped only once to 'spend pennies' two little dolls holding hands taking a path into the bush 'Like grown ups,' Sally said, insisting they go alone. We of course followed a little way behind, just to make sure. It was very funny to see Sally trying her best to help Janey who persisted in falling over at each attempt to haul down her pants. I left them to it. 'They can't manage it alone, we shall be here all day,' Jim said going over to their aid. 'I'm coming' he called, bending over double whilst running towards them. There were squeals of delight as he gave them a kiss, tucked one under each arm and carried them back to the car. We were seated in the car ready to go. As always he took my hand, placed it on his knee, patted my cheek, then off we drove in the direction of Abercorn. We arrived in full voice to the strains of 'Doggy in the window,' the 'in' song with the children at the time. We joined in heartily, mainly in an effort to distance ourselves from the cry of 'Are we nearly there,' or 'We are hungry can we have an ice cream when we get to the hotel?' This had been pretty repetitive and we were beginning to fray a little. Our cry for help had been, 'What shall we sing girls,' we often sang in the car to help things along a little.

Our choice of hotel was almost instant, we would stay at the Abercorn Hotel. It was old charming and colonial, the host and hostess were English. We were given a delightful room with a huge double bed, a single bed for Sally and a cot was installed for Janey. The porter carried our suitcases to the room. Tea, scones and fruit cake were set out for us on the veranda while we washed and tidied up a little. The girls ate ice cream! Both the hotel and its long flagged veranda were dripping in lush green creepers, fresh cool and well watered, small pools of water had settled into small shallow hollows in the flags, it had only recently been watered, the smell of wet earth, plants and blossom was enchanting. Our bedroom looked out onto a rectangle of Kikuyu grass and flower beds, in the middle of this water appeared from seemingly nowhere, running over stone steps into a round rocky pond, fish darted and jumped, the gold of their bodies glistened in the sunlight. We made a mental note to keep an eye on the children, water was like a magnet to them There were palm trees, tropical bushes and plants of all kinds. We found the place irresistible, everything invited us into its hospitable comfort. We would enjoy ourselves immensely here.

191

The hotel was quite central to the few shops in Abercorn all of which were well stocked. It was here with unbounded excitement we bought our first gramophone, a forty five record of Ella Fitzgerald, a record of Billy Daniels (the jazz and blues pianist) and Club Italiano, a splendid record for dancing to. We bought books and paints for the children and a box of paints for Liz. It was our intention to visit her at school on our way through Mbeya. After Mbeya our next stop was Iringa, and our final destination. The children were excited, and delighted with their presents, 'Please, can I carry my book mummy?' poor little Sally she was stumbling along, just able to carry herself. I gave her the book, it was not long before she gave it back to me hanging onto my hand as though her life depended on it. Such little legs to be trotting along these stony roads. Jim had Janey on his shoulders, 'Please daddy carry me now, I'se tired,' I took Janey from him, he hauled Sally onto his shoulders and we staggered, parcels and all, to the hotel, where the porter on seeing our plight rushed over to help.

I remember so well how tasty and wholesome the hotel food was. It was here the children were first introduced to peanut butter sandwiches which they ate with great relish, and have never touched since! 'But you liked them in Abercorn' I would insist. 'We don't like them now,' Sally answered for both herself and her sister. After the children had finished supper, we tucked them up and they fell asleep instantly. Returning to the dining room we enjoyed a relaxed meal of soup, fresh lake fish, baked Alaska, fruit and cheese and biscuits with a bottle of chilled South African KWV. We took it in turn to check the children. As always we wandered onto the veranda to take coffee, we had an accompanying liquor to celebrate the purchase of our little music maker.

Tunduma our next stop was not far away, it was on the border of Tanganyika, Rhodesia and Nyasaland. It was time to relax a little now. Our bedroom had a balcony, 'Shall we try the gramophone, Ella soft and low,' Jim suggested, carrying it out of the bedroom, we were both dying to hear it. 'Yes, but for goodness sake we must not wake the children,' So, we played our Ella record very softly and we danced on the tiny little balcony of our bedroom in the 'Abercorn Hotel.' Who could want for more? It was a little bit of heaven, we loved each other, we were in love with life, which to us was one and the same. I decided the years had only added to Jim's already abundant charm and magnetism, this big man with his pantherine quality and enigmatic smile filled every component of my heart. It was with great reluctance we left this quaint little place the next day, 'Farewell Abercorn, thank you for the memorable and romantic sojourn.'

Liz, Jean, Sally, Jim and Janey on leave in the Uk for Christmas

Jim and Jean, Queen's Arms in Bosley

Jim and Jean going
to a party 1956

Jane, Liz and
Sally, our
three girls

Jim aged 21

Sally, Jim, Liz and
Jean, Dar-es-Salaam

Harrison our
cook, Nyasaland

Ferry – Tete
Mozambique

Carriers with
buffalo head in camp

Jim- Buffalo 'bag'
in Camp,
Chikwawa, 1956

The Camp

Jim the first time he
gets into the boat –
will it or won't it?

Jim and Jean on the
road to Lake Nyasa

Johnny Mbegalo our
cook in Tanganyika

Jock and Jim

Fishing in our home
made boat 'Debbie'

Liwonde ferry

Jean off round 'Namisu' estate in need of guinea fowl for supper

Jim hand rearing a bush buck

Carriers resting in our camp – Chikwawa

An old workhorse –
the Landrover
which never
let us down

'Old Jock'
enjoying a
whisky

Jean and Jane

Carol, Jean and
Jim – Chirundu,
Zimbabwe

Jim and Jean –
Paraguay

Carol, Jean and
Graham Chirundu –
Zimbabwe

Ken and Jim
'Ndata' Malawi,
Nyasalnd

Lions in
N'gorogoro
Tanganyika

Jim sitting on
veranda steps –
Dar-es-Salaam

Jim tying Jane's
shoe,
Tangnayika

Namisu House

Ken and Bev

Making a boat at
Lake Nyasa

Jim, Jean and new
arrival Sally,
Nyasland 1957

A weekend in
the bush –
puncture

Above and below: The Chunga Camp in Zambia

Geoffrey in
Namisu

Old Jock out
on a hunt

Jean, Shirley and
Geoffrey,
Dar-es-Salaam

Market day at
Makuka,
January 1952

Liwonde
Ferry

On safari,
Tanganyika

Jim, Jean and Graham – Banks of the Zambezi

Another time, another picnic, Carol, Jean and Jim – Zambezi Valley

CHAPTER EIGHTEEN

Southern Comfort

'Hoi, move away from the doors you two.' I knew I had locked them, but even so I could not control the wave of apprehension which snaked through me.

'May we have a sweetie daddy?' Sally asked putting her hands on his face in order to turn his head and look him in the eye.

'For Heavens sake Sally that is very dangerous.' I gave her a few jelly babies. 'Those are for you both.'

Janey was fast becoming vocal with more words and less cooing, she was well able to register displeasure if she felt life was treating her unfairly! Our journey to Tunduma was good, these big placid countries were not difficult to pass through we loved this sunlit lovely land of flat topped acacias, bush, scrub and distant lavender blue hills. As we drove along, many small bush paths became visible leading to scattered villages where the children shrieked at play and women were bent double, with babies on their backs, hoeing and pounding maize, men sat lazily drinking chibuku in the shade. We made good time, it was still light when we reached the Tunduma Hotel.

We were greeted by a huge outlandishly dressed lady of indeterminate age, a retired doctor who had worked for many years in the country, finally choosing to retire and live the rest of her life out in Tanganyika. Surrounded by dogs and a monkey, which adeptly leapt from the back of one dog to another, she was a doyen of an aging stage post on the borders of three countries all itching for independence.

It was quaint and had a sad charm; everything screamed 'I am in need of repair.' Pink, blue and mauve 'lavatory' flowers were everywhere, so called as they were used extensively to cover a variety of drains, a very prolific flower, they ran riot. Poincettia, plumbago and lantana struggled to grow in the dry parched sand of this border post where water was in short supply. The bedrooms were basic and clean bath water from a rusty Tanganyika boiler outside forced its way through pipes which clanged, through taps which spluttered, into a bath stained by years of rust coloured water. More ochre liquid added another coat to its already pitted surface as we prepared to wash off dust from four sticky, salty bodies.

Before supper we walked the children round the garden, we found a fish pond and a huge cage containing birds of all varieties singing, screeching, squawking and flying frantically from perch to perch, tiny birds of all colours. A little further down the path we came to a prolific vegetable garden, suprisingly it had a tiny stream running through it. To the side there were citrus trees, avocado, guava trees, passion fruit and bushes of Chinese guavas. It was dusk when we turned heel and headed back to the hotel, the crickets chirruping and frogs croaking to let us know it was their time to be heard, the bush was crowding in. From the distance the cackle of a hyena echoed over the waves of a fast falling night. Lights from the hotel veranda lit up an African worker shuffling by clad in khaki shorts and a soiled, frayed coloured shirt, his feet were bare, his heels cracked. No doubt he was a labourer making his way back to the village, to his wife, or to his parents hut, tired hungry, content to greet the end of the day.

Sitting at a table by the window, we were able to look out through the open windows into sparkling Heavens and to watch the comings and goings of waiters as they walked to and fro, from kitchen to dining room, making comments and laughing heartily as they passed each other. Sometimes the talk would be of work, or there may be comments of a recent visit to the market. More often than not it was over some girl hiding shyly in the bushes. Farmers from nearby estates wandered from the bar into the dining room, always a good sign, farmers liked to eat and they enjoyed good food. Everyone appeared to know everyone else and the air of bonhomie was tangible. It occurred to me that there were far fewer remittance men in Tanganyika than there were in either Nyasaland or Kenya, young men who by their feckless and promiscuous lifestyles were encouraged to live overseas by families tired of being disgraced. They were given an extremely generous allowance and virtually told to keep out of the way.

Our supper was chicken soup, chicken and mushroom pie with fresh fruit salad to follow, nicely served and satisfying. Afterwards we put the girls to bed and popped down to drink coffee and liqueur in the lounge. We found ourselves included in the conversations of local planters, two were tobacco farmers. It was interesting, they prised a lot of useful information from Jim. Deciding it was time for bed (they were obviously intending to make a night of it) we said goodnight, expressed our best wishes for the coming season, then made our way to the bedroom. The children were fast asleep, together we said sotto voce, 'I love you,' and after a goodnight kiss, we slept.

Breakfast the next morning consisted of paw paw, toast and marmalade with freshly ground coffee. After collecting a packed lunch from reception, we piled into the car and set off for Mbeya, my hand wandered to a brown knee nearby.

How would the planters be feeling this morning? It was pretty certain they would all have sore heads. Driving along in the heat we passed many small villages, the sun was beginning to burn in a cloudless sky, people sat lethargically beneath mango trees, which threw down dense circles of shade, tethered goats bleated pathetically nearby. At the side of the road lay grey boulders of differing sizes shiny with use, all displayed assorted wares of whatever fruit or vegetable was in season at the time, almost always there were tomatoes, binongwe (spinach), and peanuts; green, ripe, shelled or unshelled. In season maize cobs by the thousand were for sale, their outer leaves and empty cobs littered the roads. Children at the roadside played, pulling along little homemade toys made from twisted wire, they called and waved. We waved back and they chased the car. 'Huyu mummy, see daddy.' Grazing in the bush nearby Sally had spotted a small herd of impala, the first game we had seen since leaving Kibondo, spoor had been in evidence for much of the way, at this time of day the animals had walked further into the bush towards water. There were snakes sunning themselves, slithering off into the bush as they became aware of vibrations from the car wheels.

This particular stretch of road was littered with termite mounds, shade trees stood around in the dry earth waiting for imminent rains, the heat was building up towards a thunderous downpour, the rains would soon be upon us, and with them the sweetest most pungent smell of all as moisture from the skies hit the hot build up of dry season sand, this is something remembered by everyone who has lived in Africa. Throughout the seasons the earth awakens dramatically to a new dawn. Jim loved the dry season, hunting and our safaris, we both did, but there is something so unbelievably intoxicating about this sweet, wet smell rising from a dry parched earth. The experience never leaves you, it hangs about in your psyche, it is one of a thousand reasons for returning to Africa.

A wild fig tree leaning over the road threw out a patch of deep shade we decided to stop as it was lunch time to eat our boiled eggs and sandwiches. I was pleased we had asked for a flask of coffee at Tunduma. Guinea fowl honked nearby, doves cooed the cicadas 'chittered' in the heat, our life in Africa was, no matter how you looked at it, one long romantic adventure.

197

'What time do you think we shall arrive in Mbeya?'

'3.30 perhaps 4 p.m. I imagine,' came Jim's reply. This would be fine, we were looking forward to seeing Liz, though unable to stay long it was almost half term and she would be with us again soon.

We had been booked into the Iringa Hotel, an East African Railways establishment. They were always good and very popular, the Department of Agriculture had reserved our accommodation. The house allocated to us was presently occupied by the District Magistrate, he was leaving for the U.K. very soon. Also, we must wait for our baggage to arrive from Kibondo. Liz stood at the top of the school drive waiting for us to arrive, we had tea on the lawn and she played games with Sally and Janey. She was very pleased with her paints and very excited at how much nearer school would be to home, when living in Iringa. When the time came to leave we 'prised' the children away, there were kisses all round. 'See you soon love,' we waved until she was out of sight then continued on to the end of the journey.

A Thumbnail Sketch of Seven Years in Iringa

Iringa was a town at the top of an escarpment 5,380 ft above sea level. The views were wide and breathtaking, looking down onto the Ruaha valley, huge boabab trees stood sentry to this kingdom of surreal grandeur where the searing heat of the dry season defied belief, blood boiling heat was how I could best describe it. Even so, we learned to love the valley. The main tribe, in the area were the Hehe, of Bantu stock. The surrounds of this great escarpment consisted of rain forest, miombo and woodland areas, there were tea estates in Mufindi, tobacco, pyrethrum, coffee and livestock in the Dabaga area. Arriving in Iringa was exciting. The streets were lined with jacaranda and flamboyant trees, the main shops were owned mainly by Greeks or Indians, they were all well stocked, colourful and welcoming. We felt we had two worlds in our hands, the bush and safaris at the bottom of the escarpment, and everything we needed at the top. The avenues of colonial bungalows all bore the names of trees.

It was decided to head straight for the post office, I had written a letter to my mother since leaving Kibondo, her sister had died. I felt she needed letters to give her some support. Jim and the girls sat in the car, I popped into the post office to buy a stamp and put the letter in the post box. No sooner had I got back into the car, than there was the most horrendous, bump, crunch, followed by the sound of breaking glass.

'Oh hell no,' exploded Jim.

I leapt out of the car and raced to the back. The back light was broken, I was absolutely incensed, frantic with anger and devastated by the thought of our lovely new car being damaged. 'My God,' I spat at the man, wagging my finger. 'We have travelled all the way from the Western Province with no problems, and you damn well run into the back of our car, why, can't you see?' I felt steam was jetting out of my ears such was my anger. 'You will of course have to foot the bill for this,' I said with blind fury.

In the desperation of the moment my whole psyche was convinced that it could never be repaired. 'Yes, I will pay,' said the man whose name we later discovered was Robello, a Goan tobacco farmer. Jim joined in 'The car will have to go to Dar-es-Salaam, I shall hold you responsible for any expenses incurred.' I could see he was inwardly seething, we were both feeling pretty despondent at this turn of events. The next morning we rung Mithani. We did not have to go to Dar as we had feared, Mithani sent the spare part, tools and instructions needed to carry out the car repair. They were put on the next plane coming to Iringa, Jim fixed it; making a point of returning the tools by air immediately the job was done. We were later told that Rebello, a vain man his grey hair dyed black, was as blind as a bat without his spectacles which he rarely wore, they interfered with his 'pulling' of the girls! Getting him to pay for the repair was like getting blood out of a stone. I had taken an instant dislike to him and it remained.

On our arrival at the Iringa Hotel we were met by Fred Barrett who was working on the tobacco project in the area. By this time we were not at our best and the children were weepy. I have no doubt that, at first glance, he wondered who on earth he had been presented with. He understood perfectly after a description of the sequence of events since our brief arrival in the town. He knew Robello well, apparently he was prone to disfiguring vehicles belonging to other people, also he was not 'au fait' with the word insurance.

On the negative side this was not a good introduction to Iringa. On the positive side, things did change and it was never the bad omen we had feared. We were to remain here for the next seven years. It was a delightful posting. There were two hotels, the Iringa Hotel and the White Horse Hotel, a library, a church and a very good hospital complete with small operating theatre and an English doctor. There was a nursery school, primary school and a secondary school for both boys and girls, they all had European teachers.

Mr Shivji was the town auctioneer, his wife (Mrs Shivji) made the most scrumptious samosas to order. We had a corner paper shop owned by Bashkar Patel, a butcher, a German chemist, two Banks; Standard and Barclays. The were many shops of all kinds, Gerry Lorandos (a Greek) sold groceries, the Iringa Stores belonged to an Indian mainly they sold Indian groceries and goods. On the opposite corner was a garage belonging to an Indian, whose name I cannot recall. Another corner shop was the Tanganyika Farmers' Coop, T.F.C, they sold all things from blankets to fertilizers and hammers to screws, in short, everything a farmer needed. | It had a European manager. Tucked round the back in one of the side streets was a repair garage owned by Garas, the Greek, his son often came into the bush with us, he eventually became an airline pilot with Olympic Airways, there was a baker's shop alongside. On the perimeter of the township Iringa had a club, where we played golf, tennis and attended dances. Burns night do's, Christmas parties, children' parties; everything was held here. If not in our home!!

Our accommodation at the, Iringa Hotel was beyond reproach, the food and service were excellent, the waiters efficient and smart. We slept like logs despite the excitement and trauma of the broken back light on our new car. After breakfast the next day, Jim went to the office to introduce himself, he was briefed and given leave to familiarize both himself and us with the town. Its layout and amenities, the avenues, and the house which had been allocated to us, we were excited by the posting, it lived up to its reputation seemingly having the best of both worlds.

Rumblings of Independence were in the air, at times we were greeted with scowls and calls of 'Uhuru na kazi,' which turned out to be a contradictory cry. Africans were gathering in groups, there was a slight tension but nothing intimidating. Life went on in its inimitable way, to date nothing had happened to quell the enthusiasm of the inhabitants of Iringa and district, nor had it in any way affected the loyalty and friendliness of the African staff who worked for the Europeans. We were in the hotel for three weeks. Our luggage arrived, the magistrate, whose name I cannot remember, went on leave. We moved into his nice big but very dirty house The situation was not ideal, nor did we feel sympathetic or drawn towards it.

Jim went off up country with F. Barrett, and was introduced to the tobacco planters – many of whom were Greek Cypriots. He familiarized himself with all the tobacco estates and their workings and he made copious notes as to the improvements he felt would be beneficial to each man. He talked and advised long and hard and was accepted by everyone, he had much to contribute to this huge tobacco area.

We employed a Nyasa house servant/cook. His wife was an ayah to our girls. Their names were Julius and Ruti. In their work they were excellent though Julius sadly was a born liar and relentless in his dishonesty and theft, a great pity but they had to go.

Not liking the location of the present house, we drove around looking for somewhere more simpatico and more to our liking, we eventually found a house which really 'clicked,' we fell in love with it immediately it had great potential and a lovely garden. There was just one snag, it was inhabited. Not to be deterred, the next day Jim went to the Dept. of Housing to ask if there was a possibility of our being allocated the house at some point in the near future should it become vacant. He was told it was presently occupied by the vet who was shortly leaving for the U.K and was due for transfer to another station. We were ecstatic. The vet left the house and we moved in. It was a happy house, a happy home, people were continually popping in for tea, supper, for drinks or just dropping in to see us.

All the men, when they visited us, went 'outside to see Africa', ie., they watered the hollyhocks, which in turn grew to enormous proportions, became brilliantly red and very beautiful they were admired by all unsuspecting persons visiting the house.

Each year there were Christmas parties and usually a big deep frozen, but very succulent American turkey ordered and bought from the local Greek grocer, it was an exciting time almost everyone had an open house. New Year parties, Birthday parties and general get togethers were held in most homes. We played 'Club Italiano' on our battery operated gramophone, dancing and laughing well into the star spangled night. There were many people in the neighbouring houses, friendly people who laughed a lot and we had wonderful times together.

Despite all the activity we had our 'quiet times,' they were made quite clear to our friends it was something we insisted upon and was always respected. Our life was heaven, passion surfacing quickly made us sing, made us laugh and it made our hearts light and full of joy, this was the way we were. Our friends knew accepted and understood; at times they smiled and shook there heads. Sometimes on Sunday we were invited to lunch at the Boddy's estate, they farmed in Dabaga. Bill was the brother of Ken our old friend from past times in Nyasaland. Bill's wife, Babs, was a volatile Scot. She was a likeable no nonsense person, and extremely able. Both Bill and Babs were very active, very strong, very big and swore like troopers. The volume of food produced for Sunday lunch made the table groan as it became overburdened with dish after dish of roasts, sauces, salads, vegetables, potatoes roast, potatoes mashed, potatoes in salad, sweet potatoes (cooked in the traditional South African way), the list goes on, servants flew in every direction. The puddings were many and varied, rich, highly calorific and delicious and of course there was fruit. Who could provide the best, biggest and most talked about spread on their table at Sunday lunchtime, seemed to be the ultimate challenge of each estate wife in the area. Babs adored Bill and she would fight tooth and nail for him though he himself was no shrinking violet.

During the war he had been a rear gunner, twelve times he had been taken prisoner and twelve times he had escaped. A local Sheik once accused Bill of pilfering his battery. Babs took great offence and flew into a furious rage slapped the accuser across his face, taking off part of his beard with her ring. 'Bastard,' she cried, not once but many times, 'You lie'. These wild stories were the norm in those days as many people tended to drink heavily, stories of their exploits were at times sad but at other times hilarious. I remember Geoff and Gypsy, who at the time were well into their 'cups', taking off from the White Horse Hotel, in a cloud of dust. A little farther down the road Gypsy felt she wanted to pee, Geoff braked and she went behind the Land Rover, having done what she had got out to do to she called, 'Okay', Geoff started the engine, put it in reverse gear and promptly ran over her, there was a terrible 'to do', fortunately the only damage was a broken arm and a grazed brow. 'You bloody nearly killed me darling.' was all she said nursing her broken arm as they sped back to Iringa hospital. After treatment and another swift whiskey and soda for the road they went on their way, back to the farm no one glimpsed them until the following week. The 'White Horse 'hotel was a meeting place each Friday from up country visitors and farmers.

Joe de Britto managed the tiny airport and airstrip of Iringa, he had planted many trees in the area; they had made this point of entry to the southern highlands most attractive and something to be proud of. For this call beyond duty, he had been awarded the MBE. Often he would pop into the 'White Horse,' for mid-morning coffee only to be radioed back to the airport because elephant were on the runway. It happened in those days! Affairs were rife and steamy, some played out openly others were more discreet. Burn's night at the Iringa Club was always a revelation, furtive glances, dodgy hand moves, couples sidling out, slinking back, stealing kisses with rapt faces, fondling, billing and cooing.

Tanganyika became Independent in 1961 and with its independence expatriates began to leave, teachers, doctors and agriculturists. Rumours were beginning to abound the hospitals, though still good, were not as efficient and staff were in short supply. The standard of education dropped enormously. Liz was the first of our girls to be sent to boarding school in England. Slowly everything began to change.

The Spell of Pawaga

Weekends were often spent on safari in the Pawaga flats. Here we were in the wild, sleeping under the stars of the African night alongside a crackling camp fire. Safari life takes you away from the real world and it's troubles, you become drunk on the spirit of the wilderness. We always camped beneath the same huge wild fig tree with a mushroom shaped crown almost reaching to the ground; its dense foliage gave relief from the heat of the flats. In the deep shade beneath this huge umbrella Jim parked the Land Rover. The river was nearby, we made liberal use of its waters. There were usually eight to ten of us on these safaris, including the children who revelled in safari life, spending a large part of the day playing extraordinary games, testing their imagination to it's farthest reaches. In the evening, with Jim at the wheel, they loved to tear over the flats in the Land Rover, screeching with delight as we chased zebra and wildebeest into the sunset, watching giraffe loping against the brilliance of the skyline. WE shot guinea fowl for food and the children 'guarded' them in the back, when darkness fell we made our way back to camp, hyena in the distance whooped cackled and whined, elephant and buffalo droppings littered the ground. In camp lamps were lit and hooked onto low hanging branches, adding further shadows to those already cast by the camp fire, our chairs etched in black stood around the leaping flames. Under a red glow from the fire, succulent meat lay roasting in a sealed tin beneath the ground sandwiched between embers placed below and the heat from the fire above, potatoes baking slowly on the perimeter were thrown into the flames a little later, for anyone who liked the outside crisp and black. Beneath the tree in the shade a couple of crates of 'Tusker' beer, sometimes we put a crate into the river to keep it cool. Sitting watching the shooting stars brilliant in the southern sky. 'This is the life,' we all agreed.

The following day the men would hunt while we remained behind to clear and organize the camp, keep an eye on the children, prepare for any game meat they may return with. Our children played with ant lions, they make tiny funnels in the soft sand lying in wait and out of sight just beneath the base of the funnel, any unwary ant having the misfortune to fall into the trap is rapidly devoured. The girls dropped in a few grains of sand, grabbing the little 'creature,' their name for them, as it came to the surface, at the end of the game counting to see who had caught the most. The girls had learnt to speak Swahili very quickly, Janey knew more Swahli than English. There were times when tribesmen of the Maasai wandered by and I never ceased to be amazed at their resting position, they always stood on one leg with the other leg wrapped around a long stick when they stopped to talk, the sticks were normally carried by herdsmen who used them mainly for walking, resting and tapping in cattle. They stood like this for hours, chatting to the children. They were always aware of any game in the district, and would tell us of their last siting. Early the next morning the men left in search of game, a red headed Scot from Fife, Graham, and a short cocky lad, Tim, whose home was in Devon. They were under the tutelage of Jim, who was endeavouring to give them an insight into bush life and bush lore, on similar lines to his initial instruction from Jock on his arrival in Nyasaland in 1947.

'Coffee for two love', called Jim as he came through the door. Graham had recently arrived to take up his post with the Dept of Agriculture in Iringa the two had been introduced that morning. He was a great surprise, his sandy hair sticking up short and straight, his face and lips red and sore from excess sun on the boat journey out to Dar-es-Salaam. His Fife accent and its rapid delivery were rather difficult to understand at times, in 1964 our family was extended, he became a member almost immediately. In 1965 his fiancee came to Tanganyika on holiday, our family then numbered seven, and have done to this day. They married and had two boys and a girl. Tim the cheeky lad from Devon arrived later he had to be repressed somewhat and encouraged to conform, he also became very close to us, meeting his wife-to-be, in Iringa. We all had so many laughs and much fun.

★★★

It was very hot in Pawaga, the men had left in a flurry of dust just as the sun was beginning to rise. We lay around in our camp beds yawning and stretching for a short time as we watched the sun come up painting the surrounding bush in brilliant pink and gold, from the distance a ground hornbill gave a haunting deep bass call, the children slept on. 'I think we had better move Carol, if the men are lucky they may find game nearby.' I muttered quietly hoping not to waken the children. One never knew how long a hunt would be, it could be anything from one hour to the whole day, I did know they would be hungry when they returned to camp. I also knew from past experience that there would be quite a lot of work to do if they were successful in their hunt.

It was mid-afternoon when the men arrived back streaked with dust and sweat and very hungry, they had been lucky they came back with an impala, gutted where it had been shot the innards left for predators. There were also three guinea fowl to be prepared for supper. We cooked them bacon, sausage and eggs while they tended to their sticky, dusty bodies in the nearby river, the children danced around in great excitement.

'Daddy can we go into the bush to see the game later?' They loved to race over the flats on a game drive before they went to bed.

'Yes, we have to cut and hang the impala first,' Jim replied twirling their curls with his finger.

'Can we help, mummy can we help.'

'Yes, if daddy agrees, you will also have to ask Graham and Tim.'

I knew they would give them little jobs to do, usually it was fetching and carrying, they loved to watch, help and ask a million questions. The smell of cooking breakfast hung mouth-wateringly on the air we washed and cooked some impala liver to add to the bacon and sausage. Carol set out the little camp table and their food was put onto warm tin plates, toast we made over the camp fire. They tucked in with lip smacking enjoyment accompanied by over the top appreciative comments, then it was smoky coffee for all. Talk at the moment was of hanging the impala, we must leave for home the next day, which was the last thing we wanted to do. Another night in the bush was always a bonus. Eventually salted and roped the impala was then hung in the tree. We took the children out over the plains for an evening drive, there were herds of zebra idly grazing, looking up inquisitive at our approach, and giraffe, some with their heads reaching up from long slender necks, into the tops of nearby thorn bushes, others loping off across the plain. Everything had been left ready for our evening meal, meat had been left to cook together with potatoes and vegetables in a tin beneath the fire, it made life a little easier on our return. Our supper was eaten under the stars, a gentle breeze had cooled down the hot air of day, round and about us in the bush the animals settled to their nightly roaming; it was a tasty meal, washed down with a beer. We had enjoyed yet another romantic interlude. Unanimously we decided an early night would be in order. Graham and Carol had their beds around the camp fire, Graham lay discussing the stars for some time. The children were fast asleep in the back of the Land Rover, we had dozed off. Suddenly I heard this dreadful crunching noise behind me, a hyena had smelled the meat, crept up and was attacking the impala head, it unsettled us for a while, we stoked the fire sent the hyena scuttling, hauled the head a little higher up the tree and went to sleep again. The next morning we ate toast, tided the camp sight, packed our loads the impala and the children then reluctantly made our way back home. How we loved the bush!

Our home was used for everything by almost everyone, skinning, cutting up, salting, cleaning and stretching the hides. Everything went on at the back of the house, cars were repaired and fiddled with, a boat was made from 5 gallon paraffin drums (debes) cut open, hammered out and soldered. We had a shed for the chickens, housed next door to a smaller wooden shed made for our pet dik dik. Half of the garage became home to a donkey. Janey had wanted a donkey. Jim and Graham went to Ifwaga one Sunday morning, to a mission where the white fathers kept beer for Sunday visitors. They bought a donkey from the mission but they had great difficulty getting the animal over the river, and brought it home in the back of the Land Rover. On this particular Sunday the house was regaled with every member of the Dept of Agriculture, the office closed. Everyone headed for our home; bodies were draped over every chair. They had come to welcome the donkey!

From morning coffee to afternoon tea, there had to be a large supply of sandwiches and a chocolate cake. I thanked the Lord for my 'all in one mix' (put-it-all-in, whip-it-all-up, cook it in the oven). Perfection. This was a new concept in 1961, a miracle for me and for Grevas, the house servant and general factotum. Grevas and Diana, the ayah, worked well together until the day Grevas took to drink and stayed with it. From that day we upgraded Johnny Mbegalo from the garden to the kitchen, where he remained with us a loyal and true member of the household until we left Tanazania. Despite all of this it was a harmonious life and each day was a bonus. Jim and I were bound at the hip, our home was peaceful and contented and this must have been the reason for people descending upon us in droves. We had music, laughter and love at all hours of the day and night.

A hole in the hedge led us to the doctor's house. It was well used. Poor Ian was called over at all hours. For example, one day Janey had been riding her bike and the front wheel had hit a stone, over the handle bars she went, and the metal flag stick on the handle bars pierced the roof of her mouth. What would we have done without Ian! There was never a dull moment; on the same afternoon, we came upon a cobra slithering up the back steps of the house towards the bedrooms.

There were also sad times. I had a dear little dog, a Pekinese, Susie Wong, she was always at my heel. We went for walks, I took her with me when I went to meet the girls from school, she stood in the kitchen with me when I was baking and she waited out side the bedroom door for me each morning. She was a faithful little dog with no vices and I was very fond of her. Each night we took her outside and walked her round the garden before we went to bed. One night I called her but no Susie Wong appeared. She had slipped out, we called, called and called again. Greyfus found her, she was on the road not quite dead. We brought her into the house and Jim tried hard to keep her alive. She did not stand a chance. I was desperate and so upset aas she had been attacked by a particularly vicious pack of dogs belonging to a Greek. This had happened to others in the past. The man in question had been warned and told to fasten his dogs up at night but ignored the warnings. I have never seen Jim so angry, he took his gun and went after the dogs.

A few people popped over for drinks one evening, this was always a very popular idea. Johnny cut up lots of fruit which we put into a huge bowl poured in half a bottle of brandy and it was left to soak for the day with other ingredients added in the late afternoon. A friend living next door who was quite advanced in her pregnancy decided just to eat the fruit; she was very poorly indeed. It was quite a party, is it any wonder the hollyhocks below the veranda grew with such vigour and colour! The downside to all this was when one poor fellow got into his car when it was time to leave and it refused to start. Thieves had taken the battery. We had not heard them; our chatter and the fact that we were obviously enjoying the evening made us oblivious to the goings on outside and had given them the opportunity they were waiting for. This sort of thing was happening more and more often, thieves took advantage of these situations.

Wonderful dances were held at the Greek Club. We played tennis at the Iringa Club, had drinks at the bar and became involved with all the local chit chat. On our way home from these events we often pondered on the possibility of a robbery in our absence! On a long weekend there was always someone who wanted to go into the bush on a hunting safari. Sometimes Jim and Graham would go off to the Bohoro flats alone. On these occasions I stayed at home with the children. I usually made them a sweetie jar of mince and bean curry. The food box contents were mainly bacon, sausage, eggs, bread and beans, almost always Johnny went with them to tend to the camp and to do the cooking.

Hunting was good in this area there were always tales to tell on their arrival home. At one point Graham said there were so many flies on his gun barrel he could not see his target and was unable to take a shot. He did however manage to bag a zebra a little later, a great shot and a great trophy. The skins, as always, were salted and stretched at home then sent to Nairobi to be cured and softened. Trophy heads also went to be cured and cleaned in Nairobi.

The Bohoro flats were alive with mosquitoes. It was not a good area and certainly not a place for the children. An Indian, whose name I cannot remember, was keen to buy the Citroen, offering us almost the price we had paid for it. We were not quite sure what to do, however we came to the conclusion, 'Why not sell?' Jim rung Mithani in Dar, who sent us up a catalogue. We chose and ordered a Citroen saloon in light yellow ochre from him. It arrived in a surprisingly short space of time. We collected the car and drove it up from Dar-es-Salaam, sadly we parted with our old 'Blue treasure'.

Jim with the help of friends made a boat, they named her 'Debbie,' she was taken to be christened in the river which ran through the Seatondale Research station at the bottom of the escarpment. This flat bottomed boat was made from beaten out five gallon paraffin tins, which were welded and bent to shape. It was pushed into the water with an unsuspecting David (a friend and neighbour), sitting with oars over his knee confidently awaiting events to take place. To say he looked a little startled when the boat promptly started to sink is an understatement, in fact he became more then a little panicky. We all moved pretty quickly, it was necessary for us to haul both David and the boat out of the water as the river was fast flowing and there was no time to spare. It was quite a feat. We laughed heartily afterwards - in fact we were hysterical. With the help of a nervous, dripping but sporty partner, we heaved it back onto the roof of the Land Rover and returned, a little deflated to the house. Undeterred, Jim acquired more tins and made outriggers, after this addition it worked like a charm and we always used 'Debbie' when we went fishing, in fact everyone used her. Why the name you wonder! A debe was a five gallon paraffin tin, many of which were used to make her.

Our life in those days consisted of tackling the most extraordinary projects and everyone got involved, it was an interest and a challenge and we all loved it. Each day we took our prophylactics but there was a day when Jim came home from the office looking simply dreadful, almost unable to lift his head. He was convinced it was going to burst and he was in a great deal of pain and felt very ill indeed. Wasting no time I called Ian Clarke, our hospital doctor, conveniently he lived next door (equally convenient was the hole in the hedge through which I frantically raced). He came immediately and diagnosed cerebral malaria. Tests proved him right. The doctor put Jim straight into his car and drove to the hospital, telling me to follow with pyjamas and anything I felt he might need. I left the children with Diana. Scared out of my wits, I was praying, 'Please God don't let it be cerebral malaria,' he was put into a quiet darkened room and when he had settled I was sent home. Ian gave him injections and stayed by his bedside for the whole of the day and that night, watching, injecting, taking his temperature and generally observing his condition. I was frantic with worry. Slowly Jim responded to treatment and the pain in his head receded. It took him a long time, despite rest, a great deal of medical attention and much fuss, to recuperate, and to get back on form. Cerebral malaria is extremely dangerous and its effects can be devastating and long term. After this we were even more careful, we used spray and mosquito nets, both at home and on safari.

The time had come for Carol to go back to Scotland and to teaching; her holiday was over. We missed her. Graham returned to normal and Jim was now quite well and full of life again. Sally and Janey had their birthday parties, I provided the food and goodies whilst Jim and Graham organized games for excited children. When it was all over, Graham left for his flat and cooked us a meal, it was the best sweet and sour pork we had ever tasted. We were lucky having Diana to look after the children, she was clean, efficient and she was strict, she insisted they behaved well and were obedient. This was vital as there were so many hidden dangers.

Our visits to Pawaga were regular. One weekend Jim shot a zebra, on another weekend a wildebeest. There were always guinea fowl for the camp pot. Sometimes we took evening trips into the bush in an open Land Rover, our children and others stood up in the back holding on to the frame everyone yelled, 'Duck,' at the sight of low branches ahead, wending our way through the bush was exhilarating, almost always we had a spectacular game drive. The most magnificent sight on our evening drives were the giraffe families, moving with deceptive speed in graceful slow motion through the thorn scrub. Babies ran alongside their mothers, legs a wobble, huge long necks swaying forwards then backwards in an hypnotic rhythm which was synchronized to their lope. Legs straddled wide, their long muscular necks reached down from huge shoulders above, small heads thrust forward to drink from the river. Those seemingly endless necks enabled them to reach high into the tops of acacia trees to nibble tasty green leaves and new growth, long muscular tongues, immune to thorns, pulled away fresh tender shoots. Necks were also used in the mating season; neck slapping echoed for great distances. Due to their reticulated pattern, these tall, graceful animals became almost invisible in the dappled, harmonizing colours of the vast areas of bush. The whole scene created the ambience of some exotic ballet

Carcasses hanging in the camp tree attracted the hyena – mocking wails and fiendish laughter rent the night and rose into the still hot air. At night their eyes gleamed as they reflected light from the camp fire as they slowly edged ever closer to the hanging meat. We waved torches, shouted and gave chase and they slunk away, usually for only a short time then whining they crept back to the direction of the smell, jaws slavering. Through the night elephant walked quietly by, gently placing huge feet down in almost total silence. Ghost-like, they have the ability to dissolve behind the smallest bush, as though they had never been. They have walked through our camp at night and we have been totally unaware of their presence until the next morning when they were given away by huge cracked footprints in the sand, their 'calling card'. They passed through unmolested as we lay on our camp beds beneath the big tree, mosquito nets gently stirred by a shifting breeze.

The Ruaha National Park

From a small office in the centre of Iringa I designed brochures and promoted the Ruaha National Park, a wonderful, wonderful game park full of game and virtually unspoilt. It was a convenient and interesting job and not too tying. It allowed me to be at home when the children arrived home from school. Diana collected Janey from the nursery school when necessary, it blended in with our life very well. Jim called in to see me when he was around in the town, I loved to see him walk tall through the door. I was always ready for the arm which crept around my shoulder and his gentle kiss 'Hello.' My love of him welled up inside me, life seemed so perfect, how lucky I was.

At times like this I reflected on our times together at school, the long-legged, mischievous rather disobedient girl with dark unruly hair. My imagination would begin to wander. I was sitting in the cinema again by the side of the tall good-looking boy with grey-green eyes and fair curly hair. I imagined the envy of all the other girls. Despite all their eye-rolling and coy expressions I was the one he had chosen, it was my shoulder his arm had been around. After all the past years I could still feel the thrill of that touch and our close proximity in the dim light of the Odeon. Really the other girls stood no chance. I know that now. Sagittarians and Arians are made for each other, everyone says so. Jim was the Sagittarian. He looked and smelled like no other person could ever look or smell, fresh, clean (and to me, an Arian) he was toe-curlingly sensual, hewn to near perfection from a little bit of Heaven, even now after all these years, entering his office, his shed, or when opening his books our girls comment 'I can smell daddy'.

On our visits to the wild Ruaha we stayed in the rondavels of 'Scottie's,' camp. 'Scottie' was an old timer trying to scratch a living in difficult times. All his money and more had gone into the making of this small camp, it was a struggle and I hoped from my little office, to be able to give it the tourist lift it deserved and needed. One of my duties was to accompany the new African District Commissioner to view the Ruaha National Park in a light aircraft. We flew over beautiful land; standing out in this wilderness were the white rondavels of Scottie's camp which lay beside the writhing Ruaha river. We could see herds of elephant, buffalo, zebra, kudu, impala and sitatunga; some standing, some running in the swamps and over the plains of this vast undulating bush below, it made the heart surge with overwhelming joy. On presenting what I felt were the possibilities of opening this vast swathe of bush as a National Park I was met with little response. Mr Chamshama continually referred to the game as meat. It was a strange occasion full of unexplained foreboding. I was not content, I felt quite convinced that simply nothing would be followed up, another project doomed to failure. I was right. This area in the south, which is so full of potential, is virtually ignored by tourists who are continually drawn like magnets to the beauty of the North. A great pity as there are so many wonderful things to see in this vast unspoilt wilderness of the Ruaha.

We spent much time, and Graham came too, wandering through this vast unspoilt part of the country in the Land Rover, blundering into a number of pretty scary situations. Sitting in camp at night, we flicked our torches backwards and forwards across the river, bright beams lit up the flashing red eyes of crocodiles lying along its banks. During the night hippos grunted, snorted and blew as they came out onto the banks to feed. We lay listening to tufts of grass being uprooted, followed by much noisy munching and muffled grunts. Scottie had planted frangipani poinsettias, bougainvillea, rose and plumbago bushes and lots of colourful zinnias round and about the rondavels so the camp was attractive, exotic and colourful. There were some problems with game, at times they came into camp and ate all his young plants, he kept a strict eye on them. They also played havoc with his paw paw trees which made him very agitated indeed.

How we loved these moonlight nights in distant lonely camps, gazing through mosquito gauzed windows at brilliant clusters of stars shining onto the mysterious bush below. The sound of branches breaking, loud and resonant in the still night air, made one wonder, 'What is out there.' Our beds were pulled together, enfolded in one another's arms we were at one with the night. Could there be a more magical place to love? I don't think so.
Yet, there were exceptions which sprang to my mind as I spoke to myself: 'under the deep still of a star studded sky, when a huge moon hangs in sultry beauty from black velvet heavens, throwing light on a sleeping earth. When the warm breath from an evening breeze plays gently over receptive, sensitive bodies enveloped in peace. Immersed in the shattering silence of magical mystery

which is the African bush'. This is irresistible and powerfully hypnotic. This is the exception.

The next day, Graham and Jim ventured a little way upstream, they pulled the boat onto the sandy shore of an island lying amongst the reeds in the midst of the Ruaha. Intrigued I watched through binoculars from the river bank as they wandered through the reeds in deep conversation not paying attention to their surrounds or indeed to anything in particular. It was rather like watching a silent film, then mouthing something, I think it was 'God Almighty,' I saw them stop rigid in their stride, immediately in front of them two sleeping crocodiles rose high on their legs with their jaws wide open, vicious teeth ready to snap. They had almost walked onto them – it was incredible to watch. I could almost hear the vicious hissing of the crocs as they dashed past them, with no hesitation they sped down to the water with lightning speed. Simultaneously the men turned their heads looked at each other mouthing the words, 'Let's go,' then turning they ran back to the boat and pushed it with great difficulty out into the river. This took rather longer than they had intended, hands and feet reacted strangely in this state of confused haste. With great relief they pushed the boat clear of the sand – neither were very keen on crocs! They paddled off rapidly towards camp. I stood on the bank still observing every move, rapt in fascination at their reaction of shock and amazement to a situation which neither had expected or anticipated.

A little later, over a cup of tea, we talked of the escapade. The children were playing heavily in the sand at 'catching creatures,' (lion ants), they had a school friend with them who seemed to be enjoying herself immensely. Janey, on hearing a little of the adult conversation, berated both Graham and Jim; 'You could have been eaten.' she grumbled. 'Daddy where is your gun? You should always have your gun.' Walking back to Sally and their game, she turned around many times, pointing and wagging her finger at the men in rebuke.

Life was never dull in the Ruaha. Graham came, red-faced and fuming back into camp one morning. He and Liz had taken a leisurely paddle down river wanting to see any game which had wandered down to drink from its banks. Rowing had been rather more difficult than either had imagined and there was an argument as to who was slacking in the rowing stakes. They had drifted further and further away from the camp. Whoever it was, Liz blamed Graham, Graham blamed Liz, we never knew who was really to blame; but the situation was eventually resolved. They came back bedraggled and wet through just in time for breakfast which Scottie's woman, who lived in a village nearby, had prepared and set out for us. Meanwhile the little ones had been fishing on the campsite shore of the river and Sally had caught a fish and was very excited. Jim was in the shower singing 'More,' this was his tune of the moment. He had a soft mellow singing voice, so had his brother Geoffrey, I often thought when looking at these two handsome men and hearing them sing, their future should have been on the silver screen.

We had decided to take an early morning drive as everyone had decided they would like to see elephant. From the camp a dilapidated, heavily tilting bridge had to be maneuvered to enter the reserve on the far side of the river. Jim was at the wheel and Graham sat on the top of the Land Rover gripping the luggage rack, he had a camera around his neck. I sat with Jim, the girls were in the back. Jolting along over these rutted treacherous tracks found over the length and breadth of Africa, it felt as though the whole vehicle would fall apart, surely every nut and bolt holding the thing together would be shaken loose. There were vast quantities of game in the Ruaha National Park. There were impala, eland, greater kudu, water buck, bush buck and zebra not to mention the many herds elephant.

The bush varied, from the riverine areas to sandy, rutted and bouldered ground, dense brush, miombo forest and mopani; rough tracks covered almost the whole area. The children despite having seen many species of game since we left camp had decided there were no elephant.

'Where are all the elephant daddy?' was the continual cry from behind us.

'Around the next corner,' came the inevitable reply, then turning to me. 'There must be elephant soon, the place is supposed to be crawling with them.'

'Elephant, on the right,' yelled Graham from above, camera at the ready.

How right he was. There were elephant to the right, elephant to the left, elephant in front and elephant behind us. A huge herd of matriarchs with their young – and they were not at all pleased to see us. All around us amid clouds of dust, branches cracked and smashed.

'God,' said Jim, 'we are surrounded.'

Not being at all helpful, I put my hands over my eyes. One cow really took exception to us, trunk up ears back she charged,screaming like a banshee from hell, out of the depths of the surrounding bush.

'Hang on Graham,' Jim called through the window, 'hang on everyone, I am heading off to the left through that piece of clear ground' We have never moved so fast in such terrain, only a Land Rover could get us out of the predicament in which we found ourselves. Fortunately Jim had a good sense of direction and seemed to know where he was heading, he was also always cool headed. The female elephant was still following in the near distance, rising dust told us the rest of the herd were in some agitation. On we went, circumstances had whipped us into a high state of tension.

'Surely these elephant have been badly harassed by poachers to be so nervous,' I managed to croak hardly daring to speak. The children were wild with wary excitement. I felt for Graham sitting on top, hanging on for dear life, he was being bounced from one side to the other knuckles white as he gripped the rack.

'Hold on tight Graham' I yelled.

Gradually we drew away from the milling herd, it was with enormous relief we heard Graham call, 'There is the river.'

Peering through the bush, we saw the glint of water ahead of us, as yet it some way in the distance.

'Take any pictures Graham?' Jim called through the window.

'You have got to be bloody joking,' replied a hoarse, shaken voice. The Land Rover rattled on, a battered, bent and due for a coat of paint, victor.

With great relief we re-crossed the ragged splintered old bridge, arriving back on the road which led us into camp.

'That was pretty bloody close Jas.' (Jim) Graham called as he jumped from the top, 'I admire your sense of direction.'

To me he sounded rather shaken and his legs appeared a bit wobbly. I know mine were. The children could not stop talking in the excitement of the moment.

'That was quite unexpected and a mite scarey,' Jim agreed.

Scottie, it seemed, knew of this particular herd. I could never understand why he had not mentioned it to us before we went off into the bush, we would then have been prepared and on the look out. We never came across the herd again, though we did hear of others who had! Jim was not in the habit of hunting elephant, he always felt they were such magnificent beasts so family orientated and sensitive. They were certainly wonderful to watch.

Later that evening we left for Iringa and home. A few minutes after leaving the camp we had a puncture! We all had identical thoughts. With a meaningful look from one to the other, we gave thanks that this had not happened earlier, amongst the angry herd of matriarchs whom we had unwittingly encountered. Arriving home was something of an anti-climax after the excitement of the weekend. Johnny helped with the unloading of our katundu (loads), and put them away in some order. Diana scooped up the children and put them into the bath and their pyjamas. Johnny had roasted a chicken and potatoes served with spinach picked from the garden. Graham ate supper with us, needless to say it was an early night for us all.

During one of our many visits to the Ruaha with friends Alec and Jo, we decided to hire a boat with a small outboard motor from Scottie. It was the dry season and the river was low. Inspired by the surroundings Alec, Jim and I had an urge to meander downstream. It was peaceful and soporific puttering along looking for game walking down to drink. There were lots of impala which we loved to watch. They paused in their drinking, they were alert with heads held high as they snorted and looked over in our direction. They gazed at us with soft, melting dark brown eyes, ears taut and tails twitching they were alert and watchful though obviously not afraid. Hippo stood about on the banks, glowering inquisitively at us over the water. Astonished, and failing to see the submerged hippo in our path, we felt the boat rise. Unwittingly we had drifted onto its back as it lay resting. Standing to its full height, the hippo rose blowing, snorting and was very angry indeed. It lifted the boat out of the water, but fortunately for us did not turn it over. It slid off the side of the hippo's slippery wet back. Open jawed, with huge pink mouth wet and dripping, its bellow echoed over the river into the surrounding bush, then rushing through the shallow water over to the other side it stood amongst the herd, shaking its great head and glowering angrily. I was convinced it would come roaring back at us. The jolt had stalled the engine and we could not get it to start. It was mayhem. We had only two tatty emergency paddles and a stick, the men moved in overdrive to get the thing moving. As self appointed cox, I gave loud instructions! Fortunately the camp was within calling distance, we could hear the children playing. The worrying thing was that the hippo was still giving us this menacing glare. My main cry was 'Forget the bloody engine, just row.'

This was to Alec, whose wife had sensibly stayed in camp with the children, he and Jim would keep trying to start the engine. I could not take my eyes off the hippo as it stood with others on the bank looking aggressive.

We paddled slowly and pushed our way back to the jetty. When I left the boat for terra firma my knees turned to water. The meaning of the term was forcibly brought home to me. Jim hauled me from the boat, hugged me and planted my feet firmly onto the ground, and I was very shaky indeed for a few minutes. The children laughed, Alec's wife was not amused at what she called 'Our foolhardy escapade.' (Looking back, it was just another little scrape amongst many.)

On another occasion, back in the Pawaga bush, there had been a shower of rain, immediately afterwards flowers appeared as if by magic. Jim and Graham spotted some wild orchids so they pulled up the Land Rover and went off to pick a bunch for me, whilst the girls and I sat waiting, they would not be long they said. It was very quiet, no sign of anything no noise, just an odd mumble from the men talking as they picked flowers. Ever so gradually they moved out of sight. I thought perhaps a 'call of nature' was the reason for this, they were prone to disappearing on these occasions.

Quite suddenly the silence was broken. We were abruptly alerted to the noise of breaking branches and ripping bark. Deep bass rumblings came and went. A breeze in the damp air carried an unmistakable smell. 'Elephant, that must be elephant,' I thought to myself. No sign of the men, 'Why, haven't they heard them?' I muttered to myself. Moments afterwards they appeared in some haste, clutching the orchids.
    'Start the engine, get into reverse and open the door.' yelled Jim.

I did all of these things at the double, but stalled the engine in my haste. The men jumped into the Land Rover, I moved over and Jim took the wheel, Graham jumped in the back and away we went in a cloud of dust. Four elephant ran from the bush, with ears flapping and trunks raised. So much for these enormous pachyderms, they can blend in and make themselves invisible behind the smallest bush. In complete silence they can appear from nowhere. Often only their 'smell' gives them away.

The next day Bob Mansfield appeared, he had called in to see if the coffee pot was on. Bob was yet another member from the Department of Agriculture. There seemed so many of them. Bob was not an easy person to get to know. He did, however, become a staunch and stalwart friend. He had the driest of humour and was great on observation – simple things could become ridiculous through his lateral thinking. We saw a lot of him although he never accompanied us on our bush safaris, often in the early evening he came to the house to quip and remark on the day's happenings, he always made us laugh. Bob had a habit of purposely whistling one tune, deliberately of course, and he caught me every time. 'Listen to the rhythm of the falling rain,' was a favourite, walking from the kitchen carrying a cup of coffee the inevitable happened. I hummed as I handed him the coffee.
    'What's that you're humming Jean?'
    'Damn it Bob you caught me again.'
The tune remained with me for the whole day – round and round it went in my head.

One evening he arrived in a state of great agitation, his wife had been taken ill she was in the Iringa hospital suffering with severe bowel pains and her condition was deteriorating fast. The hospital doctor was on safari up country and the remaining staff had done all they could under the circumstances. It seemed the only solution was to take her as quickly as possible to the big hospital in Dar-es-Salaam. She had to travel by road. Bob held her head up as they went through Mikumi, because there were elephant on the road she wanted to see them. Her condition on arrival was diagnosed as stoppage of the bowel. They operated, but she died during surgery. It did not seem possible. Poor Bob was stricken, he seemed only to be able to communicate with Jim. It was decided to give them both leave, the help would give him some comfort and support. He had much to cope with in these tragic circumstances and the deep sadness it had caused. It was an exceptionally hard time for him and difficult for us all. Jim seemed to be his only source of solace, the only person he seemed able to talk to at any length. Eventually he re-married and went to Australia, we always kept in touch, until he died in 1983.

At the bottom of the Iringa escarpment lived Ginger King-Smith, a sandy haired South African who had a parrot named 'Joey'. Ginger had been in the navy and had great stories to tell. He was loyal friend. We felt that we could trust him with our lives, our girls loved him. His wife Paulette was born in the Seychelles, spoke fluent Swahili and was an extremely good cook.

'Paulette,' at the call of her name, one never knew whether it was Ginger or the parrot.

'Ginger,' it would call.

'Yes, what is it,' Ginger would ask.

'I have not called you, it is the parrot,' Paulette would call from whereever she happened to be. Joey caused great confusion and much hilarity.

Every Sunday Ginger made a large goulash. It was always absolutely delicious, and we loved it when he invited us to join them. As everything began to deteriorate in Tanganyika they decided to leave for the UK, their three children had 'flown the nest' and two were now married. Ginger was much older than Paulette and, as everything became more difficult in Africa, she gave the impression of feeling a little insecure. I think Paulette was really the instigator of this move, and once there she was determined to remain in England. Ginger hated it, he longed for the sun. He had wanted to go back to live in the Seychelles, sadly this never materialized. We wrote to him regularly and he opened his heart in his replies. He died in England.

The community of expatriates gradually dwindled. Some felt, as Ginger and Paulette had, that now was the time to get out. Others had their posts Africanised. A few were transferred and others went further south to Rhodesia or South Africa. Many left Africa with bruised hearts and a love coupled with memories of this vast and complex continent, which would last a lifetime. Great changes came very quickly, they were not always beneficial to either man, or country. In the bush some miles from Iringa was Tosamaganga Catholic Mission. Here, along with travellers who were visiting or passing through the area, we could buy hand embroidered table mats and napkins, guest towels, plants, baskets and wooden ornaments. The proceeds from these sales went towards the upkeep of the mission. The sisters were responsible for teaching local girls to embroider, which they did with great success. First class professional work was produced, displayed and bought by eager visitors. I still have a set of finely worked mats and napkins in my linen chest. It was a warm, friendly and well organized establishment.

In the Iringa area, on a nearby tobacco farm owned by a Greek was 'Daraja ya Mungu,' Bridge of God, where the stream water simply disappeared underground at the bridge, flowing below with a rumbling echo to suddenly appear again some way further on. (Rather similar to the one we found on our 1957 safari in Nyasaland.) Sally and Janey liked to picnic here, they said it was 'Like fairyland.' They collected pretty stones, which were usually piled in a corner of the veranda when we arrived home, later to be placed around the small flower bed in the garden.

Suddenly everyone decided we should have a big barbeque, a pig on a spit. Bill and Babs Boddy would provide the piglet. It was a magnificent affair which went on well into the night. Almost everyone we knew came. The wine flowed and much food was consumed. The event was a talking point for a long time afterwards, followed by the inevitable question: 'When is the next barbeque'?

In Iringa we had one Mr Shivji. He was a tiny man with a limp, the part he played in the township was that of local auctioneer. We loved his auctions, standing for hours on Saturday afternoon (when we were not in the bush), listening to his broken chatter, intrigued by his outrageous presentations and accompanying contortions. All the expatriates leaving Iringa took their unwanted possessions to him to sell, things with which they had decorated their homes, things which had become a part of their life, many of which told a story, a little bit of history. They put their faith in Mr. Shivji. He sold well and was very popular. Everyone not intending to leave Iringa attended his sales – it was a meeting place like no other. On auction days Mrs Shivji had orders for dozens of her excellent samosas. Each week we bought her samosas – it was part of our lifestyle. The weekly get together with all our friends became a time to voice our opinions, discuss our grievances, arrange safaris, more parties and exchange chit chat. A time for men to water the hollyhocks, drink a beer or two and relax. They were splendid occasions which none of us would have missed.

Despite the mosquito situation, Jim and Graham went off to the Bohoro, or Usanga flats, armed with a huge jar of mince and bean curry, to shoot game. The mosquito situation in this particular area worried me greatly. I was so afraid of cerebral malaria after Jim's last attack. They promised to take every precaution. Certainly it never happened again. They almost always came back from this area with warthog or impala meat, much of which was shared amongst our friends. Skins and heads were salted to prevent the hair slipping. The skins were usually salted, rolled and left in my kitchen, of all places. I was assured that this was not at all unhygienic. It was a safeguard against any 'nasties' which might destroy it if left outside. After the salting period, the skins were stretched on a wooden frame and left to dry, they were either taken by road or flown up to Nairobi for curing.

Each week we bought vegetables from local farmers, who lived in the surrounding district. We were able to buy delicious farm butter, thick cream and lots of exotic fruit. All were delivered to the door. Iringa was a good, healthy posting.

My mother came to stay with us and we took her to the Ngorongoro Crater. On our way we saw a great variety of game and flocks of pink flamingo which held her spellbound. On the crater rim, we slept in log cabins and as the evenings tended to be chilly, fires were lit each day. It was an exciting time for her trundling down the almost sheer escarpment in the old Land Rover with not another vehicle in sight. We saw almost every species of game in the crater, there were lion taking their siesta and we were chased by rhino. Elephant stood under trees, hyena sloped away cringing at the sight of us and, of course, there were the tall, slim and regal Maasai who were covered from head to foot in red ochre, layers of beads around their long necks, their hair was plaited and their high red cheek bones shone in the sun. Huge rings hung from long stretched ears. Each carried a long hunting spear. They loped along with their cattle as they grazed alongside the game; zebra, impala, buffalo and wildebeest. A youth must kill a lion before he becomes a man. Dotted around on the floor of the crater were Maasai manyattas (dung and red ochre huts), around which sharp-nosed dogs lay dozing. Mother was sad to leave Ngorongoro. In fact we were all sad to leave. When the time came for her to return, to the UK and to sail back to England, she did not want to go. It was not the excited mum we had met on her arrival in East Africa. She did visit us a number of times after that. Like so many others, she had been bitten by the 'Africa bug!'

Jim made regular visits to the many tobacco estates in the district to advise and weigh up progress. All his advice was well received and applied. Farmers came in continually to ask questions about the crops during the days spent in his office in Iringa. It must have been sound – both yields and quality improved and everyone was satisfied with the prices at auction; both Greeks and Europeans. Jim was well liked and highly respected.

For some time Janey had not been at all well. She had become very thin and developed an irritating nightly cough. We took her to endless doctors and specialists but no one seemed able to give the correct diagnosis. She was given vitamins to help improve her eating, cough medicine to help her cough and antibiotics, nothing helped. We took her to Nairobi to see a specialist in tropical diseases, he gave us little encouragement and a mountain of pills, we left baffled and very worried. Our stay at the 'Norfolk' was overshadowed by the little girl's sickness. Soon after arriving home from Nairobi, we were talking to the local German vet in the bar of the White Horse hotel, we mentioned our visit to Nairobi and the reasons for going. He suggested we let him have a stool specimen on which he would do a series of tests. I followed his instructions – not really expecting any positive results. However I was wrong, he sent a message asking us to call in to see him. While having a cup of tea he told us Janey had hook worm. It was essential to dose her for this worm he said, as he handed Jim a prescription. I immediately took it to the local chemist, another German. The medicine was flown up from Dar-es-Salaam. It arrived quite quickly and after dosing her, the improvement was very obvious. This incident caused me to dose the whole family regularly, including Graham and Tim. When the time came for the second dosing I made them stand in a row and gave them each a powder. They hated the stuff, we all did it was foul. In fact it was quite an exhausting experience.

Sometimes Jim was away for days at a time on safari, visiting farms and native tobacco schemes. I was grateful for my little job in the office at these times. Immediately he arrived back from safari he popped his head around the office door and the earth moved. It always felt like a new beginning being greeted with a kiss and wide open arms. It was just a case of melting into them, my head in the crook of his shoulder. It would not have been a problem to stay there forever. The children became excited 'Daddy, daddy,' they would cry leaping into his arms. Each afternoon as he arrived home from the office, Janey waited for him, the drive of the house was in the shape of a horse shoe and at each end was a short stone pillar. She sat for hours waiting, her little face lighting up as he came along the road. When he drew up he opened the door and she jumped in giving him a whacking kiss, then driving slowly up to the other pillar he turned in towards the house. After stopping the Land Rover he opened her door, took her into his arms and carried her into the sitting room. It was for this little ride that she had waited for so long, such is the love of a little girl for her daddy. Sally was usually playing with a young boy living over the road.

Each Saturday morning, under the supervision and beady eye of Johnny, our garden worker at the time, the girls and their friends had a wonderful time cooking sausages and beans in their special frying pan on a tiny fire surrounded by stones. I gave them bread from the kitchen, they picnicked and played for hours. Talking, playing with a ball, singing, twirling on the swing and riding on their bicycles. Afterwards they headed for the small pool, which Graham and Jim had made, It was used for dipping in the heat of the day. I found them fascinating to watch and never ceased to be amazed at all the inventive games they played in the water. The swing was nearby, anchored to a branch of the eucalyptus tree.

Around this time my kitchen was overflowing with bread, Chelsea buns, currant bread and doughnuts. I made them for the expatriates and for the local boarding school of St Michael and St George where there were still a few expatriate teachers. They gave me orders for all of these goodies as the local bakery had become defunct. The reason, for these frantic baking sessions was because the British Government provided just one passage every two years for children attending school in England. I stashed away all my profits in order to fly Elizabeth out for the long summer holiday. A short time afterwards a child whose parents lived overseas was murdered on the train as she travelled from boarding school to her grandparents home for the school holidays. From this tragedy our good fortune came, afterwards passages were provided regularly for our children.

The proceeds from the last of my seasonal bakes bought a 'series one' Land Rover from our friends Don and June who lived opposite. They had bought and shipped out a 'nipple pink' Vauxhall saloon, the colour ordered had been green! Don was suffering from a horrible dose of tick fever at the time he was not at all well and lost a lot of weight. The colour of the car added to his misery! Grant their son was Sally's good chum they played together all the time. It was in this old bone rattler we had all our fun, it took us on all our hunting safaris and game spotting drives. For one of our annual holidays we drove to Kenya to spend a holiday with friends, journeying into the beautiful, wild Masai Mara, and the Serengeti. We saw game of all varieties; huge herds of wildebeest and buffalo though no more than we had come across in Tanzania. We visited Karen, Eldoret and Thika with its flame trees. I had always wanted to see the wildebeest migration but sadly never had the opportunity, even so the whole panorama was breathtaking, the animals were all in good condition and had been enjoying the fruits of the rains.

We dined with our friends in the 'New Stanley' and stayed for two nights in 'The Norfolk,' both of which were comfortable old colonial meeting places. We revelled in our stay, in the people we met, the banter we engaged in, the laughter, bawdy remarks and jokes that we shared amongst farmers who were enjoying a few days break in Nairobi. Our long journeys were always taken in the Citroen, on a number of occasions we visited Geoffrey and Shirley in Malawi and met up with old friends. This was not the country that was so indelibly writ in our minds, the country we remembered as Nyasaland. We visited most of the old places we remembered but did not go back to Namisu – it would have been much too painful. We were afraid of change and preferred to remember it as it was in all its glory. It held so much for us, such romance and so many blissful memories.

There were times when out of necessity we had to go to Dar, sometimes it would just be for a long weekend, at others Jim would have to go to Pamba House Headquarters of the Ministry of Agriculture. We loved these visits, meeting up, and sometimes staying with old friends. Leaving home before daylight, we always took with us of all things tilapia fish sandwiches. Everything was prepared the night before – we just had to lift the children and put them on a prepared mattress in the back of the Citroen. With my hand on Jim's knee we drove away in the early hours of morning. We had usually travelled some distance before Sally and Janey stirred. Hoping to pass through Morogoro we tried to make it to Mikumi before eating our sandwiches. Here we could sit by the roadside, watch the game on either side, quaking when the elephant walked over the road a few yards from the car. It was prudent to be wise and cautious. There was an abundance of all species of game in Mikumi National Park. The main road ran through it, every species of game wandered alongside the road from the surrounding bush. Giraffe often walked gracefully along near by, it was a great thrill to watch them.

The children amused themselves by counting euphorbia trees as we drove along. Spotting game was also very popular. There was a monetary reward for whoever spotted the most, the biggest or the most rare species. We sang as we travelled, songs from 'Swinging Safari,' were the in thing at the time. Little voices trilled from the back, almost word perfect. 'Ach, please daddy will you take us to the drive-in, all six seven of us, eight nine ten,' was popular, and a regular choice. We joined in it was a way of 'eating' up the miles necessary to travel from one place to another. As we approached Dar we came to the top of an incline, from here the sea was immediately visible on the horizon, glittering and golden in the sunlight. Wildly excited, the songs became louder, followed by the cry, 'Can we go into the sea daddy, as soon as we get there?'

'Hotel first,' replied Jim with a light heart.

We were all looking forward to our dip in the Indian Ocean.

The 'New Africa,' was comfortable and relaxing, it was an old colonial hotel near to the harbour, on the shore of Oyster Bay, and close to the main shops. The shops, in the now re-named, Independence Avenue, sold food and books alongside exotica from India, Zanzibar, Kenya, Uganda, Macao and the Far East There were oriental rugs, carved camphor wood chests, local Makhonde carvings, silver jewellery, precious and semi-precious stones, skins, artefacts made from different skins, saris, jewellery of gold in every carat, there was a mind blowing variety of everything. Dewhurst's had one of their butcheries in the old Acacia Avenue, now Independence Avenue. For how long could this state of affairs continue? We wondered. We were noticing many creeping changes. Our life was idyllic, much too perfect to continue we felt.

After seven years in Iringa the girls had grown and the time had come for Sally to join Liz at school in Wales. At least we were now secure in the knowledge of them spending regular holidays with us.

Mixed blessings

We were due for leave when a letter arrived. Jim looked very downcast as he turned the page.
     'What now, my love?' I asked feeling a little apprehensive on noticing his reaction.
     'I cannot believe it, a transfer to Dar, I have to work in Pamba House after our leave.'

Now, one would expect a totally different reaction given our love of the of the sea and the East African coast, however, to put things into perspective, there would be no bush, no game and no safaris

232

as we had known them in the past. Jim would be more or less confined to an office, with the odd journey up country thrown in when necessary. This was not good news. It meant leaving our lovely friendly little home in Iringa, a posting which was very dear to us. Our many friends would be left behind. We did not want to leave, but sadly we had no choice.

Graham and Carol were married whilst we were on leave, it was a very memorable wedding they looked so happy we were delighted. They would not be going back to Iringa either because Graham had been transferred to Arusha. At least we would be able to visit them. There was a tobacco area in Arusha. Even so, it was a blow to us all, things as we knew them seemed to be falling apart, the inevitable was happening. A replacement would have to be found for my little office, 'Oh dear.'

Life was to change – no more snakes in the school toilet to remain unseen by Sally but not to the next child popping in for a wee; she fled out with her arms up in the air and wet pants! Janey would no longer dash past the kitchen window screaming and threatening Neil Grieve, the little boy from next door, with mortal destruction because he had the audacity to pull and swing on Sally's pony tail, making her cry. No more visits to the friendly little library from which I had taken and read Han Suyin's *A Many Splendoured Thing,* which had a deep effect on me and made me cry. No more brains on toast made especially for me, Greek style, and handed to me at the bar when we went to the 'White Horse,' for a sundowner. It was a good tranquil life, with few very problems. There had been a great deal of happiness, we had shared such love and passion in this little station in the Southern Highlands, it had been such fun, we had so many memories. This was yet another experience we must leave behind. We had to start again. Long and hard we talked, often late into the night. We made plans, life would go on as it always had in the past. It would be different but the main thing was we were together and this way we could always make things work. We cheered up a little, Jim decided to approach the Game Department as to a possible transfer – it was something he had always been keen to try.

We spent three long months in England. It was great to see our families and they were pleased to see us. We had made a point of writing to them regularly, keeping them in touch with our comings and goings whilst we were overseas. There were lots of things for us all to talk about and they loved it. The weather in England was mainly cold, wet and miserable and it was so dark. Despite all the inevitable changes going on in Africa, we longed for the sun, the smell of the first rains, the freedom and the opportunity to relax. It would be nice to be back. At times we wondered if Africa was in its death throes.

Leaving the family behind was always traumatic. It was something none of us ever became used to. All the many hugs and tears! I attempted to adopt the 'see you soon,' attitude which rarely worked. We bought a small house in the UK for the sake of convenience – and in order that the children would have an address in the UK. The house was cared for and, at times, used by the family. Nan and Grandad eventually moved into it permanently. The children spent half terms with them and with my mother. It seemed a perfect arrangement. The children were happy, their grandparents delighted. It was always our considered opinion that the schooling we had provided for them, the family guidance, past adventures and further visits to different parts of the world, would hold them in good stead for the future.

We were on our way to the local market,
   'May I run my fingers through your hair?' A little old lady with very white hair and an enchanting smile, asked Jim.
Looking a little surprised, 'Yes do,' Jim invited, bending low.
Slowly, she drew her fingers through his curls.
   'I thought it would be,' she said, 'it is so soft, soft like a poodle's fur, thank you.'

Rapt she went on her way. I shook my head. Whatever next my love? Whatever next?' Was all I could say. As I tucked my arm into his he looked down and said, 'That was rather a nice compliment, don't you think?' He smiled in his intimate knowing way and gave me a sexy wink. Jim never ceased to amaze me he was a multi-faceted, out of this world, a very special man. The love I felt for him at times caused me a great deal of emotional upheaval, the combined masculinity and inner beauty leapt out, he was very charismatic. The girls loved and respected him, they knew he expected high standards of them and in return they were given. He was a loner, quiet, shy, gentle and often very amusing; he was sexy, seductive and passionate. I found no difficulty in either accepting his charm or reciprocating his love.

CHAPTER NINETEEN

At last the time came to return to what was now Tanzania. Zanzibar appeared to have settled down after the recent revolution, many craftsman had been slaughtered and its economy was faltering badly.

Sally had settled into school, she had Elizabeth to run to should any unforeseen problems arise. This state of affairs was to carry on into later life! We were not unduly worried about their welfare, all events were catered for and the school staff were all kind but strict; rules must be obeyed. Each Sunday they walked to church in crocodile, very smart in their blue capes, school hats and highly polished shoes.

It was necessary for us initially to return to Iringa. We had to pack and organize our luggage for shipment by rail to our new posting in Dar-es-Salaam. It was a heart wrenching move. The break up was total, almost all the friends with whom we had shared such happy years and unforgettable times, had moved on; some to Canada, Australia, South Africa and others back to the UK. Some like ourselves had been given alternative postings. A few had gravitated to Dar. It was the end of an era.

Johnny Mbegalo came with us to the coast, he jumped at the invitation. We in turn were delighted at his pleasure in still wanting to be with us. Of course he knew us and he knew our ways so there were never problems during the years he spent with us, he was a loyal servant and a true friend. We were allocated a very nice, but extremely dirty house, near to the sea. During an incoming tide we were lulled to sleep by the sound of surf pounding the shores of the Indian Ocean.'

Whilst the public works department, hosed, cleaned, fumigated, decorated, painted and then flung out the cockroach and cockroach egg infested cooker we were housed in a tiny ground floor flat in the middle of Dar-es-Salaam. All the meals of the previous occupants (the finance minister, his wife and many children) had been had been cooked on charcoal in the centre of the kitchen floor. The garden was flat, trampled, sandy and shabby with the odd lavatory flower here and there. Even so we could see it had a lot of potential.

It was a daunting task to clean and renovate the place the P.W.D. did a good job of smartening the house up. We eventually found it acceptable. Johnny helped us with the garden. He found a local helper, seeds were scattered everywhere and we begged flowers and shrubs from other Europeans. He planted, watered and nurtured them. There were many bourgainvillea and poincettia bushes in the garden and they were given water and care. In return they flowered and flourished in profusion. We bought dozens of African violets and other potted plants to give colour to the verandas and to make them 'glow'. Gradually it took shape and we came to love it, the sound of the sea as we were dropping off to sleep was sublimely soporific, a great bonus.

Janey had been ill whilst we were in the small flat, she had a wicked bout of tonsillitis. This had been during the hot season and she suffered badly. We bought a small fan which worked continuously in an effort to keep her cool. Our luggage arrived; we rooted out the mustard coloured record player, her bicycle and her favourite record, which was, 'The sound of music,' These things (and the fact that there was plenty of room for her to ride her bicycle round the flat) kept us all sane at that time, She ate little and drank a lot, it was a very worrying time, her weight dropped dramatically. As soon as we had moved into what was now a spotlessly clean, well painted, fumigated house, she started to improve. Johnny fussed about getting everything right for her, tending to every need and wish. We took her down to the sea sitting in the waves was her idea of bliss. Laughing and patting the sand.

'Mummy, daddy, come and sit here with me.' Obediently, in our relief at her improvement, we went to sit in the waves. The time came when she and Jim were to have very special times in Dar.

★★★

And now, there are times when I hear the telephone ringing during the night. It rings so clearly in my head my first thought is, 'My God, who is that?' leaping up from my bed I pick up the receiver the phone is dead, then ring 1471, nothing. Always there is nothing. Two nights ago this telephone rang. On the following night I noticed a programme was to be shown, describing the efficiency of the old steam engine during the time we were at school together, I decided to watch the programme. My imagination spun back in time, when with head out of the window I waved furiously as Jim stood on the platform. We watched and we waved peering through a cloud of smoke and steam until we could see no more. I used to make my way to the corner of the carriage feeling happy and content weaving dreams around the future life we were planning to spend together, but the daydream disturbed me, leaving a deep hole of emptiness and grief. How much I miss the warmth, the blanket comfort and shelter of those open arms which nothing can replace, those arms which melted away tension and promoted a sensation of total relaxation, dissolving any lurking worries or thoughts. Day and night they were always open for me to snuggle into. Now, without him the world seems empty, lack lustre and desperate.

On my writing desk I have a small black and white photograph taken in our younger days. Around it a small square frame transmits sparkling lights from the tiny shining diamante in its surround. Each sparkle delivers a message, a message of love, and a message of our past times together. The twinkling lights and the two faces peering from the picture inspire and encourage me to put down onto paper all I remember. To say 'Thank you my love, for the life of love, joy and adventure we have shared together.'

★★★

Office hours in Pamba House were from 7.00a.m-2.00p.m. Always up early, we were full of life and ready for the day. Usually Johnny had prepared grapefruit, followed by toast and marmalade, the latter made by me as fruit was in abundance everywhere. I also made pure lime syrup which we watered down and drank chilled with ice. The biscuit tin, bulged with homemade ginger biscuits and melting moments. Sometimes I made lots of samosas, an Indian lady in Dar had taught me how to make and fold them. We often went to the 'Drive in,' particularly when Liz and Sally were home. During the film we ate the samosas, biting off a corner and squeezing in fresh lemon or lime juice, we took along lime juice to drink It was a lovely way to spend an evening. I often met Jim at Supercortimaggiore, a petrol station-cum-coffee house, it was near to Pamba House and many of the staff popped over daily for a coffee break. The cappuccino and pizza were always delicious.

After collecting Janey from school, we almost always took a basket along to the beach and sat beneath the palms, she played in the sand with Bella, our Doberman. I read my book until Jim came along at 2.30 p.m. and it was time to eat lunch. Sometimes he went home first to put on his bathing trunks. He and Janey snorkled for hours while I sat in relaxed luxury beneath the palm trees, or was caressed by the tide on the shore line. Sometimes I looked for shells or read. Later, we ate oysters at the Oyster Bay hotel, (directly opposite the beach) with a 'sundowner,' then off we went home to wash away the sand, to change and enjoy supper prepared by Johnny. We talked, read, made plans and played scrabble with Janey until bed time. Later we lay, perhaps made love, and listened again to the sound of the sea. Healthy, glowing and tanned we were enjoying this life it was a far cry from the Iringa days which we had been so loathe to leave behind. Each in its own way, was more than we could ever have either asked or wished for. We basked in a working life of luxury.

Mostly, at the weekends Jim and Janey went to Rascomonie (spelling!), snorkelling and goggling, gliding through the caressing waters of the East African ocean. Tanganyika's clear warm waters are renowned, there are lovely corals, exotic and spectacular fish in shimmering colours of all shapes and sizes. I had never found it difficult to sit on any small part of this 15 mile coast line, or to lie on the palm-fringed sands, watching the antics of my family as they played and swam amongst the jewel bright colours of the Indian ocean. At times I read, at others I dozed, it was a delightful way to relax! Sometimes I joined them, but they were so much better at under-water swimming then me. Our youngest offspring would never want to join her sisters in England, though sadly the time would come when this must happen because education had taken a big down-turn in some of these old ex colonies

We were invited to parties, we gave parties. On warm tropical evenings we ate crab claws dipped in butter in gardens decorated with tiny lights, under a night sky exploding with stars. Accompanied by the sound of distant waves crashing on the shore, soft music played sweet in the still air, we danced slowly, rapt with deep feelings and emotion to the seductive tunes of the past 'It had to be you', 'Moon glow,' 'That old feeling.' Music that we had grown up with, made plans to and still lived with. We decided to buy a new, very smart record player shortly after our arrival in Dar-es-Salaam. By chance we had walked past a radio and record shop on Independence Avenue during a demonstration to other interested and potential buyers. We had been entranced by the resonant and mellow strains echoing through the shop, such a far cry from the old battery radio and the little mustard coloured record player which had given us such pleasure in the past. The decision was instant and we bought and installed a new record player in our home in Oyster Bay. I thought the roof would lift at the strains of the aria from 'Madam Butterfly.' Johnny happily took over our little mustard player. He invited friends round to eat, played local music and had a thoroughly good time. His small house was in the garden of our home. He was always respectful and kept noise to a minimum. Johnny was not a noisy person he liked solitude and had the odd good friend. I think that he had perhaps been influenced a little by us in this respect.

Life was never dull it always seemed to be full of nice things to do. Jim went to meetings at his Lodge. I joined him on Ladies' Night. We enjoyed every moment of our time together. On the evenings Jim was out I made dresses for myself and the children, turned collars, made skirts and blouses, baked, read and waited for him to come home.

My mother and father came to stay. My mother was still the same erect, good looking, dark-eyed woman she had always been. She had a black velvet ribbon tied round her head, her now greying hair was tucked neatly into it in a coil around her head. She was a determined person who enjoyed a challenge. My father on the other hand was of medium height and rather quiet. Mother had always told me in his hey day, and in old black and white photographs, he had looked exactly like Rudolph Valentino, and he had. A little shorter than my mother he was still slim, dark-eyed and had good features. Hearing mothers stories of her adventures in London with her sister, they were both VAD nurses, I sometimes wondered!

Most days, we walked down to the sea, spending hours on the sands and sitting under the palms, usually with a book. We had picnics and drank from fresh coconuts taken from the trees under which we sat. On spare evenings we played scrabble. At times this became a little boring. We took local leave and took mother and father on safari to the game parks. They saw so much and so many different varieties of game. My father did not like the wide open spaces of Africa – in fact we felt he suffered a little from agoraphobia he certainly would not be left alone in any open bush country. It was the one and only time he came to Africa. On mother's future visits, he stayed with my brother.

At 'sundowner' time we often went to the New Africa hotel. Sitting on the patio on balmy evenings we listened to music played by George de Souza, who incidentally looked and sounded almost exactly like Englebert Humperdinck, immediately he set eyes on us his band struck the first cords of 'More', the vocal contribution was delivered with great feeling. 'George, my mummy and daddy like 'More' – my daddy always sings it'. Janey had told him this, as she weaved her way past the podium to ask the cook in the hotel kitchen for more peanuts. From that evening onwards, he serenaded us with an all knowing look! Dreams are made up of these little things in life they turn the windmills of the mind. During the interim periods of silence there was the sound of the sea, the rustle of palm fronds and the muffled, lapping swish of water hitting dhows in the nearby harbour. We drank brandy sours, talked and dreamed on but sadly, life can not stand still.

Janey's visits to the kitchen were part of the scene and there were times when she took a little longer than usual. On these occasions she could be found standing in front of the mirror in the toilets watching herself sing. Her little voice trilled, warbled and floated out into the warm night air. In a few minutes she skipped out, curls bobbing clutching her dish of peanuts heading straight for her daddy's knee. When we had people to supper, Johnny sneaked quietly past the bookcase and down the corridor taking a bowl of peanuts to her unseen, outstretched hand.

The Boddy's who had been farming in Iringa were now employed by Tanganyika Packers, they had been sent to live on a station on the outskirts of Dar. They were also missing Iringa though eventually, like ourselves, they fell in love with Dar-es-salaam. We saw a great deal of them. On shopping days they made a habit of popping in at coffee time and we visited them. Their two elder children, always above average intelligence were now biochemists in the UK. The three younger ones remained in Dar with their parents.

Some Sundays we went to Njimweyma beach picnicing, Babs always produced vast quantities of food, all tantalizingly delicious. We had glorious, unforgettable times with them. Bill secreted his syringe from its little box deftly injecting his leg he was a diabetic, a legacy from his prisoner of war days.

Quite suddenly I was whistled off to England, it seemed I must have a hysterectomy. Little was said, I did not want to make a fuss in case Jim became desperate. I went into hospital, had the operation and wrote to him each day. I posted the pages when the whole thing was over and I had started to recuperate. On his arrival back from an up country safari he collected his post and read my letter. The whole thing was over. That was just as I had wanted it to be.

Whilst recuperating in hospital, I read in the daily newspaper of a Wilfred Boddy employed by Tanganyika Packers in Dar, having been murdered. I read and re-read the article trying to make sense of the words, 'It just could not be,' I said to myself. It was. Apparently he had been giving a lift to a group of Africans whilst on his way to pay his labour. They knocked him unconscious from behind, stole the money he carried and afterwards pushed the Land Rover into the river. His wife had been at home waiting for him to return. He never did. Jim spent much time with the family whilst I was in England. 'The whole thing was heart-breaking and quite beyond belief,' he said. Babs was hysterical, she was also filled with a great anger – this I could understand and envisage knowing them as I did. Her grief was all consuming. The effect on the children was devastating. Their life was in tatters, overcome with sorrow and disbelief they became hard and wild. It was so very sad to see. To me it did not make any sense, here was a man who had been captured and had escaped so many times, and from so many prison camps. He had been a rear gunner during the Second World War. How could his life end in this way? A flurry of activity began, I mended quickly and well, longing to be back. Life without Jim around me was not what I wanted. It was necessary for us to be together to function with any semblance of normality. I also wanted to try to help Babs and the children, if it was at all possible under the circumstances.

It was with great excitement I boarded the plane at Heathrow. My time away had seemed an eternity. The journey back was filled with emotion, so much had happened and in so many ways. At last we arrived and as the aircraft ground to its slow halt on the runway, I could see Jim clearly. He stood out amongst the crowd of squinting, searching, handover-the-eyes-from-the-glare-of-the-sun, gesticulating waving relatives and friends who stood on the balcony, each one eagerly awaiting the first glimpse of the flight weary passenger they were there to meet. As I walked across the tarmac my heart lurched when smiling Jim put up his hand indicating that he could see me below. Fortunately, I had no problems with baggage or customs. The smell of the sea, of spices, of Dar-es-Salaam, of Africa, greeted my nostrils creating an upsurge of indescribable joy. I arrived to find myself enfolded in the comfort of open arms, showered with kisses and the recipient of huge captivating smiles of joy. My luggage was taken care of. I had arrived. Now I could relax.

'Welcome back,' I was greeted by the immigration officer,.
'Memsahib, welcome back.' Johnny enthused as he seized my

hand shaking it vigorously on my arrival home. It felt so good to be together again and to have all the surgery behind me. It had been a concern to us both at the time, but that was over, we could surge ahead with life again!

Supper was laid beautifully. Johnny had made coq au vin which we ate with relish, as an accompaniment we drank a splendid bottle of chilled South African 'Johannesburger'.

My love was delighted with the blood stone ring I had brought back for him. I slid it onto his little finger as I gave him a huge kiss. It fitted absolutely. I loved everything about this man so much.

There were few people who met us who ever doubted our love or attentiveness to one another as side by side we slotted into the jigsaw of life. When we were separated we seemed in a strange way to be slightly dysfunctional, as our first point of reference in everything we did was always to each other. Our physical relationship was strong, our understanding of each other, unquestionable.

We were becoming excited as the girls were almost due to arrive home, on holiday from school. Then we would all go on 'mystery tours', none of us ever knew where we were going. We knew the venues would be places we all enjoyed visiting, and had usually at some point, been on our special request list. Only Jim knew the 'tour route'! One favourite place was the coastal town of Bagagmoyo where a large community of Arabs and Indians lived amongst the African population. The township had its origin in trade between Zanzibar and the mainland in the first half of the century. It had a good dhow harbour with a broad sandy beach uncovered for miles at low tide, superb for beach combing. Intricately carved doors lead into small dark interiors which housed people, dogs, chickens and scrawny cats. On chakiris (stoves) outside, sufarias (pans) contained fish stew and posho in preparation for evening meals. Children played, screaming and shouting in the way all children scream and shout. Old women in faded kangas, their faces resembling bits of biltong were responsible for preparing the family supper; it was a noisy affair, everyone vying to outdo the other with news of the day, each guffaw became louder and more shrill as the night progressed and the village beer took its hold. Conversation went on well into the night as dogs barked, goats bleated and the odd cock crowed. Then all became silent, until the approach of dawn, when the rituals of the day started again. The rustle of swaying palms nearby, the gentle swirl of the incoming tide as it hit the shore lent their sounds to the daily activity of village life.

The main shops belonged to Indians of differing castes each one offering a variety of goods, some essential to the needs of everyday life, others frivolous 'feel good' bits and pieces, which made the people smile. They were proud of their ownership of gaudy mirrors, bangles, beads and plastic flowers which never died, they just became covered in 'blow away' dust. The vase of glass with daubs of gilt, needed little attention glittering in the lamplight of the dark house or hut. They added a glamour to an otherwise soulless interior. One Indian shop belonging to a family of Brahmin, sold food of every kind. Soft drinks were available, we were able to quench our thirst by sipping a warm Coca Cola at a high counter courtesy of a very high stool. The girls loved it. Sometimes. power permitting, the drink would be cold, or there might even be be ice dropped into it. If the owner felt benevolent dishes of Indian titbits were placed in front of us.

Bagamoyo had an enigmatic quality about it, it was haunting and full of quiet mystery, perhaps the 1000s of slaves passing through in past years had left something of their soul behind. In contrast we, in this tiny coastal town, felt as free as birds totally relaxed, wandering at low tide to the fishermen in the far distance who were always excited to have someone buy their freshly caught fish as they hauled it in from the boats. We collected driftwood and made a small fire on the dunes. We knew we were guaranteed a succulent and extremely delicate tasty and welcome break from our routine meals.

One hot afternoon Jim arrived home from the office complaining of bowel discomfort and lower abdominal pain. We felt it must be something he had eaten – there were many foods which were always suspect. During the night he moved around a great deal in an effort to relieve the pain. It became very intense so I felt the only thing to do was for me to take him to the hospital in Dar. I was desperate with worry though I tried hard not to show it as I helped him to the car. 'Hell love, even my balls ache,' he said with feeling, as he bent over in pain. In a very short time the doctor had arrived, his examination caused him some discomfort, he diagnosed diverticulitis. Jim stayed in hospital overnight and was given medication. The next day he was able to come home. He was still bent over a little and looked pale and grey, though he had much less pain. He was given a diet to follow and overwhelmed with care, he repaired very quickly and the tenderness disappeared. My poor love was never sick, though it came into my memory that whilst on leave staying with friends in Devon he had experienced a similar pain, though it had been much less severe. I wondered if all the driving, sitting and bumping about in the Land Rover on safari work might affect him. I made sure he was in good shape before we went up to the northern region, Handeni, the Usambaras and on to Moshi and Arusha where tobacco projects had to be visited and assessed. It was a long body racking 10 day ride. Reports had to be written when he arrived back in Pamba House from notes taken whilst out in the field.

It was a good safari, we had so many friends in the area, Graham and Carol were in Arusha, Carol was now pregnant with her first child, Robin. We did love staying in the Marango Hotel, on the slopes of

Kilimanjaro where it could be quite cold. Inside huge log fires burned brightly whilst the mist swirled in a dripping wet swathe outside it was the perfect setting for 'cuddling'. Magic and mysterious, quietly haunting and a little ethereal, the trees spread out ghostly limbs, their fingers shedding glistening cobwebs lit by shafts of light from lamps on stone walls. This time we were alone, the girls were all in Wales at school and Janey was not liking it at all. We were consoled somewhat by the fact that she had her sisters with her and we knew they would give her support. I wrote to them all almost on a daily basis. They looked forward to holidays and we made plans for special things to do whilst they were with us.

One enormous disappointment during our time in Dar had been the refusal of the now African Minister of Agriculture, to transfer to Jim to the Game Department. For some time they had been wanting a game ranger for the Serengeti – this was his dream. He applied for the position, attended many interviews and meetings. His quiet excitement at the prospect of living amongst the game, learning to fly and having a home in the park I found very infectious. It would be a life of dreams. He was accepted. On approaching the Minister, both by letter and in person, he was told there was no one to replace him, the transfer was not possible. Even a letter from the Director of Parks to the Minister failed to have the desired effect. His disappointment was cataclysmic, it affected him in many ways, it was something he had wanted for us all so badly, and for so long. It had been within his grasp then snatched away. My poor love, it was difficult to console him at the time. I had hoped in time he might forget, but he never did.

One by one all of our friends began to leave Tanzania. What was left of the Boddy family went to Rhodesia where they joined Bill's brother Ken and family who were now growing tobacco in Karoi. We managed one last safari to Iringa, a few of our friends still hung on. Many shops had closed and had been reduced to battered concrete buildings with rusty corrugated roofs and neglected and pealing paintwork. The Iringa hotel was no longer functioning as we had known it. We stayed in the White Horse Hotel which was still owned by a Greek and still good value. Jim visited some of the tobacco farms – many of which were for sale. Others were making good profits on their tobacco. The farmers plied him with questions and asked when he was returning. The Iringa we had known was fast becoming a thing of the past. With sad hearts we left, staring out of the Land Rover windows as we descended the escarpment, we had to travel the 430 miles to Dar through the Ruaha valley, past the enormous baobabs standing sentries to the river, on through Mikumi with its game and back to the coast for the last time. It tugged hard.

Back in Dar it was time for the children to pay what was to be their last visit. We spent lots of time at Oyster Bay. Fishing floats bobbed about on the waves as the tide came in, porpoise played amongst the waves. Jim rescued a loose glass float, webbed with rope, which we took home. We were wildly excited at our 'catch'. It now hangs beneath the beams of Janey's patio cover, a nostalgic reminder of those magic days on the coast of East Africa. During this time in Dar we bought a Persian rug from an auction and a camphor wood chest from an Indian shop in Independence Avenue. Lots of us skinny dipped in the Indian Ocean and we had a party, held in the Marine Club on New Year's Eve.

We packed a lot into that short time amid rumours of the withdrawal of British aid. We were withdrawn. We spent a short time in the UK after which Jim was sent to Malawi as Regional Tobacco Officer. Graham and Carol stayed in Scotland, where they farmed and their family grew by two, another boy and a girl. Johnny Mbegalo returned to his village. This good and faithful friend did not go empty handed. In his last letter to us he told us he was cook to another European government official in Iringa. He also said how he missed us. It was a sad farewell to yet another African country we had learned to love and think of as home. Now, Tanzania had a place in our hearts.

CHAPTER TWENTY

Malawi

After spending eight weeks in England we flew out to Malawi. The girls were settled in school and were looking forward to flying out to Africa again for their holidays. For us it was time to start again, flying back after almost thirteen years to the country we had last known and loved as Nyasaland. The country in which we had finally come together again and the country in which Sally had been born. In its bush we had hunted, followed game, studied the stars and spent devastatingly romantic nights. Before leaving England, as we were about to board the aircraft I took out my compact to powder my nose, on the mirror was a message; 'I love you Cog.' Tears squeezed up into my eyes I was again going into the sunset with my husband, my lover, my soul mate, companion and friend. What more could anyone need or want? We settled into our flight, had sundowners before our evening meal, snuggled together and read, occasionally looking out of the window at the night sky. With my head on Jim's shoulder I drifted at first into a fitful sleep, the drone of the aircraft gradually becoming ever more faint. With a vision of Jim's face before me, I slipped into a deep comfortable sleep and I dreamt.

★★★

I was a child again. It was before the war, before my teens, before taking the train to school, before I was 'grown up.' Seeing the gas lamps and the old lamplighter. The 'midnight men,' carrying huge buckets to collect empty sewage from murky outside lavatories, before dumping it into the sewage truck standing in the dusk of the dim lamp lit road. I saw the village shop opposite my old home, the window full of goodies; huge jars of sweeties of all colours. Oh I did love pear drops, I stood on sturdy little crossed legs, curls a-bobbin' holding onto the handles of a doll's pram and gazing longingly at the array of tantalizing sweets on display. Mr. Pierpoint's shop held all the good things in life, so many things confronted me as I strained to see over the counter. There were big round cheeses, tub butter, rolls of bacon and a bacon slicer nearby. Home made jam and jellies, tea leaves in packets to be put in a warm pot and infused for two or three minutes before pouring into cups – no mugs! Biscuits in square tins, cream crackers and soup. There were trays of sticky banana split, raspberry split and plain toffee smashed with a small toffee hammer, shovelled into a small scoop, popped into a paper bag, weighed, corners twirled, and sold for one penny. I could see the biscuit cones filled with marsh mallow, hundreds and thousands covered the top, a dream in Technicolor. I would have to wait for my Saturday penny. Today mummy only needed a packet of salt.

I could see myself playing hopscotch, conkers, top and whip and performing fantastic feats with my yoyo. I was up trees in the wood, playing cricket, sledging in the snow on the slopes behind my home and skating on the lake. I played outside from dawn to dusk, making a fuss when I was called into the house. After being firmly tucked up for the night, I crept out of bed and stood on a chair to peer through the bedroom window. The 'Bleeding Wolf,' was an old red pub, there were steps, hand rails on either side leading up from the road to the entrance door. I watched people walk in and stagger out in bewildering numbers; some singing, some appearing deep in gloom, some were quite ill. I wondered why they drank beer to make them ill!

In the morning the landlord stood at the front door taking in deep breaths of fresh air, twirling a cigarette in nicotine stained fingers.

When the dray arrived, I watched huge men in flat caps wearing leather aprons heave and roll barrels down the ramp into the cellars. I skipped over the road to watch them. The cellars were to be used later as air raid shelters.

***

I felt a kiss on my forehead, 'Time to wake up love, we are almost ready to land'. I was told gently, I roused myself with much twitching, stretching and rubbing of eyes.

'Gosh, I dreamt I was a small girl again.' I murmured, giving his hand a little rub.

We were about to re-enter Malawi. We had no idea what to expect. Despite our tentative misgivings, we were greeted as we stepped from the plane by the old sweet smell of wet rain on dry earth as it mingled with wood smoke from village fires. It penetrated our nostrils plunging us immediately into nostalgia. A shower of rain before we landed had cleared the air and laid the dust. Our memories were swirling back, bringing with them a ache for a reliving of the past. Holding hands we made our way across the tarmac on a runway lined with matted grass of bright yellow ochre, then on through the muddle which was immigration. Here we joined a long line of weary passengers all squirming with an aching desire to pass through the airport as quickly as possible.

In some ways we felt we had gone back home. Geoffrey and Shirley were in Malawi, no doubt outside waiting for us at this very moment. We encountered a considerable number of undisciplined officials standing about doing very little, or doing whatever their allotted position required them to do very slowly indeed, it was a bewildering new age. This move into Independence was something we must in time, and with some difficulty, accept and become accustomed to. Passports were thumbed through, pages made dirty and bent with no attention to detail. Most officials were distracted by lengthy conversations to any passing person who made a comment or asked a question; the dialogue was a long and lengthy process, particularly if the other person happened to be female. Immigration officials were suspicious and glum. We explained our reason for being in Malawi, however we had to produce documents to prove who we were. This took a great deal of wasted time and created major frustration, it was something we had never experienced in the past but would have to get used to in the future.

A waiting Geoffrey catching a glimpse of us edged forward in greeting, his face beaming. Shirley was not with him, 'At home not at all well,' he told us. We were very pleased to see him. After much hand shaking, hugging and a kiss we piled our luggage into the car and chattering furiously, made our way to the Mount Soche Hotel in which we were to stay until our house (which was allocated by the Ministry of Agriculture) had been made fit to live in. Sitting in the comfort of the lounge, we ate a few sandwiches, drank an excellent coffee and talked endlessly.

Geoffrey took us to look at our new home on the outskirts of Blantyre. It was not quite what we had expected. The garden was large and wild, tiers of poinsettias lay on either side of a long winding drive leading up from the road. The house was basic – each room had a ceiling fan and hard furniture. When the luggage arrived we would soon put our stamp on it, make it a home and bestow on it that loving feeling. After a leisurely inspection Geoffrey took us back to the hotel and over a sundowner we reminisced eagerly. It seemed in many ways such a short time since our past life together in the Lunzu valley. After he had left we went to our room and made plans for the next day. It was strange to be in Malawi in this situation, it was such a far cry from the bliss of estate life we had experienced in previous years. Our eyes had been partly opened by happenings at the airport and through information leaked to us by Geoffrey during our conversations.

Jim and I lay down and wondered how the days would be played out during our time here. It was good to be back in this little slice of Africa. A kiss and a wink sent us spinning into a deep sleep, until it was time to shake ourselves into some semblance of order and head towards the bar and supper in the dining room.

Dr. Hastings Kamuzu Banda was now the Life President of this small landlocked country in the heart of central Africa. He was of minute stature, an old and shrunken man. A dictator who was never without his fly whisk and was always dressed in black. He wore a black trilby style hat. He possessed many ornate palaces, each one had immaculate landscaped gardens designed and overseen by David Slater, a Scot whom we had met and become friendly with whilst we were in Iringa. Dr Banda dictated the length of shorts, the length of skirts and the length of hair. He allowed no magazine which might contain anything even vaguely pornographic to enter the country. When his motorcade passed through the streets everyone must stand to attention as outriders noisily hailed his approach.

On our way from the airport to the hotel we had noticed the endless streams of people walking along either side of the road, there were people everywhere. We wondered where they had all come from. Some were apparently refugees from bordering Mozambique who were fleeing the war. The population explosion was very evident – what would our observations be in the days to come we wondered? We knew of people from Mozambique pouring over the borders into Malawi, it was general knowledge. The situation was talked of on the radio and shown on the TV, even so one had to see the numbers to believe them.

We awoke to a beautiful day in this tight landlocked little evergreen country (when compared to the rest of Africa). After breakfast we decided to spend the day familiarizing ourselves with, what was to us, a new Blantyre. In places we found it difficult to recognize this once familiar little town whose past had been burnt into our mind from past memories. So many new buildings had replaced the colonial built shops the offices and the old Town Hall, where at one time we had sat on hard wooden chairs to watch the film of the month holding hands, our eyes wide at the sight of the devastatingly beautiful Ava Gardner in 'Mogambo'. Some of the old commercial stores that we remembered still remained. From these land mark buildings we wandered out into uncharted territory, we sifted and sorted out the new from the old, remembering so much of what had been. Indeed much of the land, where once there were buildings, was now reduced to rubble. It had been left as wasteland – dry and dusty – where tenacious clumps of trodden grass were pushing their way through uneven boulders, turning the areas into dumping grounds. Here and there the odd new cinema or cola bar stood incongruously to the side. A few of the shops were still in the hands of 'old timers,' many of whom lived in shocked acceptance at the changes wrought upon them.

I walked on with my love, down some still familiar streets through the wondrous veil of our yesteryears, closing my eyes to the surrounding decay. I could not fully accept the reality and looking at Jim I could see he was swallowing hard in disbelief, at some of the things he was seeing. Goods in many of the shops were in short supply. Most of the Indian shops looked in a state of disrepair, broken down and shabby. People were worn down with fear, poverty, lack of food, lack of money, lack of everything. The whole framework of the country was in a state of disrepair and broken down and so were a lot of hearts.

Nyasaland gained Independence and became Malawi in July 1963. In 1959 we left a peaceful country, yes, there were rumours and stirrings of unrest and we did wonder about its future, however this state of affairs was beyond all belief. It had been reduced from riches to rags during our eleven year absence. The markets we visited were mostly dirty, stinking and ramshackle; rotting fruit and vegetables lying in what at one time had been storm drains. People with hugely cracked heels trudged through inches deep 'grunge', a paradise for mosquitos.

Eventually we came to a garage from the past, 'Mandala', we talked with the then still European manager, someone Geoffrey knew quite well, and we shuffled round the many cars he had on display. Mostly they had belonged to Europeans now no longer in the country. After some time we settled for a Ford Falcon. It was big, in good condition and was satisfactory for most travel and would, we were told, be easily sold on when the time came. Jim had a Land Rover for work. Our Citroen was in the process of being shipped out, it could take months and we needed transport. Wheels were set in motion we would soon be the proud owners of this rather large blue car.

The arrival of our crates with household contents was imminent. It was time to find a shop selling promising curtain material. Together we found an Indian store on the main street. After scrutinizing roll after roll of material we felt might be suitable, we chose a semi-heavy woven cloth in rich autumn colours, we gave window measurements, chose the lining and within three days they were hanging in each room of the house to great effect, reflecting a deep comforting rosy glow.

Jim went to the office to acquaint himself with the routine and work and the areas he had to cover. There were a great many farms in Namwera, a mountainous area and a major farming region up towards the lake and east of Mangochi. Ministers and Greeks had farms in this area. A huge amount of safari work was done in this region with his colleague Roger Barclay-Smith who in the past had been working on tobacco in Rhodesia. He was a very knowledgeable and a nice fellow with whom we became great friends. We also enjoyed many happy times together outside working hours. Strangely, in the past, he had known a male cousin of mine, they had been at Cambridge together. We found much to talk about, he was good company and a great raconteur. Our girls met Roger and became very fond of him.

We made our home comfortable and welcoming. The cook was named Stone, the gardener was Jimo. The cook was satisfactory, he tried very hard to make things as we liked them and mostly he succeeded. One of his all time greats were aubergine crisps – guests came from far and wide to savour this delicacy. He also made the most tasty fried tomatoes ever to be found in the world. Jimo was not good, he shirked whenever he could. Sometimes he arrived to work, sometimes he decided not to work. Despite this he kept the garden reasonably well tended, he also kept his eye on the rabbits as their breeding was becoming out of hand! It would have been useful to give the odd one or two away but Janey would not hear of it. We often wondered why on earth we had ever brought them to the house, rabbit burrows were everywhere!

Whenever I could I went with Jim, but sometimes it was not possible. Things had changed, the system was different. I hated it when he was up country for three of four nights. Eventually I decided to find myself something to do. It would be nice to have some spare cash so that we could treat the girls when they were at home with us. I also enjoyed buying surprise presents. I could not just sit at home wishing Jim was within calling distance, I could work and plan little treats for him. It was in Blantyre, in a very exclusive and modern shop housed in a new building in the main street, that I found my niche. The main clientele were farmers who came in particularly after the tobacco auctions and business people. Many goods were sold from this outlet, almost all were on display. Goods were mainly imported, from the UK, South Africa or Rhodesia. We had glassware, Royal Doulton, Wedgwood, table linen and silver. Fancy ware of every description graced the shelves It was a delightful place to be. Jim's first port of call when he came back from up country was the shop. I can see his tall figure standing silhouetted in the doorway, he was bronzed, tall and handsome, his hair curly and unruly. Dressed in khaki shorts and shirt with his boots and knee socks. Waiting for the customers to leave who were barring his way towards me, he looked, smiled and winked. When we were alone he took one or two long swift strides into the shop, I was swept me off my feet and with a kiss, twirled round. What a wondrous feeling that was. I could not wait for the shop to close, to go home and await his coming through the door from the office. When he had been on safari it was always me he came to see first. Afterwards he went to his office to write a report on the state of affairs up country.

★★★

Weekends were often spent with Geoffrey and Shirley on the estate. We had tremendous times together and so many laughs. Often as Sunday lunch time approached there would be a cry of 'Let's go over to Portuguese Mulanje.' Scooping up a few things we thought we might need such as handbags, and swimming gear in case we decided to dip into the icy cold water which poured from the mountain into the Mulange swimming pool. We piled into the car chattered non-stop. Our main decision was whether to eat piri piri chicken or garlic/chilli prawns. The prawns were simply gorgeous. Huge fat juicy prawns from the coast of Mozambique, served with hot homemade bread to dip into a dish of butter sauce. This with a bottle of wine was manna from Heaven. We sang as we approached the border which was rarely manned. A bluegum barrier had to be we lifted high to enable the car pass through. Immediately past the barrier a huge tree stood to the left of the road, in the centre of the trunk there was a natural deep broad crack which cradled a telephone. We had to lift the phone and call, I think it was the Chef de Poste telling him of our arrival into the territory. The same procedure was repeated as we left the Mozambique. From the barrier, we travelled along a very bumpy, pot holed and dusty road which we named 'Giggle mile'. Along this mile we laughed and sang our way to and from the town of Mulanje. Our return, after much good food and wine, inevitably turned to spontaneous laughter and hysterical giggles!

Usually, on arrival we popped into the restaurant to book a table, the waiters who knew us well were always polite and generous in spirit. Mulanje had small interesting shops on either side of the road, from these we bought small pieces of pottery and glass imported from Macao, toothpick holders and pretty liqueur glasses were amongst some of our purchases. I still have them, they carry such happy memories. Each time I look at them I am reminded of the pleasure we shared on those exhilarating days in Portuguese East Africa. I am reminded of the juicy prawns, the dozens of napkins used to mop up runny butter as we attempted the ungentle art of shelling, breaking, squeezing and sucking out the hot, pink, succulent flesh. How we smacked our lips in pure delight at this ambrosia from the sea. I think of the chink of wine glasses lifted to lips eager to take sips of icy cold, shining rose. Such wonderful times, I could not part with these memories.

On the odd occasion Roger joined us, he became intrigued with Mulanje, its food, wines and the icy cold pool fed by rivulets pouring down from the mountain. They delivered a goose pimply dip to anyone brave enough to venture into the water. There were seats, or rather benches, around the pool. Some people having taken a picnic settled in groups then sat in the sun. At intervals diving into the pool screaming loudly as bodies hit deep 'freezing' water, then sinking below the surface to hit the bottom On resurfacing there was much blowing, huffing and puffing, swearing and laughing, with added lewd comments made at the chill they were experiencing.

One Sunday, Jim and the children ventured into the water I sat with Roger watching the general comings and going around the pool. Many Portuguese soldiers were in evidence, they were obviously enjoying a day's leave from nearby barracks We remarked upon how well behaved they were standing in polite and dignified silence. We also commented on what the reaction there would have been from lads of the old country to all these luscious bathing belles!

Janey went up onto the diving board. I was absolutely petrified, despite the fact that her daddy was below waiting to catch her as she hit the water. I hid my face in my hands quite unable to watch. Roger was at my side patting my back and trying to reassure me.

'She will be fine don't worry, Jim is below to make sure.' I knew all of this but it did not make a scrap of difference. Of course all my fears were unfounded as she leapt from the board and landed immediately alongside a shivering Jim. They did not stay in the water long, covered in goosepimples they swam to the side, jumped out, grabbed towels and vigorously rubbed themselves down. I gave them a helping hand – their bodies felt so cold. The water in Mulanje was always very, very cold, the time of year made not the slightest difference to its temperature, the mountains had the upper hand in this.

Roger's brother Chris visited Malawi we introduced him to Mulanje. It was a good day, we ate many prawns, much chicken and drank the odd bottle of rose. Unfortunately on our way home to Blantyre, we had to push the Ford Falcon, the battery was apparently not at it's best though we did not realise it at the time. It certainly took a great deal of effort on everyone's part to push that very heavy car up to the top of the hill. Then hastily we all had to jump in, enabling it to run down the hill in order for Jim to start it. We were all exhausted. Strangely there were no complaints, merely the odd comment and a laugh or two. It was all part and parcel of our day out, these things happened in Malawi and other countries like it, we just hoped there would be no difficulty in procuring a new battery. There could be massive shortages of goods but we had not heard news of a battery shortage.

Almost every weekend held an event of some kind, either we were invited to one of the estates or I would decide to give a fillet fondue which everyone seemed to enjoy. Bob Mansfield, who had previously been in Iringa Tanzania with us, had left New Zealand and come to work on tobacco in Malawi. He was in the north of the country, where he worked alongside Jim when he visited that area. Bob at times came to the office in Blantyre and at these times he stayed with us, always practising his dry humour to the full. Each day Stone had to make fried tomatoes for breakfast at Bob's request; we seemed to eat tomatoes by the hundredweight!

★★★

Each time the children came for their holidays we made them members of the Blantyre Club where they could play tennis, swim, play table tennis and meet others their age who were on holiday in Malawi. The club was quite near to the shop enabling me to fetch and carry them with ease. During the weekends, at holiday times, we spent a lot of time with Geoffrey and Shirley on the estate, our three girls went to spend time with their cousins James and Sara who were also on holiday, all five were at school in England.

It was disconcerting to be living in this country when faced with the reality that we no longer had Jock to visit. He had been dead for some years. We could not bring ourselves to go back to the Lunzu valley and Namisu. We had been advised against it by people who had known us in those past years. We preferred to remember it as it was in 1956. 'The Flamingo,' was now much more, supposedly, 'up market'. It was absolutely the opposite to the glorious little 'beat up,' old restaurant of the past. Now it was big modern and unappealing, sometimes we called in. Tony Pope still had the place, he still served piri piri chicken with cabbage salad, it was still extremely good. Unashamedly, Jim and I felt that the only people who had remained unspoiled and untouched in the years away from Nyasaland, now Malawi, were ourselves. Over the years we had learned much and loved more. Our mutual attraction was as strong as ever, we were young at heart and life was wonderful. I had moved out from the shadow of my school desk, into his shaft of light on the opposite side of the hall. Here I had stayed and here I would remain forever. He still gives me the special slow, sexy wink of past years, I know he always will.

★★★

In Malawi the peaceful easy pace of life had almost disappeared. Noisy Presidential motorcades, outriders on enormous motorbikes to the front and to the rear, stormed from palace to palace, or from event to event – shattering any remaining peace. Sharp-eyed Africans 'all seeing,' when there was nothing to see, made an effort to climb the political ladder. Everyone had become careful not to be heard defending or offending the 'wrong' or 'right' person. Malawi had become tense, old timers whose families had lived in the country for generations could be turfed out for ever, should some disgruntled worker report them, inspite of their having a Malawi passport.

Hospitals, schools and shops had either disappeared or had fallen into disrepair. Shortages were the order of the day. It had all these shortcomings but it was still Africa and anyone who knew Africa loved it, smelled it and forgave a lot. Each Friday evening I went to a yoga session at the Blantyre Club. Our yoga teacher was tall, dark, gentle in character and extremely attractive. She had brown soulful eyes, screened by long sweeping lashes. I found yoga relaxing and was amazed at some of the positions I was able to get into under her tuition and supervision – leading to ever more advanced positions. I became very pliable and felt extremely fit. Another wonderful thing happened on Friday evening. When I arrived home a huge iced gin and tonic with a squeeze of lemon juice and a slice of lemon awaited me in the fridge. No one in the world could make a gin and tonic to equal his, only my love could mix this magic, titillating nectar. On these Friday nights my bath water was always full of bubbles waiting to receive an eager body, a kaftan was laid out on the bed, and supper organized. This prelude to the weekend resulted in total relaxation and unprecedented anticipation for us both. On Friday evenings we made our plans for the weekend and beyond.

Soon it would be the tobacco auctions. Always an exciting time the auctioneers, who were usually from Rhodesia, were a breed apart. I loved going to the auction rooms to listen to them 'sing' their sales. The speed at which they 'sang' was magical – a certainty for top of the charts. One auctioneer, Johnny Guitar, did in fact make a record of his selling skills. I have it tucked away somewhere still. One enormous fellow, Toddy Van Rensburg, was a tremendous raconteur and highly amusing; he was so large that to enter the dining room it was necessary for him to turn sideways in order to get through the door. His 'tipple' was gin with ice and water, and an occasional slice of lemon. Whenever the sales were on in the country I invited them to the house together with one or two tobacco farmers. I used to make a huge fondue, a tasty informal meal that always went down well! They were riotous evenings with so much laughter. The parties usually extended to the wee small hours. Everyone enjoyed these times, they gave us all great deal of pleasure and much needed relaxation. The auctions were a busy time.

***

Each time the girls flew home they were overwhelmed with excitement, meeting them at the airport always had an air of adventure about it. They were on top of the world to be back in

Africa, to them it spelt adventure. A downside to this was their arrival into the customs hall. Their cases were opened and searched for pornography. Janey dithered a bit, not knowing the meaning of the word. 'Have you drugs,' 'No,' they trilled, their books, school reports, letters and any other papers they carried which the officials felt might be suspect were well and truly fingered. Carrying either of these commodities would have meant immediate arrest. 'Who are you staying with while you are in our country,' 'Our mum and dad,' Elizabeth replied. The questioning always seemed trite, one had the feeling they had been programmed to ask everyone the same questions in the same order, in the same tone of voice, child or adult it made not the slightest difference.

We ventured in towards them for as far as we were permitted. They usually looked a little dishevelled after the journey but they had big wide smiles.

During their holidays, we took them to the lake and saw that there was a new bridge at Liwonde. Many years ago when Malawi was Nyasaland, the road leading to Lake Nyasa had attractive rustic native villages scattered here and there. In front of the huts huge tree trunks had lain their centres in the process of being hewn out and chiselled away by scantily clad, muscled men. Men who ate many fish, who were content and who ate well, worked well lived and slept in what comfort they needed. They had produced many children to follow them in their trade, and to keep them in old age. Armed with just an axe, they bent over chipping, carving and rubbing smooth the sides of their work. Their bodies were shining with sweat and spattered with wood dust. Chippings exploded from beneath the tool they used. Talking, calling, singing, picking their nose and scratching their crotch from dawn to dusk, until they had sculpted a canoe suitable for their fishing needs. Always, there were sounds of the villagers calling to one another. The women pounding maize, hoeing fields and tending to the needs of children; their laughter echoed over the lake and into the surrounding bush, children with dirty noses and smiling faces ran after us calling 'Morny bwana'.

Things had changed. The small Indian doukas along the roads were no longer there. The essentials provided to make life a little easier for the African had disappeared, only a few shells remained. Malawians who were not used to making a living as store owners and all this entailed had left the premises to bats and their droppings. Termites whose brown tunnels ran along the crumbling white-washed walls helped to give everything an air of neglect and decay. Sometimes in the past, on our approach to the lake, there had been huge mounds of steaming fresh elephant dung on the road then turning our eyes towards the bush alongside, a huge backside was visible disappearing into the scrub. In those days, not for nothing was the battered wooden notice erected by the public works dept., which read 'Elephant on this road.' It was a far cry from the state of affairs in these present days. Where are the elephant now? Visits to the lake, always induced gut-wrenching nostalgia.

Usually we stayed in a cottage at either Monkey Bay or Palm Beach where we lazed, fished, swam and sat under the palms reading. At times we were roused by the children into playing ball games. We ate our meals in the cottage and made full use of the kitchen.

In the back of the Land Rover was a safari box which contained all the basics and a few goodies which we felt that we might need. Supper was often a picnic on the beach accompanied by our nightly tipple. We talked until quite late, then tired from the sun and heat of the day we eventually rolled into bed. The acrid smoke curls swirling from the burning mosquito coils penetrated our nostrils. Peering through the open door of our bedroom we watched the moon's reflection on the lake, becoming hypnotized by reflected colours on the lapping water. To the gentle swish of the surrounding palm trees we drifted into a deep and dreamless sleep. The children completely worn out from the days exertions were fast asleep, bodies limp as rags, limbs spread at all angles and in every direction.

As is the nature of things, Jim and I tended to make comparisons when faced with old dreams and ghosts from the past. At times we decided to visit Cape Maclear where there was a long sandy beach sheltered by rocks. Islands nearby were within swimming distance. We lay on the beach reading and later watched the local fishermen in their canoes. Their dark backs gleaming in the setting sun as they paddled chanting towards the shore with their catch. My mind always wandered back to the time we visited the Cape with Jock, he in his baggy shorts and white vest, drinking whisky and soda, and talking incessantly of the time when foolishly I been lying in the sun for too long. I had fallen asleep during the afternoon as I lay reading, and was rewarded by an enormous water blister bouncing painfully up and down on my chest.

★★★

Elizabeth had decided she would like to learn to drive and with great patience Jim took her round and round the drive, teaching her to use the clutch, gears and brake. It was no easy task. Eventually convinced that she could manage the car alone, she was left to her own devices. We thought she would cope quite well taking the car up and down the drive and around the house. How wrong we were. Somehow she had driven the Ford Falcon between two poinsettia trees and the car was completely jammed. It took six of us to pull it from the stranglehold of the trees and the deep hole into which the two front wheels were firmly entrenched. 'How the hell did you manage to get into that position Liz?' Jim mused, shaking his head in wonder, at what seemed to us all an impossible manoeuvre. She is still often reminded of this faux pas.

Shirley decided she needed to work and moved into Mombo Road with us, each morning she left to join the other office workers who were employed by Lever Bros. Every weekend she went back to the estate. I think this lasted for three months and then she decided that 'home' was the place to be. She moved into the office with Geoffrey and helped him with surplus and urgent paperwork.

The Tea Planters' Ball was our next big event. Geoffrey had mentioned this to us before we left to go on leave. In England I scoured the shops and eventually found a satin ball gown in black and white stripes, with a little lace trim at the neck and fitted at the waist. It was very lovely in a 'Calamity Jane.' way. To enhance the image I bought a long hairpiece to match my black hair. The overall effect was dramatic. Rolling my eyes I asked for approval. In reply, Jim described it as jaw dropping. Fortunately he did approve. The Tea Planters' Ball was a huge success and so was my dress. Jim in black tie looked very handsome. Geoffrey, whose hair was rather darker than Jim's, had large brown expressive eyes, both men were tall and very good to look at. They were two very different people, yet so obviously brothers. Shirley and I were lucky. Shirley was much shorter than me. She had dark brown hair and lovely eyes set in an elfin face. Her dress was black and made her look demure. We met many people we knew and exchanged news and gossip, we drank, picked dainty morsels and enjoyed supper. Best of all we danced in 'another world.' I danced the night away with my love. We arrived home content and sleepy, in time for breakfast. It was with some relief I took off my hair piece.
  'God, that feels better.'

Jim looked at me, 'Well I must admit you look more like the old Cog now,' he laughed handing me a piece of toast and a cup of tea. Enough for breakfast today.

Undressed we flopped into bed, arms flung out, love and smiles etched onto tired faces, we fell asleep until the middle of the day. When I awoke Jim was still fast asleep, I watched him lying relaxed and handsome and as I bent to gently kiss him his arms crept around me and my heart melted as I looked into his longing grey green eyes. We fell asleep. It would soon be Christmas when the children would be home full of bounce and festive joy. I invited Bob Mansfield because we were not happy at his being alone in Kasungu and a little of his dry-as-a-bone humour which had so endeared us to him during our Iringa days would be welcome. No doubt we would visit Geoffrey, whose humour was on a par with Bob's, it all spelt good fun and much laughter.

★★★

Later I went to the north with Jim and Roger, visiting tobacco estates in Kasungu and Mchingi. Two other main areas of production were also being encouraged to expand, these were Namwera (east of Lake Malawi) mainly run by Greek farmers and Zomba and Thyolo in the south, owned mainly by white Malawians (Sir Malcolm Barrow, the federal deputy PM, Drew Henderson, who was an opposition MP and Chairman of the Tobacco Association, Don Pyman, Robin Thornycroft Conforzi and Lonrho). These areas all old and established were being encouraged to enlarge and to apply modern methods hence they were just as much in need of an extension services as those in the north. For all these reasons the Malawi Government employed a Tobacco Extension Officer, James Moss. Roger Barclay-Smith asked for two or three seasons to spend two weeks out of four in the growing season to help keep Jim au fait with the latest Rhodesian results. These times were as Roger describes them. Magic Years.

So we headed north to Namwera – a large area of fertile land settled for some time by Greeks who were very conservative and suspicious of new ideas, hence they were in great need of extension. It was a remote area so the visit was usually for a week, giving time for the farm areas to be well and truly covered. There were two factions in this community those from Crete, and the mainland Greeks, whose freely offered hospitality could have been misinterpreted by some. We preferred our independence. Jim maneuvered the long dusty potholed roads without complaint, we had to prise our sticky backsides from sweaty wet seats at each call we made.

On the road from Mangochi to Namwera was a huge forest area, in the middle of this there was a cottage. It had been built by an old resident doctor in Mangochi for his retirement. He had retired and lived there happily until he died. Afterwards the cottage had been bought by a civil servant from Zomba who also so planned to retire there. This new owner, a friend of Roger was only spending the weekends in the cottage so he was only to delighted to have someone stay in the place during the week. He suggested we use of this delightful house when in the area. There was no electricity but abundant fresh water. The buildings were old and romantic, the pictures on the wall historically fascinating. Built on a steep slope it had fresh water running through the tiny swimming pool and was surrounded by wonderful views. It was perched high above the main road and the approach was on foot. When we arrived it was usually after dark. We parked in a layby hooting madly. Before long we would see two lights approaching as they zig- zagged down the path. It usually took about ten minutes and then we would be warmly greeted by the house-boy who led the way with a light and the cook who brought up the rear with another light. In between them, to do the carrying, came four or five watchman and gardeners; one would carry a beer crate, one the food box and the others a suitcase each. They were magic times.

The resident cook made our evening meal and breakfast. I do remember sitting on a veranda which had all round protection from mosquito gauze. This was surrounded by bushes of sweet smelling frangipani, hollyhocks and bougainvillea. To the side of the house, mango trees threw shade onto patches of spiky burnt dry grass. I remember the road before the approach to the wood and the house was marred by an empty store. It was a scorched relic from the past with broken windows and peeling walls. A shell packed with ghosts from a time when the rafters groaned with brightly coloured cloth, and shelves packed with every item used by the African – when life by the very existence of these stores was so much easier for the local people. These stores were owned by Indians, generally known as douka wallahs. Outside the stores, Africans had in the past sat at treadle Singer sewing machines, making, mending, re-making, talking singing, calling the time of day to passers by and laughing. Everywhere, ghosts and memories bombarded us.

Now there were exhausted charcoal sellers in rags, pushing heavy loads of charcoal which they had forced into burlap bags on their bent and beaten up old bicycles as they were headed for the local market.

★★★

When our visits to the more remote farms were completed we made our way south towards Blantyre and the not-so-distant farms. We agreed our overnight stay must be at the 'Kanimambo' a hostelry on the borders of Malawi-Mozambique, in the highlands of Dedza. The owner was a friendly Portuguese man named Maciel, who had a large house and store nearby. The staff were a jolly crowd always ready to help and to make our stay as comfortable as possible. So, on the occasional weekend we decided to meet at the 'Kanimambo,' Roger, Bob and ourselves, we walked, talked and spent hilarious evenings together, sometimes bordering on the intellectual as we felt that we could find an answer to anything! One weekend Bob attended a hippy wedding in the open air. The ceremony was held on Dedza mountain. He had obviously been very carried away by it all, because after our short siesta we walked into the hotel sitting room to find him not only in full voice but with spectacles awry and his tie round his head with the long end hanging over one ear. This was a most un-Bob-like gesture. He was a quiet man with a quirky sense of humour, a man who normally disliked any type of demonstrative behaviour either from himself or other people. To find him sitting there warbling 'Sur le Pont D'Avignon', after a few glasses of wine taken at French nuptials celebrated on Dedza mountain, was to us beyond belief. It was a long time before he heard the last of this unbelievable escapade. He was an accomplished artist and I felt that he was in torment at times. He had to escape and let his hair down sometimes in order to relieve his unspoken anxieties. After this he could settle down and become the old Bob again.

It could be very cold in Dedza. The trees shrouded in a blanket of chiperoni mist. Excess moisture swirled to earth, saturating everything below. The wood fire blazed in the stone hearth of the hotel bar and on these days I handed over my hot water bottle to the barman – it was handed back to me on a silver tray with great ceremony at the time we said 'Goodnight'.

At these times the bedrooms were chilly and the beds felt damp. Five heavy cotton blankets did not stop our bodies from shivering. If we moved the shiver almost became a rigor. All the bedrooms had twin beds. I usually crept into Jim's bed, snuggled up and drifted into a cosy warm and delicious sleep lulled by a softly beating heart, seduced by the intoxicating scent of Old Spice, leather and gun oil. We shared the bottle!

On mornings like this we counted to five, leapt out of bed and went quickly through the necessary morning ablutions. We hurriedly dressed, dashed into the bar and stood shivering, backsides in front of the leaping flames of the fire burning brightly in the hearth. Yes, it can be cold in Africa.

271

Roger appeared as lively as ever, today he and I were eating chambo (fish) cooked in garlic butter for breakfast, much to Jim's horror. His fish was kept well away from the magic clove. We ate freshly baked bread and drank chilled white wine. A surplus to last night's needs. It was refreshing and despite the early hour, received with delight. Our unusual breaking of the fast ended after drinking strong, freshly ground coffee.

During breakfast we made plans to visit various Greek tobacco farms in the area. Usually I sat in the Land Rover reading while Jim and Roger attended to their tobacco queries, inspections and chores. At times I went in to chat and drink coffee with the wives. Some impromptu visits to farms had saved crops. As a result of this close relationships were formed.

It had been a grueling day as both men had been relentless in their determination to see each farmer in the area to check planting, weeding, topping and reaping as they occur; disease, fertilizing, tying, curing, bulking, the list of work seemed endless. At the end of the day all tired and weary we arrived back at the 'Kanimambo' where we were handed sandwiches and tooth-achingly sweet, sticky Portuguese biscuits. Sitting around the fire we discussed the events of the day, well the men did, I listened! We were given a handwritten slip of paper which passed as a menu, we are asked 'What would you like to eat at suppertime,' for a moment the conversation was diverted to the choices for supper.

Later I wandered over to the bar to let the barman know what we had decided to eat. We usually we had either chambo (fish) or chicken.

To move was to shiver, as evening approached the chiperoni took on bone chilling proportions, moist cool fingers of curling mist seemed to penetrate every pore. Walking away from the fire to the chill of the shower room was a foot dragging, mammoth task for me but the men did not seem to fare so badly, their complaints were rather less vocal! To put an end to this whole procedure, I rushed to take the first shower, a hurried affair, 'Please God don't let me drop the soap' I trilled out loud as I felt I could not bear any further draught on my wet body caused by the movement of bending. I dried myself well and hurriedly threw on my clothes and emerged glowing. Africa is a contradictory place always throwing out a challenge, hot in the valley during the day, so cold up here in the mountains during the night. I took my book from the travel case and wandered back into the bar and sat by the fire. We were the only guests. Within a short time Jim appeared, calm, glowing, fresh and good, a waft of aftershave titillated my nostrils, went straight to my head and my heart stood still. There he was kind and smiling with his wistful grey-green eyes, giving me a toe-curling look which I knew so well.

Roger bounded in, well scrubbed, shining and as ever raring to go. It was sundowner time, a time for relaxation, laughter and for making further plans. The man behind the bar, whose name I cannot remember, was a great character whose stories of night life and the good time girls of Dedza made us roar with laughter. Their establishment I seem to remember was called 'The Green Door'! Mostly we bought a jeroboam of wine, most of which was consumed over the evening accompanied by huge tins of cashew nuts.

That evening we drank Portuguese rose with our evening meal of pork and trimmings. The next day we must leave for home although we had a yen to stay one more night despite the chiperoni. However, go, we must because other previously arranged commitments prevented our capitulating to this lurking desire. In bed we lay cosily content listening to the soft patter of misty rain. A muffled sound of drums from some distant village in Mozambique rose up penetrating the heavy night air as it shrouded the mountain. Their beat at times broken by the croak of a nearby frog. All this and we were to be up at first light.

We awoke to the rattle of dishes, the cook was in the kitchen nearby and the air did not have the chill edge of past mornings. The chiperoni had lifted. We organized and packed our luggage put it into the Land Rover and wandered into the dining room. Roger was up, he had been for a short walk and was waiting for us. We ate lots of scrambled egg and toast for breakfast and drank one or two cups of coffee, hoping to sharpen our wits.

On our way home, Jim and I both remarked on the lack of game in the area. Unless we travelled to the Liwonde game area there was nothing to be seen. Chikwawa had now changed beyond belief. We could only reminisce over our past hunting safaris with Jock. Now they were no longer possible. I should explain that 'safari' is a Swahili word. In Malawi (the old Nyasaland) a journey is 'ulendo.' There were still a few impala, hartebeest, hippo, lion and elephant in Malawi, buffalo must surely still be wandering down in the bush on the Malawi-Mozambique border, though we felt certain their numbers had dwindled considerably over the years. Our vocal comparisons between now and the past rumbled on, as we travelled mile after mile over the once graded and well kept roads.

From our weekend in Dedza, we bumped back over these roads which were in need of a great deal of repair, to Blantyre. Blantyre looked shabby and old as we drove slowly through the town to our home in Mombo Road which was on the opposite side of this commercial capital of Malawi. At times it could look charming when the jacaranda was in full bloom, their flowers falling to earth shedding a lilac blue carpet to coat and cover the disarray below.

As we had passed Michiru the mountain which stands as sentry to Blantyre it sent me messages from the past. Again I step back in time looking down at my hand resting on Jim's knee. I felt overwhelmed at the way in which the world had changed. Then suddenly I had become flushed in a warm glow with the certainty that though all around us had changed, some used the term 'moved on', we were still the same. Our love, our dreams and memories would be with us forever, they were sacred and filled us with immense joy and pride. We had been privileged to live in those times to have experienced this past excitement and romance, the unknown and all that it had entailed. In fact the present was a pretty dull old place by comparison.

My hand spread out over the warmth of the golden thigh beneath. I looked up into a face broadened by a mischievous cheeky smile and twinkling eyes. We were safe, let the world throw at us what it will.

We promised ourselves that a visit to the boabab country of the Shire valley and the area of Chikwawa sometime in the near future. Our next free weekend would be spent at the Kuchawe Inn on the Zomba plateau, we realised that over the years many things would have changed. The following week Jim wrote up his reports and visited local farms in the area surrounding Blantyre. We had a very busy week in the shop from the point of view of sales and deliveries. I enjoyed unpacking and arranging all the new china and silverware, placing it in what I felt were strategic positions, where the customer could not fail but see them. Arriving home one Thursday evening from the shop, tired after a hectic day, I decided to sit and read my book on the khonde (veranda). It was a beautiful balmy evening it occurred to me that it was almost sundowner time, I would wait for Jim – he should be home soon. Almost immediately afterwards I heard the Land Rover rattle up the drive, the door was opened, the door clanged shut footsteps came towards the veranda. A tousled head atop a face covered with a film of red dust peered round the door he came striding over to plant a dusty kiss.

'If you can leave the shop a little earlier tomorrow love I think we should go to the 'Kuchawe'. I saw no problem. The lady in charge, she had been there for years, was always sympathetic to this particular type of request plus she had a 'thing' about Jim and it proved very useful. 'See how you feel. Have a bath, make our sundowners and then we can sit and talk about it' I was all for the idea. We enjoyed these weekends alone. Some trips became an obsession with us, this was one of them.

And so, the following day, we headed off towards the 'Zomba Inn'. Memories loomed large, particularly when we passed the 'Ntondwe Bar' on the road to Zomba. This once romantic little place was now a run down native drinking bar, crumbling and dirty. Very little remained of the way it had been. Glancing at it as we passed we noticed what it had become. Even so, in our minds eye we saw it only as it had been in 1956. When mesmerised we had sat together unable to believe the lot fate had handed out to us as we ate our chambo and salad, accompanied by a glass of Chardonnay. After our meal, we had left in a dream for the journey back to Limbe and my Citroen tucked away amid the blue gum trees by the cemetery wall, 'Aye, aye, aye what memories.'

★★★

Travelling the old road to Zomba, deterioration was everywhere. The town was still a conglomeration of assorted buildings, all in a bad state of repair with much surrounding squalor, the bread shop belonging to the Greek we noticed, was still producing acceptable buns and loaves each day. On the slopes of Zomba plateau was the old Gymkhana Club – a relic of the old days. Up its misty craggy sides stood the once elegant houses where the British bureaucrats had lived, now they were rather less beautiful and housed by African bureaucrats. Travelling along the winding 'one up' only road to the inn, we were always steeped in nostalgia. The sides were planted with sweet smelling fir and pine trees in soft mossy ground, bracing fresh cool air and at times light swirling mist titillated the senses. We drove into the weedy car park and glanced at each other with raised eyebrows.

At the reception desk we asked for a room overlooking the plain, a room we had always been given in the past was vacant. We were escorted along the veranda, the view was stunning, up and down one or two steps and along a short corridor to our room. It was still the pleasant room it had always been, rather more worn, but clean. Jim went to the car with the porter and helped him carry the luggage.

'Okay love'?

'Of course' I replied.

We asked for a bottle of red wine to be sent to the room then we unpacked and settled down to a pleasant evening and discussed what we fancied to eat for supper. The decision was unanimous, fresh Zomba trout. Who could ask for more? If it lived up to expectations we would have it again tomorrow.

The trout was delicious – well cooked and nicely served. The Chardonnay accompanying the meal was chilled and refreshing. Afterwards we sat for sometime drinking coffee and looking over the dark plain below, it was moonlight and the stars were brilliant, the night was dotted with lights. Jim put out his hand, I placed mine in it and we sat in silence for sometime

'I suggest we go to Namikango tomorrow, take a lunch box and make a day of it, we can walk round the estate if only to see what shape it is in.'

I was a little taken aback at this suggestion, Namikango had been the estate we had fallen in love with and failed to get after our crop failure at Namisu.

'Yes, it would be interesting, I wonder if it is occupied?' I replied, feeling doubtful and a little uneasy.

The crickets were noisy, owls hooted, night jars cried. From inside the sound of a radio playing 'music of the day' disturbed the natural sounds of night, I felt the two were not sympathetic and should not be mixed. I knew Jim's thinking matched mine.

'Come along love, time for bed'.

Arm in arm we went to the bedroom. The bedside lights had been switched on, the beds turned down. On the small table by the window stood a bottle of red wine with sparkling glasses. I noticed a chocolate had been laid on each pillow and a carafe of water on each bedside table. Completely relaxed, we sat by the window with a glass of wine. The wall lights were too low for us to read by, we would have to wait until we were in our bed where the lights were a little brighter.

The night air was becoming decidedly cooler, we decided to warm up in bed . Jim had his book peeping from beneath the covers, for the umpteenth time he was reading 'Where men still dream' by Lawrence Green. I was reading 'Last Chance in Africa' by Negley Farson. Would we ever let go of Africa? I thought not. We put down our book curled up and disappeared into another world.

Saturday we awoke refreshed, ate breakfast, collected the lunch box and headed towards Namikango. It was a bone-shaking old road. Some villages we passed were all but in ruins. There seemed to be so many people and such little activity, thin dogs and scrawny chickens scratched around for food. Goats foraged and made an awful mess and everything looked neglected. Women wore broken shoes their clothes resembled rags. Men wore torn shirts hanging from their bodies and trousers with the backsides hanging out. All they appeared to have to eat was a foul smelling grey fish soup with nishima. Mangoes grew in profusion around the villages and these were eaten with relish by everyone. Some of the women had on once bright, now faded kitenges around their waists, falling to the knees. President Banda's face stretched over wide backsides. Everywhere it is written that − Malawi is the warm heart of Africa − Tee-shirts blazing the slogan are on sale everywhere, particularly at the airport and in the hotel shops.
Eventually we arrived at Namikango, it had almost been reduced to a shell. Many of the coloured octagonal veranda tiles, if not stolen were broken and useless. We look at each other raised our

eyes to Heaven, should we laugh or cry. This estate had held so much potential. Shrugging we walked on, suddenly deciding to turn round and walk back to the Land Rover. It would be much wiser to drive it into the bush where we could still wander round and keep an eye on it at the same time. Tyres had a habit of disappearing. We wandered around the fields. There were now no peasant farmers. Jim had often wondered why he had not been asked to visit the area. Here was the answer – there were no farmers to visit! Feeling somewhat disheartened, we drove away to try to find a suitable place to have lunch. It was difficult. We eventually went back to the hotel and ate beneath the fir trees on the slope.

On our excursion we had noticed so many 'empty faced' ex-Indian shops, the unpopular owners had been expelled from their properties, which in turn had been handed over to local people who were unable to comprehend the rudiments of keeping the business as a going concern.

In the afternoon we went for a long walk on the plateau. Afterwards we lay on the bed and read, even dozed, to be awakened by crickets and croaking frogs. We lay for a while and listened to the sound of tins rattling in the kitchen, the coming and going of vehicles, dogs barking and the perpetual sound of a pump. I felt Jim looking at me, turning I smiled, he gave me his old familiar wink. Later we leapt up bathed, changed and prepared for supper – it was just as good as it had been the night before. We sat in the bar to drink our coffee, it was chilly outside. Tomorrow we were to leave, we had enjoyed our stay in Kuchawe, but had been disheartened by the shambles that was once Namikango. We had seen that Zomba was no different to the rest of the country, much worse in many ways. We had always thought it so grand in the past.

After a late breakfast we left this once flourishing community with its magnificent mountain and drove back past the Ntondwe bar to

279

Blantyre giving knowing smiles as we approached the cemetery and familiar blue gums. The time was fast approaching for our local leave. This was always spent in Africa travelling from one country to another. We had in the past, covered most of East and Central Africa and a great deal of South Africa.

★★★

As I look out of the window I am greeted by the splendour of a scene covered in a blanket of snow. How happy you would have been my love to see the trees covered by this crisp untouched whiteness, still and quiet. Deciding it was time to make a cup of tea I put on my slippers and the cosy warm dusty pink dressing gown you bought for me some years ago. In a huddle wandering through to the kitchen I put on the kettle, draw back the curtains and looked through each window at the scene outside. My hands clasp the mug, steam rises in the cool air. I am making my way back to the bedroom now, if only I was carrying a tray and two teas. Quickly I place my mug on the side table, and leap back into bed drawing up the covers around my neck, lonely as I lie thinking and wondering. Then sitting up to drink my tea. I sadly watch huge flakes fall silently onto the trees and your shed, how I wish you were by my side. I wish you were here to pelt me with snowballs, I wish you were here so I could pelt them back.

★★★

Just one week, and the girls would arrive home for their annual holiday. My mother was to arrive a week later. We must make arrangements for our safari. At the moment Roger was in Rhodesia – he had a flat I think, in Sinoia. We were invited to stay with him for a couple of days. From there we intended to travel through Rhodesia with, for the sake of comfort, two cars (his Citroen and our own). Meanwhile, we had enjoyed the break at the Kuchawe Inn we liked to go away but we were never sorry to be back at home.

Stone prepared our evening meal whilst we unpacked, bathed, changed picked some vegetables from the garden to be used that evening, then went for a stroll before settling down for the evening with a book and a sundowner. Tomorrow was Monday we must be up early. Jim was going to the office to organize his next safari to farms in Namwera and Mandimba. He thought he would leave Tuesday and would be away until Friday. I hated this!

We both had to leave the house early, the shop opened at 7.30. We could never get used to the 9.0 am opening times when on leave in the UK. The week passed by as usual, Jim called in to see me immediately he arrived back on Friday. It was good to see him – I missed him dreadfully when he was away up country. In the past I had always travelled with him, I missed these matey journeys and our chats as we travelled along dusty or muddy bumpy roads. Separation did not sit well in our soulmate existence.

Geoffrey had a meeting in Blantyre, Shirley decided to call into the shop after buying groceries and visiting the market. They ate supper with us, and as usual we talked of the past and of our weekend in Zomba. We laughed a lot and made naughty little quips. It was time to meet excited children at the airport. I was always wet-eyed with emotion on these occasions. They struggled through the airport formalities and flew out arms open to greet their grinning joyful parents. They could not get home fast enough to cut into the 'Welcome Home' cake awaiting them.

Our next visit to the airport was to meet my mother, she arrived flustered and a little cross at the treatment she encountered. The searching of her luggage, the questioning, querying and prying had irritated her nevertheless she was pleased to be with us and showed it. We put her luggage in the boot. The children linked their arms through hers. They were laughing as they came over to the car, the girls made her feel comfortable. There was a great deal of chatter all the way back to the house, when told of the trip to

281

Rhodesia voices became shrill and excited. 'Quiet girls', the noise was getting a little out of hand. On our arrival home all was chaos. Mother had noticed the curio sellers in the streets of Blantyre on her way from the airport – she would like to see what they had for sale, not yet of course, but later. We took note of this, mother tended to drop hints now and then!

★★★

This weekend we decided to take them all to Cholo which was once a pleasant, leafy place with colonial overtones and wonderful views looking over the rolling hillsides of the tea estates. Jim and I decided this might be a very good way of spending the weekend. We would visit Geoffrey! We had also decided to take my mum down the escarpment to visit the old Africa. To introduce her to our old haunts in the boabab country of the Shire valley where we had walked and hunted so many years ago. We thought it seemed like a splendid idea, there were no mosquitoes there until the rainy season, malaria was the very last thing any of us wanted before we went to Rhodesia.

We enjoyed our visit to Cholo, everything was as we had hoped it would be from scenic beauty to the cool charm of Geoffrey who supplied us with much of his dry humour and acidic wit. We took with us steak, bread, wine and various other goodies. Marko, his cook, produced an excellent meal under the beady scrutiny of Shirley. It was a good day, a lot of humour was bandied about a great deal of laughter echoed around the veranda of the old estate home, it probably reached out, echoing over the brilliant green tea bushes on the hills surrounding the homestead.

On a more serious note we turned to the present happenings in the country, mentioning the movement of the thuggish Malawi Youth, hostile, furtive and sneaky, employed by the government to spy. Our beloved Nyasaland of old no longer existed it seemed. This beautiful land was in the hands of a 'band' hell bent on destroying any semblance of the past almost everyone was mistrusted and treated as a spy. Both Jim and I had wondered whether of not to return to the UK we did not enjoy this present alien mood of Africa. It interfered with the love and joy of past memories, but even so we knew Africa despite its problems, would always be in our hearts and always retain its timeless beauty. Forever we would remember the stars dancing around a huge moon hanging in a dark indigo sky and we two lovers who had lain beneath, entranced by its magic, its beauty and our love.

★★★

The following weekend we introduced the family to the Chikwawa escarpment, the stunning views we knew so well and the vast expanse of bewildering, bewitching bush, spreading out for as far as the eye could see, to where land and sky become one. The village of Chikwawa, as we had known it, no longer existed when we had passed through, on our long trek out into the bush at the beginning of a hunting safari with old Jock. We drove around for some time trying to point things out as we remembered them but it was no use as only we knew what had once been. Nevertheless both my mother and the girls tried to understand. They enjoyed the stories we had to tell them, and asked many questions. We found an ideal place to have a picnic, under an acacia tree where there were no huts and we were away from the road. As for Jim and I we were aching with a stomach churning nostalgia for a time in the past.

Back home, Stone unloaded the Land Rover, he had a bowl of aubergine fritters waiting for us to devour before supper, which was to be piri piri chicken he said. Filled with renewed energy at this announcement we all trooped off to bath or shower, whichever one took our fancy, emerging clean, tidy, and smelling of soap. Jim's Old Spice pervaded my nostrils sending me into my usual spin. He gave me a wink followed by a kiss as he handed me a glass of wine. Stone's fritters were delicious we ate them accompanied by a glass of crisp white wine. The piri piri chicken was tasty and succulent – we demolished every morsel.

We had one week to prepare, as next week we were to make our way to Rhodesia via Mozambique. Jim and I had planned what we felt would be a simple straightforward route. It was a busy week, I had to work and Jim had to visit local farms and bring his reports right up-to-date with any forward advice which he felt may be needed during his time away. Each lunch break I drove to the house. When I left to return to the shop I took the children, and sometimes my mother back with me. From the shop they walked to the nearby club. If the girls played tennis mum found a comfortable chair and read her book until I was free to take them home. This was not late as the shop closed its doors at 4.30pm. I stipulated that it was the responsibility of each of the girls, and my mother, to pack their cases sensibly and keep things to a minimum. I was there if they needed advice. My responsibility was packing for Jim and myself. Washing our clothes en route was never a problem – each overnight stay had facilities of some kind.

After a hectic week the day of our departure arrived. Stone had been given instructions to keep watch on the house because robberies were now commonplace. I thought this was a good time for him to spring clean the kitchen and spend some time polishing and tidying the house. I gave him money to buy meat for the day we were due to return home. With breakfast over, our luggage was piled neatly into the boot of the ca. One excited mother and three excited children sat in the back We decided Janey (as the smallest) should sit in front with us. I did offer my front seat to my mother but she seemed to want to sit in the back; there was a good all round panoramic view in the Citroen which helped. We set off in an unrelenting whirl of dust, which persisted pretty well all the way to Tete in Mozambique. When we arrived in Tete we found we had missed the ferry, it was just turning around on the other side of the river to come back. The wait seemed interminable, it took almost an hour to travel over, we had to wait for cars and passengers to disembark and then there was all the fuss of scrutinizing tickets and scrutinizing us. We had to answer what seemed to be a thousand questions before we finally drove the car onto the ferry to cross the Zambezi. To say the ferry was temperamental was to put it mildly. There was a great deal of nail biting and a lot of patience to be exercised before we finally got to the other side. Some of the locals, admittedly not all, were anything but friendly. We clutched everything we were carrying tightly and made sure that the car was locked.

'This anti colonial feeling seems to be spreading fast.' Jim said a little wryly raising his eyebrows.

'I wonder what the atmosphere will be like in Rhodesia?' Ian Smith with U.D.I. seemed, to have things under control at the moment.

Eventually we arrived, grinding up onto the sand on to the other side of the river. We were beginning to doubt our wisdom in taking this route. Jim drove the car off the ferry.

'Into the car girls let's go.'

We gave mother a hand she was quite chirpy, if a little weary following the journey on the ferry.

'That is one hell of a relief,' Jim sighed settling into the driving seat prepared for the upward struggle through the Zambezi mud to the abominably rutted, potholed road above. This we decided would be a slow road to travel on. It bore all the hall marks of hell!

'Thank God for the Citroen's suspension,' I said thinking particularly of mothers comfort.

On either side of the road strung willy nilly from crooked tree to crooked tree, were the countries main telephone service wires, some taut, some hanging in long hoops almost touching the ground depending upon the angle of the tree to which they were attached. It all looked very temporary and Heath Robinson. We decided the

British colonies had the edge on the Portuguese, as we vividly remembered the telephone in the tree trunk on 'Giggle Mile'. Much later than anticipated, the ferry journey having taken so long, we decided to keep an eye open for somewhere to stay overnight, surely there would be a pousada as this was the main road from the border. Yes there it was, as we approached the next corner, facing us on the bend stood a building offering accommodation and food. It looked weathered and had splintered wooden steps up to reception. The paint on the hand rails was peeling. Jim and I went off to investigate, leaving the family in the car. We were greeted by a friendly Portuguese lady who spoke a little English. She was obviously pleased to see us, we got the impression that it was not easy to eke out a living in the present environment. Looking round I noticed it was clean if not sumptuous. Looking at Jim I gave him a perfunctory nod and we decided the sensible thing to do was stay the night. Five people, the lady of the hotel was overjoyed. We were very tired, this unexpected stop on our journey proved to be very comfortable. A great effort was made in cooking supper to perfection, the results were excellent.

'That was some ferry love.'

'I could not agree more.' Two heads on one pillow drifted into a dreamless sleep.

The next morning, we were really thrown into confusion – mother had lost her hairbrush. If she had lost her handbag and passport there could not have been more fuss, the brush had belonged to her late sister and was very precious to mum. 'Jean you must ask the staff if they have seen it.' I felt this was not appropriate. No doubt she had left it behind and had forgotten to bring it with her. I felt it unwise to spark a revolution perceived by accusation. Towns in Rhodesia were normal and well stocked, the brush would be easily replaced, the chemists I was a convinced, would have mountains of hairbrushes.

★★★

FEBRUARY 4TH, 2004

It is now three years my love since that dreadful day in 2001.

Sitting in your chair I choose and put on a film of Africa sitting back to watch, putting together pieces of our past life, watching and thinking of the times before that dark day of your departure when my love, my life and my reason for living was blown apart, leaving me like a tumbleweed rolling backwards and forwards aimlessly across a barren dessert. We are born, we live and we die. What happens in between these three phases of life depends upon fate, the realization and acceptance of recognizing your soul mate, of given love, of commitments, loyalties sacrifice and joy of laughing together and sometimes crying, through sorrow, discomfort, shortages and sickness, danger from man and from the wild. This vast, beautiful and wild wilderness I now see on the screen was so much a part of our life together, in some way I feel sandwiched between what has been, what is and what might be for us in the future. It is impossible for me to believe that our life together is over. Somehow, somewhere, there must be something mapped out for us. Or am I left with no roads running to red slushy mud? No sun to squeeze out the noise from the cicadas? No crickets to mark the oncoming of an African night? Your arms hold me back. Your smile keeps me watching and waiting.

★★★

The following day, relaxed and refreshed we re-organized ourselves and headed out towards Sinoia, we ate an early breakfast and took a packed lunch with us. If everything went according to plan, we should arrive at Roger's flat in mid to late afternoon. Again we blessed the Citroen's suspension it took the rough road very smoothly giving no-one cause for complaint. I decided to put on a tape of 'Swinging Safari'. In full voice we joined in the chorus of each song. It was a happy, uneventful journey but game was very scarce and we saw only the odd impala. As we travelled along Jim would ask, looking a little bewildered, 'Where has all the game disappeared to these days?' We had no difficulty in finding Roger – he had been very precise in his directions and we had notes and maps. His Citroen was in the car park proof that we had arrived at the right place. We were greeted with open arms so typical of Roger then ushered into the flat and organized in no time at all.

Having brought him up-to-date with all the news of Malawi over tea and biscuits, he decided we should eat supper at the club. Mother and the girls ate at the flat it – was a night out for just the three of us. We sat round the bar and we were introduced to friends. We talked, ate supper and talked again. In those times there was a great deal to talk, not least about, where all our futures lay.

Everyone was asleep when we arrived home. The sitting room had taken on a rosy glow from the electric torpedo-shaped lamp in the corner, suspended red oil was rising and falling in globules, driven up by heat from below. I was very intrigued as this was something quite new. It had a slightly mesmerizing effect and as I sat and watched, I put it on my mental list of 'Would likes'.

The next morning, after breakfast, we set off in great style with two cars. Mother and Liz went with Roger. The noise we made in our sing along safari was not quite up to mum's taste. We moved from car to car it became rather like musical chairs as whichever car the children were in rocked and rolled with mirth and song. We managed to buy a hairbrush before we left. We were heading towards Bulawayo to visit a cousin of mothers, they had not seen each other for many years but had always kept in touch, we were to stay for two or three nights on their cattle ranch on the outskirts of the town. They were Ruby and Ewart Golightly, but I cannot remember the name of the farm. It was a delightful, though tearful, reunion with emotions running high for a while. We left them to talk and organize tea whilst Roger, Jim and I together with the girls tagging along behind took a walk around the farm. At this time terrorists could be anywhere and it was prudent to be cautious and expect problems. Life was not easy on the farm. The couple had encountered many insurgencies and had cattle stolen. I remember they also had frustrations with electricity. It was a very pleasant two days. We wandered and walked around the area went and into Bulawayo there were lots of interesting sights. Despite all these set backs they soldiered on for some years but eventually they were able to take no more and they decided to live in England where Ewart's health deteriorated fast. Fortunately the Masonic fraternity found them a flat in Hove. After Ewart's death Ruby continued to visit what had now become Zimbabwe, it had been her home for many years and all her friends were there. She was very saddened at what had become of the country – rampant corruption and deterioration shrouded every aspect of a once thriving society.

We said our fond farewells after this short stay and followed the road to Salisbury. The roads were a delight they, like so many other things, had been re-built during U.D.I. everything happened in this country in those days. Alongside the roads at intervals, particularly where there were 100s of miles to travel with no break, bright bougainvillea had been planted as a snap-out-of-it measure for boredom or tiredness At regular intervals there were picnic areas – concrete tables and benches. Rubbish bins were emptied regularly. People enjoyed and respected these areas and kept them tidy. Salisbury was a hub of activity, businesses flourished, banks were numerous helpful and well staffed, hotels were out of this world'- some were tip-top venues of the rich. There was activity everywhere. Farmers played a big part in the comings and goings of this vibrant city. We dropped in on the way out and again on the way back. Meikles Hotel served a splendid coffee and lunchtime buffet.

Back on the road again. We headed to Karoi where our old friends the Boddys, grew maize and tobacco. They were expecting us and we were all looking forward to the reunion. Ken and Bev (ex-Nyasaland) with their family had Kapena farm. Living with them in a nearby cottage was Babs with her two youngest. Babs was the wife of Bill who had been murdered in Dar-es-Salaam. There was a complete uproar when we arrived, much whooping, hugging and plenty of kissing. Their kids were almost adults – our girls too. It was some time since we had last seen them and we noticed how much older we all looked, everyone had a few more lines and our hair had become a little more pepper and salt.

A fantastic party had been arranged for that night and we hardly saw the young folk. We ate and drank far too much, went to bed far too late, had a wonderful time with so much reminiscing. We played music and danced, Jim and I smooched much to the great amusement of Ken. 'You two haven't changed much.' he called. We were having a lovely time so many memories came flooding back. The next morning feeling very jaded, we decided to have an easy day and a quiet night, we talked mainly of old times. There was much waving as we left the farm on the following day, many farewells and sad faces. We all vowed to keep in touch, and we did.

Rocking and rolling we departed in the two cars, still to the strains of 'Swinging Safari' – splendid music to accompany us on the road. I think mother would have preferred something rather more sedate but she did not complain. There was no point really, our taste in safari music did not rise to light opera. In actual fact she was having the time of her life.

From the Boddy farm we moved on to Kariba, staying the night in Cloud's End hotel, at the top of the Chirundu escarpment. This was to play a big part in our future years though we had no idea of this at the time. We ate lunch, swam in the small pool at the hotel then drove down to the valley and the Kariba dam. We saw a lot of game in the bush. There were many different types of antelope, elephant and buffalo. Quite a lot of adrenalin was pumping as elephant have a habit of suddenly appearing from nowhere! We stayed the night in the chalets overlooking the valley and the distant bush. Sitting with a sundowner, we watched day turn to night, the deep firey sunset lived up to all expectations. Brilliant blinding reds of every hue, behind distant hilltops which shimmered with reflected colour. Trees and vegetation were reproduced to appear as black, intricate, cut outs against the vivid sky. We were all enchanted. Supper though good was an anti-climax after the sunset sundowner and peanuts. We walked back to our chalets beneath the panoply of stars with Roger and Jim pointing out each of the larger constellations. I knew them well from past years, my mother and the children were eager listeners. I put my arm through Jim's taking notice of all he had to say and watching his face light up as he spelt out the magic of their names.

Leaving Chirundu the next day we dragged our feet as we walked towards the cars, we were all a little loath to leave. We left Roger to lead the way – lots of back tracking seemed to be going on but he knew his way around Rhodesia. We all agreed Victoria Falls should be our next venue and everyone wanted to travel with Roger. 'Nan doesn't like the window open it makes her head cold,' was the cry so they the girls went with Roger, on a sing-along. I stayed with Jim and mother and I was allowed to open the window one inch, mum said the draught made her ear ache when the window was down, I supposed it must do or she would not complain. We followed Roger, he had the windows open and it was almost possible to see his car rocking and rolling. The girls waved to us in high glee, thank goodness the roads were good, one could actually call them highways they were pretty well dust free. As we approached the falls we were able to see the spray rising heaven wards from The Victoria Falls 'The smoke that thunders' or, as the natives call it, Mosi oa Tunya. 100 metres deep 2 kilometres long a simply spectacular sight.

We drew up at the doors of the sumptuous old colonial Victoria Falls Hotel still in a time warp from the past, wonderful well-heeled ladies and their gentlemen glided over highly polished floors glistening with reflections, to sit graciously at perfectly adorned tables sipping pink gin making small talk, discussing business and inevitably U.D.I. problems which were rearing their ugly head. No one wanted to accept the situations which may arise from internal pressure and outside interference.

A number of farmers had collected around the bar taking a drink before lunching on the pig-on-a-spit revolving over the fire where nearby tables were laid and an orchestra played from its vast and lively repertoire. The smell from the pig roasting induced much mouth watering which almost led to a dribble!
    'God, that smells good.' remarked Roger.

Jim agreed so did everyone else.
    'Yes choose a table Cog, perfect place to eat.'
    'And stay overnight' I added 'kissing his cheek.' We were given rooms overlooking the Falls.

The pork with all its accompaniments and various salads from nearby tables lived up to all expectations. The pork was rich and succulent. Our evening meal of the fish was cooked to perfection, delicious and delicate, a bottle of chilled South African wine married well with the meal.

On the rostrum in the dining room an orchestra played soft, slow music. Jim and I danced and floated back in time. Cheek to cheek and relaxed, our movements were spontaneous and natural but perhaps a little erotic! Geoffrey, had he been there, would have smiled his crinkly smile and said 'You two will never change' and we never did. I had on my Whistling Thorn dress and the huge smoky topaz ring bought for me in Dar before I had to leave for England. Jim's special natural smell and the slight fragrance of aftershave, caused things to become a little 'heady'. (Gather yourself together Jean!) Strangely my mother never questioned the way we were, unusual in a parent in those days. She knew of our chemistry, so did Roger, as a matter fact all of our friends knew.

After breakfast the next day we walked to the falls. The wet slippery path taken to actually view the waterfalls and the turbulence below, ran alongside the 'lip' of the falls in the surrounding rain forest, we all loved this invigorating walk – everyone glowed. We were wet through, and literally dripping with water. Near to the falls a fellow was offering to take people up in a light aircraft to view the falls from above.

'Who will come with me, my treat?' asked Roger. No-one volunteered.

I was amazed – Jim would face a charging buffalo but he refused the flight in a light aircraft over the falls.

'Why not love?' I asked.

'I would not be in control' was his swift reply.

I understood completely, a silly thing for me to ask, his fate would be in the hands of someone else. Mother said 'no' the children also went into reverse. Amazingly, though hating heights, I clutched Roger's hand and walked towards the tiny aircraft, we climbed into the plane and sitting with sweaty palms I allowed myself to be taken skywards, up on and over the falls, at times I held Roger's arm as I became a little nervous when we were buffeted by the turbulence. To offset these involuntary tremors I concentrated on the view below, it was astounding, quite spectacular, never to be forgotten. The cutback of rock from years of water continually eroding and wearing it down can only be seen and appreciated from above, only from this angle could the gravity of nature and its immense power be even remotely understood. The whole scenario was bewildering and in some way very humbling. We were exhilarated revelling in what we felt was a unique experience. We were dying to explain to the family on the ground what we had seen from above, though to put it into words was impossible, it was beyond comprehension it had to be seen. 'Cog, you amaze me,' exclaimed Jim as I walked over and gave him a hug.

'I would not have missed it, thank you so much Roger.'

'It gave me great pleasure,' he replied with a smile.

Our stay at the falls had come to an end. The next day came the cry, 'Come on girls, file up and fall in' from Jim telling us to put our luggage in order, he and Roger were off to get the cars.

From the Victoria Falls, we drove off into the miles of wilderness which was Rhodesia -watching illusive shadows flit from bush to bush, tree to tree and in clumps of nearby thorn thickets.

'No vultures,' exclaimed Jim looking up at the sky from the open window the sky was brilliant blue unsullied by vultures, we were not in vulture country here.

We felt there were turbulent times ahead, on many occasions we were to be bent by the wind only to straighten as it passed. Noises from the outside world were political, distorted and often scandalous. Driving along we commented that only in Africa can the heart burst free, 'Yes, we are certainly away from the madding crowds my love' Jim remarked moving his hand from the steering wheel indicating the vast empty area through which we sped.

'Yes, and only in Africa can the ears be filed with the seductive sounds of night and the beating of drums from distant villages,' was my reply. How I loved the mystery and the warm embrace of night.

Janey blew noisily into her mug as a fly had settled on the rim, we had stooped beneath a roadside tree for drinks and sandwiches. At times we had been backtracking at others we wandered off in different directions. 'It will enable you to see different aspects of the country,' Roger said. Our energies had been spent in the content of a wonderful holiday, a little deflated and in a state of anti-climax we drove on hoping not to meet angry natives on the road. Almost daily tension seemed to be mounting and we prayed that on our arrival at the ferry it would be working to time and with some semblance of order. It was our intention to stay in the same little pousada on the Tete road, we had found it comfortable and adequate on our outward journey. We spent the last night with Roger. He was shortly to return to Malawi, it was back to work for us all. We had enjoyed an unforgettable holiday.

Our journey back was uneventful despite the occasional wave of apprehension, merely the odd scowl from people standing by the roadside, two boys picked up stones and threw them at the car.

'They will break the window,' piped up a little voice. The ferry at Tete had presented no problems we gave huge sighs of relief.

Making our way back to Mombo road we sang yet again to the strains of Swinging Safari, some of us at times sung the wrong words which resulted in a little joke; 'That is wrong mummy'. Stone had supper prepared, he was cooking a joint of roast beef, aubergine crisps were waiting, there was beer in the fridge. Everything was organized until Sally (who was trying hard to be helpful) caught the clasp of her case, its contents spilled out all over the place, deflated she began to cry. Jim of course put his arm around her. 'Don't worry love it happens to us all sometimes,' he said helping her to sort out her bits and pieces. We bathed, changed and settled for the night. It had been a super holiday, now we were pleased to be back home. For some reason that night we lay in bed talking of the western province of the wonders and mysteries of this area, of the forests bordering Ruanda Urundi and the Congo, of Kibondo and the rituals and superstitions of the people.

'Mmm it was another time another place,' Jim said, 'another world another Africa, my love.' I had to agree there we had the swamps, the wilderness, the game, tetse fly, mosquitoes, isolation, quiet and untold shortages. Steam rose from the Moyowosi swamps and we had witnessed the emergence of elephant from those swamps. Livingston country, the green heart of Africa where there were forests, parrots, birds, bongo and gorilla.

We went to sleep agreeing that we had both seen wondrous sights. Lived a privileged life and what was even more wonderful, we had enjoyed all these things together. A bearded Jim had sat on the shores of Lake Tanganyika an inland sea, five miles deep. Not far away was Shiwa Ngandu the home of Gore Brown a colonial home of grand proportions. We hoped to visit it one day.

In the morning things were back to normal, time was flying by, it would soon be time for mother and the children to return to England, we were due for home leave at the end of the year, the rainy season in Malawi. Each weekend we tried to take mother and the girls out to somewhere we knew they would enjoy, somewhere they could talk to their friends about on their return home. 'The girls are changing,' Jim commented and indeed they were. Liz and Sally had long plaits, Janey's hair was still short and curly, but she was becoming quite tall.

An invitation arrived a party was to be held on Saturday by David Slater and his wife at their home. David was landscape gardener at the President's palace. The Mount Soche Hotel advertised a disco for this same night. 'Could we please go daddy?' the three of them trilled. 'Just for a short time.' They had never been to a disco, we had never encouraged it as feedback from other parents had not been encouraging.

'What are we to do, shall we let them to go?'
Jim put the ball in my court. We would be at a party. They had been invited, David had children, bring your mother along he had said.

'Alright we will take them on our way out and pick them up at 11 pm.' We could take them back to the party for a short time afterwards we had no intention of staying late. Off they went all dressed for the occasion. They were allowed a little make-up.

The party was in full swing and 11 very quickly arrived, Jim was fussing about the girls, he went to collect them. Sometime later he arrived back, the girls trailed behind looking a little jaded.

'What on earth is the matter?' I asked. 'We gave you an 11 p.m. dead line.'

'Daddy didn't like it' said Jane the spokesman.

'It was dreadful, I couldn't find them, there were lights continually flashing the noise was deafening, too many discos and they would be both blind and deaf.' So that was the end of the disco scene, they never asked to go again.

Jim did not get angry, at times he would show his displeasure and this appeared to be enough. I really don't think they were overly impressed; it was not quite what they had expected. So we learned later on.

It was quiet after they had left, the girls had not wanted to go back, they never did. My mother had enjoyed herself immensely but she was ready for her home comforts. We had told them at the airport we would soon be home on leave, with this news they perked up.

Jim came home from the office he greeted me with a kiss and 'I have a pain in my crotch area'. I had no idea what on earth it could be, I did wonder if all the travelling and bumping in the Land Rover could have anything to do with it. The next morning I insisted he go to the Seventh Day Adventist Malamula surgery. Poor love he came home looking pretty miserable. 'I have a hernia and it must be operated on' my heart sank.

'When?' I asked

'Soon, they are going to let me know.' He would have to go to Malamula hospital near to Geoffrey's tea estate

I could be nearby. Everything went through my mind, all the 'what ifs' in the world. Geoffrey got into a state. We just felt the world was going pear-shaped things did not happen to Jim. It was arranged that Jim should have the operation six weeks before leaving for the UK. He could recuperate and carry on light work locally and in the office. I asked the travel agent in Blantyre to arrange a relaxing tour lasting one month from Malawi to UK by air, it included two weeks in Cyprus with stops in Turkey Greece and Italy. I knew I would have to carry any luggage we had, or organize someone else to carry it, as Jim must not lift.

When the time came to go into hospital, Geoffrey and I went along with him. We spent two traumatic days pacing the old estate house. Shirley tried to console us without a great deal of success. It was a huge relief when they rung through to say it was all over and we could visit. We sneaked in quietly with a small bottle of whisky and soda, just what he would like we told ourselves, we were wrong. Poor Jim, his movements were very measured and slow on our first two visits, however he did improve rapidly after that.
'When can I come home?' He wailed sounding rather like a little boy.
  'I promise not to do anything silly.' We drove him home to the estate very gingerl teasing the car over every bump, after one week he must go back to the hospital to enable them to measure his progress, he was fine though still sore. The next day we went home to Blantyre and he was able to visit the local clinic. Apparently he needed a great deal of anaesthetic to send him to sleep before the operation.
  'Did you fight it?' I asked.
  'No, I'm just tough' he said.
He soon mended and we prepared for our journey home, we were

looking forward to this, Turkey was to be our first stop, then Kyrenia in Cyprus for two weeks, Greece and Italy. We organized for the Citroen to be sent home to the UK later, The government packed and shipped our household goods. We had decided quite suddenly to try our luck in England in the form of a country pub, if we could find one. We did.

Cyprus was a bonus it gave us both a much needed 'lift'. Malawi we knew was going to have big problems, in fact it already had them. We hired an open car and toured the island, which one could do in 1972. We ate well and we swam, we relaxed and read on the beach. I did not allow Jim to lift, he carried his briefcase under his arm and tended to our flights etc. We arrived home full of the joys of spring and ready to put our plans into action much to the astonishment and high glee of the family. Jim wanted to get moving immediately, I knew he could not, his body had to fully recover and it must be able to take the strain of gradual lifting. When I took him to task he gave me a smile and a wink and 'You make too much fuss love.' I had no intention of taking any risks with him. This incidentally, was not 'Goodbye' to Africa

CHAPTER TWENTY ONE –
A COUNTRY PUB

Sitting at the breakfast table scratching our greying heads, as we wondered what our next move should be and where to start .'I still think we should write to the odd brewery asking what they have to offer don't you agree?' I said. I could see no other way forward at the moment we had gone round and round talking of other possible ventures but this seemed the most feasible idea. Jim suggested that we eat lunch in a local pub not too far away, perhaps in a locality near to the Cheshire border towards Cloud End.

'Mmm, we could put out a few feelers and make a few enquiries.' I pulled him to his feet, and gave him a kiss, 'Come on get ready love.'

We were still in dressing gowns. We dressed quickly and were ready to follow up yet another challenge made on the spur of the moment. We felt quite excited at the thought of a new venture, though we did not know quite how we were going to settle into this very different environment. I felt quietly confident of Jim having grown up in an hotel and he had often helped his father at that time, surely it would all come back to him, added to which Grandy would be only too pleased to give us advice should we need it.

'You would make a splendid landlord.' He would, he had the presence and the 'right' personality. We were both essentially private people but we would manage together, Jim raised his eyes to heaven 'My Cog, what I do for you.'

As we settled into the Daimler my hand lay on a trouser covered leg. I preferred the warmth of soft skin, the feel I was familiar with. The feel which made me tingle and feel young. His hand crept over mine I turned to look at him his face was an open book. 'Not quite the same is it love?' Our thoughts went back in time.

On the roads of our chosen area we popped into one or two hotels – none of which had either customers, atmosphere or appeal. The smell of stale food penetrated our nostrils almost as soon as the doors were opened. We peered round and with a sense of guilt backed out and made our way to the next likely hotel in the vicinity. The results were always the same, we were beginning to despair. 'They can't all be like this, there has to be something different somewhere,' Jim told himself, hoping I had heard.

We were in Leek. 'That looks nice,' I said, we came to a halt and reversed our way back into the car park of a popular pub named 'The Jester.' Here things were very different. There were customers, there was no smell of stale food and everything shone, obviously a lot of loving care went into its upkeep. Sitting down we had a light drink and studied the menu listing bar snacks. A big friendly well-dressed fellow, probably our age, round faced with brown wavy hair came over to us. He introduced himself as Danny he was the owner of this free house and gave us the impression of being highly successful in this trade.

For lunch I ate escargots with crusty bread and Jim ordered Dover sole. We each had a glass of wine it was a delicious light meal.

'Have you time to have a coffee with us?' Jim asked Danny, 'Jean and I feel you might be able to help us with a plan we are hatching.' Danny sat down and asked us about our plans offering to help if he could. Danny was an easy man to talk to, and so over coffee, we settled down to talk of our past and to present our ideas for the future, not in detail of course, he was a busy man. Immediately we had explained what we wanted and where we would like it, his eyes lit up.

'Ah, ah,' he replied, 'I think I might have an answer for you.' He knew the tenant of The Queen's Arms in Bosley had a heart problem.

'Where is this place?' I asked.

'Not far from Leek on the Macclesfield road, I understand they are looking for someone to take his place and he would like to leave as soon as possible'.

Jim looked at me. 'Shall we call in on the way home?' I thought it was too late, however Danny dashed to the phone gave them our names and told them to hang on we would be along to see them within the next 15 minutes.

'The place is doing nothing at the moment but from what you have told me of your intentions, I feel it could have a future.' We thanked him and he came to the door with us, putting up his hand as we left. We saw a lot of Danny in the days to come.

Neither of us could really believe this had happened on our first day of probing into our future plans. It did not take long to draw into the car park of the Queen's Arms. The door was open so we walked in and introduced ourselves to the tenant and his wife, but I cannot remember their names. From the conversation they were obviously eager to leave the place. There were only the four of us in the bar and we noticed how clean it was although it totally lacked atmosphere. The lady who kept the place spruce Mrs Jones, lived nearby and they felt sure she would continue to help whoever replaced them as tenants. I immediately made a mental note of this. They told us they would like to leave as soon as possible and were grateful for our interest.

The lady of the house took us round the premises and we could see it had potential. Jim and I made little signs to each other as we noticed problems which would soon have to be addressed. A great deal had to be done in order to make the Queen's Arms appeal to the clientele we hoped to attract. It was on the main road with a little frontage and had a long garden to one side which could be useful when we had made it more attractive during the summer. In the field at the back Janey could have a horse because we saw that it had a big cark park and a number of farm type out buildings, one of which was a stable.

Everywhere, both inside and out, needed a lick-o-paint, the outside of the main building was pealing and ugly it had been scarred by the weather and by neglect. When we remarked on this we were told the brewery was considering making improvements. 'I see,' commented Jim, 'They look a little overdue.' They gave us the address and telephone number of the brewery and the name of the tenancy manager, we stayed chatting for a while longer before deciding it was time to leave. Then we gave them our thanks and with a 'Bye for now, hope to see you soon,' we drove away.

To say we were astounded at our luck is to put it mildly. We were certainly very excited there was so much to say, so much to tell and so much to plan. Immediately when we got home, we rang the brewery and asked to speak to the tenancy manager. 'I wonder what qualifications a tenancy manager has?' Jim said with his hand over the mouthpiece, I shrugged. The Tenancy Manager came onto the phone and we explained our movements and intentions. He asked us to write to him so of course we did. An interview followed and within ten days we received a letter from him offering us the tenancy. In what was, only a matter of weeks, probably two months. During this time we had somehow to completely disconnect from the past and reconnect to the future. We were sure that this new move would be a totally different way of life from anything we had been even remotely used to in the past. It was a very sobering thought this would really present a difficult challenge.

The brewery had promised a face lift to the hotel, they also mentioned alterations and asked us for any ideas that we might have. We did stress that we felt painting the outside must be the first priority. They agreed with us on this point. Very soon The Queen's had a smart black and white exterior. Jim and I decided to concentrate on well kept beer and good food, which would be entirely our responsibility. We approached Mrs Jones (Sheila), and she agreed to stay with us, she kept the place in ship shape and was always there when we needed her, she was loyal and totally reliable.

It was a mammoth task. To say we were traumatized was an understatement. There was so much to consider, at times Jim and I as we passed, went into a 'quickie' reconciliatory hug which usually took longer than we intended! Everything had to be re-organized or replaced. It was necessary to completely refurbish the kitchen, which meant new crockery, cutlery, grills, fryers, fridges, deep freezes and stores. It was a nightmare. But we did it. We found suppliers; a butcher, a source for vegetables, a cheese maker, a baker and a provider of materials and necessities for the trade. We developed a good rapport with them all. Our first day at The Queen's Arms known by the locals as The Queen's was a gloriously sunny day albeit with a little chill in the wind.

'I shall have to go into the cellar love, call me if you need me.' How many times was I to hear that!

'Yes,' I answered not sure that I could get my head around anything. We had gathered all the family together and made a plan for our opening day. Two benches and small tables had been put outside the front windows I had cooked a turkey in mother's oven the night before, bought crusty bread, sandwich bread, farm butter and trimmings. At lunchtime we advertised ourselves by putting a sandwich board by the front door. Asking the family to sit outside we served them with beer, turkey, salad and tomatoes they looked the epitome of satisfied customers, hail and hearty. We never looked back, the turkey was eaten and the bread finished, there were many people in the bar on our first day, we had piped music

304

– songs and tunes from the old days – we had many comments and compliments, customers on this first day introduced other. We went from strength to strength and never looked back.

The mess made by the alterations did not deter either ourselves or our bar men and certainly not our customers. When it was all finished, we re-carpeted the whole of the premises. We emptied our containers now delivered from overseas. We had our Citroen in one and many, many items of Africana in the other, skins, heads, ornaments, spears, pots, knives, fishing floats from the Indian ocean, rugs and drapes, they all looked attractive and very unusual. Our customers now went 'On safari' when they came to The Queen's.

In the garden we had peacocks, guinea fowl, pigeons and game bantams One cockerel – Adolph – and his two little wives. Adolph had ideas above his station, the kitchen door was split, a stable door, the top door always open and Adolph stood atop the bottom door crowing his head off while the two wives stood below outside content on picking up any bits he dropped as we fed him from our hand, he was beautifully coloured and very grand. The one horse in the field had graduated to three, Jim and Janey fed and exercised them, 'Lady' had a foal we named her Bula Matardi (I am not sure of this spelling), which in Swahili means Breaker of stones; in our minds Africa was never far away.

In time were recognised and starred by the A.A. we were also in the Good Beer Guide. Each year Jim and I bought 'The Good Food Guide' and lived in luxury for 10 days, we had reliable people to take over our work whilst we were away. We worked hard and were so successful we were able to keep the children in boarding school to finish their education. Elizabeth was now married The girls and the family loved having us at home the girls were fantastic during school breaks they worked hard as did our parents, everyone enjoyed doing their bit.

Jim and I were becoming more than a little grey on top, hard work and age did nothing to quell our still teenage upsurge of emotions, my hand still travelled on his knee, he still unexpectedly stopped the car to tell me he loved me and give me a kiss. I loved him as I had always loved him, not for one moment did it ever diminish.

We worked together and became excited at new ideas put them to the test, we invented recipes, we cooked them and they were ordered for lunch or supper from customers prepared to travel a great distance to eat our meals. On many mornings the guinea fowl sat on the fence making the most dreadful noise, Jim grabbed a shoe throwing it hard from the bedroom window, squarking they fled into the field. So often I have heard the clip clop of Mrs Jones feet halt for a moment as she walked over the car park, so many times I have seen her with a knowing smile on her face pick up the shoe and take it into the house. All our bills and menus had caricature elephants, Jim and I on safari with carriers, masks or spears or zebra, an artist friend called to see us he was on leave from Australia, teaching art to university students, it was his decision to contribute these drawings for our use. Our last meeting had been in Kibondo in the Western Province, he had been responsible for designing the face of the cow on 'The Laughing Cow' club tie, we did much reminiscing as he stood behind the bar and pulled a few pints for old times sake. It was a very busy pub we managed to get one or two very good and reliable people to help us both in the bar and in the kitchen.

We had a small dining room – just four tables, which had to be booked in advance. There were times in the evening when almost at bursting point we went into the hall leading to the main bar; leaning on the radiator for a few moments of breathing space listening to the chink of china and cutlery, we heard our customers comments on the food we had prepared for them and they were always complimentary. It made us feel that it was all worthwhile. Jim would look at me put his arms around my shoulders

'Let's go love, back to the fray', off we went back to the kitchen to start again, back to the orders which were all spiked numerically as they came in from the bar. We cooked until we felt we could cook no more, last orders were at 9.30 p.m. From 10 p.m. we worked on automatic pilot until 11 pm till midnight when the kitchen was in order, the last customer gone, and the barmen had left. Then we had the till to check and the cellar to attend to on most nights we did not get into bed rather we fell into it, side by side we recharged our batteries until the birds sang. After Mrs Jones arrived we managed to get out of bed, she always set the breakfast table and had the kettle on for us, what a God send she was.

After breakfast we started our mornings cooking session, together we made cottage pies ham, and pea soup with crispy spare ribs and crunchy bread to the side, field mushroom soup served with swirls of Dunster's cream and thin slivers of raw mushroom. There might be lasagne and Stone Crackers which consisted of tasty Lancashire cheese, cut from a whole round cheese, pickled onions, granary bread and farl, this with a glass of draught Guinness was manna from Heaven. We cooked splendid juicy tender sirloin steaks bought from a local butcher and served them with continental salad we also cooked crispy skinned piri piri chicken. These were the basic and most popular bar snacks. We introduced others at times to prevent boredom. Always there were pickled eggs with curry sauce. Some afternoons we were able to rest a little and read, or Jim would bring his books up to date, or we had to dash off to replenish stocks.

One afternoon, during the winter, Jim went off to Crewe alone we had orders for the dining room that evening so I remained at home and prepared the evening puddings. Snow had been forecast. We however had not taken the warning seriously and been quite unprepared. Whilst he was away it had begun to snow heavily, on his way home he had managed to reach Bosley crossroads where he had to abandon his car and walk to the garage. He arranged for them to collect the car and asked them for a crisp box, made holes in it for his eyes to see through and walked on to The Queen's. Looking through the kitchen window at the falling snow and the white covered ground, I saw this apparition with a square head approach the door. My poor love was so cold. 'The box kept my ears warm' he said sheepishly. I ran a hot bath, gave him a hot drink rubbed him hard with a large warm towel, gave him dry warm clothes patted his cheek gave him a kiss and he was a new man.

That night the place was heaving. We had people everywhere, they abandoned cars and came in for warmth to drink and to eat, there was very little left in the larder, it was an all night affair. Some of those people driving from office to home became regulars stopping for a meal mid-journey whilst others brought their families. Every person was intrigued by our African themed décor, it provided an interesting talking point.

Christmas was huge at The Queen's. We cooked for private and corporate parties and were inundated with orders. These celebrations usually finished quite late, our staff were splendid they never let us down. Janey and I made our way across the road through the graveyard to the little church, which was directly opposite, to take communion. Each year we attended church at midnight. New Year's Eve was wild. We had a fancy dress party and usually everyone came in fancy dress. I remember the first year I wore my Calamity Jane dress (the one I had worn at the Tea Planters' Ball), Jim wore his kilt, Liz wore a sari and Sally suddenly became Japanese and Janey a Mexican bandit. It was all very noisy, very wild and a far cry from the big moon, stars and quiet of a warm African night. It is said that variety is the spice of life our life was certainly very well spiced.

The time came for the girls to leave school Sally went on to Miss Wilkinson's secretarial college in Manchester whilst Janey went to

Sweden as an au pair. We and her friend J.T. (a friend from school days, who had now become a family member) took her to the port of Immingham where she boarded the boat for Stockholm. We waved her goodbye tearfully and we were all three desolate at her departure, I remember driving home in virtual silence.

During our time at The Queen's Jim had bought a Bentley, I think it was R type, I know we drove up to Scotland in it, we stayed in Good Food places and felt very grand indeed.

In 1976 I became ill, very ill, Jim sent for the doctor who seemed unconcerned and gave me an injection of largactyl, which proved useless. I became worse and was now having rigors, again Jim phoned the doctor. Immediately he saw me sent for an ambulance and phoned the surgeon. Thank God for B.U.P.A! I was whisked into hospital and operated on almost immediately, I had peritonitis. I was very poorly indeed but somehow I pulled back. I am sure it was for Jim he was absolutely beside himself. Despite all he had to do, though everyone rallied round, he came to see me each day and organized a T.V for my room.

Jim's parents were a huge support at this time, they stayed at the hotel with him. It took a few weeks for me to recover sufficiently to go home and much longer for me to get back to normal and work again The privacy and quiet of my own room in the hospital helped me to recover. Sally came to see me. 'Mummy come home soon daddy never smiles now.' This made me more determined than ever to get well quickly. Each time Jim came to visit me he tried to hug me and each time was unable to, prevented by all of the drainage tubes which I had hanging from the different orifices and parts of my body. It was a miserable time and he had all the work in the hotel and was responsible for everything, I am sure he shed the odd tear. in fact I know he did. I did recover and come home, though did not heal very well, one of the internal stitches had decided not to dissolve. Eventually I was admitted again, this time all went well.

Things were back to normal. The children were home to help Jim, the staff were all willing to work a little longer and I went with Jim's mother and father to see Geoffrey and Shirley in Malawi. I had to convelese a little I was told. They had never been to Africa and never would have gone alone. It was an emotional time for everyone, we all enjoyed it very much. I missed Jim terribly but I had to swallow my emotions and anxieties. It was with great joy I fell into his arms at the airport on our arrival home. But, I was well rested and had put on weight. He was thrilled to have me back home. Later he presented me with a Wedgewood 'Florentine' pattern dinner service and a set of silver cutlery. I was overwhelmed with the gift it was very beautiful, I had mentioned in the past how I loved the 'Florentine' china but as I had said this, it certainly did not occur to me that such a service would soon rest in my china cabinet.

A visit from the VAT man was imminent and we also needed to replenish supplies so.

'You prepare your books for the tax people love, I will go for the shopping, just relax I shall not be long.' I knew I must leave now quickly as he badly wanted to come along with me. I drove away feeling horribly guilty. I went straight to the wholesale store, picked up what we needed, selected a few things for my mother and had them put into a box she could open it after my visit, she was alone now as my father had died some years ago and when we called to see her she hated us to leave. This box of goodies to open later would help her a little.

I had to get back to The Queen's, there was always so much to see to before opening for the evening session. Jim wanted to have a break from his office before starting again in the bar, feet up, a cup of tea and a little time for us to be alone. Tonight the tug-of-war team would be in for a pint after training which was a weekly ritual. They were all local lads mainly from the farming community. They were huge heavy chaps proud of their achievements. They were the world champions and had recently been to South Africa. We were both becoming very tired mentally and physically. For some reason I felt a little despondent as I drove home. It went through my mind what an enormous success we had made of this business. We had known nothing of the machinations of catering, running a hotel, dealing with the public and all the other hundred and one things vital to its success when we went had walked through those doors five years ago The Queen's had done little before our arrival. We now know it has done little since we left.

As I drove up to the kitchen door Jim was looking through the window obviously waiting for me, I found myself smiling.
'I wonder what is he up to?' I thought.
He came to meet me at the door and his face was beaming, his smile was as wide as it could possibly be.
'Help me with these boxes love.' I opened the boot we put the boxes onto the kitchen table he was still smiling to burst.
'Why do you keep smiling?' I asked turning to pack some boxes into the cupboard. He sneaked up behind me putting his arms around may waist. 'Would you like to go to South America Cog?' I think I said in amazement. 'For a holiday, why South America?' He pulled a chair up indicating that I sit down. 'An hour ago I had a call from London. O.D.A. have asked me to consider the possibility of going to Paraguay for them.'
'For how long and when?'
'In two months time, for two years initially,' the conversation went backwards and forwards he had to spend one month in London, home for the weekends, on an intensive Spanish course.
'How the hell do we manage this?' I was truly baffled.
'We have never been beaten yet' came the reply and so we talked, considered and reinvented. It was an enormous opportunity what was even more thought provoking was that they had been the ones to approach Jim, not the other way round. He was to let them know after talking it over with me. They rang again the next day his reply was in the affirmative. Our next moves involved so much planning,

scheming and work that we hardly knew which way to turn. Quickly we bought a house, it was in fact a house we had always admired. Driving past one day we noticed it had a For Sale notice by the gate. We investigated and did a deal. Whilst Jim was in London it would be necessary for me to organize the pub, decide what we were to leave behind for the next tenant, arrange the move, decide what to take to the new house and have it transported, organize and arrange for the transportation of our baggage for Paraguay with O.D.A. Jim would have to deal with the brewery. They in fact were very helpful and understanding, a tenant to follow us was found quickly.

★★★

Today is the 12th February my love. Today I followed you as you led us to the end of our world. The day reality became unreal. The day Elizabeth read her tribute to you with such grieving and splendid dignity it brought tears to the eyes of most people who had assembled to wish you 'Farewell'. We were bent in the wind of grief. Three long years have passed, each year we stoop as the gales of realization and reality are forced upon us. It will always be this way. Yesterday my love it was necessary for me to go into Crewe and again I was overtaken by memories of the past, memories, of your sheltering arms as we stood in the draughty alley running along the side of the Odeon cinema, it is no longer there. Only its ghost remains, walking alongside me pinching, making my mind reel and my body squirm as I become overwhelmed with vivid memories. Tenderly my eyes lift to the curl on your forehead, slowly my finger moves gently to brush it away your grey-green eyes still watch and see. They make you know as I bend yet again in a breeze of sweet dreams and the wind of nightmares. Haunted by the manly beauty of my momentary loss, I shall find you again, just wait, I shall find you.

★★★

Our Africana remained with us and went to our new house 'Croxton.' The rest was sent to Paraguay, the new tenant of The Queen's took all we had decided to leave. The Bentley was sold and the Daimler put on blocks in the garage of our new house. Saying 'Farewell' to loyal customers and staff was difficult and quite tear jerking. Sheila Jones fortunately was always around for the children and the house in our absence. If we needed her when we were in England we only had to lift the phone. As I drove away from The Queen's for the last time I slowed down and lifted my hand in fond farewell. Our home for the past five years had been busy, but more importantly it had been happy and it had been successful. I moved on to 'Croxton' our home in Holmes Chapel Road, onto another new phase in our life. Each Friday evening Jim arrived home looking very chipper and well primed, with Spanish, his call on entering the house was always 'Donde esta mi mujer', or 'Where is my woman', arms open he stood in the hall, headlong I rushed into them. It was a frantic two months which we extended by a few days. Jim's work would entail meeting Government Ministers in Paraguay, with this in mind we went to Chester Barrie to buy two suits, one from the rail one made to measure. Both suits screamed comfort, particularly the latter. My goodness he looked as handsome as any man could. When my turn came to shop I went to Chester to buy both casual and 'dressy'.

It was an exciting part of our life as we knew nothing of South America and never in our wildest dreams had we expected to work there. When Jim's month in London was completed he had acquired a good working knowledge in Spanish. I had attempted to learn a little grammar without a great deal of success. I decided not to worry, I could practice with Jim. The four weeks we had together before we left for South America went by in a blur. We arranged for a decorator, and a local man was prepared to keep the garden in order. Sally and the girls were going to use the house whilst we were away. Our luggage had left and would take a month to get to Paraguay.

Elizabeth now married was living in the Cayman Islands. Janey was still in Sweden which meant Sally and J.T. were left to hold the fort. We went feeling nervous into yet another phase of our lives. It was a long flight from London to Rio de Janeiro, however, it was a comfortable flight. At one point we sat back with a glass of wine and looked at each other.

'Cheers my love, here's to us and to whatever Paraguay has to throw at us.' Jim's eyes passed over me in a slow caress this told me everything was fine.

'Cheers my love,' our glasses touched and as I took a sip tears pricked my eyelids. But they did not stop me from seeing that he was relaxed at last.

'When did we last sit together like this quietly relaxed?' I asked, my hand falling to his knee. His reply was short.

'Africa,' he said with great depth of feeling.

We flew on the Brazilian airline Varig, we ate well on the aircraft, we read and we slept, in fact when we arrived in Rio we felt very 'alive' and became quite exited. The approach to the airport was a new experience, this huge sprawling city overlooked by Sugar Loaf Mountain and the open armed statue of Christ standing 710m above sea level atop Corcovado Mountain held us spellbound. Both the approach and the landing were perfect. We were very impressed with Varig.

Our next flight was to Asuncion in Paraguay on L.A.P. the Paraguayan airline. We did not have wait long for our connection, I seem to remember wishing we could stay a little longer in Rio. The accented female voice calling us to our flight had husky vibrations, so much so that it was difficult to understand her message, we misunderstood her sequence of touchdowns.

'Come on love, time for the fray,' Jim said with a quick look of concern. We were both slightly bemused by the enormity of what we had taken on and we had to make our way in a foreign language. We boarded the plane, putting our hand baggage into the locker above Jim looked at me wide eyed.

'I have forgotten every word of Spanish I ever learned' he said with quiet concern. I could see he was nervous.

'Only momentarily love, you will be fine.' I knew exactly how he felt, who would not? Our first stop was Soa Paulo and my stomach turned over as we approached the airfield to land, to me it seemed like a very tight squeeze. Our stay was short, as we left the runway my scalp prickled.el a little intimidated at the prospect of attempting to put to rights a tobacco industry which everyone to date had failed to do; there was also a research station which had to be brought up-to-date in every sense of the word and to achieve this, Spanish was the language he must work in

'It's very hot and humid love,' I said thoughtfully. 'Very hot' came a voice from behind. Turning round I smiled at the brown eyed man with sandy hair sitting behind Jim. I had a distinct feeling he could understand English but could speak very little, he was holding a conversation in German with the young man sitting beside him.

Approaching Foz do Iguazu the steward made an announcement in rapid Spanish and we had no idea what he was telling us. As we approached Foz; we flew over the vast waterfalls featured in the 'Bond' films. 'We get off here,' I said nervously as though it was a bus! 'Come love grab the hand luggage.' We stepped from the plane and walked quickly over the shimmering tarmac handing over our documents to Immigration. 'No, no, no Asuncion next, you go back to plane'. Looking at each other. 'Sorry' I said, we turned and fled back unceremoniously over the hot sticky tarmac to the aircraft, they were just closing the doors. This was so embarrassing. We fell into our seats the man with the sandy hair and brown eyes gave us a knowing look and smiled. Our next touch down was Asuncion in Paraguay which was our destination.

CHAPTER TWENTY TWO

Paraguay – The land of lace and legend

Stepping from the aircraft in Asuncion, we found it very hot 103 degrees and extremely sticky, the humidity was 98%. Almost immediately we were wet through, the clothes we had travelled in were far too hot for this climate. Rivulets of sweat ran down our backs wetting the top of our pants, sweat ran down our legs and into our shoes. At the airport we were met by other expats like us. All appeared to be deep into their projects, mainly agriculture and veterinary. We were escorted to the Hotel del Paraguay where a room had been reserved for us. Over afternoon tea we were given a briefing and a picture of life in Paraguay.

The following morning Jim visited the British Embassy. He had to get to know or at least become acquainted with everyone within its confines. As O.D.A. we were under the umbrella of the embassy. During the afternoon he had an appointment with the Paraguayan Minister of Agriculture. Jim was given a Land Rover for work and we bought a small blue Ford car for pleasure. It was necessary for us to live in San Bernadino approximately 40 kilometres from Asuncion, which meant we were much nearer to Jim's work and the research station. Living in the capitol would have meant a death trap journey each day. The road to Caacupe was notorious.

We did not mind living in this resort for the rich alongside lake Ypacarai, in fact we were delighted but there was one big snag we had to find our own house and were responsible for the arrangements and the renting of the property – all this after just one month of Spanish conversation in London, poor Jim! I understood only the odd word here and there. We were to stay in the hotel in Asuncion until we had managed to find a suitable home and it was quite a challenge as Jim must start work immediately, which meant we had only the weekends and the odd hour here and there to look for a suitable vacant property.

We had a stroke of luck, the Hotel del Lago a large hotel near the lake in San Bernadin had an Argentinian manager, he knew everyone and all there was to know about everything in the vicinity. Jim introduced the two of us in what I deemed splendid Spanish, the reply came back in perfect English! The tall fair haired manager's name was Richard whose late father had been an Argentinian who had married a Scots lady. She had spoken to her son in English since his early years and as a result of this his spoken English had a Scots accent. He also spoke fluent Spanish and German, switching languages with such ease that we found our hesitancy in just the one language, Spanish, a little humiliating. Through Richard we found a home quite quickly, I was very pleased because I hated the thought of Jim having to drive from the hotel in Asuncion to his work along the dreaded 'ruta' (road) each day. In fact we moved into the Hotel del Lago and from there we could negotiate the rental of any property we found so much more easily

The little house we did find was a quinta type property in a backwater way off the road. It it had a small swimming pool and a tennis court, the house and its surrounds had a 'feel' of Africa.

'There is no drain from the kitchen,' said Jim glancing down and looking a little bemused. The owner had a tenant, only now did he say he would spend no more money how typical. We learned much of the South American ways over our years there.

'Don't worry love, I can dig a soak away.' I knew he had no time and anyway the soil was sandy so I dug a channel for a soak away, it proved to very efficient. I was almost reduced to a large globule of salt water in my efforts I really thought I was about to expire. 'Thank God for the pool,' I groaned jumping into its luke warm water.

A big problem was the generator – it did not generate enough power to start the air conditioner and there were no fans. Another thing, we snapped the very small flimsy bed it literally came apart. 'Cog, we shall have to find somewhere else to live.' Our only 'cool time' was a ride in the evening with all the car windows open, sweaty arms hanging out in an effort to catch some breeze. Sleep was almost impossible so we became galvanized in our efforts to improve our lot. Back to the drawing board and Richard.

It was a great pity the owner of our little home refused to make any improvements he was charging an enormous rent each month. A Rhodesian couple who smelled trouble in their country had come to Paraguay to spy out the lay of the land for a probable farming purchase. They stayed with us for two or three nights, it was fun to have them, we swam or rather hung about in the pool a lot, played tennis a little but it was too hot, talked a lot about the things we had in common and of the places we both knew in Africa. We became very nostalgic at times. During their short stay we became great friends, we were sorry to see them leave. Eventually they went to live in Australia.

We went, as we often did, to the Hotel del Lago to eat milanesa with salad. I dressed mine with lots of lime or lemon juice. Richard almost always came to sit with us, he knew of the problems we were having with regard to the house he was making enquiries as to other properties available for rent locally. Apparently he had heard of a house on the main road into San Bernadino almost opposite the army barracks. It belonged to the wife of an army colonel and she was willing to let it. There was no swimming pool at present but she would build one, we were to meet her at the house.

'Richard thank you so much,' I planted a kiss on each of his cheeks.

'When did you hear this Richard?' Jim asked carefully with restrained interest.

I knew he thought this was too good to be true, despite the cash lining the pocket of its owner each month. Any deal done in Paraguay was done with tongue in cheek. Nevertheless we met Senora Rodrigues the conversation was one of rapid Spanish punctuated with a little English here and there. She took us around the house, pointing out all the good points but missed the bad. She asked us where we would like them to dig the pool. We thought not too far away from the barbeque area. The house was quite a reasonable size, it had three large bedrooms, kitchen, storage area, dining area and large sitting room complete with television. In those days this was an added bonus. Everywhere there was air conditioning and each room had a ceiling fan. The largest bedroom had two. Everything worked, the house was fully furnished, including curtains. We liked it – although it had the one draw back, it lacked a bathroom there was just a shower.

We agreed to lease the house immediately. The kidney shaped hole for a swimming pool was rapidly dug. We liked the house it had a huge veranda to one side with a view over to the lake and this provided a slight breeze in the suffocating heat It was an ideal place to entertain a large party which was important.

Around the veranda there were lots of creepers bougainvillea and moon flowers, it was a very romantic setting.
    'What do you think about the house my love?' Jim asked.
    'I think we will be very happy here.,' I said giving a sigh. And we were.

True to their word the pool was built quickly and well, it gave pleasure to so many people not just to ourselves. Most weekends we had a pool party and a barbeque for many of the embassy staff and their London visitors who were from mainly from O.D.A

(Overseas Development Aid). We had our meal around two tables set out on the veranda on these occasions, I borrowed a waiter from Richard who often made a huge crème caramel for me, it was his piece de resistance. We lived a very pleasant civilized existence everyone seemed to be totally relaxed. It was easy entertaining.

Jim and I used the pool everyday. We had a good life, we were happy and fullfiled. At the research station there was an experimental plot which provided us with the most luscious fruit, we were inundated with huge delicious limes, lemons, enormous grapefruit, oranges, tangerines red sun-kissed mangoes and bananas. It was a fruit lovers paradise, not to mention the fantastic avocadoes. The Paraguayans are not great fruit eaters as cattle seem to benefit more from this than the local population. We sat and ate them in silent wonder juice running down our chins – fruity kisses.

It was arranged that Janey who was leaving Sweden, should go to England for a while then on to the Cayman Islands to stay with Liz, afterwards joining us for a year, to take a correspondence course in G.S.E. English language. (She had failed her English grammer at school.) Sally was in Australia, the family at this point seemed to be scattered all over the world.

Meeting Janey at the airport and watching her walk from the aircraft was a revelation, we hardly recognised her. She had left us as a girl and was returning as a young woman. We waved at the trim young blonde who had raised her hand and was waving frantically in our direction. It was so good to have her with us; she had been disciplined in her studies and passed her exams with good results. She had fun with our friends and was a great asset when I entertained. She loved water-skiing on the lake and having meals out with us in the churrasquarias and parrilladas on the streets. When we were in Asuncion we bought bags of chipitas (fat cheese biscuits). We ate toasted cheese and ham sandwiches in the café San Marcos whilst we waited for Jim on the days he visited the embassy.

Over the Christmas period we went to Puerto Presidente Strossner on the borders of Paraguay and Brazil and stayed in The Gran Hotel Casino Acaray. We stayed mainly around the pool, sometimes popping over the border to a very good Chinese restaurant on the Brazilian side. On Christmas day we ate sandwiches as we sat around the pool we loved this. Christmas celebrated in Paraguay was interesting though strange, there they tend to celebrate the days of the Saints walking to Caacupe in their thousands. People from all over the country converge upon town for the celebration of 'Virgen de los Milagros'. Janey joined this arduous walk, I think with Frances our home help, Franny as we called her. She became a great and loyal friend.

One very hot day day Jim picked up the mail and read that his mother was very ill and in hospital so he had to fly home. He was devastated and my heart ached for him because he loved her dearly. I remained in Paraguay, Jim's mother died whilst he was in England. I understand he arrived at the hospital just in time for her to recognize him, she gave him a faint smile. He was heartbroken. On his arrival back he he was very quiet and for some time he buried himself in his work. But was consoled by the fact that he had gone home in time to see her. We looked after him, made a fuss of him and were there when he needed us most. Time helped, gradually he healed and was able to laugh again.

We travelled up country to outlandish farms covering hundreds of miles along undulating roads as they snaked off into the distance for as far as the eye could see. It was a relief to turn off into the side and drive along the bumpy little tracks which led to the farms where we could stop for a drink and a sandwich or to stretch our legs as we walked and moved away from the suffocating, debilitating wearing heat of the Land Rover. There were times when we had to travel to the far north through the lush tropical forests, I shall never understand how Jim found his way around this maze. Even the Paraguayans admired his sense of direction. Hernando who was a member of the embassy staff, said to him 'Jim I admire your sense of direction,' when one day they went on one of their farm visits to Encarncion. The amazing thing about Jim was that he always did what he had to do, he did it well and he never complained.

There were many artists in Paraguay and I became friendly with one of them. Her name was Ysanne Gayet, she actually originated from Cheshire. She knew I had painted in the past for pleasure so she suggested that I take up my brushes and have a go! I valued her support. I was rusty but determined. In Paraguay I painted in watercolour; flowers, villages, and landscapes were all loved by the Paraguayan people. The embassy organized an exposition (exhibition) of my paintings, most of which were sold. One was bought by a millionaire for his home in Brazil. The proceeds from this enabled me to fly home for a short time when our daughter Sally, now back in England, gave birth to her first daughter.

We went to the races in Paraguay, and although not quite up to Epsom standards they were good enough to lose the odd pound or two. We went along with friends and took Janey who enjoyed it. We all had fun. Afterwards we went back home to San Bernadino, swam, sat around the pool and enjoyed a barbeque. Jim took a huge piece of flesh from his finger on a tile in the bottom of the pool. I went totally weak and could not look. Derek our friend drove him to the doctor who put stitches in it, Liana, Derek's wife and the children stayed with me until the men came back. Even now I go hot and cold at the thought of it.

One day whilst out shopping in San Lorenzo we met a German couple with their two little girls. We stood chatting in the shop for a while – we had both gone in to buy a chicken. The woman's name was Elke and we immediately became firm friends. They lived on a small farm on the Asuncion Road which was not far from our home in San Bernadino. Elke prepared lots of homemade goodies which we all enjoyed and looked forward to. We often called to see each other the girls loved to come over to us for a swim in the pool whilst Elke and I sat drinking tea, eating biscuits and talking. We often talked of the failure of her relationship with her husband, she had a problem with Peter. I could understand, though felt ill-equipped to advise her, the fact that I listened seemed helpful in itself. They eventually left to go back to live in South Africa and I really missed her. We are still in touch, we write letters and make the odd phone call to catch up on the news and talk of old times. Now there is no Peter as they are divorced.

Liz came over for two weeks from the Cayman Islands with her two children Kate and Ben, we had lots of lovely times together. We went up country to visit the Paraguayan farms, had picnics, went into Asuncion shopping and into the cafes. We swam, ate barbeques, messed about on boats on Lake Ypacari and in the evenings often went to the Hotel del Paraguay and ate milanesas with Richard, who joined us on most evenings. The days went by very quickly, and soon it was time for them to leave, Janey flew back to England with them. It was a sad time for us, the house seemed very empty.

Frances a Paraguayan school girl came to help me when she was just fifteen years old. She came during the weekends when she had time off school and during her holidays. She was a gem and we did everything together. I tried to teach her to speak English and soon she became more than someone who helped me, rather more a part of the family. She was quick to learn, very understanding and extremely kind. She was intelligent and passed all her exams which she deserved because she worked so hard at her studies.

One morning when Janey and I had been sitting on the veranda drinking our coffee, a tiny sunbird flitted in and out hovering amongst a creeper sipping nectar from its flowers. The most gorgeous little thing we had watched it for a while then lost sight of it. When we next noticed it, it was fluttering before a minuscule nest in a corner beneath the roof. Sometime later we decided to investigate; this tiny nest had been made from Jim's hair. I always cut his hair as he sat on a chair outside. Obviously the bird had collected single hairs and woven them intricately to form this perfect little nest, inside the nest there were two of the smallest eggs I have ever seen – they were no bigger than the nail of a little finger. How, I wondered, could they ever hatch and develop? But they did. We had watched them discreetly until the babies had flown. We found the whole procedure absolutely fascinating. Later we removed the nest carefully and we still have the little treasure in a cabinet with our other precious items.

My love and I were alone this Christmas of 1980, our first year without any of our girls or a member of the immediate family. Last year Janey had spent Christmas with us. We decided we would go to The Acaray again. I awoke with a start – something was different; of course it was Christmas Eve. I gave Jim a good morning kiss, he snuffled, grunted held his face up for the kiss and turned over. I pattered off barefoot to the kitchen switched on the kettle then I laid the tray whilst stifling a yawn and waited for the kettle to boil. The atmosphere felt airless, hot and humid. It was refreshing to go back into the bedroom with its air conditioning, the tiles were cool and smooth. I put the tray on the side table, Jim's side. 'Your tea is poured love'

'Will just leave it a minute to cool' says he.

I sat on the edge of the bed and drank mine gratefully. It was time to get dressed and start the day we had a long way to go and must call at one of the tobacco trials on the way. Whilst I packed our picnic of roast chicken, boiled eggs, olives, cheese and tins of sardines, Jim went up to the bakery in the village for hot crusty

French bread. We also took butter, onions to slice, salt, napkins, openers and a few tins of Brahma Chopp beer, we had very efficient cool boxes. Our cases had been packed the night before which was a great relief.

We called to see Elke and Peter on our way our and exchanged Christmas presents. They were spending Christmas with the South Africa Military attache in Asuncion. We said our fond farewells and arranged to meet them on our return. Jogging along in a diesel Land Rover makes conversation almost impossible however I did manage to scream, 'Jim we forgot to turn the water off at the mains.'

'Oh hell,' he said turning in at the next petrol station so that we could ring Peter to ask him to turn it off at the gate. There is tremendous pressure on the water in San Bernadino and it had caused a burst in the house before.

'Okay, no problema,' Said Peter. We sighed with relief, thank God he had been in.

A large truck tore past us, killing a pig as it was crossing the road. I did not like this at all and covered my eyes.

We passed a sign 'Se vende carne' (we sell meat) written on a large board featuring the caricature of a grinning cow. There were two blonde children, obviously of German descent, selling bags of oranges. Thump, bang, bump, we turn off into the bush, my hand was jerked from Jim's leg. After 6 kilometers we arrived at a little Quinta and Jim's plot. It is siesta time, one child calls the father who emerges from the bedroom area pulling up his trousers.

'Buenos tardes senor', off they went to his tobacco trial.

I meanwhile climbed into the driving seat and reversed the Land Rover beneath a mango tree, it was 3 p.m. It was an attractive little quinta. The veranda draped in the shadow of a vine, chickens pecked about and piglets ran hither and thither. A very hot and red faced Jim and a very hot Paraguyan returned, I noticed the farewell was brief and formal.

'How was the tobacco?' I asked.

'Absolutely fine, for God's sake can we stop for a cold beer and a sandwich Cog?'

So out of sight of the farm we stopped beneath a tree, Jim looked at me, 'Oh love what a relief.'

Back to the tarmac and we eventually arrived at the Acaray Hotel we were taken to our room which had a fridge in it. 'Hooray' we shouted.

We collapsed on the bed for some time, had a dip in the splendid pool, took a shower, changed, then went over the border to our favourite Chinese restaurant. On the way to the border post we called in at a supermarket to buy chestnuts, brazil nuts and figs. We ate our lovely meal at the Chinese restaurant then went back to the hotel and flopped into bed, we read for a while then fell fast asleep to the soft burr of the air conditioner. On Christmas Day, Jim opened one eye and we wished each other a Happy Christmas with lots of hugs and an exchange of presents. What were the family doing we wondered. Then in leisurely fashion we dressed and went into breakfast. This huge hotel was almost empty as they did not encourage Christmas traffic. We could more or less do as we liked, so we took advantage of this situation.

We spent the rest of the day by the pool beneath a tree. Our lunch was in the cool boxes beside us. We lazed, we swam, read and had a lovely time until the end of the day when we returned to the Chinese restaurant, simply because the food was so much better than the hotel. I ate huge fat juicy prawns, Jim had an omlette with prawn filling. We did actually dress for the occasion – after all it was Christmas Day.

On Boxing Day we left for home – me with my scent, Jim with his tapes – our gifts to each other. We chugged along the road and were passed by a bus bearing the words 'Rapido Caaguazu' (Rapidly or quickly to Caaguazu) emblazoned along the sides. When we eventually arrived in Caaguazu it was getting very hot. We saw a man sitting with his wares alongside the road beneath a grass shade. He sat in a semi-recumbent position on one of the chairs he hoped to sell and was totally utterly and completely relaxed wearing his hat askew over one eye.

The Paraguayans are able to perfect the art of complete relaxation no matter what their surroundings, their position or the noise. Really quite extraordinary! Had we stopped to buy a chair, he would have leaped up as though stung by a bee and immediately afterwards he would have returned to his old position, closed his eyes and fallen to sleep again. We decided not to stop; it was far too hot we were wet through in the cab of the Landover. Our main aim now was to get home. We had enjoyed our break, now it was time to get back to San Bernadino. My hand was wet on the damp hot leg beneath! That evening we did not unpack we were too tired; a quick shower and bed, tomorrow was another day.

There were vast quantities of work for Jim to do on our return, we had a visitor from Rothamstead research station who was coming to stay with us which seemed to put even more pressure on him. The amount of data flying backwards and forwards from England to Paraguay and vice versa seemed to me to be endless, but he just went on calmly, surrounded by what appeared to be yards of paper covered in numbers! He designed and ordered machinery from England for his research work, virtually rebuilt the tobacco research station in Caacupe. After that he decided that the farmers needed easily accessible information, so he carefully wrote a handbook which covered the whole sector from seeds through to selling and the Ministry of Agriculture agreed to help. The title of the manual was 'Tobacco Production in Paraguay' written in Spanish, each farmer was given one of these handbooks.

Paraguay is mainly a country of haughty military and needy campesinos, a country where a particular herb drunk in hot water is called mate and when cold it is called terere. This traditional drink peps up the tired and gives spirit to those who lack it. Paraguay is a country where hides, timber, cotton and soya bean are produced. The land of golden lapacho trees, the wild Chaco region and the Acaray dam. It is a land a for gossiping; the place where nanduti and Aho poi lace are delicately produced and where proud, beautiful, dark haired, red lipped girls walk in sparkling clean snow white dresses, from huts with red earth floors and grass roofs. Here the rich are very rich and the poor are very poor. It is the land of the bottle dance, sopa Paraguaygo and parrilladas. It is a land of contraband, half- truths and broken promises.

Add to this past wars and their military history, the Guarani Indians, promiscuity and song. Asi es Paraguay. This is Paraguay.

It was necessary for us to go into Asuncion between the hours of 7 a.m 11.30 a.m to buy things we needed from the shops which had to be bought between these hours. Everything closed and everyone slept after midday, even the dogs. It was siesta time, the heat had by this time become unbearable. On the other hand, though not really having seasons as we know them, it could be icy cold, winds eating into the bones. The name I chose for them was the Falkland winds, there seemed to be no way of getting even remotely warm when they blew. To look at the lake or the swimming pool at these times sent shivers down ones spine.

It was almost time for us take our long leave, we had planned to go to the Cayman Islands to stay with Liz and her family for two weeks before flying home to the UK. A short time before we left for leave, I was taking a shower singing 'Raindrops keep falling on my head' I liked the echo in the shower room. Suddenly I felt a tingle, the water was heated by an element in the shower head.

'The senora will have to do something about the shower' I had complained to Jim, this had been happening a lot recently. There was always a feeling of doubt as to the stability and the safety of the electricity in Paraguay, wires hung like ribbons of spaghetti all over the place. I had the distinct feeling the landlady was becoming complacent. She was probably wanting more rent as we were comfortably settled and were planning to return to her house after leave. This however was not on the cards, I had mentioned it to Jim and his reply had been a grunt of disapproval.

We were paying her a great deal of money each month in dollars. We did not want to move house our time had been happy in 'Teresita', nevertheless, just in case we had started to put out feelers. On making a few enquiries we heard of a house in a quiet spot which was surrounded by trees, almost on the lake shore so we decided to investigate. It belonged to a German lady whose family had The Gran Hotel del Paraguay. It was here we had originally stayed on our arrival in the country, we now knew her quite well due to our long stay in the hotel. We often popped in for coffee on our visits to Asuncion. Jim mentioned our concern to her, explaining that we were about due to leave for the UK and during our converstion discovered that she was willing to lease the house and build a pool. It was a very big open house, fully furnished with all amenities. There was a bathroom in the house and outside showers for use after swimming in the lake, we were also delighted to hear there was a small boat for use on the lake. We arranged to view the property.

Arm in arm we walked around the house. A raised veranda ran alongside and to the back of the house, looking out onto the lake. It was a wonderful place to sit and paint. The swimming pool would be built just below. Many of the trees that surrounded the pool area were covered with magnificent native orchids growing on them. We decided it would be superb to sit there together in the warm glow of evening with our sundowner, watching the sun go down over the lake.

'Shall we say yes love?'

'Yes' I replied immediately.

It was quite a new house, the lawns had not yet been planted. Franny and I decided we could manage to do this while Jim was at the office. We would be all set for the move on our return from leave. We had tried to explain to the previous senora that unless 'Teresita' was brought up to scratch and certain conditions were met, a move to another house was imminent, now she was back tracking but it was too late!

We left Franny in charge whilst we were away on leave, she may have been young but she was very capable. It felt like second honeymoon. Off we flew to the Cayman islands, we had drinks, food, read our books then dozed of with our heads together and smiles on our faces as we looked forward to seeing Liz, Richard and the children.

When I awoke my hand was on Jim's leg, his hand was over mine. Some would say what's new!

'Would you like an orange juice?' The stewardess asked as she passed.

'Yes please' it was cold and refreshing.

'We shall soon be landing in Grand Cayman,' announced the pilot. Approaching the island, which is only 22 miles long and 8 miles at the widest point, it seemed impossible to land without overshooting it and dropping into the sea.

'I suppose there is room to land?' knowing full well how silly this must sound. After all it had been done thousands of times before.

Jim flipped my nose and squeezed my hand. 'Yes Cog there is room to land' he said with a smile. It was in fact a very good landing.

It was lovely to see the family looking so bronzed, fit and well. We embraced each other, bursting to pass on chit chat, it was difficult with everyone talking at once. We piled our luggage into the boot and made our way to their delightful single storey home by the sea. Which had a jetty at the end of the garden. We were going to enjoy this holiday it had a feel good factor. That evening we had our sundowners in the brilliant glow of an island evening followed by a scrumptious clam chowder. Later content, well fed and happy we made our way to bed.

Next morning the light was brilliant and already the air was hot. The birds were singing, the children were chattering as Liz urged them to get ready for school. She brought us in a cup of tea before taking them. Richard had left for the office where he was the director of water and sewage on the island.

'Good morning my love,' I said sleepily, delivering our daily kiss. Our hair was becoming quite grey. 'Oh dear,' I thought, though it did nothing to dampen our sparkle. Liz was teaching that afternoon so Jim and I decided to explore the far end of the island it took us no time at all to get there. We sat on the hotel patio by the sea on blue and white striped deck chairs which were covered by umbrellas of the same colour and listened to the light swish of waves as they hit the shore. We drank a lager and ate a light lunch, we had our books with us so we lazed, read, talked and held hands until we were all aglow and it was time to return to the family. That evening we took them out to a meal.

Walking along the sea shore the next day we stopped to chat to some seamen who were just bringing in their morning catch, observing Jim's obvious interest in their way of life they invited him to join them the next day.

'Yes I think I would enjoy that.' Despite his enthusiasm I could see he had some doubts, but I knew he would enjoy the experience. I knew also and he knew that his swimming reputation was next to none but his eyes would always be directed towards the shore line. Instinct told me he would have a plan, his hunting days had taught him so much of survival. In the afternoon we sat on deck chairs on the house jetty. Jim's nose was burnt I stuck a lint cover over it, he decided he would like to 'Just sit in the nude' these were his words. Laughing he covered his 'bits and pieces' with a spotted red hanky, then some time later a gust of wind whisked it away. I retrieved it with a 'Jolly good job we are in isolation,' quip. 'Cover me up love, all this skylarking is not good for us!' he had a cheeky look his face, which I loved.

The next morning Jim was going to join the fishermen, he was a little hesitant because boat trips made him sea sick and I knew he would hate that under the circumstances; in fact in the company of these hardened old fishermen he would be covered with embarrassment. Later he told me he felt very queasy on the boat and asked the captain 'Is there a cure for seasickness,' 'Yes land,' came the terse reply. The boat went on and the men caught fish. With eyes forever in the direction of the shoreline Jim enjoyed his morning at sea, eventually he beccame a little less queasy. I felt when the time came, he was not sorry to be getting off the boat.

'Well that was some experience' he said slightly in awe and full of admiration for the men who went out to sea each day. I looked at him. 'How lucky can I be?' I thought, he would always have a go, he was quite extraordinary. Though he had drawn a line at flying over Victoria Falls in a light aircraft.

During that afternoon, I lay and read my book, Jim and Liz went to do a little shopping they wanted something to cook with the fish he had brought home. I had dozed and on hearing voices I awoke with a start, jumping up to put on the kettle, make tea and butter some of Liz's scones. During tea I was handed three small presents, a pair of black coral earrings, a gold necklace with tiny balls of gold placed equidistantly along the chain, they were so beautiful tears came into my eyes.

'Oh thank you so very much I shall always love them,' and I have.

Later Liz handed me a tiny box, inside were earrings to match the gold neck chain, I was quite overwhelmed and after trying them on I was determined to wear them tomorrow evening, when a friend of Liz's had asked us all to supper.

Our days were flying by. Jim decided to go to the beach. 'Come on love, we'll go to the seven mile beach this was a heavenly place – the sea like a shining blue millpond. Palm trees lined the sandy shore. I grabbed our books and popped them into the beach bag and like everyone else, off we went pretty scantily clad. Jim took the wheel and I could feel the muscle of his leg under my hand. I looked at his hands as we drove along, neat smooth hands with well formed nails, hands I loved. He must have sensed my look probably even my thoughts. 'I love you Cog.'

Content we went to what had become our favourite spot on the seven mile beach. Mid-afternoon although we had a bottle of water, I felt I would like a rum punch. I like this drink, it was always very good and so refreshing that it sent tingles down my spine, when I told Jim his reply was, 'Just be careful.' I drank it rather quickly and thought perhaps another glass would be nice. Jim went over to the little shack with some reluctance I thought, to buy me another rum punch. 'Make this one last, apparently they are strong,' he said handing me the iced nectar. I did drink it slowly and enjoyed every drop. However, the effect of the second drink was mind blowing. I was not wobbly and I was not incoherent, I was not dizzy nor was I loud, I just seemed to be on another planet. I seemed to have become a zombie, very quiet and uninteresting and this evening we were out to dinner. I did manage to pull myself together and become a little more vocal as the night went on. Later we were told that this particular chalet was renowned for the strength of its drinks, I was living proof of that, it took me days to feel normal. I have not had one since nor have I managed to live it down. The family will not let it die. 'Remember the rum punch mum?' After our meal we sat around drinking coffee and the talk, inevitably in those days, turned to the British Empire. It was unanimously agreed by us all that the British were good, fair and efficient in their colonies and one of the better colonizers. I could not have agreed more the trouble was I felt so 'odd' I thought it better to just sit and listen. We may have taken a lot out of these countries but we had also given. It was not all bad we had given them a lot and had taught them a lot and many were grateful.

The days went by quickly, we were relaxed brown and very loathe to leave, however the time came and we had to wave a tearful goodbye to our family before boarding the plane bound for Miami and on to the cold climate of Europe. While waiting to embark in Miami, we sat in a vast air-conditioned lounge staring out through the tinted windows, wondering at the mass of white distant clouds hanging in the heat haze. 'UK here we come'.

Our flight to London on, I think it was British Airways, was fairly comfortable. At Heathrow we had to board a smaller aircraft to Manchester. The names of these airlines have changed so often I find it almost impossible to remember the old names. Nor can I remember who actually met us at this homecoming I think it was Sally and Janey and perhaps Jim's father? We all went to Croxton, where the distant echoes of 'Donde esta mi mujer' rang in our heads as we walked through the door. The girls went to bring my mother who had not been well; that night we sat and sorted out the world.

Most of this leave was spent tending to our remaining parents but we visited Graham and Carol in Scotland, plus a few other relatives and friends, but mostly our time was spent in the family circle. The weather was not good but we tended the garden though the girls had looked after it very well. J.T. and Jane had done a splendid job; they had even planted a chestnut tree for daddy and it was growing very well. Nuts were always Jim's favourite, we went far and wide to collect them from beneath the trees in Cheshire. A few running repairs were needed on the house. Jim divided the very large garden at the back by planting a hedge across it with an archway in the middle; then he planted honeysuckle and a rambling rose at its base. At the far side of the hedge on the left hand side was a huge oak tree where we slung hammocks; this end of the garden was made into an orchard on one side and a vegetable garden on the other. We had a summerhouse around which Jim planted rambling rose and an, 'Italian sky' which had glorious blue flowers. I cleaned the whole place up, and made little blue check curtains to hang in the windows.

We shopped for things to take back with us and arranged for a carport to be erected in front of the garage. This was a sudden last minute decision.

The time came quickly for our return to Paraguay. It was a tearful and emotional time each parting became more difficult. We had each other we were lucky; our remaining parents had lost their partners and neither of them was well, however we knew our girls would look after them and Jim's sister lived nearby so she was able to see her father quite often.

We flew back to Paraguay with sadness when we thought of our aging parents but we were pleased we had spent five years at home with them during our time at The Queen's, their life had been very full. I had always felt we were meant to be in England at that time. Both my mother and Jim's father were content in the knowledge that we, in our love, had something special and they were grateful for that. Sadly we walked arm in arm over the tarmac to board the plane for Paraguay, we had a feeling in our bones and it was not a good feeling.

Our return flight was good and uneventful, this time we stayed firmly in our seat at the touch down in Foz, On arriving in Asuncion we called a taxi, collected the Land Rover, bought a few items we felt we might need then drove home to San Bernadino. Franny had everything ready for us even the beds were made. We did little other than turn on the ceiling fan tumble into bed and sleep. The following day was Saturday so we were up early. I went with Jim to the research station to collected citrus fruit, while he went to make sure everything was still ticking over and in order. Afterwards we went home to make marmalade!

Apparently the house by the lake was ready for us to move into it was for us to decide when. By this time the senora, realising that we had meant what we said was relenting, she tried her best to make us change our mind and made all kinds of promises if only we would just stay. It was hardly surprising really when one considered the dollars she was about to lose. If we had signed another contract with her we could be pretty sure she would renege on her promises. Gradually we moved into our new house where the pool was in the process of being built. It was a much larger and deeper than the pool at Teresita. They were building it whilst the weather was a little cooler, which encouraged us to put the house in order and not yearn for our daily dip as we did during the heat. With Franny I arranged the house and we made an office for Jim to use at home when it was necessary for him to work late. He felt the ambience of the home environment would perhaps help with the writing of his manual.

Life continued on as usual; people came and went and we still entertained our embassy friends, their friends and their visitors. On the other side of the coin we visited them when we were in Asuncion, we met at parrilladas and at restaurants and sometimes on Sunday at church. Sally and her family had decided they would like to spend Christmas with us now that she had two little girls. We were looking forward to this and made plans for their visit. We thought we would make our usual Christmas trip over the border to stay at the Panorama Hotel on the Brazilian side and visit Foz do Iguazu, whilst with us they must see the falls.

We were making these plans when Jim was told of his father's illness and his fast deterioration which we had almost expected. Plans were made and Jim flew home but his plane arrived too late for the funeral. Poor love, he was desperately sad. Perhaps all the organization he had to do during his stay in England helped to take his mind off things a little. He had all the arrangements to make, including negotiating for our house to be put up for sale. Nan and Grandad had been living in it. During this time at home he had a chest infection and was in bed for one or two days when Janey looked after him.

Sally was unable to attend the funeral because she was flying out to Paraguay. What a miserable time it was for us all. When she did arrive she had a temperature and was not well for some days. I sponged her down and gave her some potion prescribed by the local doctor. Franny looked after and played with the children. The pool was finished so we were able to cool them off in the water, rubber rings firmly under their arms. Jim was away for two weeks so Franny and I had finished planting all the grass indeed, everything looked very good but sadness hung over us for a long time. My poor love looked so tired when he came back; he was badly in need of a little tender loving care.

It took some days for him to settle after the ordeal, Sally, Franny and myself did all the packing for Foz whilst Jim went into the office but sent one of the senior Paraguayan staff in the research station up country, to assess the trial plots. Our journey to Puerto Presidente Strossner was hot and tiring, we were carrying all the usual bits and pieces, however we had decided to stay at the Panorama on the Brazilian side, which meant we carried less food as only a picnic was needed.

Liz and Harriet, Sally's two daughters were very good, the pools big and small at the hotel were sparkling and inviting and the food was good, we visited our favourite Chinese restaurant once but mostly we sat around the pool drinking 'Kia piringas' (spelling). Cane spirit, fresh lime juice and soda water, the sugar 'iced' rim of the glass glittered in the sunshine, inside the glass ice cubes danced, chinked and sparkled in this delicious confection. The Panorama, is the only place I have ever come across this drink though I am sure others must serve them, they are wonderfully refreshing in the heat of day.

It was a great Christmas, the children had a lovely time, we were a little loathe to face the journey home – a long way for little ones to travel in the heat. We set off in the early morning, it was hot even then. We stopped once for a picnic and arrived home in the early evening. After showering and changing we drifted up to the Hotel del Lago to eat supper and to chat with Richard. Another Christmas had passed. I wondered how many more we would spend in Paraguay. Whilst Sally and family were with us we had a number of pool parties, everyone from the Asuncion crowd came. We had a lot of fun with much jumping in and out of the pool and a great deal of laughter. There was always lots of food and enough to drink. Sally did not want to leave us when it was time for them to go back home, we did not want her to go. We seemed to be continually saying goodbye to members of the family it was a merry-go-round of goodbyes.

Franny had been so good with the children – very kind and understanding. She was (is), a girl who was intent on getting on with her life. For a village girl in Paraguay she was exceptional, she was outgoing, keen, hard working and at school she passed each exam she took. To give her a break it was decided that when we left Paraguay she should accompany us to England. It was suggested that she could care for Sally's children for 18 months, during which time she could learn to speak English fluently and see a little of the world. This was unheard of really, only girls from military families were given these opportunities. Franny was delighted, the village/town of San Bernadino was agog at the huge

338

decision she had made. Going off with strangers! We had lived in San Bernadino for over four years and yet still, if we went into the paper shop short of change they would not let us take a paper, such was their mistrust of strangers and we only lived half a mile away. They relaxed this attitude six months before we left. I often wondered what they thought we would do with Franny.

In England she learned a lot, she spoke English when she left and whilst with us she visited Italy and the Vatican, she helped us in everyway she could. We were very sad to see her leave, in those days the immigration people were keen and on you like a ton of bricks if you overstayed your time. Now Franny is a credit to her country. She sells property and is working with a notary of German descent who lives in Asuncion. She has her own car, travels all over country and is very involved in business. I believe she is buying a plot of land and eventually hopes to build. She seems to be a prop for Gudrun and the family. This is 2004 ans she may come to see me this year, I hope so, she rings me each month.

After Sally and family had left we settled into our old routine and a quiet life, enjoying walks along the lakeshore and paddling along in the boat. Jim spent a lot of time writing, whilst I sat on the veranda painting, occasionally lifting my head and gazing out over the lake. The grass we had planted was lush and green the sprinkler had taken care of that. Together we went to any up country trials, always with the cool box. Some visits were really out of the way. We travelled along root (ruta) on our way to the Encarnacion distric. This was the most boring trip we ever made, we disliked travelling the hundreds of miles 370km on this straight grey road which appeared to continually wander off into infinity at the top of every incline. Each time, there it was again, another undulating snake of a road for as far as the eye could see. On each side of this road lay stark empty bush which was completely devoid of game; the only game was in the Chaco area of Paraguay, here there were puma, deer, tapir, jaguar, rhea and anaconda. Travelling in the countryside, or in Asuncion, if you were signalled to stop by the military or the police, it would be very foolish to disobey, they usually asked about your destination and checked the vehicle, they asked for your papers or carnet, If you have diplomatic status this is issued by the Ministry of Foreign Affairs. If you are told to go to the police station you go without question. They all carry guns.

Jim fidgeted in the sweat-wet seat of his pants, the plastic was sticking to his shorts and the tops of his legs, the Land Rover was like an oven, he fidgeted but did not complain, I fidgeted and cursed the heat. The hotel Tirol in Encarnacion was built into a hillside, we were looking forward to arriving. Tomorrow we were to visit the trials in the area. Meanwhile we settled in at the Tirol. We always had the same room, was it 24? We asked for this because it had a large shower room with a splendid full force shower which was always hot and the bed was comfy. Unfastening the case and sorting out our clothes I could not fail to hear exclamations of sheer bliss coming from the shower room, so much swishing of water so many 'Ohs' and 'Aahs'. 'Cog give me a towel please?' 'Okay', I called back bobbing my head around the door and handing him the towel, dear Jim with his tousled hair and sunburnt face.

The Tirol belonged to a German family rumoured to be ex-Nazis, it was the only place to stay in Encarnacion, overnight pensions were mainly houses of ill repute paraded by 'Ladies of the night'. As I understand it we could not claim expenses for our stay, despite the fact that Jim was working, due to the shady past of its owners. I have to say it was well run and comfortable, extremely good food was carried through the swing doors into the dining room. In the breakfast room the floor was made of thick glass, beneath the floor a stream rippled its way over pebbles, stones, and sand waving grass was flicked by gleaming fish as they darted along. It was fascinating stuff over which to cast the eyes whilst eating toast, slices of cheese and drinking home ground coffee with lots of milk.

There was a very large, extremely cold at first, swimming pool all set in dark stone. The whole ambience I suppose was darkly spooky but we liked it. We felt after travelling along the whole of route 1 to Encarnacion in the strangle hold of Paraguayan heat and humidity, a little comfort at the end of the journey was not too much to expect. A small Mennenite settlement in the area gave way to a tidiness, which would otherwise have seemed quite extraordinary. I felt for these people who wore dark heavy looking robes which must have been excruciating in the heat. There was also a large Mennenite community in the Chaco they were always such busy people, very productive with many fingers in all sorts of pies. Mostly they spoke in German though all could converse in Guarani and Spanish. Most noticeable at night were the dogs, everyone possessed dogs which barked, snarled, yelped and howled, mostly they hunted in packs through the night, at times the noise was quite overwhelming. I found them disturbing, in fact they worried me far more than they did Jim, on moonlight nights it sometimes seemed pointless going to bed. There were two 'Ds' dogs and donkeys, there were an awful lot of them, the donkeys were used for everything, carrying loads, sitting on and working in the fields.

It took Jim three days to cover the trials then we returned home, jogging along that boring unending road. It was a great relief to turn into the home drive. We had not been home long when all of a sudden I felt so ill I thought, 'Oh dear, this is bad. I had bronchial pneumonia, my love, a pale shade of grey with worry, took me to the splendid Sanatorio Aventista which provided first class medical care, they very quickly cured the problem thank goodness. I think I was in hospital for a week. I do remember I felt very ill. Franny kept her eye on me when I went home any problems and she would very quickly have gone to the doctor in San Bernadino. Medical facilities were very good in Paraguay.

In the summer of 1982 my mother, despite her age of 84, was using shears to cut her hedge, this caused a heart problem and as a consequence of this it was necessary for her to go into hospital. Sally and Janey looked after her and she was given medication and sent home. This time it was my turn to fly home alone to my sick mother we were almost due for UK leave.

After I arrived in the UK I stayed to nurse her in her own home however she deteriorated and had to go back into hospital. I visited her each day and could see the gradual deterioration, though there were days when she was very perky and 'with it.' Mother had always been the pillar of the family she was intelligent, upright and had enormous strength of character. She could also be very funny and I hated to see her sinking and so did the girls, we were very troubled by it. I sent word to Jim and he came home a little earlier than planned. She was so pleased to see him and he seemed to calm her in her trouble. Sadly she died just before her birthday. It was a sorrow-laden day for all the family. After her burial we had to get on with life, though for a while it was difficult. We could not get used to the idea that she was not around to give us advice, nor could I go to see her or phone her in order 'tell' her something which I knew she would have found interesting. I really cannot remember what we did during this leave, mostly we took out the girls and went to Scotland to see Carol and Graham.

We flew back to Paraguay, not quite able to believe our parents were no more, they would not be there on or next visit home to greet us with smiles of joy. It was a sobering thought for us both. Fortunately we had each other, we could console in our close knowledge of each other, we managed well as we knew they would want us to, picking up all the pieces and moving on. This was to be our last tour in Paraguay and it was in every sense of the word a busy time. Staff at the research station had become competent, after a lot of negotiation Jim had managed to send one of them to a university in America for an insight into research and extension work. The manual he had written was invaluable, he had chosen men whom he felt would be efficient in the field to visit each trial in the country after which they had an assessment report to write on their visit to each trial, Jim assessed and followed up their work. One evening he came in from his office, seeing me his smile widened to a grin.

'We have an invitation love,' a little taken aback at this sudden announcement.

'What to?' I asked after a tiny silence.

We walked towards each other sitting down on the sofa, he put his arm around me I kissed his cheek.

'To join the Ambassador for the Burns night dinner dance'.

'Did you accept?'

'We shall receive a formal invitation, Bernard mentioned it to me when I called in to see him this morning'.

We had actually become on first name terms with Bernard and Sonya, a firm friendship had grown between us.

'That would be really nice, how do you feel about it?

'I am all for it' came the reply. It was settled.

'How about a sundowner?' Another good idea I thought.

An even better one was. 'I think it we should have supper at the Hotel del Lago tonight.' What bliss I had not even given our evening meal a thought.

In Paraguay either Jim or I did the cooking, often we did it together sharing the chores it was not like Africa and we missed not having a cook. Burns night was a huge success we laughed and danced the night away, the haggis was piped in, a contingent of Scots had arrived from the Argentine they gave even more 'wellie' to the affair. Most of the guests at the Ambassador's table were Spanish speaking diplomats this stretched my knowledge of the language to its limits and it was a strain, as the evening wore on I became a little more eloquent perhaps it was the wine! Suddenly I felt Jim standing by my side his hand out 'Dance Cog?' it was a slow foxtrot, the song 'When I fall in love' do I need to say more?

It was one of those evenings when everything had fallen into place, another time to be stored in the memory.

Jim had been summoned to the residency and I watched him walk to the car. He had on a dark suit and looked extremely handsome, at the time I was sitting with friends having tea and sandwiches and a wave of excitement surged through me. After what seemed to be one hell of a length of time we wandered out into the garden I began to wonder where he could be and what could be so important to take up all this time. In the house a little later as I looked through the window, I saw him stride up the paved path to the front door. I noticed a curl had fallen over his tanned forehead, he had a wide smile for me but said nothing, he chatted for a while soon indicating the time had come for us to leave. With a 'Thank you, we shall probably see you next week,' we gave the customary peck on each cheek to our friends got into the car and headed in the direction of San Bernadino.

'I think I shall take you to the Hotel del Paraguay – we can eat there tonight.' felt a little mystified. He drove the car into the hotel car park.

'What did the Ambassador have to say?' I asked unable to mask the curiosity in my voice, looking into his face I could see he was dying to tell me something. Putting his hands on my shoulders he looked deep into my eyes and smiling said, 'Cog, I have been awarded the MBE. In the Queen's Birthday Honours list.' I think I stood there unable to utter a word for a few moments and then my eyes filled with tears of joy, I swallowed the lump in my throat, put my arms around his neck.

'My love, that is wonderful I am so proud of you', an overwhelming happiness and love for him surged through my veins. We ate a wonderful meal that night and drank a splendid bottle of wine. Driving back to San Bernadino we were in a blissful state of euphoria tinged with an edge of disbelief. This was earth shattering news, I was so proud of the boy who had sat in the shaft of sunlight on that day many years ago. I was so pleased I had been the girl sitting on the other side in the shade. If only his mother and father, and my mother had known, how thrilled our girls would be.

Asuncion the capital city of Paraguay is a paradox, a wealth of religious pomposity rises above the poverty of the Guarani Indians living in slums alongside the Rio Paraguay selling and begging in streets which in the main are named after generals of the Chaco war. In the shops anything can be purchased from lace to leather and from knives to guns. Shoes are made from any material you choose, in any style you like or desire and handbags are made to match. Opticians are there to test your eyes they have a wide selection of frames spectacles are ready within the hour. Often when shopping in Asuncion we visited either San Jose or the Pettirossi market, the stalls were numerous selling everything from paper flowers to pet monkeys; from fruit and vegetables to painted pottery, rope and hammocks.

Everywhere in Paraguay campesinos dressed in ponchos and sombreros strummed harps singing with heart-wrenching sincerity of love, passion, patriotism and folklore. People talked continually of the War of the Triple Alliance and of its effects on the country.

In Asuncion we browsed amongst the shops of the many streets, huge showrooms had imported cars for sale alongside electrical goods, other smaller stores sold antiques, souvenirs, leather goods, pottery, ponchos of every variety, woodcraft, religious statues, the list is endless and fascinating. Cafes and restaurants were on every corner they all sold 'specialist' helado (ice cream) which was very sweet and savoured and revered by the Paraguayans.

Hardware shops were everywhere, there were so many corners to poke into, so many shelves to scour and so many drawers to 'ferret' around in. Sadly such items of intrigue were no longer obtainable or to be found in the west, we spent hours in these stores. Jim was in his element, dragging his feet when we had to move on. Always he came out with a bag of goodies, his name for useful bits and pieces of ironmongery.

Again we had to visit Encarnacion area. 'Coming with me love I have to go to the Coronel Oveido trials?' Of course I was going with him. On this journey we visited the ancient Jesuit ruins in Trindad. He knew what my answer would be before he asked. We eventually ate our sandwiches sitting amongst the huge stones and boulders scattered around the ruins. Coronel Oviedo was a place to us which had nothing to give, despite the fact that it was supposed to be one of the fastest growing towns in Paraguay. We had to go on from this town to a small place named San Estanislao. During even a short downpour this road was closed, it was a heart-in-the-mouth journey as one never knew what condition the road would be in at any given time. It was a case of pot luck! Fortunately, at the road's end there was a place to sleep at the Hotel Alborada they also provided an average meal. This was not an area to dally in; we did what had to be done, then left for the long journey home.

We paid another visit to Ciudad Puerto President Strossner, calling at numerous farms both on the way there and on the way back. We went once more over the Bridge of Friendship into Brazil and on to the Iguazu Falls. This time we went to the Hotel des Cataratas, or to give it our name the 'Iced Cake.' The reason for this was because it was painted sugar pink and resembled a castle. It served an elaborate enjoyable buffet, all tables overlooked the falls which were breathtaking.

For the last time we walked hand in hand down the spray wet slopes to these vast falls, on to the wavering bridge bordering Argentina, eyes down we looked into the angry, churning, rolling, maelstrom below, aptly named 'The Devil's Throat,' it was a awe inspiring sight, its force and power sent shivers down the spine. I clutched Jim as we edged our way over the wet slats of the bridge,

346

the sides had little support – the rope hand rail did nothing to quieten my wildly beating heart. I wonder what improvements have been made over the years.

The following week we sat relaxing after supper when the phone rang. 'I had better see who that is' Jim ruminated.

'Hello.' a short conversation followed, then Jim glanced over.

'Peter,' he mouthed.

'What on earth does Peter want?' I wondered, hoping all was well.

'Peter would like our permission to marry Janey.'

What a shock, we had absolutely nothing against their becoming engaged, in fact we were delighted, we liked Peter. Jim gave his permission. 'If that is what you both want, best wishes and love from us both we shall be home soon.'

They became engaged on the 21st October 1983.

After Pete's proposal I decided to buy my wedding outfit from a bespoke tailor in Asuncion. Both my shoes and handbag were of the same colour and material, patent leather in duck egg blue, these also were were made by a shoemaker in the capital, they were actually very smart, ideal for the wedding. My outfit was unusual and won Jim's approval. Eventually our time in Paraguay came to an end in March 1984. Friends held a farewell party for us and when the time came they were all at the airport to wave us Goodbye. We were on the move again. Franny flew home with us. For most of the first three months Jim disappeared daily into his Croxton office to write a full report on Paraquay.

London

On the 15th June 1984 with our hearts in our mouth we left for London. We had previously made a reservation in The Royal

Horse Guards Hotel, for that night. On the 16th June 1984 a large black limousine drew up at the front doors of the hotel to take us to Buckingham Palace where Jim met the Queen and was presented with his MBE. From the balcony, the band of the Welsh Guards played rousing music in an effort to relax the tense and waiting relatives below. What a day of mixed emotions this was. Later Sally and Liz joined us, this was a surprise for daddy. We enjoyed a champagne celebration, it was all quite overwhelming. Jim certainly grew in stature during those nervous moments at the award ceremony, tears rolled down my cheeks with pride.

Peter and Janey were married on 13th April 1985, as near to my birthday on the 18th April as was possible. It was a glorious day we have never forgotten, the look of sheer love for Janey in Peter's eyes as he made his vow. An evening party and dance were held in a local black and white hotel The Black Swan. Their honeymoon was in Corfu.

Another Time Another Place

The National Tobacco Company (NATCO) of Zambia needed a tobacco adviser, Jim was chosen from a list of applicants; the then President Kenneth Kaunda was a great admirer of Her Majesty Queen Elizabeth II had noticed the MBE alongside his name.

Off we went to the Ford agent in our home town and arranged for a small green hatchback to be shipped out to Zambia for personal use. In September 1985 we boarded the plane to Zambia, we upgraded ourselves from business class to first class, feeling it was well deserved.

Once more we sat side by side on our way back to Africa and simultaneously we gave a huge sigh and looked at each other with a smile of joy, wondering what changes we would find. We knew there would be many.

Zambia (Northern Rhodesia)

What a comfortable flight we had to Zambia. From wine to food to comfort, first class air travel can be recommended. Arriving at Lusaka we looked out of aircraft window our eyes settling on the surrounding landscape. The old familiar sand lay everywhere covering each permanent structure in sight. The landscape was sparse and dry with spiky brown grass alongside the runway. Wood smoke and dust mingled to rise up into the wide open sky. The sweet, sour, hot smell of Africa stroked our faces and penetrated our nostrils. This smell we knew so well could be given only by the land we loved.

A member of the Embassy staff met us at the airport to ensure that we had smooth passage though customs and passport control. Amongst the many bent and broken trolleys we eventually managed to find one prepared to move in approximately the right direction, but only when pushed hard and tilted to one side to ease it from the wobbling badly bent wheel so desperately in need of oil. Given any slight pressure it was almost impossible to steer. Jim looked at me rolling his eyes – it made me smile I knew this look so well. Most of the passengers were frustrated and exhausted as it had been a long flight, they would be pleased to be out of the airport away from the concerted nose picking, and watchful eyes in the faces of questioning airport officials.

Our luggage was offloaded into the boot of the awaiting car and we were whisked off to the Ridgeway Hotel where we were to stay for a few nights. A house was soon to be vacated in the Leopard Hill area of Lusaka. Transport would be available and delivered to us at the hotel the next day when Jim must introduce himself to the Managing Director of NATCO. Our luggage was taken to the room. We flopped onto the bed feeling a trifle bewildered and endeavoured to gather our wits together.

'So, this is Northern Rhodesia,' Jim said dubiously his voice a little tight.

'Yes, this was Northern Rhodesia, we must remember it is now Zambia' came my reply with an odd display of logic.

'Mmm, I get the impression it is very different.' Jim stretched and gave a little yawn.

Zambia had become independent in 1964, emblazoned everywhere was the slogan 'One Zambia, One Nation' and pictures of Kenneth Kaunda stared from posters from every conceivable corner. This was an African country with which we were not familiar we had never been to Northern Rhodesia.

That evening we sat on the veranda overlooking the pool. We picked on salted peanuts, alongside two brandy and sodas fizzed with tiny bubbles. Lights around the pool twinkled onto a dark ruffled surface, fish darted golden in the light. We sat holding hands in the old familiar glow of evening, a glow made rusty orange by the suspended dust and pollution of Lusaka as the light penetrated through the branches of surrounding trees and shrubs. Looking at the bar menu we decided to eat supper outside; it would be nice to listen to the crickets again. Soon heavy eyes and anti-climax all indicated an early night. We slept like logs.

The following day began in the brilliant gaze of the sunrise accompanied by the sound of bird song. A loud clattering of dishes made by the waiters was muted by the laughter and chatter of African voices. For some time we lay and dozed, I put my head on Jim's chest where I could hear the soft slow beat of his heart. I felt safe, loved and very happy.

On our first day in Zambia, with our arms around each other, we looked tentatively out of the window. There were African workers everywhere. They were tending the borders, mowing the grass and sweeping away litter from the night before with a broom made out of twigs. Jim stood at the door his hand outstretched waiting to take mine, content we wandered down to breakfast. A message was brought into the dining room and pinned onto a bill board. Attention was drawn to it by an African ringing an attached bicycle bell. 'There is a message for Mr. Moss in reception'.

'Back in a min love.'

'I wonder who wants him?' A few moments and my silent question was answered.

A vehicle had been delivered to the hotel, an African driver sat at the wheel as he was waiting to take him to NATCO. He drank his coffee quickly, gave me a hasty kiss on the cheek then he went off to face yet another new challenge. I sat for a while reading the local newspaper before going to organize our untidy bedroom. One or two items should be locked away. This done I wandered around the hotel and into a few shops situated in the hotel complex. There was a craft shop with carvings, locally made pottery, jewellery, pictures painted by local artists and tie died materials, some of which had been made into very attractive and unusual dresses. The shop owner was a European, the wife of a farmer living a little way out of Lusaka. There was also a bookshop, here I browsed for what seemed a very long time. We had books with us which dampened down the urge to buy. I did however buy one or two cards to send home.

It was a very hot oppressive day with a feeling of impending rain, though as yet this year no rains had fallen in Zambia. Cicadas were very much in evidence and some people called them rain beetles. Sitting in the shade on the veranda I ordered coffee, sat back with my book and wondered who Jim would be talking to and what would be going through his mind. I was full of curiosity hoping he would he would be back at lunchtime with lots of news. It was becoming very hot and humid. As midday passed the cicadas dry rasp almost piercing the ear drums, geckos ran up the wall, around the pool lizards lay in wait to tongue-thick flies. Sweat ran down the back of my legs and my skirt stuck to the chair seat, time to get up and take a walk, perhaps to the car park. Jim may be on his way back.

In no time at all, there he was and I did not have long to wait, a hand waved from a passing car. I was beneath the shade of a bougainvillea covered arch. He looked hot I noticed as I walked towards him, he would be pleased to shower and to change his suit for shorts and a thin loose shirt.

'Come on Cog I am off to change'

His smile told me his meeting had gone well, I decided to bite my tongue until we were in the cool of the bedroom.

Immediately we were through the bedroom door. 'I am the only white man in the company, and seem to be responsible for pretty nearly everything.'

'What do you mean everything?' I asked.

'Field, factory and office.'

I could only say 'Oh,' he certainly did not seem to be in the least bit intimidated at the prospect of this, which amazed me

'The M.D. has a very good house for us in Kabalonga, it is big and has a tiny pool.'

He had been to see it and was quite impressed, we would have to wait but it would be there for us in three months time. It merely meant moving into the house in Leopard's Hill for a short time. When our crates arrived, we would leave them untouched until our final move. Hard furnishings were in the house and we could manage with the rest.

'A lot of time will be spent on safari. Also...'

'Also what love?' I queried.'

'We have to go to Ndola to pick up a Range Rover,' he looked very pleased to tell me this as we were so used to being thrown hither and thither in hot sweaty Land rovers! Going to Ndola would be an interesting introduction to a country of which we knew absolutely nothing. Life was going to be a bit hectic, up country visits to tobacco farms and schemes, work in the office, meetings to attend, staff to organize and the factory to keep ticking over.

'God love that is a bit awesome.'

'Not at all, I delegate.'

'How can you do that?' I asked. 'You have to know who to delegate to.'

'Wait and see.' I did and he was right.

We spent two weeks in the Ridgeway the people leaving the house kindly left bits and pieces which they felt we might need whilst moving from one house to the other. We also gave a home to their two dogs, which saved them a lot of heart ache. Everyone used dogs in Zambia as a deterrent, there were so many robberies and so much armed theft and so many murders. It was all a far cry from our past years in Africa. The bush, the game, the beauty of the African nights, the stars were all still the same. The feel of these things and the smell of Africa were just as they had always been. They were moved from the violence of civilization in the townships and the grinding filth surrounding them.

I bought some mangoes from a street seller, Jim would love these. The only sensible place to eat mangoes is in the bath the orange coloured juice runs in uncontrollable rivulets from mouth to chin to clothes, it spreads over cheeks and finds its way, complete with juicy bits, up the nose. I have seen our children's faces covered with ripe mango, their clothes spattered orange and sticky with juice, even so we continued to eat mangoes with great relish.

'You are not going to believe this,' Jim announced looking perplexed as he walked through the kitchen.

'What has happened,' my stomach turned over.

'The boat, carrying your little Ford has sunk off the coast of Mogadishu.'

I stared in disbelief. 'Do boats still sink in this day and age, you are joking?'

'Nope, your little car is no more, it's lying somewhere covered in sea water.'

I was seized with panic and seeing this, he came over to put his arms around my shoulders.

'Don't worry Cog. It is covered by insurance and the M.D. is quite willing to let us fly down to South Africa to the Ford agent, choose a car and drive it back to Zambia.'

I was considerably cheered by this piece of news, it could become quite an adventure with just the two of us driving through miles of bush seeing lots of game and staying in hotels on the way back through South Africa's Transvaal. We had to go to Johannesburg and travel back through Zimbabwe, it would be like a honeymoon.

'When are we going?' I asked eagerly.

'Just as soon as it can be arranged.'

It was all arranged very quickly, there was no problem with the insurance. We just had to go ahead, book a flight, contact the Ford agent, select a car in the same price range and ask them to prepare it for collection on a given date.

We were still in our first house and were not yet really into the swing of things. Undeterred, Jim organized the whole affair in no time at all. Suddenly we were at the airport waiting for the plane to take us to Jo'Burg, I looked at him and smiled.

'You don't waste any time do you love?'

'No,' he put his arm through mine and we walked out to the aircraft. We were off on another adventure.

A Car Drive From Johannesburg

It was our intention to contact Michael (the hairdresser), our friend from long ago in the old days of Nyasaland whilst we were in Johannesburg. He had moved to South Africa as the situation in the country began to deteriorate. He and Poppy now had a thriving business in soft furnishings in the city, their home was outside in the suburb of Germiston.

Our flight lunch arrived on a small tray. We tucked into this happily we were both feeling a little puckish; a small bottle of wine accompanied it.

'This little trip is worth losing the car for,' quipped Jim. Snuggling up I could not have agreed more. It seemed that no sooner were we in the air than we began to descend.

'What colour would you like?' Jim asked. Blue, had been mentioned so had sand and green, we thought perhaps blue, we seemed to have a penchant for blue cars.

As we landed we could see the skyscrapers of Johannesburg nestling in the hazy, shimmering heat of the city. I was amazed at its sprawling hugeness and the opulent suburbs over which we flew. Each home seemed to have a swimming pool glittering turquoise in the sunlight, it was possible to see lawns surrounded by huge patchworks of bright flora and trees, all kept crisp and bright by huge sprinklers.

We filed out of the aircraft without encountering any problems in immigration and customs and headed towards a kiosk in the lounge. We explained our need of an hotel within the vicinity of the Ford garage, the name of which I cannot now remember, it was in the centre of Johannesburg. Ah! The Carlton Hotel It was highly recommended we hailed a taxi and were rapidly transported to a many storied, edifice which was the forecourt of a very grand shopping centre. On stepping out of the taxi we were greeted by a doorman in full livery. His face was like polished ebony and shone deep bronze. Our luggage was put on to a trolley and we were escorted to reception. A smart heavily made up lady behind the desk directed us to a room with a panoramic view of the city. The whole of the hotel – from the foyer through the lounge to the tea room with a raised dias housing a baby grand – had a luxurious, relaxing ambience. From the balcony the eye was drawn to the tall, mirrored windows of the Johannesburg stock exchange, people and vendors scurrying below all resembled puppets on a string.

Arm in arm we wandered around the hotel. On the top level we found an enormous swimming pool, we would enjoy this. The pool was surrounded by tables and chairs on an Astroturf area shaded by enormous umbrellas. There were massage and aromatherapy parlours all covered by a discreet transparent sliding roof. On each floor were huge ice cube makers. The reception room lead to a sitting area on the mezzanine floor, here people relaxed with afternoon tea and sandwiches or in the evening a drink catching up with the news out of Africa in the local *Johannesburg Times*, it was moody, slightly melancholic but relaxing. We sat in the huge body-grabbing easy chairs of soft leather, reflections caught on the highly polished floors, scattered here and there were Indian rugs. Smartly dressed waiters drifted from table to table tending to various needs of hotel patrons. From a rostrum in the middle a pianist played soft music on a grand piano, the overall ambience was one of relaxation.

'Shall we go to our room? We must try to ring Michael.' Jim mused.

We were loathe to leave the comfort.

'Sadly, I suppose we have to move,' was my lazy reply.

We called Michael from the bedroom, I could hear his screech of delight from where I was sitting as he realized who was on the other end of the telephone.

'Of course I shall come to the Carlton lobby we must have a sundowner together give Jean my love.'

We rested and read for a short time. Jim phoned the garage to tell them we would collect the car in the early morning. All the paperwork had been attended to so it was merely a case of collecting a shiny blue Ford. Washed and appropriately dressed we prepared to go back to the lobby. Stepping from the lift we walked towards the foyer but as we glanced in the direction of the swing doors, we were astounded, we had not seen Micheal for some time. Could this short grey haired, slightly stooped man in the almost ankle length dark coat be Michael? It was. Alongside him stood his son Chris, immediately he saw us, he approached with arms outstretched. 'Jeemy, Jeemy' he rushed towards us hugging Jim he was almost swallowed in the embrace of the bigger man, he kissed me on each cheek then held me at arms length to get a better view, 'Lovely,' was all he said, I found his remark pleasing. Chris was now a young man – it almost seemed impossible.

The change we saw in the other each was inescapable. The years had changed us all, though our hearts and minds were just as they had always been. Michael had a problem with his heart and it showed. We talked until late of the past present and of the future, then we walked him to the car promising to stay with him on our next visit to South Africa. After a pensive 'Goodbye,' Jim and I walked arm in arm through to the lift and the privacy of our bedroom in a state of wistful yearning for the past years and the joy of Namisu.

Breakfasting the next day had a dreamlike quality, water cascaded softly over the whole of one wall in the breakfast room, it produced a calming almost soporific effect. A soothing, cooling and relaxing start to the day before our long journey north. With a jolt back to reality it occurred to us that we really had no time to daydream, ahead of us there was much to do and a long way to travel. The luggage was brought down into the foyer whilst we settled our account, afterwards we walked the few blocks to pick up the car.

There it stood, a small blue hatchback polished and shining waiting to be driven away over the stony rugged roads of Africa to Zimbabwe and on to Zambia. We had a number of security measures built into the car which made us feel less anxious from the point of view of theft. How things had changed! With a road map under our arm we got into the car and drove to the Carlton. We drove slowly almost feeling our way through the traffic. We collected the luggage from the foyer, tipped the porter and made our way out of Johannesburg, heading north towards the Limpopo river. The journey was without problems. We went through the northern town of Louis Trichardt on to Messina and the border post at Biet Bridge, we had decided to travel on to the Ruins of Great Zimbabwe at Masvingo (Fort Victoria), supposedly the greatest historic relic in Southern Africa. Here there was a lodge in which we could stay. It was hot and dusty our bottles of water were working overtime. It was quite late when we arrived. Food and bed were very welcome after the long hot days drive. We slept the sleep of the weary but we were happy.

Up bright and early the next morning we ate breakfast then took to the road. It was necessary for us to be back as soon as possible, Jim had a great deal of work to attend to, both in the office and on up country farms. The house in Sable road was now empty so we had to view it and arrange for the NATCo decorators to move in and clean the place up, also the pool had to be emptied of rubbish, cleaned and then painted.

The next day we were at sparrow, and making our way to Harare (once Salisbury), having decided to stay at Meikles Hotel which proved to be a far cry from the Meikles of the past. Security here was a priority, food and service were mediocre and lax. In Harare muggings and robberies were the order of the day. Our little car was parked in a secure car park with a guard at the gate and a high wall topped with barbed wire, it was loaded with luxury goods bought in South Africa, from pillows to feta cheese. On awakening the next morning we decided to check the car before breakfast only to find the Mercedes alongside had been broken into and the locks rendered useless. Fortunately for us, our Ford had not been tampered with. It was with great relief that we ate and enjoyed our breakfast despite feeling very sorry for the occupants of the next door car who were not up yet and oblivious to what awaited them.

Having collected our overnight luggage we made our way over

the still very good roads to the Zambian border stopping over at Clouds End a small hotel at the top of the Chirundu escarpment. All the chalets in this small establishment ran alongside a swimming pool. At the back each chalet had a bewitching vista of the valley, near and far distant mountains, playing out the drama of a setting sun as its rays lit up the evening sky. Brilliant light playing on the surface of the range picking out its peaks in glorious technicolour. The sky was aflame and eventually would be devoured by the deep indigo of the African night. Game wandered all around it was a splendid place to sit and meditate, hold hands and enjoy a 'sundowner' it was very much a rest-a-while place, and difficult to say goodbye to.

The following day we left for the Zambian/Zimbabwe border where things had begun to deteriorate badly and rapidly. The border post itself was a positive nightmare on both sides. The dirt, the smell and the rubbish were nauseating. There was disorganization, confusion and frustration accompanied by designed antagonism. We emerged red in the face but unscathed from the fray and noise. In the passport office some European travellers were being given an extremely hard time, I think they wished they had stayed at home. The questions they were asked were impossible to understand or to answer, unless you had lived in Africa for some years. Only then would you know the gist of how to reply. Giving a great sigh of relief we got into the car and drove through the gates over to the other side to Zambia. Here to they were guarded, however we were lucky and unquestioned they let us through.

On the Zambian side we had to be very careful, the roads were very rough and pot holed, there was a particular lack of game in this part of the country, mainly due to poaching. This distinct change happened immediately after leaving the border post, it hardly made sense. The Zimbabwe side of the border which we knew so well was a very different kettle of fish. In Mana Pools and on the slopes of the Chirundu escarpment, elephant and buffalo were almost always in evidence, sometimes grazing alongside, or crossing the road, it was a magical part of the country.

Travelling through the valley we had noticed how the drought had affected both landscape and game. Coming out of South Africa we had also noticed the Limpopo, it had been dry and bare. Here the game in the Chirundu valley stood limp and thin, even the hardy warthog had lost some of its cheeky arrogance – it was a bad sign. During the past year the rains had been scant. Presently there was hope, heavy cloud had built up on the horizon though as yet it had come to nothing. Moving along the Zambian roads up from the valley, over the escarpment and on and towards Lusaka in the dry heat was uncomfortable in the extreme. Goats fled across the road dashing from bare bush to bare bush stripping everything in their wake, bleating pathetically and throwing up dust in their wake as they ran hither and thither in search of food. Maize stood dry in the fields – a few shriveled cobs remained their leaves hanging dry. In the heat of day they resembled scrunched up wash leather.

My hand lay on a damp hot leg, fine hair on moist arms glistened. My hair hung wet on the back of my neck, the little fan in the car worked overtime. It had seemed a long, long way from the border to Lusaka, particularly as we had, at times, been held up and searched by the military who stood at tin pot security posts dangerously waving their AK 47s. What had happened to Africa?

It was almost dark when we eventually pulled into the drive and arrived home. The car was quickly emptied and locked. We had a shower, a sandwich and a glass of wine and then we flopped into bed. Kaput. Advancing years, and the frustrations of present circumstances in a land we both loved were difficult to come to terms with. However, despite all the changes and challenges we had to overcome, there was a magic to be found here which no other continent had to offer.

Jim was up early the next day and off he went to the office. I put away our South African purchases and went to buy fruit and vegetables from the Cathedral market, a shop in the basement of the cathedral selling produce from local farmers including butter cream and eggs. The supermarket shelves this month were full of toilet rolls and glass tumblers whilst next month, it might be toilet soap, writing paper and pens; quite bizarre. Everything came up from South Africa but we often wondered who put in the orders. The outdoor African markets were now dirty and chaotic with stale unsold goods piled alongside cheap imported plastic ware.

I made bread, we ate salads, meat, sausage and borewors bought from the Woodleys, Minnie and George who had Fringilla farm out on the great north road towards Ndola. They also provided us with milk and cream. Later when we moved to Sable road, George delivered these things in his car to us and to others living in the same area. Sometimes we visited them and bought things we needed from the farm at the same time. We became great friends.

At last we moved to Sable road it had been cleaned up, painted and the carpets laid. The curtains were hung, the garden was dug and weeded and scattered with tobacco scraps. The pool was emptied of the garden rubbish left by the previous occupier. It had been painted blue and filled with water. We bought a small pump and crystals to keep it fresh and clean. Pool crystals could be bought anywhere, food could not! At one end of the pool there was a huge sausage tree, beneath it we put a table and chairs which gave the garden a certain ambience and certainly gave us much pleasure. We made the house comfortable, even buying a television for the limited viewing. Going out at night was difficult, all sorts of danger lurked out there on the streets; there were muggings murders robberies. We did at times venture out to one of the 'better' hotels. I suppose we were lucky as our garden backed on to the garden of a security policeman, a New Zealander. He was used by the President and had a license to kill, he would always keep his eye on the house when we were away, which was often as I always went up country with Jim and everyone knew and understood this. We went together on all safaris and did things together, it did not interfere in any way with the work he had to do, in fact when we visited the farms, the families were always pleased to see us and a bed was always assured should we need one.

Here Come Graham and Carol

We had not been in Sable road long when we had a letter from Carol, she and Graham were coming to Zambia to work for Landell Mills, Graham was to set up an area for growing Cashew nuts and he would be responsible for seedlings, planting, harvesting and finding a market for the nuts. He was to be stationed in Mongu. This had been great news for us. It was a long trek from Mongu to Lusaka but we knew they would have to come into town at times and they could stay with us. On the other hand we could stay with them when Jim was in the Mongu area working on tobacco. It would be a very different life from the one we had known together in Tanganyika/Tanzania.

The changing times of Africa. Jim and I had gone from Nyasaland, now Malawi, to Tanganyika, now Tanzania, then back to Malawi. On to Paraguay in South America and now here we are in Zambia, once Northern Rhodesia. We have visited many of the other countries in Africa since Independence and on each occasion have been saddened at the changes, grinding poverty and break down of law and order.

We made the most of everything, we always did. We laughed, loved and talked as we had always done. We were however very aware of the dark forces at work and of the damage they were causing in this magnificent continent which had so much to offer to the world.

The many tobacco trials on the Great West road drew us to Chunga camp for nightly accommodation. Chunga camp was situated on the Kafue river. A long, pot-holed sandy road into the bush from the main road west led us there. Considerable game roamed the Kafue; elephant, lion, cheetah, impala, warthog and in the river many crocodile and hippo. Monkeys and baboons were all over the place. To get to the camp, it was necessary for us to cross the river by boat to reach the promontory on which it was sited. We always carried a drum of diesel to enable us to cross to our chalet on the other side. More often than not the village pump this side of the river was empty!

People rarely went to Chunga but Jim and I loved it, it was total isolation with only the inevitable bush sounds and game to break the silence. The camp had a cook, of sorts. We took our own food, usually meat and potatoes, which he cooked in the evening over a camp fire. Later on, snorts from hippo nearby would echo over the water, a lone male lion as it passed by the camp might give a deep throated grunt. The huts were on stilts and each one had two beds with mosquito nets and little else. The approach to the door was up rickety wooden steps. Hippo came into the camp through the night to graze, we often lay listening to them munch their way around the chalets.

Jim and I were adept at finding these little bits of paradise away from the madding crowds – the refinements of running water and electricity meant little to us. The camp shower had three sides, an open topped affair into which water was piped from the river to a battered temperamental rose which either dripped pathetically, or the water shot out with the force of a fire hose. To sit around the camp fire at night after a shower was Heaven, this was the Africa we knew and loved; the haunting unforgettable sounds, the moving shadows in the surrounding bush, sparks flying high from the fire when we stoked it. I propped my feet up onto Jim's knee. Looking at him my heart jumped as he smiled and stroked my foot and an overwhelming surge of love rose up to bring a lump to my throat. In the distance a hyena cackled and we wondered why as it persisted in its spine chilling laugh. Our supper in the bush that night was steak and baked potatoes and a bottle of lager from the cool box. We slept well despite the incessant noise of the crickets.

The next morning we crossed the river in the boat, keeping an eye on the enormous crocodile drifting alongside. A local African had kept watch over the Range Rover for the night. Jim paid him well for his work. This man always appeared when word reached him of our approach to camp, he attracted the attention of the cook and cleaner on the other side by banging an old tin drum as the echo was loud and clear and carried over the water. He unloaded our Katundu (baggage) and reloaded it on our return.

After leaving Chunga there were a number of trials still to visit so we hoped we would not be too late arriving back in Lusaka. On Saturday my love wanted to spend time in his garden. It was quite a large garden and was coming along splendidly. There were many vegetables of every kind alongside paw paw and avocado trees.

The shadows were lengthening, Jim put his foot down harder on the accelerator as we approached Lusaka as we were still not used to the comfort of the Range Rover, it was so much more luxurious and comfortable than the basic old Land rovers, our transport in the past.

On our travels, most bridges were manned by militia. We were held up regularly by these people who waved AK47 rifles as we approached. The vehicle was searched. The men smelt of native beer and were very offensive, eventually they became used to the sight of us as we travelled these same old roads so regularly. At times even a joke would pass between us, at others we were waved through with. 'Ah Mr. James Moss how are you today?' One never quite knew what their reaction would be. This was life after independence. In the house a rape gate separated the living area from the bedrooms and was firmly locked at night whilst security lights blazed and heavy duty curtains kept out their harsh light. An alarm was to be installed in the house which went direct to the Embassy. The cement on the high wall around the house held wicked shards of glass.

Driving up to the house tooting as we approached, the guard opened the gate helping Amelia the housemaid to unload the vehicle. Waiting for the potatoes to bake we had a well earned sundowner. We could hardly wait for our bacon, eggs and baked potato. The T.V. programmes were rubbish we chose to sit outside on the veranda and watch the stars, bats flitted back and forth into and through the light then back into the night. This was not the estate life we loved and could get lost in, but it was Africa. Our life was good in Lusaka and our home was comfortable. Our real joy were the safaris in the bush amongst the game, taking pot luck in our camp sites, watching the sun sink down into a brilliant red sky with a drink in our hand. The smell of cooking from an open fire which always stirred up mouth watering sensations impossible to experience in another setting. Being in love under the romance of the stars, enveloped in a warm breeze is the most wonderful thing in the world. It cannot be imagined it has to be the right time, the right place, the right partner and a love which will last forever. For Jim and I these were the ultimate sensations in life. A bolt of lightning in a deadly quiet, a thunder of hearts in a breaking storm while the world ticks on and the stars wink up in the sky. This was us this was Africa.

★★★

As I write these words my senses reel knowing that this life is past, this love has gone, it has been taken away from me and I cannot re-direct my emotions, my love, or come to accept that my life and future will be empty of Jim. The upheaval of this emotion leaves me hollow and bereft. Can I write myself out of this, can I empty my grief with words? I shall try. As water hurtles over a precipice so my thoughts and feelings tumble from my pen. Our happiness together had been one that description could not reach.

★★★

Before eating breakfast we checked the Range Rover it still had four wheels and appeared not to have been tampered with during the night, over bacon and eggs we decided today must be good; tomorrow it was back to Lusaka work and chaos. Graham and Carol were coming down from Mongu so there was no chance of our being bored for the coming week. It was a typical dry season day, clouds had started to build up over the distant hills we were nearing the approach of the rains and the air was very hot, a dry rasp from the cicadas hit the ears in constant waves. As we walked into the bush taking photographs, mainly for use in my game paintings, a lion crossed the path in front of us – heavy bellied and full, it must have killed nearby during the night when hyena were cleaning up the carcass their cackles intermingled with resonant howls came over the air on their approach to the kill. A little earlier Jim had to stop in his tracks to avoid stepping on a puff adder, one of the mostly deadly snakes in Africa, but rather slower than most.

I thought of Old Jock with his keen eye and attention to bush lore and detail, his training of one young man many years ago had not gone unheeded, my instruction almost daily when in the bush was to look, listen and observe. We walked back to the Range Rover and attacked the cool box; hard boiled eggs, a couple of tins of sardines, rolls from the hotel washed down by a can of beer, in these surroundings it was a meal as ambrosial as any in a five star hotel. We were under a tree looking out onto the river, entertained by resident crocs, hippos and visiting antelope which had come to the water to drink.

On the way back elephant had held us up on the escarpment road, we were quite late getting into Clouds End, the bar was buzzing with farmers from nearby farms and we joined in the conversation and listened to their concerns at the sudden turn of events in the political scenes of Zimbabwe. White Rhodesians, we were given to understand, were to be moved from their lucrative farms after which the farms would be handed to black Mugabe sympathizers, there had been talk of this for some time, but now 'accidents' were happening to more and more white farmers. We trundled into supper feeling somewhat downbeat, affected by the gloomy predictions of the farmers, we had many farmer friends growing tobacco in Zimbabwe some of whom we had known for many years. Our friends, the Boddy's from the old Nyasaland days, had moved to the then Rhodesia; living with them in a small cottage on the farm were Babs and her family, she had moved to be near Bill, her husband's brother, after Bill's murder in Dar-es-Salaam. We decided to go father into Zimbabwe when we next came over the border as apparently they were in Tengwe, we were concerned at the danger and the possibilities of what could so easily happen to them, the whole situation was very disturbing.

On the following day we went through usual drama at the customs post then sped back to Lusaka and home. It was good to see Graham and Carol. Both were a little fraught after the long journey from Mongu, made even more tedious by the condition of the roads. At least 200 miles of road had to be slowly manoeuvered due to huge potholes which unless treated with respect could do serious damage to any vehicle, no one would want to break down on this road running through the middle of a game park, it was here unfortunately that the most dangerous and broken up parts happened to be.

What a hectic week for the men. Jim went to local farms each day and Graham tended to various chores in Lusaka and the office. I stayed with Carol, we went off in my car to see if she could find anything in the shops worth taking to Mongu we called in at the Ridgway hotel to idle away the time, mooching around the small gift cloth and souvenir shops within the complex of the hotel grounds.

One evening we took the bull by the horns and went to the Chinese restaurant situated behind the walls of the Agricultural showground. It was wise to be on guard at night as people had been subjected to every crime in the book. We hoped it would not be our turn tonight, our car doors were locked at all times as traffic lights and badly lit areas were potential crime spots. It was a tasty meal and the night was, thank goodness, uneventful, and we relaxed as we went through the gates of home.

The garden had been planted up with every different kind of vegetable, salad leaves, herbs, cucumbers, chillies and lots of tomato plants which were all waiting for the rain, having to water them each day was not always convenient particularly if we were up country and had to leave the guard to do it. Everything was fast growing and lush during the rainy season. There were four chickens, laying eggs each day to accompany George's 'Fringilla' farm bacon, always a good start to the morning. To one side of the vegetables was an avocado tree and three or four paw paw trees. At this time there was not a lot to buy in the shops, it was a search and hope situation, fortunately we were able to use the duty free sho where we were able to buy the odd luxury item, some tinned foods, cheese, beer and oil. There were cheeses available at the cathedral shop, chickens and poussins were brought in to order. They were our favourite safari food – roasted and kept in the cold box. It was our custom to buy tubs of feta cheese from wherever we could get it, I made a little. If I give the impression that we were obsessed with food we were not, many items were difficult to get so we had to think ahead, in past years it had not been a problem but this was another era. At last the rains came, our visits to Mana pools had to come to a halt for the season, the garden flourished and we divided excess produce with neighbours and friends.

Christmas In Malawi

When Christmas came along we went to Malawi to spend the holiday with Geoffrey and Shirley. I took along a Christmas cake made from fruit we had bought at the duty free. It took a lot of persuasion to get the customs officers to let me take it through, it was necessary to explain what it was. I was asked why I was taking it, where we were going and for how long, the conversation extended to an explanation of its tradition. Our reason for carrying it was to share our goodwill with the brother of Mr. Moss, we waved a passport beneath their noses once more and eventually they let us drive through.

Driving up to the front of Sayama house we were greeted by Geoffrey, Shirley and the dogs, it had been so many years since we were last together, it brought great joy and the mood continued throughout our time with them. We could no longer go over the border as we had in the past as Mozambique was at war and in chaos 'Giggle mile' was out of bounds – in fact it had ceased to exist (apparently there was little left of Portuguese Mulanje). Going into into Blantyre and Limbe to buy what we felt might be needed we discovered there was more to buy here than in Lusaka, we called in at the Mount Soche hotel, met one or two old friends talked of old times over a drink. Many asked 'When are you coming back?' our reply could not be in the affirmative sadly. It was exhilarating to meet all the old tobacco growers and farmers it was also very soul searching when the time came to say goodbye. Christmas Day we spent on the estate, a lazy gift giving day we laughed a lot and took a walk into the lush green lines of tea, Geoffrey took us round the factory. Some of the Africans were working though not the full contingent if I remember rightly. I do remember how we roared with laughter all the time when we were together, it was very infectious as Jim and George's humour was so dry.

Marko, the major domo at Sayama estate, had been with them for years, he was conscientious, willing, polite and very loyal, he had moved with them from tea estate to tea estate, we knew him of old he never changed. It was a gracious life even at this time though standards had inevitably fallen as they had in every corner of the old Empire. Even so, how we had grown since those days of the late 1950s, we had aged visibly but our hearts' desires and needs were just as they had always been – perhaps they were even more intense now as in some ways we had less pressure. In all honesty I can only relate to the attitudes and emotions between Jim and I as we were still as passionate and tender towards each other as we had always been. We were also great companions, we depended upon each and were always there for one another. Our young love was as strong as it had been when we sat beneath the projection lights of the Odeon cinema so many years ago, it was different but it was still 'heady' – the power of his hand still gave me shivering goosepimples, it always would.

Most of holiday we had talked of the past of how Jim and I had flown in the face of convention – so aware that there was no alternative to our being be together, this was a meant to be situation and we had seized it with both hands and through our life had never regretted one moment. We discussed and wondered at the hard financial times we had gone through, of where our work had taken us, and of the children. It was a family holiday and we talked of family things. Of course we ate too much food and no doubt drank too much wine, we became nostalgic as there were so many things to dream on. Christmas went very quickly, perhaps we were having too good a time reminiscing, indulging in dreams, leg-pulling, banter and laughter. To soon it was time to leave, time again to close a chapter of the book in which we had all played a part. It was a tearful goodbye, though in fact we were to see them again quite soon.

Back to Zambia

The rains came, they were patchy and not at all what everyone had hoped for. Graham was working himself to a standstill in

Mongu and he was having fantastic results, never doing anything in half measures, sometimes to his detriment. Sheer determination drove him on, stress and overwork took their toll, he was not at all well and a series of tests confirmed that he had adult diabetes. It was not an easy time either him or Carol, we did what we could to help, though sometimes we stood on the sidelines helpless.

A successful tobacco crop was sown, grown, reaped and sold. There were good yields as the crop did not like too much rain. The NATCO factory was in full swing, Jim made a great success of what he had set out to do, next year would be easier he thought as the Africans appeared to have understood his teaching and were applying most of what he had taught them. Everyone appeared to be pulling their weight so far.

Here Come Janey And Peter

Janey and Pete came for their holiday in June. The weather was 'moody' mostly warm during the day with a marked temperature drop in the evening and during the night. This did not deter them, they were enjoying every minute of their holiday, it was magic to have them with us. We all went on safari with Jim to the tobacco trials and farms. Peter was a farmer and interested in all aspects of agriculture overseas, he met an old friend from college days who was managing a mixed farm for a big rancher in Zambia.

It was a family get together none of us would ever be tempted to forget, we enjoyed and appreciated each others company and it was a great joy to us to be able to introduce Peter to Africa. Janey three months into her pregnancy was as perky as ever, she loved the family, daddy was really very special to her, from a tiny girl he had been her 'everything' and he had initiated her into such a wonderfully exciting life, particularly in Dar-es-Salaam when her two elder sisters were schooling in the UK. She loved picnics in the bush and we indulged in them whenever possible.

One steaming hot weekend we took them to the David Shepard camp on the Teshi Teshi dam in the Kafue National Park, a delightful camp in a delightful situation. On our first day, in the early morning, Jim took them off into the bush. I remained behind not feeling up to scratch which was sad. They came upon a lion kill – a huge well mutilated buffalo – quite a number of lion were on the kill there was much blood and gore but it was exciting and something they had never seen before, this would be a fireside story for years to come.

Arriving back for breakfast late, faces shining in anticipation of telling me their good luck story, they avidly shared the gory details between them. We all went out again later in the day and saw the remains of the kill, there were many other species of game, mainly antelope and zebra browsing in the dry scrub. Sitting on the khonde of the camp that evening we watched the sun settle down in the western sky to a brilliant glow. The whole spectrum from yellow and orange through every shade of red lit up the sky and reflected onto the lake, slashing through the middle by a shoreline of black on the opposite side. Two natives rowing fishing boats passed by, ripples from their oars breaking the surface struck jet black against the firey background, the falling of sudden darkness taking over from this flood of colour was an anti-climax suddenly the scene was no longer there we were at the day's end.

A delicious supper arrived, the cook had gone to great pains to prepare it and it was really very good, a cup of coffee followed afterwards we went to bed to read; a generator chugging outside fed each room with electricity. Our safari around the Kafue Park the next day was delightful. It was a slow drive, we meandered in and out of the bush unhurried savouring each passing moment, there was always something new to see, something unexpected in this vast wilderness. An amazing sight was a snake leaping through the air, whipping itself from bush to bush, a distant leopard turned looked at us and walked away, our lunch was eaten watching a herd of waterbuck grazing lazily nearby, occasionally lifting their heads to make sure we were where they thought we were. Lunch over we toured the waterholes, every tree was alive with the sound of noisy weaver birds flying in and out of their nests busy with a little repair work, we watched and took many photographs. Pete's camera was red hot and his photographs were exceptionally good.

On our leisurely and long drive back there were hippo standing on the banks of the dam alongside buffalo slaking their thirst with an evening drink, some snorted, turned to take a look at us shook their great heads and carried on drinking.

'Once upon a time you would have had a bead on those love.'

'Yes, and I would have had to walk miles to find them in Chikwawa; those were the days,' Jim replied with quiet finality.

Smiling he gave my hand a squeeze and there was a tiny silence

'Seems strange, we cannot even carry a gun in the bush to defend ourselves now, it makes no sense when game is being slaughtered by Africans with AK.47s on a daily basis.' I commented.

Everything seemed so topsy turvy and contradictory these days, there was much killing going on in the Zambezi valley mainly for rhino horn exported to the East.

A herd of impala crossed the road just as we were turning into camp, they looked fat, well fed, and in very good condition we drove slowly past them to our chalets. The cook made a pot of tea. We were thirsty and drank eagerly, sitting on the khonde we watched the fishermen draw in their nets on the dam, their little dug outs rocked crazily with each tug. After this came a cool a shower followed by reading on the bed until sundowner time. Jim looked tanned, and so peaceful as he lay relaxing. What a tranquil life this was.

'Love you,' I said leaning over to give him a kiss.

'Love you to', he smiled reaching over to put an arm around me.

Over a sundowner and during supper we watched an almost replica sunset of the previous night, breathtakingly vivid and beautiful.

All were sad to leave the next day, Janey and Peter repeatedly looked back in an effort to burn the scene into their memory, we decided to go back via the Kariba dam, we would like to do some shopping and look round the tourist area, where the Africans sold crochet work of all kinds, articles big and small, from bedcovers to tray clothes were for sale. Peter was eager to see the Kariba dam. Looking at the dam from the eyes of a layman it appeared to be in need of considerable repair, it was nevertheless of great interest to him and he took endless films. The border post at Kariba was cleaner and rather more organized than the Chirundu post, of course there was not the volume of traffic passing through and no enormous trucks thundering through from the south laden with sanction busting imports whilst the rest of the world stood by sanctimoniously, refusing to trade with South Africa. To most people living in Africa the whole thing was a farce. Meanwhile white farmers were being stripped of their farms and assets by tyrannical dictators of the day. These were the thoughts invading the minds of most white people, particularly old settlers to whom none of it made sense.

We were delighted to show the youngsters the bush of Zambia, they would take home such wonderful memories. Janey remembered Zimbabwe as Rhodesia a country consisting of huge lucrative ranches and estates. Zambia of course had been Northern Rhodesia, a country rich in copper and cobalt with a smaller farming community. The journey home was full of questions chatter and laughter from the back Janey piped.

'You always put your hand on daddy's knee don't you mum?'
'Yes always,' I replied.

At home we ate most of our meals on the khonde at the back of the house. It overlooked the vegetable garden, sometimes the chill sent us inside at this time of the year though we much preferred to eat outside, to the right of the khonde and opposite our bedroom window an enormous bamboo rustled and creaked, it was here we batted a ball backwards and forwards keeping our eye on the barbeque at the same time. Amelia baked the potatoes and set the table. Jim collected salads from the garden for me.

On the odd day Jim took Peter to NATCO as his enquiring nature gave him an interest in everything. On these days Janey and I got into my little car and went to the Ridgway or the Intercontinental browsing in the hotel complex, usually stopping for coffee, sometimes we all met and ate lunch out. We had to take the youngsters to our piece de resistance the Zambezi valley and Mana pools. The tobacco crop pressure was off things were reasonably quiet, Mr. Kabwe the M.D. of NATCO had no objections to Jim having a few days in the valley with the family. We prepared for our journey. Cool boxes were packed with goodies and drinks, our clothes put into two cases and we were ready to go. Before leaving we asked Ken, the security fellow next door, if he would keep an eye on the house though there was little trouble in this immediate vicinity due to him living in the neighbourhood. He had an awesome reputation amongst local criminals, keeping his eye open for us we had little to worry about.

Saturday morning we packed the Range Rover to the hilt and left for the valley. We left instructions for the staff, piled into the car tooted the horn and the watchman came to open the gate, we roared through heading for Kafue, Luwanshya and the endless small developments leading to Chirundu. The big escarpment road was hugely rutted, some of the drops had ground trucks and trailers to a halt. African drivers were destined to sit waiting for days until help came, often some passing vehicle would be responsible for informing the main depot, they eventually sent mechanics out to repair the damage but it was a time consuming exercise. Often the women of a nearby village carried food to the road setting up a kitchen for the drivers and their mechanics, it was an ideal way of making a little money, needless to say the nights were not wasted!

The landscape was scrappy at times; dry maize, villages and goats and scattered Africans were mainly the scene, baobabs had begun to appear which meant we were nearing the valley, another smaller, less chaotic, escarpment offered a stunning vista of the land lying below over into Zimbabwe. Janey and Pete were enthralled In Chirundu the scene was as chaotic as ever, a number of trucks and their drivers held up in customs defied belief, how did anything ever reach its destination? Fortunately we had no problems, though I think the younger contingent of our little party were a little bewildered by it all.

'How does this work daddy'?

'I have no idea, let's go,' Jim quickly made his way to the customs shed door.

'Thank God we are out of that,' he burst out as we headed for the car and the barrier.

We handed over our pass and the barrier was lifted now we could all breathe out.

'Food,' came a cry from the back of the car.

'Yes, a few miles and we shall be able to stop at our usual picnic spot in the park,' I explained.

These picnic spots in the days of the old Rhodesia had been extremely smart and organized, concrete benches and a table in their midst and a bin for rubbish, usually round and about there had been bougainvillea planted and almost always there was a baobab nearby. We arrived at our stop, there was a bin and concrete stool albeit they were a little the worse for wear, the table I always covered with a cloth carried especially for the job. Quite often we saw elephant on this part of the road, warthog had also entertained in the past as we had sat eating. It would be the icing on the cake if this happened now. And so we sat beneath the big old baobab, Janey and Pete could hardly contain their excitement as opposite there were one or two impala grazing, they took little notice of us we took and spread out the cloth, our plastic plates, bread, cheese and pickles; a bush lunch fit for a king. Taking a long time over our meal we each had a can of Lion beer, the conversation revolved around the childhood safaris in Tanzania and Malawi, to present times and our plans for the future.

'Tell me when you want to move,' Jim muttered in a lazy fashion.

'Not yet daddy let's just for stay a while to see if the elephant come,' so we waited but they did not come.

The odd warthog wandered past, the elephant we thought were up river. Time to make our way to the Cloud's End, we could perhaps drive down the escarpment again before dusk we had often done this in the past.

'There could possibly be game on the road at this time, we may even see buffalo. What do you think my love?'

'Yes, I am all for it,' I said, thinking yet again 'What a wonderful world.' So often this sentence would come into my thoughts. Each day something happened to make me realize how lucky I was.

We chose our chalets the outlook was west over the valley towards Kariba and the distant hills. After unpacking we decided to take it easy for a while. We lay on the bed resting and read our books. There were small heaters on the wall which we switched on to warm up the chalet, it could be chilly in the evening at this time of year, particularly at the top of the escarpment; after a quick shower we wandered up to the sitting room where a welcoming log fire lay crackling in the hearth, in relaxed fashion we sat around the table with a pot of tea accompanied by home made cake, it was decided unanimously that we go back down the escarpment in search of game. Not far from our motel we saw elephant on the road and in the near distance buffalo milled around in the scrub, we were delighted on behalf of the children at this immediate success. It was said there were rhino in the Mana pools area, they were heavily poached which was obviously why we had never seen them. Poachers from Zambia came over the river armed with AK47s, they were generally shot by the Zimbabwean game scouts who at that time were very keen on protecting their rhino.

As the the sun would soon be setting we wanted to get back to watch its descent behind the hills, sitting in our camp chairs in front of the chalet with a 'woollie' round our shoulders and a sundowner. Who could resist watching the gradual descent of this shining golden orb splashing the horizon with golden light? Black hills jumped forward, starkly etched before the panoply of brilliant orange, red and crimson. The African sunsets were dazzling, they filled on lookers with incredulity and awe. The bar was, as ever, a prop for nearby farmers, we listened to their problems nodded in agreement at their grievances exchanged views then afterwards went into the dining room feeling deeply sorry for them in their plight. Where would they be in a few years time? Not on their farms if Mugabe and his government had anything to do with it. We could hear the buzz of their conversation and concerns from the bar as we ate supper.

'Are you ready?' The Voices from Janey and Pete as they were raring to go to Mana.
We were actually up and dressed trying to decide what to eat for breakfast.
'Coming, go to the dining room we shall follow in a few minutes.'
'Don't be long,' piped Janey.

We found them sitting at the breakfast table, breakfast already ordered with (thank goodness) a cup of tea waiting for us. I really cannot remember what our breakfast consisted of – it was usually bacon and eggs.

Our descent down the escarpment was slow, the side grass had been blackened by past bush fires, fresh green grass was pushing its way through, guinea fowl flew across the road, Jim took a bead with his finger, 'Good for lunch' he remarked.

Buffalo lifted their heads as we drew down towards the road leading to the actual pools, they were a long way into the bush taking some considerable time to reach as the road deteriorated badly further in. This was exciting, there was always something to see on the road. Impala leaped from one side to the other, some stood looking and snorting before dashing over. Marabou stork resembled old men as they ambled along shaking their heads, at times from side to side at others up and down. Monkeys sped from tree to tree some with babies on their back or under their bellies. The road was dusty and rough, a huge baobab split the road, we went around one side of the tree, the road becoming one again after passing the last of the thick roots.

Approaching the river, the pools at Mana began to shine on the landscape, beneath masasi, acacia and mopani trees elephant stood quietly, only the flapping ears gave them away. Herds of zebra galloped over the plains suddenly to stop and gaze our way. On we went, more elephant were on the opposite side stripping the bark from a tree, driving through a wooded area we suddenly came within sight of the Zambezi river gleaming in the sun and on the far side the hills of Zambia. In the shallows elephant were drinking and cooling off, the roads had deteriorated and were very rutted Jim so nursed the Range Rover along over dried swamp, manoeuvring deep holes previously made by elephant. We drove up to our favourite place beneath a huge tree and settled down to view the scenes around us. At one point Peter had been taking photographs of elephant with a zoom lens oblivious to just how close they were when Jim had said 'I think we had better move Pete,' his face as he took his eye away from the camera was startled, he had not realized just how close the big bull was.

Out came the camp table and chairs, we pulled down the tail of the Range Rover but did not take out the boxes in case we had to make a hasty retreat, This in no way interfered with our picnic. We watched the crocodiles lying on the sandy banks of the river and the hippo wandering in and out of the river. A snake slithered into the water nearby. Finding an elephant skull, Jim pulled out one of its teeth, it is now in the UK amongst the paraphernalia decorating the hearth alongside a piece of iron hard driftwood; everything has a story. It was an unforgettable day. We ate a leisurely lunch, basking in the surrounding magic listening to the bush sounds, watching the game, admiring the flora and enjoying our picnic and each other's company. Afterwards all our katundu, (boxes) were put away and we sat for a while just enjoying the peace, somewhere in the distance a ground hornbill gave its guttural call, not far away from us the call was returned. At the far end of the park we saw a leopard. It had seen us but was unconcerned, it merely stretched and lay down on an incline beneath a mopani tree, we had not been aware that there were leopard in this area.

We had been in and out of every type of terrain, Jim's driving was beyond reproach. Marshland was a menace, at times I wondered how the vehicle held together. Occasionally we piled out to pee, Janey in her condition was more prone to bladder problems. 'Stop daddy,' with a huge grin she disappeared behind a nearby bush. Her hat pushed down on her head, face beaming, she returned in a few moments buttoning up her trousers, she was obviously in her element doing exactly as she had done when a little girl, then, she had tagged along behind Sally, hand in hand they used to run behind a bush, curls bobbing and a red ribbon in their hair.

It was time to leave Mana, we must sign at the barrier to prove we were out of the park before dark, on the way back we saw huge herds of impala and zebra, Peter said he would like to take the wheel after a few miles so we decided to have a beer, parked, opened up the back and took out a tin from the cool box. Round and about us there were small bushes on the roadside, Pete pulled the tab and raised the beer to take a drink just as an elephant stepped out from behind a nearby bush, I have never seen anyone so taken aback, what a picture. 'Bloody hell Jim a tembo.' Looking up we could almost have stroked it. Leaping into the Range Rover, Peter stalled the engine in his haste to get away, with a great sigh of relief we noticed the elephant had veered over a little and was crossing the road behind us, it was a little too close for comfort. Peter tells the story to this day. At the foot of the escarpment Jim took over the driving again, buffalo dung was all over the place we passed quite a large herd to the side of us on the way to Cloud's End, the view over the escarpment was staggeringly beautiful, the bush land punctuated by bulky baobab trees disappearing gradually to merge into a distant lavender sky.

We had a lazy evening, showered, watched another magnificent sunset go down through its gradual brilliant phases until darkness fell, then we went to eat supper and soon afterwards went to bed. The holiday was passing very quickly we had yet to go to Victoria Falls. It was a splendid time to go, the falls were roaring and in full spate, walking along the tiny path along the lip we were all wet through from the spray, again Peter took lots of photographs one of all of us by Livingstone's statue which stands overlooking the falls, now it is more commonly known as 'Moshi o Tunya,' The Smoke that Thunders, it can be seen rising Heavenward for many miles.

Before leaving for Lusaka we were sitting outside having an enjoyable breakfast on the hotel veranda. Peter put out his hand to take up a piece of toast from his side plate, at exactly the same time a monkey swung from a nearby tree and grabbed it from him, Peter almost jumped-out-of- his-skin. They will never forget that holiday. We had packed quite a lot into the month they were with us. Janey was devastated when they left and we felt so sad. It was reminiscent of the times we had to put her on the plane to go back to school in the UK – how we had all hated it, but it had to be, she had always been more affected by the separation than the other two girls.

Sally and family also came to us for a holiday in Zambia. Their itinerary followed almost exactly that of Janey and Peter. In the valley Sal's two girls were very good in the back of the Range Rover. There were hundreds of 'bite flies' as they called them, tetse flies to everyone else, I must say they dealt with them very effectively, as they landed on the window they pushed them down behind and beneath the rubber into the door casing, counting each one and screaming with delight at their success. They loved the animals and were amazed at the size of elephant dung, it was a great pity they were not just that little bit older as they would have remembered so much more. Sally loved it, but then Sally loved everything about Africa, after all she had been born here and Africa takes a firm hold, whether or not you want it to has nothing to do with it, somehow in someway it becomes a part of you. This was not such a sad goodbye as we were due for home leave soon.

An Unwanted Trip To Malawi

Tramp the dog killed a chicken. Jim rushed after him, there had been a shower of rain and he slipped. I could not grasp what was happening and rushed out to help him, he seemed fine though a little shaken, later he was obviously in considerable pain, I remember saying 'Oh my love, what have you done?'
'Nothing much,' he replied.

I knew he was in pain, it was unreal things like this did not happen to Jim. I had a feeling he had damaged his ribs, off we went for an x-ray it revealed little, it was suggested we go to Malawi to Malaomula Mission hospital. We did this but Jim refused to go over the border until he had visited the tobacco farms in the Chipata region on the Zambia/Malawi border, there was only one place to stay the Chipata Hotel it was only just a hotel and extremely run down. Fortunately I always carried spare bed linen and towels, in this day and age the beds were dirty and very unsavoury so while my love went off to the farms I stayed behind to change the beds and organize a meal from our cool boxes. In the late afternoon I heard a car draw up and the engine switch off I knew it was Jim and went out to meet him, he looked dreadfully weary and his eyes were discharging. I ran a bath full of water, he lay and soaked visibly relaxed in the warmth, afterwards I rubbed him down, we had supper and he slept well.

The next day we went over the border and on to Geoffrey and Shirley who made an immediate appointment with the Mission, it was nearby. Poor love he had three broken ribs, I wondered how he had managed to visit the farms in Zambia walking the whole day over rough ploughed fields, but then he rarely complains. We took it easy for a time knowing that only patience heals broken ribs. I felt 'if only it could have been me,' I did not want him to hurt. Driving back to Zambia something alerted me to a crack in his armour, something was not quite as it should be. I loved this man so much that when he hurt, I hurt. It came as a great relief to know we were due for leave. I knew if he was in Zambia he would work, and work meant continual arduous travel over rough, corrugated roads. At home I could look after him until he had healed, afterwards we could go back to Zambia and the life we both loved.

So we flew home for leave, the girls met us at Manchester airport wildly excited at having us home for two months, they took our luggage and fussed about Jim not letting him lift or exert himself in any way. He did try to tell them he was not an invalid it fell on deaf ears, they would have none of it. Liz had managed to come up from Stratford where she was teaching in a private school and living in a hamlet not far from the town. Unfortunately her husband had strayed, leaving a long string of 'has beens' behind him, she was presently involved with an astute and dreadful man who was a 'freeloader' and my goodness did he freeload. Eventually he was forced to leave, she is now happily married. Jim's ribs healed he became fit, exercised and spent a lot of time in the garden, our girls were always popping in, tending to what they felt were our needs and making sure we were comfortable.

Often we went into Wales, we stayed at our favourite hotel the Tyn-y-Cornel opposite was a small lake and the property of the hotel, people came from far and wide to fish, the hotel was used for climbers of Cader Idris in the Snowdonia National Park. From our bedroom one of a block of converted stables, we had often sat at night arms around each other looking at the moon as it hung over the mountain opposite, lighting up the lake turning it into a shimmering sheet of silver, lighting the way home for the barn owl hooting eerily through the night.

After breakfast the next day we decided to walk around the lake, in the full knowledge that someone to love is the answer to life, we linked arms tightly and set off, we walked around the lake, climbed over stiles and said 'Hello' to the sheep, we picked a few flowers to press, cherishing all of these moments we marked them down in our memory, the wink and the smile as I was helped over the fence all the magic was still there. Driving to the coast nearby, the wind whipped through our hair, reddened our noses, and made them run, we cuddled together to keep out the chill and we walked along the promenade in the cold air it was bracing and a little extreme after the heat of Africa. Windswept and feeling pretty cold we went back to the hotel to read our books, a log fire was burning in the sitting room, the large picture window looked out over the lake. Food in the Tyn-y-Cornel was ambrosial, huge portions were served breakfast and dinner were ample, lunch was usually out of the question. We did enjoy being here the scenery was magnificent, the ambience of the place completely relaxing, it appealed to our inner peace and romantic senses.

On the day we left to return home we called at the village shop to buy Welsh bacon for breakfast on the morrow. Now the time had come to turn our minds to sleeping in our own comfortable bed we looked forward to this, it was always this way we loved both home and our breaks away from home, equally we loved Africa, and because we loved each other as we did, we loved life.

On leave in England we went to the auctions and house sales to buy small pieces of furniture and antiques for our home, this time we bought a Tantalus for Jim's office, books were also always high on the list of interests. We visited friends in Scotland staying in unusual and comfortable hotels both on the outward journey and on the way home, there were times when we found the traffic daunting after the long almost empty roads of Africa. Janey and J.T. had at Jim's request planted chestnut trees in the garden some time ago, he was desperate for them to grow and produce nuts to roast by the fire in the chill nights of autumn when we eventually retired. At the bottom of the garden was a huge beautifully shaped oak tree, half of the garden had been planted with fruit trees, it looked out onto fields of grazing cattle.

The time quickly came for us to fly back to Zambia it seemed no time at all since we had arrived. Everyone came to the airport to see us off, there was the usual sadness – goodbyes were a thing we never became used to and all the years of parting had not blunted the sharp edges of departure despair. They took us to Manchester airport, we never eased to be amazed at all the extensions and advances made over the years, when we had first flown from Manchester it was from a Nissan hut named 'Ringway'. All the improvements had taken place in our absence overseas, we found it staggering. We felt a little empty after leaving the girls. This would be our last tour overseas having reached O.D.A. retirement age, we were unsure after living abroad for so long just how retirement would effect us, no doubt their would be a solution somewhere and the family goodbyes would cease.

This was not the time to dwell upon retirement, we gave a final wave to three forlorn looking little figures in the distance and boarded the plane to Heathrow, where we hung around for quite some time before taking off for Zambia. I suppose we spent the flight head to head reading or hand in hand sleeping – with an odd break for the refreshment tray. It was a good comfortable flight we had more room in those days. After disembarking there was the usual officious nose picking, crotch scratching behaviour by over zealous officials in immigration and customs. Amongst the throngs of waiting people we saw Chewa a member of NATCO who worked alongside Jim, he was sharp and keen to learn, his home was in Mbala – the old Abercorn – the town on the borders of Tanganyika and Zambia, where we had bought our first little mustard colour record player, now there was virtually nothing there. We often wondered what had happened to the old colonial Abercorn Hotel, we never asked as we preferred to nurture our old memories rather than face the realities of now.

★★★

It had been a day of memories, disbelief and deep sadness. I went to bed and had the same recurring dream, in front of me stood a ladder which I was compelled to climb looking up I saw it went into a sky full of vaporous cloud, in a clearing above the cloud stood Jim hands out waiting for me to reach the top. Such a long ladder such a difficult climb I was determined to clutch the outstretched hand waiting to help me, to touch the familiar face smiling down with a look I knew so well. Suddenly I realised I had reached the last rung this was not the end of the ladder, now there was nowhere to put my feet, I was unable to climb further the rungs were broken . Jim was waiting his hands open. I could go no further I reached up hoping his hands would clasp mine to lift me over the gaping void, he reached down, our fingers touched our tears fell, the cloud enveloped him I reeled this time we had almost made it. In a frenzy I awoke alone in an empty bed, until the rain beating down on the windowpane brought me back to reality.

★★★

Chewa met us and took us back to our home in Sable road. Everything was almost as we had left it, the guard had tended the garden and made use of the vegetables while we were away, the dogs had been fed and looked after and a friend living nearby had paid them a daily visit. On our return they ran round in gleeful circles tails wagging furiously at the sight of us. Amelia had kept the house aired and clean. I remarked to Jim on how thin she appeared to have become, he raised his eyebrows. 'Yes, I had noticed,' his reply was a little grim, more problems for us if our fears were proved correct. We settled into the house and quickly became organized, Chewa took Jim to collect the Range Rover which had been on blocks while we were away, we went to the market to buy potatoes, eggs, tomatoes and a few salad greens which we could use for supper tomorrow. We would go to Fringilla for meat etc., and visit the duty free shop.

Jim had a busy schedule it was seedbed time, each and every trial in the country had to be visited and inspected, attention to detail was all important each year, this had to be pressed home to the African farmers and Africans in charge of trials, again another manual was produced spelling out the 'musts' and 'must nots' of growing a tobacco crop, he certainly put his back into his work. There were also a large number of European farmers who asked for visits should problems arise. At times this work could be very demanding.

Presently there was a fuel shortage in the country which made travelling extremely difficult. We mixed work with pleasure, when visiting trials in the Kafue area we stayed in Chunga camp and moved out from there until the area had been covered. We never actually ran out of fuel as Jim carried full jerry cans for emergency use; when shortages were very bad he caught up with the inevitable overflow of office work his secretary had waiting for him. It was rare that this happened as NATCO had pumps at the factory and priority was usually given to government vehicles at the petrol stations. Whenever Jim went up country I went with him. If there were any problems we intended to be in them together and to be alone in a house in Lusaka at night was not to be recommended. Visiting trials in Chipata was vital despite the fact there was absolutely nowhere to stay other than the Chipata Hotel which was something we really did not want to face again, the last visit was still etched into our memory. There was another guest house on the way to south Luangwa National Park, on one occasion we had foolishly chosen to try this place for the night, the Chipata Hotel was good by comparison. I shudder when I think of this rest house, we were bitten by bed bugs, we had one portion of scrambled egg between the two of us for breakfast, there was no bread for toast, the of pot tea was taken from our own food box. The name of this 'gem' was Crystal Springs!

On this next visit we decided to travel the rough road into south Luangwa, there were a number of chalets for tourists and people visiting the valley it was a return to the true wild and we loved it. We stayed in a camp, the name escapes my memory, which had a waterhole immediately to the front and endless bush to the rear, the food was frugal but adequate they had gin in the bar though nothing to add to it. At this time, the park was advertised by tour guides and blown up by the elaborate facilities on offer, which rather made us smile. Fortunately we carried tonics for the gin! As we lay in bed asleep we were suddenly awakened by sheer mayhem.

'It sounds as though lion have brought down a buffalo,' muttered Jim hardly compus mentus.

'It sounds as though it's outside the bedroom window,' I replied quizzically.

'It's near my love, very near', the noise was unbelievable.

The poor buffalo was bellowing and snorting as it tried to free itself from the vice like jaws of the lion, undoubtedly around the animals throat, we peered through the window but could see nothing it was out of eyeshot.

After more scuffling and snorting the noise began to abate, that is to say it changed, the snorts had now become growls and snapping. From the distance a roar indicated other lion were approaching. Now in relative silence the feast had begun, there was chomping, crunching, snarling as the lion defended territory from unwanted intruders. In the distance hyena had smelled blood and were approaching the kill with a mincing cowardly gait, suddenly making the night hideous with their bloodcurdling unearthly howl starting low and ascending to resemble a doleful cackle as they approached the scene, powerful bone crushing jaws ready to muscle in on the bloody carcass snapping and slinking away at any retaliation from the lion, then back to try again. Jackal alerted to the smell yelped on the sidelines. We had very little sleep after this episode towards morning we dozed and again we were awakened by noise outside the bedroom, this time mainly by birds, vultures, hornbills and maribou storks, jackal and hyena, bloodied horns lay in the dry grass, other than this there was very little left of the buffalo. The kill was in the immediate vicinity of the camp, a few yards away from the Range Rover; on the following morning we rushed to investigate the site of the kill.

We decided to leave early having managed to buy a few bread buns from the lodge, which we ate with a tin of sardines somewhere in the bush on the way back to Lusaka. Three times we were held up by military police each had an AK47, at one stop everything was taken out of the vehicle. Deciding, after unpacking everything, taking two beers, and finding nothing more, to let us through the barrier – one just never knew it was disconcerting. Jim was quiet and patient; I always became uselessly angry and highly stressed in my efforts to keep things under control. Back in the Range Rover Jim patted my hand 'Good girl' was all he said relieved at my silence. We were pleased to arrive home there were problems on the streets of Lusaka.

'ONE ZAMBIA. ONE NATION' we had passed the bronze statue of an African breaking the chains of colonialism, Zambians were running amok.

'I think the time has come.' Jim said.

Meaning the time had come for us to retire and go home, we were getting a little long-in-the-tooth for all this nonsense, we could not imagine any other life after the happy years in Africa and our time in South America, we felt bemused and utterly saddened at the present chaos in Africa.

Our visit to the Western Province carried us through to Graham and Carol in Mongu. Sunday we took a day trip up the Zambezi on the boat of the Zambian Cashew Company, it was a hot day though in the early morning it was necessary to wear a light jacket for our journey on the river. After going for some way the water widened and was divided by a largish sand bank.

'We'll moor here' said Graham, 'Good place to have lunch.'

I looked at him 'What about crocodiles?' I asked.

'None here,' Jim looked at me in some concern.

'Are you sure Graham?'

'Yep,' was his reply.

We decided he knew this part of the river far better than we did, so said nothing more, Carol backed him, which was a plus. We took out our chairs and food boxes, there was not a scrap of shade and it was now very hot. Graham took out his radio and decided to listen to the news. We ate a light lunch, held light conversation with much spontaneous laughter; we saw no crocodiles. On the way home someone suggested I take the wheel – a foolhardy suggestion I went onto a sandbank and the boat ground to a halt.

'Didn't you see the thing?' Graham queried a little angrily.

'No sorry.' I was so cross to have done this. After much tinkering and many expletives the engine spluttered and came to life, this was the first of four such incidents; at one point we had ropes around our waist, to prevent the boat moving away down stream as the men were trying to moor the thing, they were in the process of tying it to a sapling on the river bank. It was decided to leave it there until the following morning. The lights of Mongu flickered in the near distance far better to carry out repairs in daylight; our last effort to bring the engine to life had been attempted by the light of my make-up mirror as we did not have a torch. I felt a little foolish, having brought our day to this disastrous conclusion,

'Not to worry, it could have happened to any of us,' they assured me. My feelings must have been obvious from my expression; Jim hugged me. 'Chin up love, smile for us' he said. After the walk home, the men climbed into the Land rover and took a watchman to guard the boat for the night, bringing back our cool boxes and other equipment. Jim and I must leave early the next day it was a long hard drive, over the roads to Lusaka.

Soon after this catastrophe, there came an S.O.S from the girls. I had to take a short trip home as there had been a water burst in Croxton, our home in Cheshire and there was considerable water damage. There were certain things only either Jim or myself could attend to, and this was one of them. I did not want to leave him alone, I hated the farewells and separations which had cropped up in our lives. Going up the steps of the aircraft I was determined not to be away for any length of time. The girls met me at Manchester, we immediately started work on cleaning up of the house, insurances etc, fortunately there was not a hold up and there were no problems with the insurance. I did what I had to do and left it more or less ship shape. The girls would attend to whatever remained. In ten days

I was hauled back to Manchester by the girls, they waved me off I was back on the aircraft and on the way to Zambia.

For some reason I became very perturbed on the flight, I had a premonition that something had gone awry. I was still feeling acutely unsettled as I stepped from the aircraft and walked across the tarmac to the airport building. Formalities over, with a fast beating heart I went towards the beaming face and familiar figure standing out amongst the crowd, he walked over to me, immediately I noticed he had a distinct limp he took me in his arms.

'It is good to have you back Cog,' his face was pale and a little drawn; my heart flipped.

'What has happened my love?' I asked, half afraid of the answer.

'Nothing much, I went to the loo in the night, tripped and fell into the bath.'

'And?' I asked knowing there was more to come.

'I could not move my leg the next morning.'

Graham and Carol had arrived and managed to get him to the doctor who examined his upper leg and thigh and announced that this was the biggest haematoma he had ever seen, calling his colleague from the next room. Poor Jim he was given crutches and told to rest, he was to go to the clinic in two days time.

We called a porter who took my luggage to the car alongside the driver's seat was a walking stick he had not brought the crutches, he was meeting me.

'I thought you would have a fit if you saw me walking on crutches.' All I could say as I hugged him was 'Oh! Jim,' somehow I had to control my emotions I could not take my eyes off him, I think I was waiting for a grimace of pain or a give away of some sort, there was no chance of that.

This was the first thump of a battering ram, which had crept insidiously like a thief in the night, to rob him of his iron like grip on life, though neither of us knew this at the time.

'What did you trip over, how did you fall?' He had no answer. Graham and Carol met us at the door I was very pleased to see them, someone to lean on and it was needed. Life went on, nothing untoward happened. The doctor was not, or did not, appear to be overly concerned, he had two weeks rest from road travel seeming rapidly to become his old self.

The work load increased, north, south, east and west, supervision and advice must be given to both African and European growers, where he went so did I. The roads were long and at times monotonous we were companions having travelled many thousands of miles together. The growers always welcomed us and the farmers' wives greeted me with great warmth. I think they would have found it strange had Jim arrived alone, it was my wish to be with him and his wish that I should be by his side, they understood this, our lives had been spent in this way. Often we ate and spent the night with the European farmers. Our visits to the African trails were rather different there it was picnicing under a tree in the evenings we made our way to the nearest rest camp, Chunga was our favourite overnight stop.

The last Christmas in Africa was again spent with Geoffrey and Shirley in Malawi, this was our last 'get together' in Africa, the next was destined to be in England. Much of our conversation this Christmas in 1988 was of past years, what all those years had meant to us, how quickly they had passed. They held so many memories, so much joy, we had worries, and laughter and the inevitable financial dilemmas it all seemed like yesterday.

It was a quiet Christmas, just the four of us, quiet and full of ghosts. We were older, our hair was grey – but our hearts and minds were young and our love enduring. Life has a habit of throwing up the unexpected, Jim did have to visit Malawi again, he was called to a consultancy and this time I was not able to go with him. Graham was in Lusaka when he left, I went back to Mongu with him and Carol to spend time with them while Jim was away; ten days later they took me home, Jim returned the same evening. It was an enormous relief to see him – it filled me with such great joy. We ate at the Ridgeway that night, then tumbled into bed and slept like the dead. Apparently the Malawi schedule had been tight, but he had managed to visit the Sayama Estate again and to spend a night with Geoffrey and Shirley. I felt he had been away for months. I don't think either of us were meant to do things alone though, through the course of life there were times when this had to be. Jim had reached sixty-three years of age and I was sixty-two, our time overseas was coming to an end the children were preparing for us to go home.

Before leaving we spent a lot of time with our friends; George and Minnie bought our little Ford car, we spent the weekend with them at Fringilla. An old friend, Jose, flew up from South Africa to stay with us, she helped me with my packing; she was sad at our leaving Africa thinking she would never see us again but she did, many times. A fishing match was arranged by George, Minnie and friends in a dam over the road from Fringilla it was to be held in October, we were invited and there were many people we knew, we were introduced to many others whose names we had heard in conversation with others but had never actually met. It was all great fun there was much laughter, lewd comments were flung in every direction we laughed with the young and commiserated with their parents. Some fished from the side of the dam others stood in the dam intent. Determined and competitive, each catch was weighed often there were comments from overzealous onlookers. At one point we stood in the dam, I felt a little concerned. What about bilharzia? The snails were almost always in still and stagnant water. It was a very hot day, the reflection from the water coloured our faces to bright red. Thank God for the grass roof shelters so we could sit in the shade on bales of grass and select food from a long trestle table. We looked around at all the familiar faces the thought of leaving Africa became even more poignant, there was such camaraderie amongst everyone that it was so easy to forget that we were surrounded by crime, poverty and despair.

NATCO gave a farewell party for us, Mr. Kabwes' thank you speech for Jim was very moving, surprising and a complete revelation as to the appreciation of his input. Each member of the company appeared to be genuinely saddened at his leaving, he was presented with a Zambian-mined copper coffee table and a copper wall clock in the shape of the country. Our huge packing crates were collected and taken away by truck, I wondered if we would ever see them again. We stayed at the Intercontinental Hotel for our last few days. Graham and Carol joined us and came to wish us goodbye at the airport. With deep sorrow we left our chosen life, our chalice was full, the young fruits of love had ripened on this continent the continent we had always loved from the days of our awakening. Another life was about to begin for us all. We were still propelled by the same love, fascination and chemistry, coupled with the inability to exist without each other, the addiction was as alive as ever. We flew home in October 1989 to new ventures with new problems of a different flavour. In 1986 Janey gave birth to her first son James, the baby she had carried whilst holidaying with us. Just before our arrival home, she gave birth to her second son William.

Thank you, Jim – my Love – for all the love, patience, understanding and joy you have given me through the many years we have spent together. Thanks for carrying my satchel, hockey stick and gas mask each day from school to Crewe station in the 1940s. What a life.

Lightning Source UK Ltd.
Milton Keynes UK
20 August 2010
158739UK00001B/41/A